EQUALITY *and* LIBERTY
in the Golden Age of
State Constitutional Law

EQUALITY *and* LIBERTY
in the Golden Age of
State Constitutional Law

JEFFREY M. SHAMAN

OXFORD
UNIVERSITY PRESS

OXFORD
UNIVERSITY PRESS

Oxford University Press, Inc., publishes works that further Oxford University's
objective of excellence in research, scholarship, and education.

Copyright © 2008 by Oxford University Press, Inc.
Published by Oxford University Press, Inc.
198 Madison Avenue, New York, New York 10016

Oxford is a registered trademark of Oxford University Press
Oxford University Press is a registered trademark of Oxford University Press, Inc.

Library of Congress Cataloging-in-Publication Data
Shaman, Jeffrey M.
  Equality and liberty in the golden age of state constitutional law / by Jeffrey M. Shaman.
    p. cm.
  Includes bibliographical references and index.
  ISBN 978-0-19-533434-0 ((clothbound) : alk. paper)
  1. Civil rights—United States—States. 2. Constitutional law—United States—States. 3.
Equality before the law—United States—States. 4. Liberty. I. Title.
  KF4749.S53 2008
  342.7302—dc22   2007038783

Note to Readers:

This publication is designed to provide accurate and authoritative information in regard to the subject matter covered. It is based upon sources believed to be accurate and reliable and is intended to be current as of the time it was written. It is sold with the understanding that the publisher is not engaged in rendering legal, accounting, or other professional services. If legal advice or other expert assistance is required, the services of a competent professional person should be sought. Also, to confirm that the information has not been affected or changed by recent developments, traditional legal research techniques should be used, including checking primary sources where appropriate.

(Based on the Declaration of Principles jointly adopted by a Committee of the
American Bar Association and a Committee of Publishers and Associations.)

You may order this or any other Oxford University Press publication
by visiting the Oxford University Press website at www.oup.com

The author and publisher gratefully acknowledge permission for use of the following material:
Excerpts from Jeffrey M. Shaman, *The Evolution of Equality in State Constitutional Law*,
34 Rutgers Law Journal 1013 (2003);
Excerpts from Jeffrey M. Shaman, *The Right of Privacy in State Constitutional Law*,
37 Rutgers Law Journal 971 (2006).

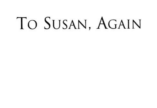

To Susan, Again

CONTENTS

Preface   *xi*

Introduction: The New Judicial Federalism   *xiii*

Chapter One: Equality   *1*
    The Federal Model of Equality   8
    The State Conception of Equality   15
        Special Privileges or Immunities   *28*
        Equal Protection of the Laws   *38*
    Conclusion   42

Chapter Two: Classifications   *45*
    Racial Classifications   46
    Gender Classifications   53
    Classifications Based on Sexual Orientation   61
    Classifications Based on Age   70
    Conclusion   76

Chapter Three: Rights and Privileges   *79*
    Educational Financing   79
    Economic Rights   86
        Tax Laws   *88*
        Damage Caps   *93*
        Allocation of Economic Benefits   *96*
        Regulatory Legislation   *101*
        Special Entitlements   *106*
    Criminal Law   107

Disparate Penalties   *108*
Prosecutorial Discretion   *113*
Disparate Treatment of Men and Women   *115*
Juvenile Offenders   *116*
Conclusion   *119*

Chapter Four: The Right of Privacy   *121*
The Federal Model of Privacy   *125*
The State Conception of Privacy   *136*
The Right to Be Let Alone   *138*
The Millian Principle   *143*
The Inherent and Unalienable Cornerstone of Liberty   *148*
Penumbrae Redux   *153*
Spatial Privacy: The Home as Sanctuary   *155*
Constitutional Situs and Methodology   *158*
Conclusion   *160*

Chapter Five: Family Rights   *163*
Reproductive Freedom   *163*
Public Funding of Abortions   *163*
Abortion Rights of Minors   *168*
Informed Consent and Waiting Periods   *171*
Family Relations   *174*
Parental Rights   *174*
Adoption   *176*
Cohabitation as a Family   *181*

Chapter Six: Civil Unions and Marriage   *185*

Chapter Seven: The Right of Intimate Association   *211*
Sexual Relations Between Consenting Adults (Married or Not)   *211*
Gay and Lesbian Sexual Relations   *215*
Public Health   *222*
Social Morality   *224*
Other State Interests   *225*
Conclusion   *226*

Chapter Eight: The Right of Bodily Integrity   *229*
  The Right to Refuse Medical Treatment and the Right to Die   *229*
  The Right to Ingest Food, Beverages, or Other Substances   *235*

Chapter Nine: Backlash and Advancement   *243*

Table of Cases   *255*

Index   *267*

PREFACE

The teaching of constitutional law in American law schools focuses primarily—in fact, almost exclusively—on decisions rendered by the United States Supreme Court interpreting the Federal Constitution. For teachers of constitutional law who believe that equality and liberty are quintessential to a free society, this has come to be a disheartening affair, as the Supreme Court of the United States has become increasingly conservative and antipathetic, if not hostile, to the recognition of individual rights. What a pleasant surprise it was, then, when some ten or twelve years ago I began to teach state constitutional law and discovered that in a number of the states the courts had broken free of federal dominance of constitutional law and actually were hospitable to the aggrandizement of equality and liberty. State constitutional law, I soon learned, was where the real action was and where social justice was moving forward, not stagnating as it was in the federal realm. State courts were engaged in an exciting enterprise, interpreting their own state constitutions with an evolutionary vision that held extensive promise for the future of constitutional law.

This book is an attempt to examine the progressive conception of equality and liberty that has developed in state constitutional law throughout the nation. In writing this book over the last five years, I have benefited immensely from comments and suggestions from a number of colleagues. As always, Erwin Chemerinsky, an eminent constitutional scholar and good friend, provided invaluable advice. Robert F. Williams, the law's foremost scholar of state constitutionalism, was also extremely helpful. Stephen Siegel, Alan Tarr, and Mark Weber offered excellent suggestions that improved my work. I am further grateful for the helpful research assistance provided by the following students: Robert Augenlicht, Mary

Butterton, John DeKoker, Virginia Fuller, Joshua Greene, and Keri McGuire. In addition, I have been very fortunate to enjoy the support of Glen Weissenberger, Dean of the DePaul University College of Law, who appreciates research and scholarship and has done a great deal to encourage it at DePaul.

Having been involved in writing this book for some time now, it will be difficult to bring that writing to a close. It is comforting, though, to know that I will continue to teach state constitutional law and thereby continue to be engaged in the pursuit of liberty and equality.

INTRODUCTION

THE NEW JUDICIAL FEDERALISM

Beginning in the 1950s, the United States Supreme Court, under the leadership of Chief Justice Earl Warren, emerged as a dynamic force in the expansion of constitutional rights. Through several decades, the nation's high Court established new individual rights under various provisions in the Bill of Rights. The most shining example of the Court's commitment to protecting the rights of the individual is, of course, *Brown v. Board of Education*, in which the Court interpreted the Equal Protection Clause of the Fourteenth Amendment to outlaw racial segregation in public schools.[1] With that momentous decision, followed by others adhering to its principles,[2] the Court rendered racial discrimination the well-deserved status of a constitutional pariah. Casting a wary eye at other forms of discrimination as well, the Warren Court ushered in a new era of egalitarianism that revitalized American constitutional law.

Equality was not the only focus of the Court's concern; other individual rights were expanded or even created anew as the Court became ever more sanguine in its reading of the Constitution. In the area of criminal procedure, for instance, the Court extended the rights of criminal defendants in state trials to be free from unreasonable searches or seizures, to be advised of their right to remain silent, and to have assistance of counsel for their defense.[3] In the area of religion, the Court construed the Establishment Clause of the First Amendment to prohibit state-sponsored bible reading or prayer recitation in public schools.[4] At the same time, the

---

[1] Brown v. Board of Education, 347 U.S. 483 (1954).

[2] *See, e.g.,* Loving v. Virginia, 388 U.S. 1 (1967); Palmore v. Sidoti, 466 U.S. 429 (1984).

[3] *See* Duncan v. Louisiana, 391 U.S. 145 (1968) and cases described therein.

[4] Engel v. Vitale, 370 U.S. 421 (1962); Abington School District v. Schempp, 374 U.S. 201 (1963).

Court read the Free Exercise Clause of the First Amendment in a new way that expanded the right of individuals to observe their religious beliefs.[5] The Court also interpreted the Free Speech Clause of the First Amendment in an expansive vein to protect the right to criticize the government and to belong to organizations that advocate subversive practices.[6]

These decisions and others of the Warren Court recognizing new individual rights or liberties were not always greeted with approval in the public arena. Indeed, a number of the Court's decisions in this period of time, particularly those regarding criminal procedure and school prayer, were highly controversial and some remain so to this day. Nonetheless, it is undeniable that for twenty-five years or so the United States Supreme Court was the most active force of government—be it local, state, or federal—concerned with the protection of the constitutional rights of individuals.

In the 1970s, as the composition of the Supreme Court was in transition—the Warren Court was becoming the Burger Court—a majority of the justices who were still willing to use the Equal Protection Clause in an active way relegated gender discrimination to a disfavored constitutional status and struck down a number of state and federal laws discriminating on the basis of sex.[7] Then, in *Roe v. Wade*, the same justices took the extraordinary step of interpreting the Due Process Clause of the Fourteenth Amendment to protect a fundamental right of privacy that encompasses the right of a woman to decide to have an abortion.[8] Subsequent decisions would further enlarge the right of privacy to include the right to marry and to live as a family.[9] Nonetheless, the Court's commitment to individual rights was steadily waning. Although there were some exceptions, with each new appointment to the Court, it was becoming increasingly conservative and less committed to the protection of individual rights.

The Burger Court remained antipathetic to racial and gender discrimination, but accepted many other forms of discrimination as

---

[5] *E.g.*, Sherbert v. Verner, 374 U.S. 398 (1963).
[6] *E.g.*, New York Times Co. v. Sullivan, 376 U.S. 254 (1964); Elfbrandt v. Russell, 384 U.S. 11 (1966).
[7] *E.g.*, Frontiero v. Richardson, 411 U.S. 677 (1973); Craig v. Boren, 429 U.S. 190 (1976).
[8] Roe v. Wade, 410 U.S. 113 (1973).
[9] *See* Zablocki v. Redhail, 434 U.S. 374 (1978); Moore v. City of East Cleveland, 431 U.S. 494 (1977).

constitutionally permissible. During this period the Court ruled, for example, that the Equal Protection Clause was not contravened by statutory classifications that disadvantaged the poor[10] or the elderly.[11] The Court also moved to curtail the recognition of fundamental rights under the Equal Protection Clause. Whereas the Warren Court used the Equal Protection Clause to protect the fundamental right to vote,[12] to gain access to the justice system,[13] and to migrate from one state to another,[14] the Burger Court ruled that neither the right to an education,[15] to housing,[16] to employment,[17] nor to subsistence,[18] were fundamental. Unmistakably, the Court was taking steps to cut short any further expansion of the reach of the Equal Protection Clause to guard against discrimination.[19] As this trend continued, the Court made it clear that the guarantee of equal protection would not be extended to new areas,[20] and if anything, would be retracted here and there.[21]

While the Burger Court re-affirmed its decision in *Roe* on several occasions, over time the dedication of the Court to the right of a woman to choose to have an abortion seemed to be fraying around the edges. In a series of cases, the Court upheld government refusals to fund abortion, even when medically necessary to protect the health of a woman,[22] and dissenting opinions grew increasingly critical of *Roe*.[23]

As other new justices were appointed to the nation's highest tribunal and William Rehnquist was named its Chief Justice, the Court's view of the right of privacy fluctuated considerably. Chief Justice Rehnquist

---

[10] James v. Valtierra, 402 U.S. 137 (1971).

[11] Vance v. Bradley, 440 U.S. 93 (1979).

[12] *See* Harper v. Virginia State Board of Elections, 383 U.S. 663 (1966).

[13] *See* Griffin v. Illinois, 351 U.S. 12 (1956).

[14] *See* Shapiro v. Thompson, 394 U.S. 618 (1969).

[15] *See* San Antonio Independent School District v. Rodriguez, 411 U.S. 1 (1973).

[16] *See* Lindsey v. Normet, 405 U.S. 56 (1972).

[17] *See* Massachusetts Board of Retirement v. Murgia, 427 U.S. 307 (1976).

[18] *See* Dandridge v. Williams, 397 U.S. 471 (1970); Jefferson v. Hackney, 406 U.S. 535 (1972).

[19] *See* Massachusetts Board of Retirement v. Murgia, 427 U.S. 307 (1976).

[20] *See* Mills v. Habluetzel, 456 U.S. 91, 99–100 (1982).

[21] *See, e.g.*, Shaw v. Reno, 509 U.S. 630 (1993).

[22] Harris v. McRae, 448 U.S. 297 (1980); Williams v. Zbarez, 448 U.S. 358 (1980). The laws in both cases did allow funding of abortions when medically necessary to save the life of a woman.

[23] *See* Akron v. Akron Center for Reproductive Health, 462 U.S. 416, 452–62 (1983) (O'Connor, J., dissenting); Thornburgh v. American College of Obstetricians and Gynecologists, 476 U.S. 747, 786–97 (1986) (White, J., dissenting).

proved to be a vigorous advocate for overturning *Roe v. Wade*, as did Justice Antonin Scalia upon his appointment to the Court. Although a majority of the Court continued to support *Roe*, the opposing camp on the high tribunal steadily gained ground. While the Court continued to recognize that the right of privacy encompasses certain family rights, reproductive rights, and even a right of intimate association,[24] the commitment of the Court to privacy wavered significantly. The Court placed definitive limits on family and reproductive rights and also refused to extend the right of privacy to other spheres, most notably the right to physician-assisted suicide.[25] Today, there is scant agreement among the justices of the Supreme Court concerning the right of privacy. As a result of the Court's equivocation in this area, the scope of the right of privacy under the Federal Constitution is considerably uncertain.

Chief Justice Rehnquist left the Court in 2005, shortly after the retirement of his colleague, Sandra Day O'Connor. In quick succession, John Roberts joined the Court as its new Chief Justice and Samuel Alito was appointed to fill the other vacancy. Their previous records revealed them both to be deeply conservative in viewpoint, and disinclined to favor any further expansion of civil rights or liberties. Indeed, if they favored any movement at all in this area of the law, it would be to retract certain incidents of equality and privacy previously established under the Fourteenth Amendment. The Roberts Court, then, can be expected to continue the trend of equivocation and diminished commitment to equality and liberty.

Since the early 1980s, the Supreme Court has been predisposed to curtail the recognition of new rights or liberties and to even rescind some that were previously granted. While there certainly have been some notable exceptions along the way, the trend of the Court clearly has been a restrictive one. Nonetheless, the impact of the Warren Court in the expansion of rights and liberties should not be underestimated. The Warren Court revolutionized constitutional law by opening new vistas of civil rights and liberties that mesmerized a generation of lawyers and judges.[26] Lawyers and judges in state courts were hardly immune from this phenomenon. Inspired by the Warren Court and provoked by the diminished

---

[24] *See* Chapter Four at notes 22–92.
[25] *See id.* at notes 70–72.
[26] Robert F. Williams, *Equality Guarantees in State Constitutional Law*, 63 Tex. L. Rev. 1195, 1196 (1985).

commitment of the Burger Court to equality and liberty, state judges were moved to begin a "revolution" of their own, which would come to be known as the "New Judicial Federalism."

Stirrings of the New Judicial Federalism began in the early 1970s and intensified a few years later as the Warren Court revolution started to subside.[27] By that time, some state courts had not only become accustomed to Warren Court doctrine enhancing civil rights and liberties, they had come to appreciate it considerably. So, they were displeased when the Supreme Court, with a new majority of justices, had a constitutional change of heart and began to curtail the advances of the Warren Court. Given the Supreme Court's diminished commitment to equality and privacy, it was hardly surprising when a number of states stepped into the breach to revitalize those rights. State constitutions, after all, are an important source of protection for individual rights and liberties, including equality and privacy. Hence, state courts began to rediscover their own state constitutions, and interpret them to afford protection of rights beyond those offered in the Federal Constitution.[28] Then, in 1977, Justice William Brennan, who had been the principle theoretician of the Warren Court revolution but now found himself in a distinct minority as a surviving justice on the Court, wrote an article entitled *State Constitutions and the Protection of Individual Rights*[29] that fanned the flames of federalism. Justice Brennan reminded the state courts that state constitutional law is independent of federal constitutional law, and that state courts no less than federal, are and ought to be the guardians of our liberties.[30] He also proclaimed that:

> (S)tate courts cannot rest when they have afforded their citizens the full protections of the federal Constitution. State constitutions, too, are a font of individual liberties, their protections often extending beyond those required by the Supreme Court's interpretation of federal law. The legal revolution which has brought federal law to the fore must not be allowed to inhibit the independent protective

---

[27] *See* Robert F. Williams, *Foreword: Looking Back at the New Judicial Federalism's First Generation*, 30 Val. U. L. Rev. xiii (1996).

[28] *Id.*

[29] William J. Brennan, Jr., *State Constitutions and the Protection of Individual Rights*, 90 Harv. L. Rev. 489 (1977).

[30] *Id.* at 491.

force of state law for without it, the full realization of our liberties cannot be guaranteed.[31]

It was a rousing call to action that many state courts heeded. Indeed, by 1988 it was being claimed that state supreme courts had interpreted their state constitutions to confer more rights than the federal constitution in well over 400 cases.[32] The New Judicial Federalism, it was said, had become mainstream.[33] With their newfound independence, the state courts granted expansive protection under their state constitutions in a variety of areas: freedom of speech, religion, criminal procedure, privacy, due process of law, and equality.

The New Judicial Federalism differs significantly from the older variety of "Our Federalism."[34] The older version consisted primarily of federal court sensitivity to state prerogatives. The idea was that in our federal system, while federal law was supreme, the states were sovereign in their own right, and state authority was entitled a degree of respect and autonomy. The old practice of Our Federalism is effectuated through measures such as the abstention doctrines[35] and the doctrine of comity and equitable restraint,[36] by which the federal courts avoid passing on state law issues believed to be best left to the state courts. It also is reflected in the federal court's practice of minimal scrutiny (or rationality review) used to defer to state authority in certain areas thought to be of particular state concern.[37] The old strain of Our Federalism is still practiced in the federal

---

[31] *Id.*

[32] David Schuman, *The Right to "Equal Privileges and Immunities": A State's Version of "Equal Protection,"* 13 Vt. L. Rev. 221, 221 (1988).

[33] *Id.*

[34] "Our Federalism...represent(s) a system in which there is sensitivity to the legitimate interests of both State and National Governments, and in which the National Government, anxious though it may be to vindicate and protect federal rights and federal interests, always endeavors to do so in ways that will not unduly interfere with the legitimate activities of the States." Younger v. Harris, 401 U.S. 37, 44 (1971).

[35] *See* Charles Alan Wright, *the Law of the Federal Courts* 8–52 (5th ed. 1994).

[36] *See id.* at 8–49.

[37] "Our scrutiny will not be so demanding where we deal with matters firmly within a State's constitutional prerogatives." Foley v. Connelie, 435 U.S. 291, 296 (1978) (quoting Sugarman v. Dougall, 413 U.S. 634, 648, (1973) and applying rationality review to uphold a state law barring the employment of aliens as state troopers). *See also*, Ambach v. Norwick, 441 U.S. 68 (1979) (applying rationality review to uphold a citizenship requirement for public school teachers); Sosna v. Iowa, 419 U.S. 393, (1975) (noting that domestic relations has long been regarded as a virtually exclusive province of the States, *id.* at 404, and applying minimal scrutiny to uphold a durational residency requirement as a condition to obtaining a divorce.).

courts, and in recent years has even been extended to additional corners by expanding the sovereign immunity granted to states under the Eleventh Amendment of the Constitution.[38] While still extant, however, the Old Federalism has been joined, if not surpassed, by a new branch of federalism that offers a different perspective on matters of sovereignty. Whereas the old species of Our Federalism stresses federal deference to state authority, the New Judicial Federalism emphasizes state independence from federal oversight. It is as if (to mix metaphors) the Old Federalism passes the baton to the states, and the New Federalism has the states taking the ball and running with it. So, the New Federalism manifests a reawakening of the idea that in our federal system of dual sovereignty, state constitutional law is autonomous of federal constitutional law. Sovereign in their own right, the states are empowered to adopt their own constitutions and to interpret them as they see fit, independent of federal constitutional law.

An early and dramatic example of the New Judicial Federalism occurred in California, when the supreme court of that state decided *Serrano v. Priest*.[39] In 1971, the California high court issued its decision in *Serrano I*, ruling that the state system of financing education primarily through local property taxes that resulted in disparate funding from one district to another violated the Equal Protection Clause of the Federal Constitution as well as the equal protection clause of the state constitution. Two years later, in *San Antonio Independent School District v. Rodriguez*, the United States Supreme Court ruled that a similar school funding system in Texas did not violate the Equal Protection Clause of the Federal Constitution.[40] Shortly after the nation's highest court announced its ruling in *Rodriguez*, California state officials petitioned the state supreme court to overturn its *Serrano* decision in light of *Rodriguez*. The California Supreme Court declined to do so, and further ruled that its previous decision had been founded on the equal protection clause of the California Constitution as well as the Equal Protection Clause of the Federal Constitution.[41] The court said that while *Rodriguez* effectively overruled that portion of the California court's decision based on the Federal Equal Protection Clause, it had no effect upon that portion of the court's

---

[38] *See* Alden v. Maine, 527 U.S. 706 (1999); Kimel v. Florida Board of Regents, 528 U.S. 62 (2000); Federal Maritime Commission v. South Carolina State Ports Authority, 535 U.S. 743 (2002).

[39] Serrano v. Priest (I), 487 P.2d 1241 (Cal. 1971).

[40] San Antonio Independent School District v. Rodriguez, *supra* note 15.

[41] Serrano v. Priest (II), 557 P.2d 929 (Cal. 1976).

decision based on the California equal protection clause, to which the court still adhered.

Serrano II is an early illustration of how the New Judicial Federalism operates to expand state constitutional rights beyond equivalent federal constitutional rights. Along the way, it offers a ringing endorsement of the New Judicial Federalism:

> In the area of fundamental civil liberties . . . (protected by) the California Declaration of Rights . . . we sit as a court of last resort, subject only to the qualification that our interpretations may not restrict the guarantees accorded the national citizenry under the federal charter. In such constitutional adjudication, our first referent is California law and the full panoply of rights Californians have come to expect as their due. Accordingly, decisions of the United States Supreme Court defining fundamental rights are persuasive authority to be afforded respectful consideration, but are to be followed by California courts only when they provide no less protection than is guaranteed by California law....

On the other hand, the older version of Our Federalism played a role in the United States Supreme Court's decision in *Rodriguez*. In that case, among other reasons for refusing to employ anything more than the most minimal judicial scrutiny, the Supreme Court professed a reluctance to intrude upon state prerogatives. The court said that equal protection claims raise implications about the federal-state relationship and that questions of federalism are present in the process of deciding whether to accord the traditional presumption of constitutionality to state legislation or to apply rigorous judicial scrutiny. While federalism concerns are always present in a case asking a federal court to strike down state legislation, "it would be difficult to imagine a case having a greater potential impact on our federal system than (this one), in which (the Supreme Court is) urged to abrogate systems of financing public education presently in existence in virtually every state."[42] In other words, for the Supreme Court to find an equal protection violation in *Rodriguez* would have a significant impact upon the education systems in every state of the union. The Court's concerns about federalism in this case led it to back away from any sort of critical oversight of state educational systems.

---

[42] San Antonio Independent School District v. Rodriguez, *supra* note 15, at 44.

A majority of the Court thought that anything other than extremely deferential review would be too much federal intermeddling with state prerogatives. Hence, federalism concerns contributed to the Court's decision to use minimal scrutiny to review and uphold the state education financing scheme in question.

In sharp contrast, in state court when a state educational financing system is challenged under a state constitutional provision, there are no federalism concerns. Not only is the state court free from federal doctrine about the meaning of federal constitutional provisions, the state court further is free from concerns about overstepping the prerogatives of some other sovereign. A state court might have concerns about separation of powers so it might decide to defer to the state legislature about a particular matter, but those are concerns about the allocation of authority among the various branches of state government and are not concerns about federalism. As the California Supreme Court explained in *Serrano II*, while the constraints of federalism are necessary to the proper functioning of the federal courts, they simply are not applicable to a state court in determining whether its own state system of financing education runs afoul of the state constitution.[43]

With the New Judicial Federalism, constitutional law becomes a multi-sided dialogue between one state and another and another, as well as the federal side. Any number of voices, state and federal, may join the dialogue. Constitutional rights, then, need not be shaped by pronouncements on high from the United States Supreme Court or by isolated state court decisions. With each voice that joins the dialogue, it becomes more vibrant and responsive to the concerns of an evolving society.

Within the dialogue, however, each state may function as a separate constitutional laboratory, deciding for itself what rights and liberties are important for its citizens. While trends involving a number of states certainly may develop, if one state sees fit to go it alone on a particular issue, it is entitled to do so. Unique state traditions or values may lead one or another state to elevate a certain right to preferred constitutional status, even though no other state does the same.[44] Indeed, this may be considered a sign of a well-functioning federal system, wherein each state is sovereign in its own right. At other times, a pioneering state decision may

---

[43] Serrano v. Priest (II), *supra* note 41, at 950–52.
[44] The phrase "unique state traditions" is from Robert F. Williams, *State Constitutional Law Cases and Materials* (4th ed. 2006) 184.

lead other states or even the Supreme Court to follow suit, as occurred when the Supreme Court of Kentucky ruled that a state statute making sodomy a crime was unconstitutional, setting an example that a number of other states were quick to follow, eventually leading the supreme court to overrule its previous decision to the contrary.[45]

It is important to note that it is somewhat misleading to speak of the new federalism as an exclusively judicial phenomenon. In some states the expansion of constitutional independence has been instigated in no small part by the enactment of state constitutional amendments, expressly creating new individual rights that have no counterpart in the Federal Constitution. In the 1970s, while the Equal Rights Amendment (ERA) prohibiting the denial or abridgement of rights on account of sex failed to gain passage as an amendment to the Federal Constitution, no less than fifteen states were pleased to adopt the ERA as part of their state constitutions.[46] Similarly, while the Federal Constitution makes no mention of a right of privacy, in modern times five states have chosen to amend their constitutions to expressly protect the right of privacy. These constitutional amendments and others protecting individual rights, enacted, as they are, by the citizens of a state, manifest the voice of the people and thereby stand as strong directives to state courts charged with the responsibility of enforcing constitutional mandates.

Eventually the New Judicial Federalism would find its strongest impact in the protection of the most basic of individual rights: equality and liberty. In rediscovering their own state constitutions and re-invigorating their sovereign independence, state courts would see fit to countenance a variety of individual rights of equality and liberty beyond those recognized by the United States Supreme Court under the Federal Constitution. Equality and liberty, then, would become the centerpiece of the Golden Age of State Constitutional Law.

---

[45] Commonwealth v. Wasson, 842 S.W.2d 487, 500–501 (Ky. 1992).
[46] *See* Chapter Two at note 61.

CHAPTER ONE

EQUALITY

Equality is a principle that enjoys a long history in state constitutional law. Some of the earliest state constitutions, which are the oldest political documents in America, proclaimed: "All men are born equally free and independent, and have certain inherent and indefeasible rights."[1] Today, that sentiment can still be found in a number of state constitutions, but is more likely to be expressed as: "All people are created equal and are entitled to equal rights and opportunity under the law."[2] A number of the early state constitutions also contained provisions prohibiting the granting of unequal privileges or immunities.[3] These provisions, too, along with their close counterparts banning special entitlements, can be found in many state constitutions today.[4] After the Civil War and the enactment in the Federal Constitution of the Fourteenth Amendment guaranteeing equal protection of the laws to all persons,[5] some states were moved to follow suit by adding equal protection clauses to their constitutions when the opportunity arose.[6] The civil rights movement of the 1950s and 60s

---

[1] Pa. Const., art. I, §1 (1776). *See also* Va. Const. Bill of Rights, §1 (1776) ("All men are by nature equally free and independent....").

[2] Wis. Const. art. I, §1 (1982).

[3] *See, e.g.,* Va. Const. Bill of Rights, §4 (1776) ("That no man, or set of men, is entitled to exclusive or separate emoluments or privileges from the community....").

[4] *See, e.g.,* Ore. Const. art. I, §20 (1999) ("No law shall be passed granting to any citizen or class of citizens privileges or immunities, which, upon the same terms, shall not equally belong to all citizens."); Ill. Const. art. IV, §22 (1870) ("In all...cases where a general law can be made applicable, no special law shall be enacted.").

[5] "(N)or shall any state...deny to any person within its jurisdiction the equal protection of the laws." U.S. Const. amend. XIV, §1.

[6] Fifteen state constitutions contain provisions guaranteeing equal protection of the laws. *See infra*, note 263.

inspired some states to add provisions to their constitutions prohibiting discrimination against persons in the exercise of their civil rights.[7] And after the Equal Rights Amendment (ERA) prohibiting discrimination on the basis of sex failed to gain passage at the federal level, some states adopted their own versions of the ERA.[8] It is worthy of note that long before the conception of the ERA, both Utah[9] and Wyoming[10] enacted state constitutional provisions guaranteeing equal civil, political, and religious rights and privileges for "male and female citizens."[11]

Furthermore, in a number of state constitutions there are provisions that grant specialized protection for various kinds of equality. For instance, a few state constitutions provide for "free and equal elections."[12] There are provisions in three state constitutions that expressly bar segregation.[13] The Alaska constitution states that "No exclusive right or special privilege of fishery shall be created or authorized in the natural waters of the State."[14] Some state constitutions expressly prohibit certain forms of

---

7 *See* Robert F. Williams, *Equality Guarantees in State Constitutional Law*, 63 Tex. L. Rev. 1195, 1200 (1985). For example, Pennsylvania's constitution states: "Neither the Commonwealth nor any political subdivision thereof shall deny to any person the enjoyment of any civil right, nor discriminate against any person in the exercise of any civil right." Pa. Const. art. I, §23 (1967). The Michigan constitution provides: "(N)or shall any person be denied the enjoyment of his civil or political rights or be discriminated against in the exercise thereof because of religion, race, color or national origin." Mich. Const. art. I, §2 (1963).

8 Some of these state constitutional provisions apply only to sex, while others include other forms of discrimination. For example, the Texas constitution states: "Equality under the law shall not be denied or abridged because of sex, race, color, creed, or national origin."

9 "The rights of citizens of the State of Utah to vote and hold office shall not be denied or abridged on account of sex. Both male and female citizens of this State shall enjoy equally all civil, political and religious rights and privileges." Utah Const. art. IV, §1 (1896).

10 "The rights of citizens of the State of Wyoming to vote and hold office shall not be denied or abridged on account of sex. Both male and female citizens of this State shall enjoy equally all civil, political and religious rights and privileges." Wyo. Const. art. 1, §3 (1890).

11 It should also be noted that article I, §8 of the California Constitution of 1879 provided that: "A person may not be disqualified from entering or pursing a business, profession, vocation or employment because of sex, race, creed, color, or national or ethnic origin."

12 *E.g.*, Del. Const. art. 1, §3 (1897); Wyo. Const. art. I, §27.

13 Conn. Const. art. I, §20 (1965); Haw. Const. art. I, §9 (1978); N.J. Const. art. I, §5 (1947).

14 Alaska Const. art. VIII, §15 (1972). The complete provisions states: "No exclusive right or special privilege of fishery shall be created or authorized in the natural waters of the State. This section does not restrict the power of the State to limit entry into any fishery for purposes of resource conservation, to prevent economic distress among fishermen and those dependent upon them for a livelihood and to promote the efficient development of aquaculture in the State."

discrimination in the private sector as well as the public one.[15] Other state constitutions contain so-called "uniformity clauses" that call for taxes to be uniformly levied within the same class of subjects.[16]

It is important to mention that a number of state constitutions contain a combination of equality provisions.[17] In some cases, the combination of provisions included in a state constitution amounts to a comprehensive mandate for equal treatment under the law.[18] Perhaps the Connecticut constitution contains the most comprehensive protection of equality by declaring that:

> All men when they form a social compact, are equal in rights; and no man or set of men are entitled to exclusive public emoluments or privileges from the community … No person shall be denied the equal protection of the law nor be subjected to segregation or discrimination in the exercise or enjoyment of his or her civil or political

---

[15] *E.g.*, Cal. Const. art. I, §8 (1879) ("A person may not be disqualified from entering or pursuing a business, profession, vocation or employment because of sex, race, creed, color, or national or ethnic origin."); Il. Const. art. I, §17 (1970) ("All persons shall have the right to be free from discrimination on the basis of race, color, creed, national ancestry and sex in the hiring and promotion practices of any employer or in the sale or rental of property."); Mont. Const. art. II, §4 (1973) ("Neither the state nor any person, firm, corporation, or institution shall discriminate against any person in the exercise of his civil or political rights on account of race, color, sex, culture, social origin or condition, or political or religious ideas.").

[16] *E.g.*, "All taxes shall be uniform upon the same class of subjects with the territorial limits of the authority levying the tax." Del. Const. article VIII, §1.

[17] *See* Randal S. Jeffrey, *Equal Protection in State Courts: The New Economic Equality Rights*, 17 Law & Ineq. 239, 252, n. 65 (1999).

[18] *E.g.*, "All persons are free by nature and are equal in their inherent and inalienable rights. Equality of rights under the law shall not be denied or abridged by the State on account of sex. No person shall be deprived of life, liberty or property without due process of law, nor be denied the equal protection of the laws, nor be denied the enjoyment of the person's civil rights or be discriminated against in the exercise thereof because of race, religion, sex or ancestry." Haw. Const. art. I, §§2, 3, 5.

"No person shall be denied the equal protection of the laws. No law shall discriminate against a person because of race or religious ideas, beliefs, or affiliations. No law shall arbitrarily, capriciously, or unreasonably discriminate against a person because of birth, age, sex, culture, physical condition, or political ideas or affiliations. Slavery and involuntary servitude are prohibited, except in the latter case as punishment for crime." La. Const. art. I, §3.

"We hold it to be self-evident that all persons are created equal. No person shall be denied the equal protection of the laws; nor shall any person be subjected to discrimination by the State because of race, color, religion, or national origin. No person or set or persons is entitled to exclusive or separate emoluments or privileges from the community but in consideration of public services." N.C. Const. art. I, §§1, 19, 32.

rights because of religion, race, color, ancestry, national origin, sex or physical or mental disability.[19]

At the opposite end of the spectrum, there are some state constitutions that contain no language expressly addressing equality or that only briefly refer to it.[20] Nevertheless, other language in those constitutions may be interpreted to encompass a guarantee of equality.[21] The Maryland Court of Appeals, for example, has ruled that although the Maryland Declaration of Rights does not contain an express equal protection clause, the concept of equal protection is embodied in the due process article of the Declaration of Rights.[22] Similarly, the West Virginia Supreme Court of Appeals has held that although the phrase "equal protection" is not found in the state constitution, the principle of equality is an integral part of the state's constitutional law, inherent in the due process clause of the West Virginia Bill of Rights.[23] And the Minnesota Supreme Court has recognized that the law of the land provision in the Minnesota Bill of Rights[24] embraces principles of equality synonymous to the Equal

---

[19] Conn. Const. art. I, §§1, 20 (1974).

[20] Jennifer Friesen, *State Constitutional Law: Litigating Individual Rights, Claims, and Defenses* 3-8 (3rd ed. 2000).

[21] On the federal side, the United States Supreme Court has interpreted the due process clause of the Fifth Amendment to encompass an equal protection component. Bolling v. Sharpe, 347 U.S. 497 (1954). Thus, even though the equal protection clause of the Fourteenth Amendment is addressed solely to the states ("No State shall...deny to any person within its jurisdiction the equal protection of the laws") and does not by its terms apply to the federal government, the due process clause of the Fifth Amendment embodies a guarantee of equal protection that applies to the federal government. *Id.*

[22] State Administrative Board of Election Laws v. Supervisors of Elections of Baltimore City, 679 A.2d 96, 100, n. 6 (Md. 1996). The due process article, art. 24 of the Maryland Constitution states: "That no man ought to be taken or imprisoned or diseized of his freehold, liberties, or privileges, or outlawed, or exiled, or in any manner destroyed, or deprived of his life, liberty or property but by the judgment of his peers, or by the Law of the land."

[23] Israel v. West Virginia Secondary Schools Activities Commission, 338 S.E.2d 480, 486–87 (W. Va. 1989). Article III, §10 of the West Virginia Constitution states: "No person shall be deprived of life, liberty, or property, without due process of law, and the judgment of his peers." The West Virginia constitution also contains a clause proscribing special legislation, W. Va. Const. art. VI, §39, and at one point the West Virginia Court of Appeals took the position that the principle of equal protection was part of that clause. State *ex rel.* Longanacre v. Crabtree, 350 S.E.2d 760 (W. Va. 1986). Subsequently, the court decided that the concept of equal protection was better located in the due process clause of the state constitution, and squarely held that equal protection was inherent in the state due process clause. Israel v. West Virginia Secondary Schools Activities Commission, 338 S.E.2d at 487.

[24] "No member of this state shall be disfranchised or deprived of any of the rights or privileges secured to any citizen thereof, unless by the law of the land or the judgment

Protection Clause of the Fourteenth Amendment to the Federal Constitution.[25]

The state constitutions, then, are a rich source of protection for equality.[26] Sadly, however, for a long period of time state equality guarantees lay relatively dormant, ignored by state courts or enervated by them of their potential vitality. The state courts, it seemed, had little inclination to interpret the equality provisions of their own constitutions in a forceful way. This would change one day, but not until the United States Supreme Court showed the way.

Beginning in the 1950s, the United States Supreme Court emerged as a dynamic force in the expansion of constitutional rights, including the rights of equality. Under the leadership of Chief Justice Earl Warren, the nation's high Court embarked on a constitutional revolution that celebrated equality as its centerpiece. The most shining example of the Court's commitment to equality is, of course, *Brown v. Board of Education*, in which the Court interpreted the Equal Protection Clause of the Fourteenth Amendment to outlaw racial segregation in public schools.[27] With that momentous decision, followed by others adhering to its principles, the Court rendered racial discrimination the well-deserved status of a constitutional pariah.[28] Casting a wary eye at other forms of discrimination as well, the Warren Court ushered in a new era of egalitarianism that revitalized American constitutional law.

---

of his peers. There shall be neither slavery nor involuntary servitude in the state otherwise than as punishment for a crime of which the party has been convicted." Minn. Const. art I, §2.

[25] State v. Russell, 477 N.W.2d 886, 889 n. 3 (Minn. 1991).

[26] The courts in forty-eight states have ruled that their constitutions contain some sort of provision guaranteeing equality. Randal S. Jeffrey, *supra* note 17, at 251. Only in Delaware and Mississippi have the courts failed to find that their constitutions contain a provision guaranteeing equality. *Id.* at 251 n. 57. In those two states, of course, the federal equal protection clause must be applied by the state courts as well as the federal courts. Moreover, the Mississippi constitution does contain a due process clause and the Delaware constitution does contain a law of the land clause. These clauses could be interpreted to encompass an equality component, as was done in Maryland, West Virginia, and Minnesota. *See supra*, at notes 21–23. In Delaware, the state supreme court once was asked to decide if the law of the land provision in the state constitution encompassed an equal protection component, but the court found it unnecessary to rule on that question since the case could be decided on the basis of the federal equal protection clause. Hughes v. State, 653 A.2d 241 (Del. 1994).

[27] Brown v. Board of Education, 347 U.S. 483 (1954).

[28] *See, e.g.,* Anderson v. Martin, 375 U.S. 399 (1964); Loving v. Virginia, 388 U.S. 1 (1967).

In the 1970s, as the composition of the Supreme Court was in transition, a majority of the justices still willing to use the Equal Protection Clause in an active way relegated sexual discrimination to a disfavored status and struck down a number of state and federal laws discriminating on the basis of sex.[29] At the same time, however, a newly emerging majority was moving toward cutting short any further expansion of the Equal Protection Clause. As the transition continued and a new Chief Justice, Warren Burger, was appointed, it became apparent that the Court's commitment to equality was steadily waning. While the Burger Court remained antipathetic to racial and gender discrimination, it accepted many other forms of discrimination as constitutionally permissible. During this period the Court ruled, for example, that the Equal Protection Clause was not contravened by statutory classifications that disadvantaged the poor[30] or the elderly.[31] The Court also moved to curtail the recognition of fundamental rights under the Equal Protection Clause. Whereas the Warren Court used the Equal Protection Clause to protect the fundamental right to vote,[32] to obtain access to the justice system,[33] and to migrate from one state to another,[34] the Burger Court ruled that neither the right to an education,[35] to housing,[36] to employment,[37] nor to subsistence,[38] were fundamental. Unmistakably, the Court was taking steps to cut short any further expansion of the reach of the Equal Protection Clause to guard against discrimination.[39] As this trend continued, the Court made it clear that the guarantee of equal protection would not be extended to new areas[40] and if anything, would be retracted here and there.[41]

---

[29] *See* Stanton v. Stanton, 421 U.S. 7 (1975); Craig v. Boren 429 U.S. 190 (1976); Orr v. Orr, 440 U.S. 268 (1979).

[30] *See* Dandridge v. Williams, 397 U.S. 471 (1970); Ortwein v. Schwab, 410 U.S. 656 (1973); San Antonio Independent School District v. Rodriguez, 411 U.S. 1 (1973).

[31] *See* Massachusetts Board of Retirement v. Murgia, 427 U.S. 307 (1976); Vance v. Bradley, 440 U.S. 93 (1979).

[32] *See* Harper v. Virginia State Board of Elections, 383 U.S. 663 (1966).

[33] *See* Griffin v. Illinois, 351 U.S. 12 (1956).

[34] *See* Shapiro v. Thompson, 394 U.S. 618 (1969).

[35] *See* San Antonio Independent School District v. Rodriguez, 411 U.S. 1 (1973).

[36] *See* Lindsey v. Normet, 405 U.S. 56 (1972).

[37] *See* Massachusetts Board of Retirement v. Murgia, 427 U.S. 307 (1976).

[38] *See* Dandridge v. Williams, 397 U.S. 471 (1970); Jefferson v. Hackney, 406 U.S. 535 (1972).

[39] *See* Massachusetts Board of Retirement v. Murgia, 427 U.S. 307 (1976).

[40] *See* United States v. Kras, 409 U.S. 434 (1973); Ross v. Moffit, 417 U.S. 600 (1974).

[41] *See*, Washington v. Davis, 426 U.S. 229 (1976); Ambach v. Norwick, 441 U.S. 68 (1979); Personnel Administrator of Massachusetts v. Feeney, 442 U.S. 256 (1979).

The impact of the Warren Court revolution was extensive. Federal constitutional law in many areas, particularly the area of equality, came to enjoy a preponderant influence on state constitutional law, and all but subsumed it. As an eminent constitutional scholar observed, the federal equal protection doctrine developed by the Warren Court "mesmerized a generation of lawyers and judges."[42] In interpreting their own equality provisions, state courts obediently followed the federal framework for putting the Equal Protection Clause into effect. While this at first had an expansive effect of protecting equality in the states, it also meant that state equality guarantees were given no wider a scope than the Federal Equal Protection Clause. Precious few state constitutional rights of equality were recognized beyond those already protected by the Federal Equal Protection Clause. In fact, during this period of time many state courts were antipathetic to equality. They had no choice but to acknowledge those rights established by the Supreme Court under the Federal Equal Protection Clause, but otherwise were unwilling to use state constitutional provisions to go any further than required by the Federal Constitution to enhance equality. Even state provisions barring special entitlements that pre-dated the Federal Equal Protection Clause were often equated to the Equal Protection Clause and shackled to its federal framework. That state provisions barring special entitlements were worded differently than the Equal Protection Clause and had a very different history than the Equal Protection Clause were for the most part unmoving to state courts. As the state courts saw it, federal constitutional law was the model to follow and state constitutional law offered no protection for equality beyond the federal model. Indeed, many states equated their equality provisions—whether they were prohibitions of unequal privileges or immunities, proscriptions of special legislation, or guarantees of equal protection—to the Federal Equal Protection Clause. These states submissively followed federal equal protection doctrine in lockstep; they conformed to federal equal protection analysis and recognized no rights of equality beyond those required by the Federal Equal Protection Clause. Thus, state equality guarantees were "federalized" and given no meaning of their own independent of federal constitutional law.

This situation, however, changed dramatically with the flowering of the New Judicial Federalism, a movement that saw state courts exercising

---

[42] Robert F. Williams, *supra* note 7, at 1196.

their sovereign independence to break free of the federal model of equality.[43] Beginning in the early 1970s, state courts began to focus their attention on the equality provisions in their own state constitutions. At the same time, they became increasingly willing to eschew or even reject federal constitutional doctrine in favor of developing their own state-based doctrinal analysis of equality. As the New Judicial Federalism gained momentum, more and more state courts exercised their sovereign prerogative to be free of federal doctrine in interpreting the equality provisions in their state constitutions. As a result, a number of state courts embraced new rights of equality beyond those that the Supreme Court was willing to countenance under the Federal Equal Protection Clause.[44]

No longer antipathetic to claims for equal justice, state courts began to develop their own conceptions of equality that differed significantly from the federal model. It is true that some states resisted the new order and continued to march in lockstep with federal rulings, refusing to recognize any rights of equality beyond those mandated by federal law. On the other hand, a growing number of states, opting for constitutional independence, broke free of the federal mold. The states were rediscovering the equality provisions in their own constitutions and taking them in new directions beyond the federal terrain.

The Federal Model of Equality

Before rediscovering their constitutional independence, the state courts adhered to the federal model of equality. In the federal system, an elaborate structure had evolved to effectuate the Equal Protection Clause. Developed over the years by the United States Supreme Court in cases involving a variety of constitutional provisions, but most prominently the Equal Protection Clause, this structure now consists of three distinct levels or tiers of judicial review, referred to as strict, intermediate, and minimal scrutiny.[45] When first devised, this structure consisted of only two tiers—strict and minimal—but after some years a third tier, intermediate, was added. The levels of scrutiny amount to different methods and

---

43 The New Judicial Federalism is discussed more fully in the Introduction.
44 Robert F. Williams, *supra* note 7, at 1216–17.
45 For a detailed description and analysis of the federal model of equal protection and the levels of scrutiny, *see* Jeffrey M. Shaman, *Constitutional Interpretation: Illusion and Reality* ch. 3 (2001).

standards that the Supreme Court uses to evaluate the constitutionality of government action. The differences between strict, intermediate, and minimal scrutiny are not merely rhetorical; they are real differences that have decisive consequences. In fact, the practice of judicial review varies considerably under each level of scrutiny, and the results of cases often are determined by the operative level of scrutiny.[46]

Under minimal scrutiny, which sometimes is called "rationality review," there is a presumption in favor of legislation, and the Court will not strike it down unless the party challenging it can prove that it is completely irrational—that is, that it bears no rational relationship to any legitimate state interest at all.[47] Under minimal scrutiny, the ends of legislation need be nothing more than valid, and there need be no more than a rational relationship between the ends of legislation and the means chosen to accomplish them. Thus, when this low level of scrutiny is employed, both the ends and means will be subject to a minimal criterion of reasonableness or rationality.

In practice in the federal system, there are two varieties of minimal scrutiny.[48] One variety, which obtains in the vast majority of cases, operates as virtually no scrutiny at all. While the Court professes to require a modicum of rationality in legislation, in reality the Court blindly accepts the legislative judgment under review with no genuine examination. This sort of minimal scrutiny functions as a rubber stamp for legislation, by providing a pretense of rationality. The other variety of minimal scrutiny, which is rarely, though occasionally evoked, invests rationality review with a bit of "bite."[49] In other words, it is true to its name; judicial scrutiny is minimal, but not nonexistent. Under this variety of minimal scrutiny, legislation must be supported by something more than a mere pretense of rationality.

Minimal scrutiny resides at one extreme of the federal approach, while strict scrutiny resides at the other extreme. With strict scrutiny, legislation will be struck down unless the government can prove that the legislation is precisely tailored to achieve a compelling state interest.[50] In other words, there is a presumption against the legislation that can only be overcome by showing an extremely strong justification—a compelling

---

46 *See id.* at 71.
47 *See id.*
48 *See id.* at 88.
49 *See id.* at 81.
50 *See id.* at 72.

state interest—to support it, as well as the closest possible fit between legislative means and ends.

Minimal scrutiny operates by granting deference to the legislature, but under strict scrutiny such deference is inappropriate either because legislative action is tainted by a suspicious property or because it impinges upon the exercise of a basic right of constitutional magnitude. So, if legislation contains an invidious suspect classification, such as race, or affects a fundamental right, such as the right to vote, strict scrutiny will be used.

Strict scrutiny is not the only tier of heightened judicial review; an intermediate tier also exists.[51] As its name indicates, intermediate scrutiny is somewhere between strict and minimal scrutiny. While strict scrutiny starts off with a finger on one side of the scale and minimal scrutiny starts off with a finger on the other side of the scale, intermediate scrutiny supposedly starts off with an equal balance. While strict scrutiny asks if there is a compelling state interest and minimal scrutiny asks only if there is a valid state interest, intermediate scrutiny asks for something in between—an important or substantial state interest. While strict scrutiny asks if the legislative means are absolutely necessary to accomplish their ends and minimal scrutiny asks only if the means are reasonably related to the ends, intermediate scrutiny requires a close, though not perfect, fit between means and ends. Intermediate scrutiny, which is used to evaluate "quasi-suspect classifications" such as gender, seems to offer more flexibility than strict or minimal scrutiny; it suggests a meaningful form of judicial review, less predisposed to one side or the other of a constitutional issue.

Race is the prototypical suspect classification, and as such it exemplifies the essential characteristics of a suspect classification. A classification may be considered suspect when it is directed at a "discrete and insular minority"[52] that has been subject to a "history of purposeful unequal treatment."[53] Suspect classifications often operate to stigmatize people with a "badge of inferiority."[54] Frequently, they are the result of prejudice and are based upon group stereotypes that are not truly indicative of an individual's abilities.[55] Suspect classifications may focus on an immutable trait that is an accident of birth for which an individual should bear no

---

[51] See id.
[52] United States v. Carolene Products Co., 304 U.S. 144, 152–53, n. 4 (1938).
[53] San Antonio Independent School District v. Rodriguez, 411 U.S. 1, 28 (1973).
[54] See Brown v. Board of Education, *supra* note 27, at 494.
[55] See Palmore v. Sidoti, 466 U.S. 429, 432 (1984).

responsibility.[56] They tend to be irrational and irrelevant to any proper governmental purpose.[57] Given their history of abuse, their irrelevance to any bona fide purpose, and their prejudicial and discriminatory nature, certain classifications are suspicious and therefore are subject to the most exacting scrutiny to determine their constitutionality. The Supreme Court also has ruled that classifications based on national origin or alienage are suspect, and, like those based on race, are therefore subject to strict scrutiny.[58]

In the 1970s, the Supreme Court began to see that classifications based on gender bear many of the invidious characteristics of a suspect classification.[59] Nonetheless, a majority of the Court was unwilling to declare that gender was a suspect classification, in all probability because at that time some of the newer members of the Court were wary of expanding the scope of strict scrutiny.[60] Finally, the Court resolved to place gender classifications in an intermediate tier of scrutiny. In effect, the Court decided to treat gender as a "semi-suspect" classification to be reviewed under a heightened, though not strict, standard of scrutiny. A few years later, the Court decided to take the same tack with classifications of non-marital children, ruling that while such classifications were not suspect enough to warrant the most exacting scrutiny, they certainly were irrational enough to call for more than minimal review.[61] Thus, classifications of non-marital children also were considered semi-suspect and hence subject to intermediate scrutiny.

That, however, marked the end of heightened review, whether strict or intermediate, of classifications.[62] Henceforth, the Court would adamantly refuse to recognize any new suspect or semi-suspect classifications. Classifications based on race, national origin, or alienage were suspect; classifications based on gender or against non-marital children were semi-suspect; and there the list ended. This brought to an end the possible

---

[56] *See* Fullilove v. Klutznick, 448 U.S. 448, 496 (1980) (Powell, J., concurring).

[57] *See* Bolling v. Sharpe, 347 U.S. 497, 500 (1954); Harper v. Virginia State Board of Elections, 383 U.S. 663, 668 (1966).

[58] *See* Hirabayashi v. United States, 320 U.S. 81 (1943); Korematsu v. United States, 323 U.S. 214 (1944); Oyoma v. California, 332 U.S. 633 (1948); Graham v. Richardson, 403 U.S. 365 (1971); Sugarman v. Dougall, 413 U.S. 634 (1973); Nyquist v. Mauclet, 432 U.S. 1 (1977).

[59] *See* Reed v. Reed, 404 U.S. 71 (1971).

[60] *Id.*

[61] *See* Mathews. v. Lucas, 427 U.S. 495 (1976); Trimble v. Gordon, 430 U.S. 762 (1977); Lalli v. Lalli, 439 U.S. 259 (1978).

[62] *See* Mills v. Habluetzel, 456 U.S. 91, 99–100 (1982).

expansion of protection provided by the Equal Protection Clause that previous decisions had suggested.

Thus, after initially acknowledging the suspect attributes of classifications based on wealth,[63] the Court changed its mind and cast wealth classifications into the lowest confines of minimal scrutiny.[64] The Court refused to treat classifications based on age as even semi-suspect, sloughing them off to the most deferential version of minimal scrutiny.[65] The Court bypassed several opportunities to rule that sexual orientation is suspect or quasi-suspect (although in the last instance the Court did strike down a law that discriminated against gay and lesbian persons).[66] The Court side-stepped one opportunity to hold that mental illness was a suspect or quasi-suspect classification,[67] and later adamantly refused to recognize mental retardation as a suspect or quasi-suspect classification (although striking down a zoning law that discriminated against persons who were mentally retarded).[68] Brushing aside the dubious properties of these classifications, the Court has been unwilling to find that any one of them is suspect or quasi-suspect.

As noted above, the Supreme Court will apply strict scrutiny if legislation contains a suspect classification or if it impinges upon a fundamental right. The Court first used the Equal Protection Clause to protect a fundamental right in 1942 in the case of *Skinner v. Oklahoma*.[69] In that case, the Court struck down a compulsory sterilization statute on the ground that it impinged upon the fundamental right of procreation. In subsequent cases, the Court used the Equal Protection Clause to protect other fundamental rights: the right to vote,[70] the right of equal access to the justice system,[71] and the right of interstate migration.[72] Beginning in the 1970s, however, the Court moved to curtail the recognition of further

---

[63] *See* Griffin v. Illinois, 351 U.S. 12 (1956); Harper v. Virginia State Board of Elections, 383 U.S. 663 (1966); San Antonio Independent School District v. Rodriguez, 411 U.S. 1 (1973).

[64] *See* James v. Valtierra, 402 U.S. 137 (1971); San Antonio Independent School District v. Rodriguez, 411 U.S. 1 (1973).

[65] *See* Massachusetts Board of Retirement v. Murgia, 427 U.S. 307 (1976); Vance v. Bradley, 440 U.S. 93 (1979).

[66] *See* Doe v. Commonwealth's Attorney, 425 U.S. 901 (1976); Bowers v. Hardwick, 478 U.S. 186 (1986); Romer v. Evans, 517 U.S. 620 (1996).

[67] *See* Schweiker v. Wilson, 450 U.S. 221 (1981).

[68] *See* City of Cleburne v. Cleburne Living Center, Inc., 473 U.S. 432 (1985).

[69] *See* Skinner v. Oklahoma *ex rel.* Williamson, 316 U.S. 535 (1942).

[70] *See* Harper v. Virginia State Board of Elections, 383 U.S. 663 (1966).

[71] *See* Griffin v. Illinois, 351 U.S. 12 (1956).

[72] *See* Shapiro v. Thompson, 394 U.S. 618 (1969).

fundamental rights under the Equal Protection Clause. Hence, the Court ruled that neither the right to an education,[73] to housing,[74] to employment,[75] to subsistence,[76] or to physician-assisted suicide[77] are fundamental. These rulings, like the Court's refusals to recognize new suspect or quasi-suspect classifications, are indicative of the Court's resoluteness to contain the scope of heightened scrutiny.

As put into operation by the Supreme Court, the multi-tier system has proven to be unduly rigid.[78] This rigidity was most pronounced during the days of the Warren Court before the emergence of intermediate scrutiny or minimal scrutiny with bite. At that time, a "sharp difference" developed between the two extant tiers of review.[79] Scrutiny that was supposed to be strict in theory turned out to be fatal in practice, while scrutiny that was supposed to be minimal in theory turned out to be illusory in practice.[80] As a result, the ultimate acceptance or rejection of government action was determined by the level of scrutiny chosen in a given case. In situations calling for minimal scrutiny, government action was almost automatically sustained; while in situations calling for strict scrutiny, it was almost automatically struck down. Eventually, this state of affairs led to the formulation of an intermediate tier of review, which provided a degree of flexibility to the overall structure.[81] However, the presence of intermediate scrutiny did little to reduce the rigidity that remained within the other two tiers. This was particularly acute in the lowest tier of review. With minimal scrutiny functioning in reality as virtually no scrutiny, the Court had no other option but to uphold legislation that in truth was irrational. While the creation of intermediate scrutiny was able to elevate some cases from the rigidity of the lowest tier, it did nothing to enhance the options available in those cases that

---

[73] *See* San Antonio Independent School District v. Rodriguez, 411 U.S. 1 (1973).

[74] *See* Lindsey v. Normet, 405 U.S. 56 (1972).

[75] *See* Massachusetts Board of Retirement v. Murgia, 427 U.S. 307 (1976).

[76] *See* Dandridge v. Williams, 397 U.S. 471 (1970); Jefferson v. Hackney, 406 U.S. 535 (1972).

[77] *See* Washington v. Glucksberg, 521 U.S. 702 (1997); Vacco v. Quill, 521 U.S. 793 (1997).

[78] *See* Jeffrey M. Shaman, *Constitutional Interpretation: Illusion and Reality* 103–5 (2001).

[79] *See* Gerald Gunther, *Foreword: In Search of Evolving Doctrine on a Changing Court: A Model for a New Equal Protection*, 86 Harv. L. Rev. 1, 12, 20 (1972).

[80] *Id.* at 8.

[81] *See* Jeffrey M. Shaman, *Constitutional Interpretation: Illusion and Reality* 103–4 (2001).

remained subject to the minimalism of rationality review. Thus, the inflexibility within the minimal tier of scrutiny persisted. Finally, this moved the Court in a few cases to invest minimal scrutiny with some bite.[82] While this reduced the rigidity of rationality review in a few cases, it also led to confusion in the law, because it is difficult to determine when the Court will evoke the upgraded variety of minimal scrutiny.[83] Moreover, the enhanced form of minimal scrutiny is utilized only on rare occasion, which means that in a high majority of cases rationality review continues to be nothing more than a pretext.

As put into effect by the Supreme Court, the multi-level system also has been beset by internal inconsistency.[84] There are legislative classifications which appear to fit the Court's own definition of being suspect that the Court has declined to acknowledge as such. Certainly, the Court's refusal to recognize gender as a suspect classification is questionable. The Court's failure to realize the suspicious aspects of classifications based on wealth or age is problematic, as is the Court's treatment of classifications based on sexual orientation, mental illness, or mental retardation. Brushing aside the dubious properties of these classifications, the Court has been unwilling to find that any one of them is suspect or quasi-suspect. Unwilling to abide by its own definition of a suspect classification, the Court takes classifications which, according to the Court's own logic, should be grouped together, and randomly scatters them among the various tiers of review.

Internal inconsistency also afflicts the Supreme Court's treatment of fundamental rights under the Equal Protection Clause.[85] There is no logical way to explain why, for example, the right to procreate or the right to vote in a state election (neither of which are mentioned in the Constitution) are considered fundamental, while the right to an education or the right to employment are not. The Court's rulings in this area simply reflect the fact that at some point a majority of the justices decided to put a freeze on the recognition of fundamental rights under the Equal Protection Clause.[86] Rights previously recognized as fundamental would continue to enjoy that status, but henceforth precious few if any rights would be deemed fundamental.

---

[82] *Id.* at 104.
[83] *Id.*
[84] *Id.* at 106–8.
[85] *Id.* at 107.
[86] *Id.* at 247.

At this point in time, the federal model of equal protection, comprised of three tiers of review, is relatively static.[87] Minimal scrutiny, except on those rare occasions when it is slightly amplified, is nothing more than a pretext for deference to the legislature. The heightened forms of review—strict and intermediate—are decidedly more meaningful, but apparently the scope of heightened scrutiny under the Federal Equal Protection Clause is frozen in its current posture.

The State Conception of Equality

There is no denying that the federal model of equality still exerts a strong influence over state constitutional law. In applying their own state equality guarantees, some state supreme courts still follow the federal model of equality in virtual lockstep with the doctrine set forth by the United States Supreme Court. Even those state supreme courts that have asserted some independence from the federal model of equal protection nevertheless borrow a good deal of federal doctrine concerning equal protection of the laws. In construing their state equality provisions, these state supreme courts typically use a tiered approach similar, if not identical, to the federal model. In addition, these courts usually borrow the federal concepts of suspect classifications and fundamental rights, although the state courts may apply these concepts differently than the United States Supreme Court applies them. The fact is, though, that federal thinking about equality still dominates state constitutional law, although some states have made significant changes to that thinking. Indeed, some state supreme courts have afforded their state equality guarantees a wider scope than the Federal Equal Protection Clause in order to protect rights beyond those recognized in the federal arena.

In interpreting equality provisions in their state constitutions, some state supreme courts continue to adhere strictly to the federal model.[88] These states adamantly refuse to extend state equality provisions to any area beyond that protected by the Federal Equal Protection Clause. Some states still cling to the federal model even if their state constitutional equality provisions are worded more strongly than the Federal Equal

---

[87] *Id.* at 237–47.
[88] *See, e.g.,* Kelly v. State, 525 N.W.2d 409, 41 (Iowa 1994); Gora v. City of Ferndale, 576 N.W.2d 141, 145 (Mich. 1998).

Protection Clause. In Michigan, for example, the state constitution not only provides that "No person shall be denied the equal protection of the laws," it goes on to add that "nor shall any person be denied the enjoyment of his civil or political rights or be discriminated against in the exercise thereof because of religion, race, color or national origin."[89] Despite the expansive language in the Michigan Constitution, the Supreme Court of that state has ruled that the Michigan guarantee of equality was intended to duplicate the Federal Equal Protection Clause and offers no more protection than its federal counterpart.[90]

The lockstep approach of state conformity to the federal model of equal protection has the effect of rendering state equality guarantees superfluous. Where the Federal Equal Protection Clause already extends to a particular area or protects a particular right, the application of a state equality provision to that area or right would be a mere redundancy, and all the more so given the dictate of the federal supremacy clause that makes federal law supreme to state law. Hence, by conforming to the federal model of equality, state supreme courts consign their own equality guarantees to obscurity.

Since the rise of the New Judicial Federalism, however, more and more states have exercised their independence by breaking free of the federal model of equal protection. Some state supreme courts have recognized that it makes little sense to conform to the federal model of equality when state equality provisions differ significantly in language, purpose, and history from the Federal Equal Protection Clause. The Supreme Court of Vermont, for example, in asserting its independence from the federal approach, noted that the equality provision in the Vermont Constitution[91] "differs markedly from the Federal Equal Protection Clause in its language, historical origins, purpose, and development."[92] Indeed, as the court explained, Vermont's commitment to equality extends back to its days as

---

[89] Mich. Const. art. I, §2 (1963).

[90] Doe v. Department of Social Services, 487 N.W.2d 166 (Mich. 1992). *See also*, North Ottawa Community Hospital v. Kieft, 578 N.W.2d 267, 272 n. 11 (Mich. 1998)("Our state constitution provides equal protection guarantees similar to those contained in the United States Constitution."); Crego v. Coleman, 615 N.W.2d 218, 223 (Mich. 2000) ("This Court has found Michigan's Equal Protection provision coextensive with the Equal Protection Clause of the federal constitution").

[91] "(G)overnment is, or ought to be, instituted for the common benefit, protection, and security of the people, nation, or community, and not for the particular emolument or advantage of any single person, family, or set of persons, who are a part only of that community...." Vt. Const. ch. I, art. 7.

[92] Baker v. State, 744 A.2d 864, 870 (Vt. 1999).

an independent republic and the state equality provision, which was part of the Vermont Constitution of 1777, predates the Federal Equal Protection Clause by nearly a century.[93] This led the court to conclude that while the Federal Equal Protection Clause may supplement the protection afforded by the Vermont equality provision, it "does not supplant it as the first and primary safeguard of the right and liberties of all Vermonters."[94]

There is, then, a significant trend toward state independence from the federal conception of equality. In some instances, the move to independence is tentative; a state supreme court may proclaim that in interpreting its own state equality guarantee it is under no obligation to follow federal equal protection doctrine, and then go ahead and do exactly that.[95] In other states, though, the assertion of independence is more forceful. At least twenty-one states have ruled that their state equality guarantees afford greater protection than the Federal Equal Protection Clause.[96] Some states have retained the basic two or three-tier structure, but have increased the scope of one or another of the upper tiers by recognizing various classifications or rights calling for heightened scrutiny that are not recognized as such in the federal system. A number of states, for example, have upgraded gender classifications from intermediate to strict scrutiny.[97] An Oregon court ruled that sexual orientation was a suspect classification.[98] Some state courts have ruled that education is a fundamental right that calls for strict scrutiny of school funding systems.[99]

Several states have departed from the federal model by enhancing rationality review under various circumstances. In 1996 (a few years before abandoning the multi-tier system altogether), the Supreme Court of Vermont gave some bite to rationality review in striking down a statute that denied adopted persons the right to inherit from collateral kin.[100] That adopted persons historically have been a target of discrimination led the court to invest rationality review with an edge that it ordinarily

---

[93] *Id.*

[94] *Id.*

[95] *See, e.g.,* Collins v. Day, 644 N.E.2d 72 (Ind. 1994).

[96] Randal S. Jeffrey, *supra* note 17, at 254.

[97] *See* Chapter Two.

[98] Tanner v. Oregon Health Sciences University, 971 P.2d 435 (Or. Ct. App. 1998). *Tanner* is more fully discussed in Chapter Six.

[99] *See* Chapter Three.

[100] MacCallum v. Seymour, 686 A.2d 935 (Vt. 1996).

does not possess.[101] In other states, rationality review of certain kinds of economic legislation is somewhat more forceful than it is under the federal approach.[102] Although no state has been willing to elevate the level of review of economic legislation to strict or even intermediate scrutiny, a few states have been willing to sharpen rationality review when considering laws that pertain to economic matters.[103]

In New Mexico, there has been an interesting reconfiguration of the federal structure of equality. For a while the New Mexico Court of Appeals, recognizing the need for an upgraded version of minimal scrutiny, adopted a four-tiered equal protection analysis.[104] Applying an enhanced variety of rational basis review, that court in one case struck down a law prohibiting state and county officials from acting as bail bondsmen[105] and in another case struck down a statutory cap on the recovery of attorney's fees by worker compensation claimants.[106] Subsequently, however, the supreme court of the state expressly overruled the Court of Appeals' adoption of a fourth tier of review, while professing that the rational basis test used in New Mexico "subsumes that fourth tier."[107] Thus, in New Mexico the possibility of rationality review with bite apparently still exists.

Other states, though not many, have abandoned the multiple-tier system in favor of what they believe to be a more flexible process. In Alaska, the state supreme court has adopted a "sliding scale" approach to equal protection, similar to the approach that was often championed by Supreme Court Justice Thurgood Marshall in concurring and dissenting opinions.[108] Although Justice Marshall could never convince a majority of the high Court to adopt the sliding scale,[109] his analysis of equal protection methodology has been extremely influential.[110] Justice Marshall

---

[101] *Id.* at 939.

[102] *See* Chapter Three.

[103] *Id.*

[104] *See* Alvarez v. Chavez, 886 P.2d 461 (N.M. Ct. App. 1994); Corn v. New Mexico Educators Federal Credit Union, 889 P.2d 234 (N.M. Ct. App. 1994).

[105] *Alvarez*, 886 P.2d at 461.

[106] *Corn*, 889 P.2d at 234.

[107] Truillo v. City of Albuquerque, 965 P.2d 305, 314 (N.M. 1998).

[108] State v. Erickson, 574 P.2d 1, 11–12 (Alaska 1978).

[109] In Plyer v. Doe, 457 U.S. 202 (1982), Justice Brennan's opinion for a 5–4 majority seems to adopt a sliding scale approach, but without calling it such. Otherwise, though, Justice Marshall's calls for a sliding scale have been rebuffed by the Court.

[110] *See* Jeffrey M. Shaman, *Constitutional Interpretation: Illusion and Reality* 102–11 (2001).

maintained that, rather than two or three levels of scrutiny, there should be a sliding scale of scrutiny that more finely calibrates the interests to be balanced on both sides of a controversy. The sliding scale system of judicial review can be expressed by a uniform criterion that inquires whether there is "an appropriate governmental interest suitably furthered by the differential treatment."[111] On a sliding scale, the operative degree of scrutiny depends on a mix of factors: the nature of the classification in question, the constitutional and societal importance of the individual interest adversely affected, and the strength of the state interest asserted in support of the law under consideration. By gauging the level of scrutiny by degrees rather than two or three tiers, the sliding scale offers a more flexible mode of review that eliminates the rigidity of the tiered system. Moreover, it is a more realistic method of review that promotes greater accuracy in the appraisal of both individual and governmental interests. The sliding scale method of review, then, brings both flexibility and precision to the constitutional process.

The benefits of a sliding scale approach to equality were apparent to the Supreme Court of Alaska, which began expressing "increasing dissatisfaction" with the tiered system of review beginning in the early 1970s.[112] In 1978, that court expressly adopted the more flexible sliding scale method of review.[113] With a sliding scale methodology, the court later noted, the Alaska equal protection clause "may be more protective of individual rights than the Federal Equal Protection Clause."[114] The Alaska system operates through a "uniform balancing test" that creates "a continuum of available levels of scrutiny" that range from rationality review to the functional equivalent of strict scrutiny.[115] The Alaska sliding scale contemplates a three-step process. First, it must be determined at the outset what weight should be afforded to the constitutional interest impaired by the challenged enactment.[116] Second, the purposes served by the challenged law must be examined.[117] Finally, an evaluation must be

---

[111] Police Department of the City of Chicago v. Mosley, 408 U.S. 92, 95 (1972).

[112] See State v. Wylie, 516 P.2d 142, 145 n. 4 (Alaska 1973); State v. Adams, 522 P.2d 1125, 1127 n. 12 (Alaska 1974); Lynden Transport, Inc. v. State, 532 P.2d 700, 706–7 (Alaska 1975); Isakson v. Rickey, 550 P.2d 359, 362–63 (Alaska 1976).

[113] State v. Erickson, 574 P.2d 1, 11–12 (Alaska 1978).

[114] Williams v. State, 895 P.2d 99, 103 (Alaska 1995). See also, Pan-Alaska Construction, Inc. v. State, 892 P.2d 159, 162 (Alaska 1995).

[115] Alaska Pacific Assurance Company v. Brown, 687 P.2d 264, 269 (Alaska 1984).

[116] Id.

[117] Id.

made of the state's interest in the particular means used to accomplish its purposes.[118] The weight afforded to the constitutional interest in step one "is the most important variable in fixing the appropriate level of scrutiny."[119] Depending upon the weight of the constitutional interest involved, the state will have a greater or lesser burden in justifying its purposes and the means chosen to accomplish them.[120] With this sliding scale system, Alaska has created a balancing test that is both more flexible and more finely attuned than a construct that relies upon two or three tiers of scrutiny.

Other states, also, have opted for a more flexible approach on the order of a sliding scale system. The Supreme Court of New Jersey has adopted a flexible uniform standard, which it sees as less rigid than the federal multi-tier approach.[121] In applying this flexible uniform standard, the New Jersey courts look to three factors: the nature of the affected right; the extent to which the governmental restriction intrudes upon it; and the public need for the restriction.[122] Analysis under the standard requires "a real and substantial relationship between the classification and the governmental purpose which it purportedly serves."[123]

Along the same lines, the Supreme Court of Vermont has also rejected "the rigid categories utilized by the federal courts under the Fourteenth Amendment" in favor of a more flexible, "relatively uniform standard" that asks whether the law in question bears a reasonable and just relation to a government purpose that serves the common benefits of the community.[124] In applying this uniform standard, the Vermont courts, too, look to three factors: the significance of the benefits and protections of the challenged law; whether the omission of some members of the community from the benefits and protections of the challenged law promotes the government's stated goals; and whether the classification under review is significantly underinclusive or overinclusive.[125]

Other state supreme courts may be more willing to take a dynamic view of the state constitutional guarantee of equality when it can be used

---

[118] *Id.*
[119] *Id.*
[120] *Id.*
[121] Rutgers Council of AAUP Chapters v. Rutgers, 689 A.2d 828, 832 (N.J. 1997).
[122] *Id.*
[123] *Id.* at 832–33.
[124] Baker v. State, 744 A.2d 864, 873, 878–79 (Vt. 1999).
[125] *Id.* at 879.

in combination with another state constitutional mandate. So, for example, a number of state supreme courts have been able to strike down school financing systems that result in unequal funding from school district to school district[126] by combining an equality provision with the dictates of the education article in the state constitution.[127] These courts have used a strongly worded education article to establish that education is a fundamental right under the state constitution, and then used strict scrutiny under an equality guarantee to assess the constitutionality of the funding system.[128]

Education is not the only subject that lends itself to using equality guarantees in connection with other constitutional provisions. In *Butte Community Union v. Lewis*,[129] the Supreme Court of Montana combined the state equality guarantee with another constitutional provision in deciding to strike down a state statute that eliminated certain welfare benefits. In this case, the Montana high court turned to, in conjunction with the state equal protection clause, another constitutional provision, Article XII, section 3(3), which reads: "The legislature shall provide such economic assistance and social and rehabilitative services as may be necessary for those inhabitants who, by reasons of age, infirmities, or misfortune may have need for the aid of society."[130] The trial court in the case had concluded that this article established a fundamental right to welfare.[131] The state supreme court, however, had a somewhat different view of the matter. As the higher court saw it, Article XII, section 3(3) did not establish a fundamental right to welfare. To be considered fundamental, the supreme court reasoned, a right must be found in the Montana Declaration of Rights or be a right without which other constitutionally guaranteed rights would have little meaning.[132] Article XII, section 3(3), the court said, was neither.[133] Article XII, section 3(3) was located not in the Declaration of Rights but in another part of the Montana Constitution that deals with the authority and obligations of the legislature. And welfare, the court continued, is not the kind of right that other constitutionally guaranteed

---

[126] Educational financing is discussed in Chapter Three.
[127] *See* Serrano v. Priest, 557 P.2d 929 (Cal. 1976); Sheff v. O'Neill, 678 A.2d 1267 (Conn. 1996).
[128] *Id.*
[129] Butte Community Union v. Lewis, 712 P.2d 1309 (Mont. 1986).
[130] *Id.* at 1310.
[131] *Id.*
[132] *Id.* at 1311.
[133] *Id.* at 1312.

rights depend upon; in fact, it is more properly characterized as a benefit.[134]

Although the court concluded that under the Montana Constitution there was not a fundamental right to welfare, the court did not think that rationality review was the appropriate standard to follow in the case. In fact, the court went on to use intermediate scrutiny and found that the statute violated the state equal protection clause.[135] While admitting that a right to welfare was not contained in the Declaration of Rights, the court nonetheless believed that it was significant that the constitution did direct the legislature to provide assistance to the misfortunate. A benefit lodged in the state constitution, the court stated, was an interest whose abridgement requires something more than a rational relationship to a governmental objective.[136] Given the importance of equal protection of the law, the court saw a need to develop a meaningful mid-level analysis, because "the old rational basis test allows government "to discriminate among classes of people for the most whimsical reasons."[137] Hence, the court concluded that "Welfare benefits grounded in the Constitution itself are deserving of great protection."[138]

The Montana Supreme Court's decision in *Butte* is an eminently sensible example of combining a state equal protection guarantee with another constitutional provision in order to elevate the level of scrutiny operative in a particular case. The court's point is well-taken that benefits enunciated in a constitution, even though not situated in a declaration or bill of rights, ought not be left languishing in minimal scrutiny. Rationality review, which allows discrimination "for the most whimsical reasons," provides insufficient protection for benefits that possess an explicit constitutional status. The joinder of constitutional provisions effectuated in *Butte*, then, was well-founded.

In another area, a few courts have been willing to combine two constitutional provisions to evoke a heightened level of scrutiny in order to review statutes that restrict the recovery of damages in tort actions against the state or its subdivisions. This is a departure from the norm; in most other states where similar challenges have been made to statutes restricting the recovery of damages against state tortfeasors, the courts have adamantly

---

[134] *Id.*
[135] *Id.* at 1313–14.
[136] *Id.*
[137] *Id.* at 1313.
[138] *Id.* at 1314.

refused to apply anything other than minimal scrutiny, under which the statutes are invariably upheld against claims that they are unjustly discriminatory.[139] The supreme courts of Montana and New Hampshire, though, have taken a different tack by using a combination of constitutional provisions to elevate the level of scrutiny used to review such statutes. In Montana, the state supreme court reasoned that the right to recover was a fundamental right by virtue of a provision in the state constitution guaranteeing that all persons shall have a "remedy ... for every injury of person, property, or character."[140] Given the presence of this fundamental right, the court applied strict scrutiny under the state equal protection clause[141] and concluded that the statute violated the Montana Constitution.[142] A slightly different approach was taken in a New Hampshire decision in which that state's highest court struck down a statute granting municipalities complete immunity from certain tort liability.[143] Pointing to a state constitutional provision guaranteeing the right to a remedy, the court concluded that while the right to recover for one's injuries is not a fundamental right, it is an important substantive right under state equal protection provisions.[144] Accordingly, the court applied an intermediate level of scrutiny in concluding that the statute violated the state guarantee of equality.[145]

It also is possible to combine constitutional provisions in order to enhance rationality review. For instance, in a case involving a classification based upon age, which most courts review with the most minimal scrutiny, the Supreme Court of Utah was willing to put some bite into rationality review in part because the statute in question granted unlimited discretion to state officials.[146] Legislative grants of authority unaccompanied by guidelines offend the principles of separation powers, and in this instance the complete absence of standards in the statute in combination with the state equality guarantee led the court to strike down the law under an enhanced version of rationality review.[147]

---

[139] *E.g.*, Estate of Cargill v. Rochester, 406 A.2d 704 (N.H. 1979); Rivera v. Gerner, 448 A.2d 508 (N.J. 1982); Lienhard v. State, 417 N.W.2d 119 (Minn. 1987).

[140] White v. State, 661 P.2d 1272, 1274–75 (Mont. 1983).

[141] The court evoked both the state and the federal equal protection clauses. *Id.* at 1274.

[142] *Id.* at 1275.

[143] City of Dover v. Imperial Casualty & Indemnity Co., 575 A.2d 1280, 1281 (N.H. 1990).

[144] *Id.* at 1284.

[145] *Id.* at 1284–85.

[146] State v. Mohi, 901 P.2d 991 (Utah 1995).

[147] *Id.* at 999.

In addition to upgrading the degree of judicial scrutiny, equality guarantees can be used in combination with other constitutional mandates in order to extend the reach of an equality mandate to situations it might not otherwise cover. This occurred in *Sheff v. O'Neill*, a decision in which the Connecticut Supreme Court ruled that the state constitution prohibited *de facto* racial segregation in a public school system.[148] Although *de facto* discrimination is not ordinarily considered to be a constitutional violation unless proven to be intentional, in this instance the court concluded that *de facto* discrimination in public schools, whether intentional or not, was indeed a constitutional violation when considered in light of both the state education article and the state equal protection clause.[149] Each of those constitutional mandates was worded quite strongly, and especially when considered together led to the conclusion that *de facto* discrimination in a public school system was an affront to the Connecticut Constitution.[150]

As might be expected, state courts are more willing to engage in an active brand of review when equality provisions are expressly worded to prohibit a particular form of discrimination. For example, in *Sheff v. O'Neill*, one of the factors that led the Connecticut Supreme Court to take a more active stance against *de facto* segregation in the schools was that the equal protection clause of the Connecticut constitution expressly bans segregation.[151] To mention another example, some state supreme courts have opted for strict rather than intermediate scrutiny to review classifications based on sex because their state constitutions were amended to expressly prohibit the denial or rights "on account of sex."[152] Thus, an explicit proscription directed to a particular kind of discrimination appropriately may be the occasion for more searching judicial review.

Along the same lines, state courts are more willing to engage in active review when equality provisions are specifically designed to protect a particular kind of right. In the State of Washington, because the state constitution contains a provision specifically stating that "All elections

---

[148] Sheff v. O'Neill, 678 A.2d 1267 (Conn. 1996).
[149] The decision in *Sheff v. O'Neill* is discussed in more detail in Chapter Two.
[150] *Id.* at 1281.
[151] "No person shall be denied the equal protection of the law nor be subjected to segregation or discrimination in the exercise or enjoyment of his or her civil or political rights because of religion, race, color, ancestry, national origin, sex or physical or mental disability." Conn. Const. article first, §20.
[152] *See* Chapter Two.

shall be free and equal,"[153] the supreme court has adopted a more precise standard of equality for election district voting rights than is required under the Equal Protection Clause of the Federal Constitution.[154] In New Jersey, when the supreme court ruled that the state system of financing schools was unconstitutional, the court pointed to the fact that schooling was one of the expressly enumerated categories in the state constitutional provision prohibiting local or special laws.[155]

There is one state supreme court that has formulated an uncommon approach to the equality provision in its state constitution. The Supreme Court of Oregon has developed a novel design for applying the state constitutional requirement of equality that differs significantly from the federal model.[156] The Oregon Constitution provides that "No law shall be passed granting to any citizen or class of citizens privileges, or immunities, which, upon the same terms, shall not equally belong to all citizens."[157] Until 1976, the Oregon courts treated the state guarantee of equality and the Federal Equal Protection Clause as interchangeable.[158] In fact, the highest court of the state unequivocally professed that state and federal constitutional principles of equality corresponded to one and other and that the scope of the state and federal equality provisions was exactly the same.[159] In 1976, however, the Supreme Court of Oregon took its first step in departing from the federal model by recognizing that the mode of analysis under the Federal Equal Protection Clause might not be appropriate under a state equality provision and that the Oregon guarantee of equality might have a broader scope than the Federal Equal Protection

---

153 Wash. Const. art. I, §19.

154 Foster v. Sunnyside Valley Irrigation District, 687 P.2d 841 (Wash. 1984).

155 Robinson v. Cahill, 303 A.2d 273, 288 (N.J. 1973).

156 The Oregon model of equality is fully described in David Schuman, *The Right to "Equal Privileges and Immunities": A State's Version of "Equal Protection,"* 13 Vt. L. Rev. 221 (1988).

157 Or. Const. Art I, §20.

158 David Schuman, *supra* note 156, at 227–28.

159 The Supreme Court of Oregon stated that: "We have repeatedly and explicitly held or unequivocally inferred that the scope of the equal protection clause of the Oregon Constitution and the Fourteenth Amendment is the same." Olsen v. State *ex rel.* Johnson, 554 P.2d 139, 142 (Or. 1976). In a previous case, the court said: "The controlling principles which guide courts in determining questions of alleged unconstitutional discrimination or class legislation are the same whether it is the Equal Protection Clause of the Fourteenth Amendment of the Constitution of the United States which is invoked, or the privileges and immunities provision in Art. I, s 20 of the Oregon Constitution." Plummer v. Donald M. Drake Co., 320 P.2d 245, 248 (Or. 1958).

Clause.[160] In following years, the Oregon high court diverged further from the federal model and eventually devised an unusual approach to the guarantee of equality that borrows partially from the federal model, but that differs substantially from it.[161] Though inventive, the Oregon model is not without its own flaws.

According to the design formulated by the Oregon Supreme Court to effectuate the state guarantee of equal privileges and immunities, the Court ascertains whether the government action in question discriminates against a "true class," a "*de jure* class," or an individual.[162] This designation, in turn, determines how the Court will evaluate the government action, there being different lines of inquiry for each designation. A true class is one that exists independently of the law and is widely recognized as forming the basis of a socially meaningful classification, based on characteristics such as race, gender, nationality, or geographic residence.[163] A *de jure* class is one that is established by the law itself, or, to put it another way, "is a group of people whose existence *as a class* derives from the statute or policy being challenged."[164] Some examples of *de jure* classes are: persons who are charged by information rather than indictment, persons who fail to meet a statute of limitations, and persons who pay income taxes.[165] According to the Oregon Supreme Court, opticians constitute a *de jure* class when they challenge a law that licenses opticians and optometrists to perform different functions.[166]

Under the Oregon approach, there are no levels of scrutiny like the ones used with the federal model of equal protection. Instead, there are different lines of inquiry depending on the designation assigned to the discrimination in question. In cases involving true classes, the court will inquire whether the classification in question is suspect—that is, whether

---

[160] *See* Olsen v. State *ex rel.* Johnson, 554 P.2d 139, 143–45 (Or. 1976).

[161] David Schuman, *supra* note 156, at 228–29.

[162] David Schuman, *supra* note 156, at 230–33. As preliminary matters, the court decides whether the state action in question impinges upon a state privilege or immunity and whether it is properly authorized under state law. *See id.* at 229–30 and cases cited therein.

[163] State v. Clark, 630 P.2d 810, 816 (Or. 1981).

[164] David Schuman, *supra* note 156, at 237 (emphasis in original). Professor Schuman uses the phrase "pseudo-class" instead of "*de jure* class." *Id.* at 229, n. 52.

[165] *Id.* at 232–33, 237–38.

[166] State v. Clark, *supra* note 163, at 816. *Cf.* Williamson v. Lee Optical of Oklahoma Inc., 348 U.S. 483 (1955), in which the United States Supreme Court used extremely minimal scrutiny to uphold a law that treated opticians differently than ophthalmologists and optometrists.

it is based on an immutable trait—and whether it is invidious—that is, whether it is based on prejudicial or stereotypical thinking rather than genuine differences.[167] If a true classification is found to be both suspect and invidious, it will be considered a *per se* violation of the Oregon equal privileges and immunities clause.[168] In cases involving *de jure* classes, the court will inquire whether the classification in question amounts to a deliberate and unfair limitation on access to a privilege or immunity.[169] In most instances, this inquiry will hinge on whether the class is "open to anyone to bring himself or herself within the favored class on equal terms."[170] Finally, in cases concerning discrimination against an individual, the court will inquire whether the state action under review is "purely haphazard or otherwise on terms that have no satisfactory explanation."[171]

The Oregon approach is highly formalistic, and allows for little, if any, balancing of interests. The concepts of true and *de jure* classes are formal categories. As such, they are artificial, tend to overlap, and in some instances lead to tenuous distinctions. It might well be questioned, for example, why the court considers opticians to constitute a *de jure* class, while nationality is thought to be a true class. And why should a law directed at opticians be subject to a different line of inquiry under the equal privileges and immunities clause than a law directed at aliens? The formalistic nature of the Oregon approach offers few satisfactory answers to questions such as these.

Moreover, the Oregon approach is a deliberate attempt to minimize any balancing of interests. In situations concerning true classes, no balancing of interests, compelling or otherwise, will be made; the law in question will either be struck down as a *per se* constitutional violation or upheld because it is not a *per se* violation. Where the challenge is to a *de jure* class, little balancing occurs, the main inquiry being whether the class is open to anyone to enter. It is only where discrimination is directed at an individual that the Oregon approach calls for balancing by inquiring whether there is a satisfactory explanation for the law under review. Otherwise, the Oregon model offers scant, if any, opportunity to balance interests.

---

[167] David Schuman, *supra* note 156, at 233–37.
[168] Apparently, under the Oregon approach, a true classification will not be found to violate the Oregon equal privileges and immunities clause unless it is both suspect and invidious. *See id.* at 235–37.
[169] *Id.* at 238–39.
[170] State v. Clark, *supra* note 163, at 816.
[171] State v. Edmonson, 630 P.2d 822, 823 (Or. 1981).

The Oregon Supreme Court's aversion to balancing is unfortunate, because balancing offers the only genuine means of analysis for evaluating if the distinctions made or lines drawn by a law are well-founded.[172] It simply is not possible to properly decide whether a law that denies an equal privilege or immunity is *justifiable* without evaluating the ends that the law serves and the means by which it is effectuated. Balancing is a necessary element of meaningful, purposive adjudication.[173] Formal approaches, such as the one adopted by the Oregon Supreme Court, are a poor substitute for balancing. Balancing is a realistic mode of adjudication that is capable of bringing true rationality to the law, while formalism is an artificial mode of adjudication that provides, at best, the mere illusion of rationality.[174]

Special Privileges or Immunities

State constitutional proscriptions directed toward precluding unequal privileges or immunities have a long history in the United States. Some of the earliest state constitutions contained provisions aimed at prohibiting exclusive entitlements similar to royal privileges.[175] For instance, the Bill of Rights in the Virginia Constitution of 1776 stated that: "No man or set of men, is entitled to exclusive or separate emoluments or privileges from the community, but in consideration of public services."[176] Similarly, the Massachusetts Constitution of 1780 provided that: "No man, nor corporation, or association of men have nay other title to obtain advantages, or particular and exclusive privileges, distinct from those of the community, than what arises from the considerations of services rendered to the public."[177]

In the early days of the nation some state courts combined constitutional proscriptions with the principles of natural law to bar the legislature

---

[172] *See* Jeffrey M. Shaman, *Constitutional Interpretation: Illusion and Reality* ch. 2 (2001).
[173] *Id.*
[174] *Id.*
[175] *See* Robert F. Williams, *supra* note 7, at 1200. Much of the following description of early constitutional proscriptions against special privileges draws on Professor Williams' excellent study.
[176] Va. Const. art. I, §4 (1776).
[177] Mass. Const. part 1, art. IV (1780).

from granting special privileges.[178] Thus, in 1814 the Supreme Judicial Court of Massachusetts declared that:

> It is manifestly contrary to the first principles of civil liberty and natural justice, and to the spirit of our constitution and laws, that any one citizen should enjoy privileges and advantages which are denied to all others under like circumstances; or that any one should be subjected to losses, damages, suits, or actions, from which all others, under like circumstances, are exempted.[179]

Antipathy toward special entitlements has carried over to modern constitutions, and remains an important aspect of state constitutional law.[180] Today, a number of state constitutions contain provisions prohibiting unequal privileges or immunities.[181] Some state constitutions contain multiple provisions prohibiting special entitlements. The constitution of the State of Washington, for example, has no fewer than four provisions barring special privileges or immunities.[182] This has been seen as "but a few variations on a dominant theme" of the Washington Constitution as well as other state constitutions passed around the same period of time, namely, that laws should be general in application and that powerful individuals or groups should not be allowed to procure special privileges or unjustified immunities.[183]

---

[178] *See* Robert F. Williams, *supra* note 7, at 1200–1.

[179] Holden v. James, 11 Mass. 396, 405 (1814).

[180] "The State, it is to be presumed, has no favors to bestow, and designs to inflict no arbitrary deprivation of rights. Special privileges are always obnoxious, and discriminations against persons or classes are still more so...." Thomas M. Cooley, *Constitutional Limitations*, vol. 2, p. 816 (1927).

[181] *See* Ala. Const. Art. I, 22; Ariz. Const. Art. 2, §13; Ark. Const. Art. II, §18; Cal. Const. Art. I, §7(b); Conn. Const. Art. I, §1; Ind. Const. Art. I, §23; Iowa Const. Art. I, §6; Ky. Const. Bill of Rights 3; N.M. Const. art. IV, §26; N.C. Const. Art. I, §32; N.D. Const. Art. I, §21; Okla. Const. art. 5, §51; Or. Const. art. I, §20; S.D. Const. Art. VI, §18; Tex. Const. Art. I, §3; Va. Const. Art. I, §4; Vt. Const. ch. I, art. VII; Wash. Const. Art. I, §12.

[182] "No law shall be passed granting to any citizen, class of citizens, or corporation other than municipal, privileges or immunities which upon the same terms shall not equally belong to all citizens, or corporations." Wash. Const. art. 1, §12 (1889). "No law granting irrevocably any privilege, franchise or immunity, shall be passed by the legislature." *Id.*, art. 1, §8. "No hereditary emoluments, privileges, or powers, shall be granted or conferred in this state." *Id.*, art. 1, §28. "The legislature is prohibited from enacting any private or special laws... (f)or granting corporate powers or privileges." *Id.*, art. 2, §28.

[183] Jonathan Thompson, *The Washington Constitution's Prohibition on Special Privileges and Immunities: Real Bite for "Equal Protection" Review of Regulatory Legislation?*, 69 Temp. L. Rev. 1247, 1255 (1996).

Closely related to state constitutional provisions barring unequal privileges or immunities are state constitutional provisions that forbid the enactment of "special" or "local" laws.[184] Many of these provisions were first enacted as part of the populist movement of the mid-1800s. As noted by an eminent legal historian, "The persistent theme of the limitations written into state constitutions after the 1840s was the desire to curb special privilege."[185] Provisions barring the enactment of special or local laws often are situated in the legislative articles of state constitutions, directed, as they are, toward prohibiting the legislature from enacting laws that bestow favored treatment upon specified parties or localities. Originally, these provisions were aspects of the trend that began in the 1850s toward curbing legislative power.[186] The constitutional bans on special and local laws were prompted by a growing public mistrust of the legislature, especially the susceptibility of the legislature to undue influence by special interest groups. As state legislatures increasingly came under the influence of big business—in particular, the railroads and banks—amendments were added to state constitutions restricting legislative authority.[187] A variety of constitutional devices were adopted to limit legislative power, foremost among them being constitutional amendments banning "special" and "local" laws.[188] In some instances, these amendments contained detailed proscriptions listing particular topics that could not be addressed by way of special legislation.[189] Typically, the list would culminate with a general proscription stating something like: "In all other cases where a general law can be made applicable, no special law shall be enacted."[190] In more recent times, in keeping with the tendency toward more streamlined constitutions, the detailed list is usually omitted, in favor of a comprehensive general prohibition, such as the Illinois provision which states: "The General Assembly shall pass no special or local law when a general law is or can be made applicable."[191]

---

[184] *See* Robert F. Williams, *supra* note 7, at 1209–10.
[185] J. Willard Hurst, *The Growth of American Law: The Law Makers* 241 (1950).
[186] *See* Lawrence M. Friedman, *A History of American Law* 348–50 (2d ed. 1985).
[187] *Id.*
[188] *Id.*
[189] Ill. Const. art. IV, §22 (1870).
[190] *Id.*
[191] Ill. Const. art. IV, §13 (1970).

Antipathy toward special entitlements also is reflected in state constitutional provisions that guarantee the right to a remedy for redress of legal injury or that insure access to the courts for redress of injury.[192] These provisions descend from the Magna Carta, which, to counteract the practice of King John's courts of selling writs to the highest bidder, contained a clause stating "To no one will we sell, to no one will we refuse or delay, right or justice."[193] Like their antecedent in the Magna Carta, right to remedy provisions are directed toward precluding the courts from granting special treatment to favored parties.[194] Thus, they can be considered complementary to state constitutional provisions that proscribe special legislation.

Constitutional proscriptions of special and local laws, like their close counterparts barring exclusive privileges or immunities, are founded on the principle that the government may not bestow special favors or entitlements to anyone, nor may the government saddle anyone with special disabilities.[195] According to this principle, the law should be impartial, both in its content and its administration. Political preference of any kind is frowned upon.[196] Laws that discriminate, either in favor of or against individuals or groups, are forbidden. Special class legislation is impermissible.[197] Neither royalty nor big business nor anyone else, for that matter, is entitled to special treatment from the government. The principle of equality proscribes favored treatment or status under the law. This means "not only that everyone enjoy equality before the law or have an equal voice in government but also that everyone have an equal share in the fruits of the common enterprise."[198]

---

[192] *E.g.*, "(E)very man shall have remedy by due course of law for injury done him in his person, property or reputation." Ore. Const. art. I, §10 (1999); "The courts shall be open to every person for redress of any injury, and justice shall be administered without sale, denial or delay." Fla. Const. art. I, §21 (1968).

[193] *See* David Schuman, *The Right to A Remedy*, 65 Temp. L. Rev. 1197, 1199 (1992).

[194] That is not to say, however, that right to remedy provisions have no application to legislation that restricts remedies or limits access to the courts. To the contrary, it has been held that such provisions apply to the legislature as well as the courts. Commonwealth v. Werner, 280 S.W.2d 214 (Ky. 1955); *but see* Meech v. Hillhaven West, Inc., 776 P.2d 448 (Mont. 1989).

[195] "A law which is partial in its operation, intended to affect particular individuals alone, or to deprive them of the benefit of the general laws, is unwarranted by the constitution, and is void...." Vanzant v. Waddel, 10 Tenn. 260, 269 (1829).

[196] Baker v. State, *supra* note 92, at 875.

[197] "It is one of the purposes of American constitutional law to prevent all such special class legislation." Anderton v. City of Milwaukee, 52 N.W. 95, 96 (Wis. 1892).

[198] W. Adams, *The First American Constitutions* 188 (1980).

It is not surprising, then, that state constitutional law manifests a strong aversion toward state-created monopolies. Of the fifty state constitutions, North Carolina's probably evinces the strongest condemnation of monopolies by proclaiming that "Perpetuities and monopolies are contrary to the genius of a free state and shall not be allowed,"[199] in addition to expressly prohibiting "exclusive or separate emoluments or privileges."[200] Provisions in other state constitutions that proscribe special entitlements, though less explicit in targeting monopolies, nonetheless are meant to interdict them. After all, a monopoly granted by the state is the prototypical special entitlement, and therefore would seem to be at the very core of state constitutional provisions banning special privileges or immunities.

It is said that special legislation advances private rather than public interests. Laws that are special or partial often are equated to private laws, that is, laws directed to private interests. Such laws are partial for the very reason that they are addressed to private interests. So, for example, the Supreme Court of Tennessee declared that "Every partial or private law, which directly proposes to destroy or affect individual rights ... is unconstitutional and void."[201]

By banning special entitlements, state constitutional law requires that legislation be in the public interest. In other words, that it be for the benefit of the public rather than for special interest groups. As one scholar put it, "Legislatures were supposed to work for the public interest; they were not to pass narrow, selfish laws, nor to act as tools of railroads and banks."[202] It can be seen, then, that constitutional proscriptions of special entitlements are rooted in a philosophy of civic republicanism, according to which government action must promote public purposes, rather than private or special interests.[203] In other words, the *raison d'être* for government

---

[199] N.C. Const. art. I, §34.

[200] N.C. Const. art. I, §32. The North Carolina Constitution also provides that: "No person shall be denied the equal protection of the laws; nor shall any person be subjected to discrimination by the State because of race, color, religion, or national origin." N.C. Const. art. I, §19.

[201] Vanzant v. Waddel, 10 Tenn. 260 (1829); *see also.* Railroad Co. v. Morris, 65 Ala. 193 (1880); Anderton v. City of Milwaukee, *supra* note 197, at 96.

[202] Lawrence M. Friedman, *supra* note 186, at 350.

[203] *See* Cass Sunstein, *Naked Preferences and the Constitution*, 84 Colum. L. Rev. 1689, 1690–91 (1984); Howard Gillman, *The Constitution Besieged: The Rise and Demise of Lochner Era Police Power Jurisprudence* 53–60 (1993).

is to serve the commonweal. Thus, the Constitution of Vermont, which dates back to 1777, declares:

That government is, or ought to be, instituted for the common benefit, protection, and security of the people, nation, or community, and not for the particular emolument or advantage of any single person, family, or set of persons, who are a part only of that community ....[204]

Echoing the same sentiment, the Rhode Island Constitution of 1842 proclaims that:

All free governments are instituted for the protection, safety and happiness of the people. All laws, therefore, should be made for the good of the whole; and the burdens of the state ought to be fairly distributed among its citizens.[205]

The notion that the government exists to serve the public is also manifest in state constitutional provisions that require that public funds only be spent for public purposes. For instance, the Illinois Constitution states that "Public funds, property or credit shall be used only for public purposes."[206] In some states, notwithstanding the absence of any express constitutional language, the courts have read a "public purpose doctrine" into their state constitutions.[207] In Wisconsin, for example, the public purpose doctrine is a well-established constitutional tenet, even though it is not recited in any specific clause of the state constitution.[208] Indeed, the Supreme Court of Wisconsin, after noting that the public purpose doctrine cannot be traced to any explicit language in the state constitution, nevertheless declared that "An expenditure of public funds for other than a public purpose would be abhorrent to the constitution of Wisconsin."[209] Thus, the principle that legislation must be directed to a public, as distinct from private, purpose runs deep in state constitutional waters.

---

[204] Vt. Const. ch. I, art. 7.

[205] R.I. Const. art. I, §2 (1842). *See also* Mich. Const. art. II, §1 (1908), which states: "All political power is inherent in the people. Government is instituted for their equal benefit, security and protection."

[206] Ill. Const. art. VIII, §1 (1970).

[207] *See, e.g.*, Sharpless v. Mayor of Philadelphia, 21 Pa. 147 (1853).

[208] State *ex rel.* Warren v. Nusbaum, 208 N.W.2d 780, 795 (Wis. 1973).

[209] *Id.*

It has been said that constitutional provisions proscribing special entitlements and constitutional provisions guaranteeing equal protection of the laws are the "antithesis" of one another, in that the former forbid special treatment of favored individuals or classes while the latter extend equality of treatment to disfavored individuals or classes.[210] It is more accurate to say, however, that provisions barring special entitlements and those mandating equal protection are mirror images of one another.[211] There is, after all, a close kinship between the two types of provisions: they both prohibit unequal treatment under the law.[212]

On the other hand, the historical roots of provisions barring special entitlements and those guaranteeing equal protection of the laws are significantly different. The former were designed to prevent the bestowal of preferential prerogatives to favored individuals or groups, while the latter were designed to prevent malevolent discrimination against disfavored minorities.[213] It has been suggested that, given their different historical aims, the two kinds of provisions might be applied in different ways.[214] Provisions barring special entitlements might be applied with stronger force (strict scrutiny) in instances where favoritism is shown toward a relatively small group of persons, while provisions requiring equal protection of the laws might be applied with stronger force (strict scrutiny) in instances of discrimination against minorities.[215] As one commentator aptly puts it, for those who challenge statutory classifications, the anti-favoritism thrust of provisions barring special entitlements puts an extra arrow in their quiver that may not be on hand with provisions guaranteeing equal protection of the laws.[216] Still, despite their dissimilar historical development, at their core proscriptions of special entitlements and

---

[210] See Hale v. Portland, 783 P.2d 506, 515 (Or. 1989); Collins v. Day, 644 N.E.2d 72, 74 (Ind. 1994).

[211] See Jennifer Friesen, *supra* note 20, at 3-6.

[212] David Schuman, *supra* note 156, at 224; Jonathan Thompson, *supra* note 183, at 1251.

[213] One commentator in Vermont (a judge) takes a more cynical view of that state's constitutional proscription of special advantages or emoluments, known as the "common benefits clause": "Unlike the Fourteenth Amendment, whose origin and language reflect the solicitude of a dominant white society for a historically-oppressed African-American minority..., the Common Benefits Clause mirrors the confidence of a homogeneous eighteenth-century group of men aggressively laying claim to the same rights as their peers in Great Britain...." F. Mahady, *Toward a Theory of State Constitutional Jurisprudence: A Judge's Thoughts*, 13 Vt. L. Rev. 145, 151–52 (1988).

[214] Thompson, *id.*

[215] *Id.*

[216] *Id.* at 1262–63.

guarantees of equal protection share a striking conceptual similarity. In essence, both kinds of provisions are directed to the same goal: preventing the state from treating individuals or classes unequally. As the Supreme Court of the State of Washington has noted:

> The aim and purpose of the special privileges and immunities provision of article 1, section 12, of the State Constitution and of the Equal Protection Clause of the Fourteenth Amendment of the Federal Constitution is to secure equality of treatment to all persons, without undue favor on the one hand or hostile discrimination on the other.[217]

Distinguishing a special law from a general one can be a complicated matter that perplexes courts. Early cases took a highly formal approach, positing that a general law was one that comprehends a *genus*, while a special law was confined to a *species*.[218] This amounted to little more than tautology and was not a sensible way of deciding cases. As legal thinking advanced, the courts stopped referring to *genus* and *species*, and those formal concepts no longer are used in connection with special legislation.

In more modern times, a body of doctrine has evolved around state constitutional provisions that ban special legislation or unequal privileges or immunities. This doctrine derives from federal principles used to interpret the Equal Protection Clause in the Federal Constitution. In fact, some state supreme courts are quite frank about adopting the federal approach and expressly equate their state constitutional provisions banning special legislation or unequal entitlements to the Federal Equal Protection Clause.[219] Other state supreme courts merely incorporate the federal approach without acknowledging its federal genesis.[220] And at least one state supreme court, in interpreting the state prohibition of unequal privileges or immunities, has proclaimed its independence from

---

217 State *ex rel.* Bacich v. Huse, 59 P.2d 1101, 1104 (Wash. 1936) (rev'd. on other grounds, Puget Sound Gillnetters Association v. Moos, 603 P.2d 819 (Wash. 1979).

218 Dundee Mortgage, Trust Investment Co. v. School District No. 1, Multnomah County, 19 F. 359, 371 (C.C.D. Or. 1884).

219 *See* Illinois Housing Development Authority v. Van Meter, 412 N.E.2d 151, 155 (Ill. 1980); Washington Statewide Organization of Stepparents v. Smith, 536 P.2d 1202 (Wash. 1975).

220 *See* Alabama State Federation of Labor v. McAdory, 18 So.2d 810 (Ala. 1944).

federal constitutional law, while at the same time adopting a stance that borrows a important portion of the federal structure.[221]

As derived from federal doctrine, there is general agreement that a state constitutional prohibition against special legislation or unequal privileges or immunities does not preclude the legislature from making classifications.[222] All that is required is that a classification "be natural and reasonable, and appropriate to the occasion."[223] So long as a classification is rationally related to its objective and applies uniformly to everyone within the class, it will not be considered invalid.[224] Moreover, according to the courts, the question of whether a classification is reasonable is primarily for the legislature to decide.[225] The courts will presume that a classification is reasonable and will uphold a classification if any rational purpose can be conceived to justify it.[226]

This, of course, is pure minimal scrutiny, lifted in whole from federal "rationality review" under the Equal Protection Clause. All that it requires is a minimal assessment by a court to determine that legislation has a modicum of rationality. As described above,[227] minimal scrutiny can be put into effect in two ways, which differ significantly from one another. In the vast majority of federal cases, minimal scrutiny operates as no scrutiny at all.[228] It eviscerates judicial review by pretending to follow a standard of reasonableness while turning a blind eye to legislation that is patently unreasonable. On the other hand, on rare occasions in the federal system, minimal scrutiny will be invested with what has described as a small amount of "bite."[229] Under this approach, legislation that in fact has no rational basis will be struck down. This slightly enhanced version of minimal scrutiny offers some deference to the legislature, while the more common form of minimal scrutiny grants absolute deference to the legislature.

As originally used in the states, rationality review followed the federal model by functioning in a high majority of cases as virtually no review at

---

[221] See Collins v. Day, 644 N.E.2d 72 (Ind. 1994).

[222] See e.g., Mandell v. Haddon, 121 S.E.2d 516, 524 (Va. 1961).

[223] Id.

[224] Adams v. North Carolina Department of Natural and Economic Resources, 249 S.E.2d 402, 407 (N.C. 1978).

[225] Mandell v. Haddon, supra note 222, at 524.

[226] Id.

[227] See supra, at notes 48–50.

[228] See Jeffrey M. Shaman, Constitutional Interpretation: Illusion and Reality 78–81 (2001).

[229] See id. at 81.

all, that is, a rubber stamp to validate even highly questionable legislation. Still, on some occasions the legislature abuses its discretion and the courts, at first almost reluctantly, have been moved to enhance minimal scrutiny to strike down legislation that cannot be shown to have a truly rational purpose.

In more recent years, there have been an increasing number of instances in which the state courts use the more searching variety of rationality review to invest it with some bite. Consider, for example, *Bierkamp v. Rogers*,[230] an Iowa decision striking down a state guest statute on the ground that it violated the equal privileges and immunities clause of the Iowa Constitution.[231] In the federal system, guest statutes that are challenged as violating equal protection routinely are given the most minimal scrutiny, which can lead only to a finding of constitutionality. In *Bierkamp*, the Supreme Court of Iowa deftly brushed aside the federal line of guest statute cases with the observation that the decisions of the United States Supreme Court construing the Federal Constitution "are instructive, but not binding" on the Iowa court in construing analogous provisions in the state constitution.[232] Investing minimal scrutiny with more stringency than is available under the federal model, the Iowa court went on to conclude that the guest statute in question did not rationally advance the interest asserted for it (preventing collusive claims against insurance companies) or, for that matter, any other legitimate state interest.[233] *Bierkamp*, then, is a clear instance of a state court's willingness to invest rationality review with a degree of bite that would not be forthcoming in the federal system.

Some state constitutions prohibit special legislation when "a general law is or can be made applicable," and further state that "whether a general law is or can be made applicable shall be a matter for judicial determination."[234] Such language amounts to an express authorization of non-deferential judicial review of the question of whether a general law is or can be made applicable. Thus, when such a provision was adopted in

---

[230] Bierkamp v. Rogers, 293 N.W.2d 577 (Iowa 1980).
[231] All laws of a general nature shall have a uniform operation; the General Assembly shall not grant to any citizen, or class of citizens, privileges or immunities, which, upon the same terms shall not equally belong to all citizens. Iowa Const. of 1857 art. I, §6 (1857).
[232] *Bierkamp*, 293 N.W.2d at 581.
[233] *Id.* at 585.
[234] Ill. Const. art. IV, §13 (1970).

the 1970 Illinois Constitution, the Supreme Court of that state recognized that the new provision enlarged the scope of judicial review and was directed at reversing the court's previous practice of deferring to the legislature, but only in regard to the question of whether a general law is or can be made applicable.[235] Apparently the court was none too pleased with its enlarged authority, and went on to rule that for all other questions regarding the prohibition of special legislation, it would adhere to "those well-settled equal protection principles developed prior to the 1970 Constitution."[236] Accordingly, in reviewing the reasonableness of the classification in question, the court applied minimal scrutiny and deferred to the legislative judgment.[237] In subsequent decisions, the Supreme Court of Illinois has followed the same deferential tack, applying "rational basis" review to classifications challenged as special legislation.[238]

Equal Protection of the Laws

Enacted in 1868, following the Civil War, the Equal Protection Clause of the Fourteenth Amendment to the Federal Constitution proclaims that: "No state shall...deny to any person within its jurisdiction the equal protection of the laws."[239] As envisioned by its framers, the central purpose of the Equal Protection Clause was to eliminate hostile discrimination against the newly freed slaves.[240] The clause is directed toward the interdiction of unjust discrimination against minorities by mandating that they not be denied the equal protection of the laws. Obviously, the primary aim of the Equal Protection Clause is to prohibit racial discrimination. The overriding impetus for the Civil War Amendments was to counteract the tragic history of racial discrimination that plagued the nation. Flowing from prejudice and malice, the agent of inequality and oppression, racial discrimination is considered especially invidious.

---

[235] *In re* Belmont Fire Protection District, 489 N.W.2d 1385, 1387–88 (Ill. 1986).

[236] *Id.* at 1388.

[237] *Id.* at 1388–89.

[238] *See* Cutinello v. Whitley, 641 N.E.2d 360 (Ill. 1994); Miller v. Rosenberg, 749 N.E.2d 946 (Ill. 2001).

[239] U.S. Const. amend. XIV, sec. 1 (1868).

[240] "(It is) a historical fact that the central purpose of the Fourteenth Amendment was to eliminate racial discrimination emanating from official sources in the States." McLaughlin v. Florida, 379 U.S. 184, 192 (1964).

Race is the paradigm suspect classification and lines drawn on the basis of race demand no less than the most exacting judicial scrutiny.[241]

For many years after its enactment, the Equal Protection Clause lay relatively dormant, rarely used to strike down legislation or other governmental action.[242] In 1927, Justice Holmes could accurately describe the Equal Protection Clause as "the usual last resort of constitutional arguments."[243] Looking back at this period, Justice Powell was moved to admit that the Equal Protection Clause had been "relegated to decades of relative desuetude...."[244] All of that changed, however, in 1954 when the Supreme Court decided *Brown v. Board of Education*, a unanimous decision ruling that racial segregation in public schools violated the Equal Protection Clause.[245] The import of *Brown* cannot be overstated. Although it would be many years until southern states dismantled their systems of segregated schools, *Brown* revolutionized the law in America and eventually led to monumental change in American society. The catalyst for reform in this movement was the Equal Protection Clause. Through the evocation of the Equal Protection Clause, *Brown* triggered the civil rights movement[246] and awakened the realization that racial discrimination as well as other kinds of discrimination—against ethnic minorities, religious minorities, persons with disabilities, elderly persons, women, gay and lesbian persons—simply was wrong and could be challenged under the Equal Protection Clause.

Although there has been a long and unfortunate history of discrimination against women throughout the nation, it was not until the 1970s that the Equal Protection Clause was used to combat gender discrimination.[247] In the mid-1970s the Supreme Court finally got around to recognizing that classifications based on gender should be subject to heightened scrutiny, settling on intermediate scrutiny as the appropriate level of review for gender classifications. To this day, the court has declined to use

---

[241] Korematsu v. United States, 323 U.S. 214 (1944).

[242] The equal protection clause was "virtually strangled in infancy by post-civil-war judicial reactionism." Joseph Tussman & Jacobus tenBroek, *The Equal Protection of the Laws*, 37 Cal. L. Rev. 341, 381 (1949).

[243] Buck v. Bell, 274 U.S. 200, 208 (1927) (upholding constitutionality of state law providing for compulsory sterilization of "mental defectives").

[244] Regents of the University of California v. Bakke, 438 U.S. 265, 291 (1978) (Powell, J.).

[245] Brown v. Board of Education, 347 U.S. 483 (1954).

[246] *See* Jack Greenberg, *Crusaders in the Courts: How a Dedicated Band of Lawyers Fought for the Civil Rights Movement*, 12 (1994).

[247] Frontiero v. Richardson, 411 U.S. 677, 684 (1973).

strict scrutiny to review gender classifications, although the Court has intensified intermediate scrutiny of gender classifications by requiring that they rest upon an "exceedingly persuasive justification."[248]

While the principal purpose of the Equal Protection Clause clearly is to proscribe racial discrimination, the language of the clause is universal: the clause expressly states that equal protection of the laws shall not be denied to "any person." Accordingly, the Equal Protection Clause functions to bar other forms of discrimination as well as racial discrimination. The clause may be offended by classifications addressed to other discrete and insular minorities who historically have been the target of prejudice and discrimination.[249] Classifications based on ethnic origin— the close cousin of invidious racial classifications—are considered suspect and subject to strict judicial scrutiny,[250] as are classifications based on the status of alienage.[251] Classifications based on gender are subject to heightened judicial scrutiny under the Equal Protection Clause,[252] as are classifications directed at nonmarital children.[253] The Equal Protection Clause may even be violated by discrimination against a "class of one" if the discrimination is irrational.[254]

The Equal Protection Clause prohibits the government from singling out unpopular groups for disfavored treatment for no other reason than that they are disliked. As the Supreme Court explained, "A bare desire to harm a politically unpopular group cannot constitute a legitimate governmental interest."[255] Adhering to this principle, the Supreme Court has struck down laws that discriminate against "hippies,"[256] persons who are mentally retarded,[257] and gay and lesbian persons.[258] This axiom has been described as the "Pariah Principle," a principle that bars the government from designating any group, whether entitled to special constitutional

---

[248] United States v. Virginia, 518 U.S. 515, 531 (1996) (citing Mississippi University for Women v. Hogan, 458 U.S. at 724).

[249] United States v. Carolene Products Co., 304 U.S. 144, n. 4 (1938).

[250] Korematsu v. United States, 323 U.S. 214 (1944).

[251] Graham v. Richardson, 403 U.S. 365 (1971).

[252] Craig v. Boren, 429 U.S. 190 (1976).

[253] Trimble v. Gordon, 430 U.S. 762 (1977).

[254] Sioux City Bridge Co. v. Dakota County, 260 U.S. 441 (1923).

[255] Romer v. Evans, 517 U.S. 620, 634 (1996).

[256] United States Department of Agriculture v. Moreno, 413 U.S. 528 (1973).

[257] City of Cleburne v. Cleburne Living Center, Inc., 473 U.S. 432 (1985).

[258] Romer v. Evans, *supra* note 255; *but see* Bowers v. Hardwick, 478 U.S. 186 (1986).

protection or not, as untouchable.[259] According to this view, the Equal Protection Clause prohibits the government from targeting people for who they are rather than what they do. In other words, the government may not treat people as pariahs; it may not penalize people simply because they are disliked.

While the primary focus of the Equal Protection Clause is on the basis by which laws classify people, that focus need not be exclusive, and the clause also may be used with an eye to protecting fundamental rights.[260] Laws that impinge upon fundamental rights, such as the right to marry or have children, the right to vote or to migrate from one state to another are subject to strict judicial scrutiny under the Equal Protection Clause.[261]

For many years, a large majority of the states saw no need to include in their constitutions a provision modeled after the Federal Equal Protection Clause. Given that the Equal Protection Clause of the Fourteenth Amendment was binding on the states, it appeared unnecessary to add a duplicative provision to state constitutions. It further appeared unnecessary to add an equal protection clause to state constitutions because almost all of them already contained some sort of equality provision, such as a ban on special privileges or immunities. So, until 1970 only seven states saw fit to enact an equal protection clause in their constitutions.[262] Even today, the constitutions of but fifteen states contain provisions similar in wording to the federal one that prohibit the denial of equal protection of the laws.[263]

When the occasion arose, some states decided to reaffirm their commitment to equality by adding an equal protection clause to their constitutions.[264] This usually occurred at constitutional conventions when

---

[259] Daniel Farber & Suzanna Sherry, *The Pariah Principle*, 13 Const. Commentary 257 (1996); *see also* Akhil Reed Amar, *Attainder and Amendment 2: Romer's Rightness*, 95 Mich. L. Rev. 203, 208–10 (1996).

[260] Jeffrey M. Shaman, *Constitutional Interpretation: Illusion and Reality* 240–47 (2001).

[261] *Id.*

[262] Frank Grad, *The State Bill of Rights*, in *Con-Con: Issues for the Illinois Constitutional Convention* 30, 35 (Victoria Ranney ed. 1970).

[263] Cal. Const. art. I, §7(a); Conn. Const. art. I, §20; Ga. Const. art. I, §1; Haw. Const. art. I, §5; Ill. Const. art. I, §2; La. Const. art. I, §3; Me. Const. art. I, §6-A; Mich. Const. art. I, §2; Mont. Const. art. II, §4; Neb. Const. art. I, §3; N.M. Const. art. II, §18; N.C. Const. art. I, §19; N.Y. Const. art. I, §11; R.I. Const., art. I, §2; S.C. Const. art I, §3.

[264] For example, the delegates to the 1950 Hawaii constitutional convention took the position that while the Equal Protection Clause of the Fourteenth Amendment applied to Hawaii and made it unnecessary to include a similar provision in the Hawaii

states were framing new constitutions. In 1868, when it adopted a new constitution as a condition to being readmitted to the Union, Georgia became the first state to enact an equal protection clause.[265] In 1910, the constitution forged by New Mexico to gain admission to the Union included an equal protection clause.[266] States such as South Carolina in 1895, New York in 1938, Michigan in 1962, Connecticut in 1965, Illinois in 1970, Louisiana in 1974, and Rhode Island in 1986, included equal protection clauses in their freshly-minted constitutions.[267] In 2000, Nebraska earned the distinction of becoming the latest state to enact an equal protection clause when it adopted a new constitution.[268]

Over the years, the state courts have developed a considerable body of doctrine, some of it borrowed from federal case law, in interpreting their own equal protection clauses. Equal protection concepts have had a great influence upon thinking about other types of equality provisions, such as bans on special entitlements or prohibitions of unequal privileges or immunities. In fact, as time passed, doctrine generated under equal protection clauses has merged with doctrine generated under other species of equality provisions. Undeniably, the Equal Protection Clause has had a tremendous impact upon the conception of equality in state constitutional law.

Conclusion

With the rise of the New Judicial Federalism, a number of states have exercised their sovereign independence to create a conception of equality that transcends the federal model of equal protection of the laws. State

---

constitution, such a provision should be included in the Hawaii constitution in order to reaffirm the Hawaiian commitment to equality. Proceedings of the Constitutional Convention of Hawaii 164–65 (1960). Along the same lines, the delegates to the 1970 Illinois constitutional convention decided to include an equal protection clause in the new constitution to reaffirm that equal protection of the laws was guaranteed to all Illinois citizens. Sixth Illinois Constitutional Convention Transcript, 1496–1523 (June 4, 1970).

[265] Georgia Journal of Proceedings of the Constitutional Convention 216–17 (1867–68) (card 3 of 7).

[266] New Mexico Ter. Constitutional Convention 1–3 (1910). Proceedings of the Constitutional Convention (1910) (card 1 of 3).

[267] See supra note 263.

[268] See Jason W. Hayes, Amendment One: The Nebraska Equal Protection Clause, 32 Creighton L. Rev. 611, 611–17 (1998).

constitutional equality builds upon the federal model, but remolds it and expands it into new areas beyond the scope of federal equal protection.

Many states have seen fit in cases involving equality to reconstitute the multi-tier system of review developed in the federal courts.[269] In some instances, this has been done by expanding the scope of strict or intermediate scrutiny to encompass classifications or rights which in the federal courts are assigned to lower regions.[270] State courts have upgraded gender classifications from intermediate to strict scrutiny[271] and have ruled that classifications based on sexual orientation are subject to heightened scrutiny.[272] State courts have taken the position that education is a fundamental right and therefore public school financing schemes are to be reviewed with strict scrutiny.[273] And state courts have held that strict scrutiny should be applied to determine the constitutionality of laws that deny funding for abortions.[274] In other instances, the tiers of review have been reconstituted by intensifying rationality review to give it an edge lacking under the federal approach.[275] State courts may sharpen rationality review to assess the constitutionality of economic legislation that denies benefits for no apparent reason, interferes with fair competition, or grants special entitlements to a favored few.[276] On occasion, state courts may enhance rationality review to examine the constitutionality of criminal laws that provide differential penalties or treatment for similar offenses.[277] A few state courts have put bite into rationality review to strike down classifications based on age,[278] and one state court even used a sharpened version of rationality review to invalidate a statute that discriminated against adopted persons.[279]

Some state courts have taken a more radical approach by abandoning the multi-tier system in favor of a less rigid methodology that relies upon either a sliding scale of review or a uniform standard that can be calibrated by many degrees rather than a few tiers.[280] Using this sort of flexible

---

[269] *See supra* at notes 96–107.
[270] *See supra* at notes 96–99.
[271] *See* Chapter Two at notes 61–72.
[272] *See id.* at notes 124–37, 145–52.
[273] *See* Chapter Three at notes 3–10, 21–24.
[274] *See* Chapter Five at notes 10–25.
[275] *See supra* at notes 99–108.
[276] *See* Chapter Three at notes 113–29, 134–71.
[277] *See* Chapter Three at notes 172–84, 195–208.
[278] *See* Chapter Two at notes 191–212.
[279] MacCallum v. Seymour, 686 A.2d 935 (Vt. 1996).
[280] *See supra* at notes 107–25.

approach, the Supreme Court of Vermont struck down a state law that excluded same-sex couples from the benefits of marriage.[281]

Other state courts have been able to go beyond the federal model of equality by using a state equality guarantee in combination with another provision in the state constitution.[282] This approach has been used in state courts to strike down statutes that eliminated welfare benefits,[283] restricted the recovery of damages in tort actions,[284] gave undue discretion to prosecutors to treat juvenile offenders as adults,[285] or that led to *de facto* segregation in public schools.[286]

While the federal conception of equality has become relatively static, its state counterpart is dynamic and, hence, responsive to the evolving needs of a changing society. In recent years, it has been the state courts that have led the movement to recognize new rights by expanding the guarantee of equality. In state courts across the nation, doctrine developed under various equality provisions is consolidated, with the result that a prohibition of unequal privileges or immunities, a ban on special entitlements, a guarantee of equal protection of the laws are equivalent to one another. The various kinds of equality provisions inform one another. Underlying principles pertinent to one equality provision give meaning to another equality provision and the favor is returned. There is a coalescence of meaning among equality provisions. The meaning of an equality provision grows as part of a common undertaking from jurisdiction to jurisdiction.

The concept of equality is no longer an exclusively federal construct. To fully understand the meaning of equality in the United States, state constitutional law, as well as federal constitutional law, must be thoroughly considered. Constitutional equality is now a joint federal and state enterprise.

---

[281] Baker v. State, 744 A.2d 864 (Vt. 1999). *Baker* is discussed in Chapter Six.

[282] *See supra* at notes 125–55.

[283] *See supra* at notes 129–39.

[284] *See* Chapter Three at notes 96–101.

[285] State v. Mohi, *supra* note 146.

[286] *See supra* at notes 147–50.

CHAPTER TWO

CLASSIFICATIONS

It often is said that the Equal Protection Clause does not prohibit a state from making classifications in its laws so long as there is sufficient reason to justify differential treatment.[1] As the Supreme Court put it in a 1920 decision, a classification will not be struck down if it is reasonable, not arbitrary, and rests upon some ground of difference having a fair and substantial relation to the object of the legislation, "so that all persons similarly circumstanced shall be treated alike."[2] Many state courts have adopted the principle that equal protection requires equal treatment of persons similarly situated, while allowing differential treatment of persons who are not similarly situated.[3] As early as 1921, the Supreme Court of California declared that a law will not be declared unconstitutional because of discrimination, "unless it improperly discriminates between persons similarly situated."[4] Since then, state courts have frequently adhered to the principle that "equal protection requires that persons who are similarly situated be treated similarly."[5]

In many instances, however, it simply is not enough to ask whether persons are similarly situated without also inquiring whether any purported dissimilarity between them "rests upon some ground of difference having a fair and substantial relation to the object of the legislation." Frequently the more pertinent matter is to determine if the dissimilarity at hand is one that justifies differential treatment. It almost always is

---

[1] Thomas Cooley, *Constitutional Limitations* 812–17 (8th ed. 1927).

[2] F.S. Royster Guano Co. v. Virginia, 252 U.S. 412, 415 (1920).

[3] State v. Freeland, 667 P.2d 509, 519 (Ore. 1983); Israel v. West Virginia Secondary Schools Activities Commission, 388 S.E.2d 480, 484 (W. Va. 1989).

[4] *In the Matter of Girard*, 200 P. 593, 594 (Cal. 1921).

[5] Kelly v. State, 525 N.W.2d 409, 411 (Iowa 1994).

possible to find some distinction between people, but not necessarily a distinction that makes a difference. Indeed, it often begs the question to say that persons are not similarly situated; the real question should focus on whether their dissimilarity is one that calls for differential treatment. For instance, in *Powell v. Pennsylvania*, decided in 1888, the Supreme Court found no violation of the Equal Protection Clause in a statute prohibiting the sale of oleomargarine.[6] In the Court's view, the statute did not deny equal protection of the laws because it placed the same restrictions upon all persons in "similar circumstances."[7] The statute preserved the principle of equality, the Court said, by applying to all those engaged in the same business.[8] This, of course, is pure sophistry. As Professors Tussman and tenBroek perceptively noted, "What is striking about (the Court's) statement is the easy dismissal of the equal protection issue on the grounds that the law applies equally to all to whom it applies."[9] The more important inquiry was whether the lines drawn by the statute between various businesses were justifiable. The Court's decision in *Powell* illustrates that often it is not sufficient to ask whether parties are similarly situated; there also should be an inquiry of whether any purported basis of dissimilarity rests upon a ground that truly supports differential treatment under the law.

Racial Classifications

For many years, litigation on behalf of racial minorities in the state courts was overshadowed by litigation in the federal courts.[10] During the chief justiceship of Earl Warren, the Supreme Court took the lead in opposing racial discrimination, striking down various forms of racial discrimination as violating the Equal Protection Clause of the Fourteenth Amendment.[11] The high Court designated race a suspect classification subject to strict judicial scrutiny. Indeed, few, if any, racial classifications

---

[6] Powell v. Pennsylvania, 127 U.S. 678 (1888).

[7] *Id.* at 684.

[8] *Id.* at 687.

[9] Joseph Tussman & Jacobus tenBroek, *The Equal Protection of the Laws*, 37 Cal. L. Rev. 341, 345 (1949).

[10] *See generally*, Jennifer Friesen, *State Constitutional Law: Litigating Individual Rights, Claims and Defenses* 3-8 (3d ed. 2000).

[11] *See, e.g.*, Brown v. Board of Education, 347 U.S. 483 (1954); Anderson v. Martin, 375 U.S. 399 (1964); Loving v. Virginia, 388 U.S. 1 (1967).

could withstand the strict scrutiny with which the Court assessed their constitutionality. While the Supreme Court and other federal courts struck down one racial classification after another, most state courts seemed content to sit on the sidelines in the struggle for racial equality.[12] Eventually, however, as the composition of the Supreme Court changed, so did its commitment to racial equality, with the result that the Court found some limits to the capacity of the Equal Protection Clause for proscribing racial discrimination. The Court ruled that only intentional racial discrimination would be subject to strict scrutiny, while government action that was not shown to intentionally discriminate on the basis of race would be subject to the most deferential sort of minimal scrutiny.[13] Racially neutral laws that have a racially discriminatory impact would not be reviewed with strict scrutiny unless it was demonstrated that they were enacted with a racially discriminatory purpose.[14] In cases involving school desegregation, the Supreme Court drew a distinction between *de jure* and *de facto* racial segregation, holding that the latter amounted to a violation of the Equal Protection Clause only when proven to be the result of an intent to discriminate on the basis of race.[15]

It was at this juncture that a few state supreme courts stepped into the breach and found that their state equal protection clauses could be extended beyond the point where federal equal protection ended. In California, the state supreme court ruled in a series of cases that, irrespective of what federal law might or might not require, the California equal protection clause prohibits *de facto* as well as *de jure* racial segregation in public schools and school boards have an affirmative obligation to eradicate racial segregation in the schools whether it is *de facto* or *de jure*.[16] In fact, the California court made it clear that the constitutional obligations of school boards in the state entail more than simply the avoidance of intentional discrimination.[17] Even in the absence of gerrymandering or other intentional discriminatory conduct, the state may be

---

12 Friesen, *supra* note 10, at 3-3.
13 Washington v. Davis, 426 U.S. 229 (1976); Arlington Heights v. Metropolitan Housing Corp., 429 U.S. 252 (1977).
14 *Id.*
15 Keyes v. School District No. 1, 413 U.S. 189 (1973); Columbus Board of Education v. Penick, 443 U.S. 449 (1979).
16 Jackson v. Pasadena City School District, 382 P.2d 878, 881 (Cal. 1963); San Francisco Unified School District v. Johnson, 479 P.2d 669, 682 (Cal. 1971); Crawford v. Board of Education, 551 P.2d 28, 33–36 (Cal. 1976).
17 *Crawford*, 551 P.2d at 34.

obligated to provide relief if there is substantial racial imbalance in a school.[18] In the court's view, given the right to equal educational opportunity and the harmful effects of racial segregation, the school boards in California bear an affirmative duty to undertake reasonably feasible steps to eliminate racial segregation regardless of its cause.[19]

The force of these rulings, however, subsequently was nullified through an initiative amending the state constitution.[20] The amendment, enacted in 1979, added a provision to the state equal protection clause declaring that, with respect to pupil school assignment or pupil transportation, nothing in the California Constitution imposes any obligations or responsibilities upon the state which exceed those imposed by the Equal Protection Clause of the Fourteenth Amendment to the United States Constitution.[21] This obviously curtailed the ability of the California Supreme Court to rectify racial discrimination in the public schools. Nevertheless, the California experience serves as a powerful example of a state court willing to recognize that its state equal protection clause may provide more extensive protection than the Federal Equal Protection Clause against racial discrimination. When the United States Supreme Court faltered in its commitment to racial equality, California's highest court carried on the endeavor for racial justice.

Racial imbalance in public schools has also been the subject of an important decision in Connecticut. In *Sheff v. O'Neill*, the Supreme Court of Connecticut ruled that the public schools in Hartford, Connecticut were in violation of the state constitution because they were racially segregated.[22] The court's opinion in *Sheff* is extremely interesting, in that it relies upon some uncommon language in the state equal protection clause and then combines that clause with another constitutional provision to resolve that racial imbalance in public schools violates the Connecticut constitution.

The facts recited near the beginning of the court's opinion describe the extent of segregation in the Hartford schools: While the statewide

---

[18] *Jackson*, 382 P.2d at 881.

[19] *Crawford*, 551 P.2d at 34–35.

[20] Cal. Const. art. I, §7(a) (Amended Nov. 6, 1979).

[21] *Id.* The amendment also provided that no court of the state may impose upon the state any obligation or responsibility with respect to the use of pupil school assignment or pupil transportation except to remedy a specific violation that would also constitute a violation of the federal equal protection clause and that a federal court would be permitted under federal decisional law to remedy in that manner. *Id.*

[22] Sheff v. O'Neill, 678 A.2d 1267 (Conn. 1996).

percentage of children from minority groups was 25.7% of the public school population, in the Hartford schools 92.4% of the students were members of minority groups.[23] Fourteen of Hartford's 25 elementary schools had a white student enrollment of less than 2%.[24] If anything, this pattern was continuing, and the percentage of minority children in the Hartford schools was likely to increase rather than decrease.[25]

In finding that this situation violated the state constitution, the court pointed to two provisions in the Connecticut Constitution, the education article and the equal protection clause. The education article states:

> There shall always be free public elementary and secondary schools in the state. The general assembly shall implement this principle by appropriate legislation.[26]

The equal protection clause states:

> No person shall be denied the equal protection of the law nor be subjected to segregation or discrimination in the exercise or enjoyment of his or her civil or political rights because of religion, color, ancestry, national origin, sex or physical or mental disability.[27]

The issue in the case revolved around the fact that the Hartford schools were not intentionally segregated. There was no showing that the government had intentionally caused racial imbalance in the Hartford schools, so this was an instance of unintentional *de facto* racial segregation.[28] Hence, the state argued that so long as it had substantially equalized school funding and resources, there could be no constitutional violation in the absence of a showing of intentional segregation of the schools. The court ruled, however, that even in the absence of intentional discrimination, a racially segregated school system may violate the state constitution.[29] In fact, the court concluded that "the existence of extreme

---

[23] *Id.* at 1272.

[24] *Id.* at 1273.

[25] *Id.*

[26] Conn. Const. art. 8, §1.

[27] Conn. Const. art.1, §20.

[28] *Sheff*, 678 A.2d at 1289. The court noted, though, that the state had nonetheless played a significant role in the concentration of racial and ethnic minorities in the Hartford public school system by creating and maintaining the boundaries of school districts. Indeed, the court said that the state districting statute was the single most important factor contributing to the racial and ethnic concentration in the Hartford schools. *Id.*

[29] *Id.* at 1281.

racial and ethnic isolation in the public school system deprives school children of a substantially equal educational opportunity and requires the state to take further remedial measures."[30]

The court reached this conclusion by reading the education article and the equal protection clause in conjunction with each other. It said that it was persuaded to do so by two factors, the special nature of the education article and the explicit language of the equal protection clause.

Concerning the former, the court noted that the education article places an affirmative obligation on the state to provide substantially equal educational opportunity.[31] This differs from most constitutional provisions. Constitutions, the court said, "rarely contain provisions that explicitly require the state to act rather than refrain from acting."[32] In saying this, the court was building on its previous decision in *Horton v. Meskill*, where the court had ruled that the Connecticut system of financing public schools, which resulted in disparate funding from school district to district, violated the state constitution.[33] In *Horton*, the court pointed out that the education article created an affirmative obligation on the state to provide education, and the court interpreted this to be an affirmative obligation to provide substantially equal educational opportunity.[34] In *Sheff*, the Court said that what was previously articulated in *Horton*— the affirmative obligation to provide equal educational opportunity— was not limited to financing.[35] So, the court extended the state's affirmative obligation to provide equal educational opportunity to the inequality caused by racial isolation.[36]

The second factor that persuaded the court to interpret the education article and the equal protection clause jointly was the fact that the equal protection clause explicitly prohibits segregation. In the court's view, the express inclusion of the term "segregation" in the Connecticut equal protection clause had "independent constitutional significance."[37] Accordingly, the scope of the state's constitutional obligation to provide

---

[30] *Id.*
[31] *Id.*
[32] *Id.*
[33] Horton v. Meskill, 376 A.2d 359 (Conn. 1977).
[34] *Id.* at 375.
[35] *Sheff*, 678 A.2d at 1280.
[36] *Id.*
[37] *Id.* at 1282.

substantially equal education opportunity was "informed and amplified by the highly unusual provision in the state equal protection clause that prohibits segregation not only indirectly, by forbidding discrimination, but directly, by use of the term "segregation."[38] Therefore, the court concluded that at least in conjunction with the education article, the equal protection clause prohibits unintentional *de facto* segregation as well as *de jure* segregation.[39]

The court noted that linguistically, the term "segregation" as used in the Connecticut equal protection clause is neutral in regard to intent.[40] That is, the constitutional proscription of segregation does not specify whether the segregation must be intentionally caused by the state.[41] The court concluded, though, that whatever the equal protection clause may mean in other contexts, in the context of public education, where the state has an affirmative obligation to monitor and equalize educational opportunity, the state's awareness of severe racial and ethnic isolation imposes upon the state the responsibility to remedy racial segregation in the public schools.[42] So the court held that textually, the education articled as informed by the equal protection clause requires the legislature to take affirmative responsibility to remedy segregation in the public schools, regardless of whether that segregation has occurred intentionally or unintentionally.[43]

Equality provisions in state constitutions also have the potential to be used to challenge affirmative action programs that utilize racial classifications to favor minority groups. Usually constitutional challenges to affirmative action are based upon the Federal Equal Protection Clause or, in the few states that have adopted them, constitutional amendments proscribing affirmative action programs.[44] However, in *Malabed v. North Slope Borough*, a 2003 decision, the Supreme Court of Alaska ruled that a borough ordinance granting a hiring preference to Native Americans was

---

[38] *Id.* at 1281. Connecticut is one of three states whose constitutions contain a provision expressly prohibiting segregation. The other two states are Hawaii and New Jersey.

[39] *Id.* at 1283.

[40] *Id.* at 1282.

[41] *Id.*

[42] *Id.*

[43] *Id.* at 1283. Moreover, the court thought that its interpretation of the education article and equal protection clause was consistent with the intent of the delegates to the 1965 constitutional convention that drafted and proposed these two provisions. *See id.*

[44] In 1996 the voters of California approved an initiative amending the state constitution to ban affirmative action. Similar measures were enacted in Washington in 1998 and in Michigan in 2006.

in violation of the state equal protection clause.[45] The plaintiff who challenged the ordinance asserted that it contained a racial classification or, alternatively, a classification based on national origin in violation of the Alaska Constitution. Justice Matthews, in a concurring opinion, also thought that the ordinance amounted to a racial classification, as evidenced by the fact that the ordinance frankly acknowledged that its goal was to benefit a racial group, Inupiat Eskimos.[46] Accordingly, Justice Matthews would have applied strict scrutiny to the ordinance to find that it violated the Alaska equal rights provision (a separate provision from the Alaska equal protection clause) that expressly prohibits the denial of civil or political rights because of race.[47]

A majority of the court, though, thought otherwise and chose to take a different route in striking down the ordinance. Because the ordinance defined "Native American" as including any person belonging to an Indian tribe under federal law, the court assumed for purposes of deciding the case that the ordinance was based on a tribal or political classification and did not discriminate on the basis of race.[48] Therefore the court decided to assess the ordinance under the state equal protection clause rather than the equal rights provision. In making that assessment, the court used the Alaska three-step, sliding scale approach that places a progressively greater or lesser burden of justification on the state, depending on the weight of the individual interest impaired by the law in question, the importance of the governmental purpose underlying the law, and the appropriateness of the means employed in the law to accomplish its ends.[49] The court determined that the individual interest affected by the classification was the right to obtain employment within one's profession, which in the court's view, was an important right, calling for close scrutiny of the law, requiring the borough to show that the ordinance properly served an important governmental interest.[50] The borough offered several reasons in support of the ordinance: reducing unemployment of the largest group of borough residents, strengthening

---

45 Malabed v. North Slope Borough, 70 P.3d 416 (Alaska 2003).
46 *Id*. at 428 (Matthews, J., concurring).
47 *Id*. at 428–29 (Matthews, J., concurring). Justice Matthews did not suggest that racial classifications were invalid *per se* under the equal rights provision, but that they were subject to strict scrutiny.
48 *Id*. at 420.
49 The Alaska three-step, sliding scale approach is described in Chapter One, at notes 112–20.
50 *Malabed*, 70 P.3d at 421.

the borough's economy, and training its workforce.[51] While agreeing that these purposes were important, the court concluded that the ordinance sought to achieve them in an illegitimate manner, that is, by favoring one class of Alaskans over another.[52] In the court's view, conferring an economic benefit on one class of persons while denying it to others who are similarly situated was impermissible under the Alaska equal protection clause.[53]

Gender Classifications

In 1893, the Indiana Supreme Court decided *In re Leach,* holding that a statute prohibiting women from the practice of law was a violation of the state equal privileges and immunities clause.[54] An individual's right to choose a profession, the court said, should not be denied on account of sex.[55] The decision in *Leach,* however, was a rare exception. In fact, the court noted that it was "not unmindful" that Illinois, Wisconsin, Oregon, Maryland, and Massachusetts previously had upheld statutes similarly barring women from the practice of law.[56] Moreover, until the 1970s precious few laws of any kind that treated men and women differently were found to be unconstitutional. Prior to that time, the vast majority of state courts, not to mention the federal courts, were extremely tolerant of laws that differentiated on the basis of sex. Traditionally, the courts endorsed differential treatment of men and women under the law as an accepted way of life, and once the levels of scrutiny were developed, classifications based on gender were sloughed off to the lowest tier of review. The states, in lockstep with the federal model, used the most minimal scrutiny to review gender classifications, invariably seeing nothing improper about them.

In the 1970s, the Supreme Court of the United States realized that classifications based on gender share many of the invidious characteristics of a suspect classification.[57] At one point, a four-person plurality of

---

[51] *Id.*

[52] *Id.* at 421–22.

[53] *Id.*

[54] *In re* Leach, 34 N.E. 641 (Ind. 1893).

[55] *Id.* at 642.

[56] *Id.* The court neglected to mention that 20 years earlier the United States Supreme Court had also upheld the constitutionality of a statute barring women from the practice of law. Bradwell v. State of Illinois, 83 U.S. (16 Wall.) 130 (1873).

[57] *See* Frontiero v. Richardson, 411 U.S. 677 (1973); Craig v. Boren, 429 U.S. 190 (1976).

the Court agreed that gender should be treated as a suspect classification calling for strict scrutiny, but a fifth vote could not be mustered for a majority.[58] In a separate concurring opinion, Justice Powell, joined by two others, suggested that the question of whether gender is a suspect classification should be postponed because the proposed Federal Equal Rights Amendment (ERA), which would prohibit the denial or abridgement of rights on account of sex, would resolve that very question.[59] The ERA, however, narrowly failed to gain passage on the federal level, and the Court eventually decided that gender classifications should be reviewed in an intermediate tier of scrutiny.[60] In effect, the Supreme Court resolved to treat gender as a "semi-suspect" classification subject to a heightened, though not strict, mode of scrutiny.

Meanwhile, the states were proving more hospitable to adopting the ERA. Between 1970 and 1978, some fifteen states adopted constitutional amendments modeled in whole or part after the Federal ERA that specially prohibit discrimination on the basis of sex.[61] They joined three other states—California, Utah, and Wyoming—whose constitutions have contained provisions expressly prohibiting sexual discrimination since the late 1800s.[62] Today, some twenty state constitutions contain equality provisions that specifically prohibit discrimination on the basis of sex.[63] As might be expected, the language of these provisions varies from state to state. Some of them include other forms of classification, such as race, color, creed, national origin, or religion, in their proscriptions.[64] Others simply state that: "Equality of rights under the law shall not be abridged or denied because of sex."[65]

In most states whose constitutions contain a provision expressly proscribing discrimination on the basis of sex, the courts take a strong stance against gender classifications. Perhaps the strongest statement in this regard was made by the Supreme Court of Washington in declaring that:

---

[58] Frontiero v. Richardson, *id.*

[59] *Id.* at 692 (Powell, J., concurring).

[60] Craig v. Boren, 429 U.S. 190 (1976).

[61] Paul Linton, *State Equal Rights Amendments: Making a Difference or Making a Statement?,* 70 Temp. L. Rev. 907, 908 (1997).

[62] Cal. Const. art. I, §8 (1879); Utah Const. art. IV, §1 (1896); Wyo. Const. art. 1, §3 (1890).

[63] The provisions are collected in Jennifer Friesen, *supra* note 10, at 3-51 (Appendix 3).

[64] *See id.*

[65] Md. Const. art. 46.

The ERA absolutely prohibits discrimination on the basis of sex and is not subject to even the narrow exceptions permitted under traditional "strict scrutiny"....The ERA mandates equality in the strongest of terms and absolutely prohibits the sacrifice of equality for any state interest, no matter how compelling ....[66]

Several state supreme courts have held that the purpose of the ERA was to eliminate the use of sex as a basis for making legal distinctions between individuals.[67] In *Henderson v. Henderson*, the Supreme Court of Pennsylvania stated:

The thrust of the Equal Rights Amendment is to insure equality of rights under the law and to eliminate sex as a basis for distinction. The sex of citizens of this Commonwealth is no longer a permissible factor in the determination of legal rights and legal responsibilities. The law will not impose different benefits or different burdens upon the members of a society based on the fact that they may be man or woman.[68]

A few courts in other states take a nearly absolutist approach to their ERAs by holding that gender classifications are strictly disallowed except when necessitated by physical differences between the sexes.[69] In other states that have an ERA, the courts reason that given the express constitutional prohibition of sexual discrimination, gender classifications must be considered suspect and therefore subject to exacting scrutiny.[70] As a Texas court explained, the ERA elevates sex to a suspect classification and any law that classifies persons for different treatment on the basis of sex is subject to strict judicial scrutiny.[71] In the view of the Supreme Court of Illinois, the conclusion is inescapable that the ERA was intended to supplement and expand the guarantees of equal protection and requires that

---

[66] Southwest Washington Chapter, National Electrical Contractors Association v. Pierce County, 667 P.2d 1092, 1102 (Wash. 1983). The court did allow that benign gender classifications intended to ameliorate the effects of past discrimination do not implicate the ERA. *Id.*

[67] *See* Henderson v. Henderson, 327 A.2d 60, 62 (Pa. 1974); Attorney General v. Massachusetts Interscholastic Athletic Association, 393 N.E.2d 284 (Mass. 1979).

[68] Henderson v. Henderson, *id.*

[69] Henderson v. Henderson, 327 A.2d 60 (Pa. 1974); People v. Salinas, 551 P.2d 703 (Colo. 1976).

[70] *E.g.*, Page v. Welfare Commissioner, 365 A.2d 1118 (Conn. 1976); Attorney General v. Massachusetts Interscholastic Athletic Association, 393 N.E.2d 284 (Mass. 1979).

[71] Low Income Women of Texas v. Bost, 38 S.W.3d 689, 696 (Tex. Ct. App. 2000).

a classification based on gender be considered suspect and subject to strict judicial scrutiny.[72]

Not all states, however, are so forceful in applying provisions that expressly bar discrimination based on sex. At first, the Colorado Supreme Court seemed to adopt an intermediate level of scrutiny for claims brought under the ERA,[73] but later suggested that strict scrutiny was the more appropriate level of review.[74] The Supreme Court of Louisiana used intermediate scrutiny in applying a state provision that expressly bars discrimination on the basis of sex.[75] In Virginia, after the enactment in 1971 of a new constitutional provision expressly proscribing discrimination on the basis of sex, the state supreme court originally took the position that the provision was no broader than the Federal Equal Protection Clause and called for no more than rationality review.[76] Ten years later, still in lockstep with the federal approach, the Virginia high court upgraded the level of review under the provision to intermediate scrutiny.[77] This sort of adherence to the federal standard of intermediate scrutiny is questionable in states whose constitutions have been amended to expressly proscribe discrimination on the basis of sex. The enactment of such provisions seems to be a definitive step that goes beyond the federal conception of equality and that calls for nothing less than strict scrutiny to review the constitutionality of classifications based on sex.

In states whose constitutions do not contain a provision expressly barring sex discrimination, the courts tend to follow the federal approach of using intermediate scrutiny to review classifications based on gender.[78] Some of these states have found that, as is true in the federal system, intermediate scrutiny can be an effective means to combat sexual discrimination. In New Jersey, for instance, using an intermediate standard of review, the courts have struck down the practice, whether utilized by prosecutors[79] or defense attorneys,[80] of exercising peremptory challenges

---

[72] People v. Ellis, 311 N.E.2d 98, 101 (Ill. 1974).

[73] Lujan v. Colorado State Board of Education, 649 P.2d 1005 (Colo. 1982).

[74] Civil Rights Commission v. Travelers Ins. Co., 759 P.2d 1358, 1363 (Colo. 1988).

[75] Pace v. State, 648 So.2d 1302 (La. 1995).

[76] Archer v. Mayes, 194 S.E.2d 707, 710–11 (Va. 1973).

[77] Schilling v. Bedford City Memorial Hospital, Inc., 303 S.E.2d 905 (Va. 1983).

[78] E.g., Israel v. West Virginia Secondary Schools Activities Commission, 388 S.E.2d 480 (W. Va. 1989); Franklin v. Hill, 444 S.E.2d 778 (Ga. 1994); Friehe v. Schaad, 545 N.W.2d 740 (Neb. 1996).

[79] State v. Gilmore, 511 A.2d 1150 (N.J. 1986).

[80] State v. Chevalier, 774 A.2d 597, 2001 WL 506235 (N.J. Super. A.D., 2001).

on the basis of gender. The Supreme Court of Georgia employed intermediate scrutiny to invalidate a law that created a civil cause of action for seduction when committed by men, but not when committed by women.[81] Intermediate scrutiny, however, has its limits, and on occasion it is employed to uphold gender classifications that in all probability would not be able to withstand strict scrutiny.[82] Though demanding, intermediate scrutiny is a less exacting standard than strict scrutiny.

Florida has taken an unusual stance in regard to classifications based on gender. In 1998, several amendments were made to the equality provision in the Florida Constitution, including one amendment that added the phrase "female and male alike," so that the introductory sentence in the provision read: "All natural persons, *female and male alike*, are equal before the law ...."[83] Notwithstanding the new language, a Florida appellate court later ruled that gender classifications would not be subject to strict scrutiny.[84] The court's conclusion was based on commentary of the Florida Constitution Revision Commission pointing out that the original proposal to amend the equality provision, which was intended to secure equality for women, would have added the term "sex" to the list of protected classes at the end of the equality provision.[85] That proposal was dropped for fear that it might lead Florida courts to require recognition of same-sex marriages, as had previously occurred in Hawaii.[86] So, instead of adding "sex" to the list of protected classes at the end of the equality provision, the Commission added "female and male alike" to its introductory sentence. Because other new classifications were added to the list of protected classes while sex was not, the Florida appellate court concluded that classifications based on sex should not be subject to strict scrutiny.[87] The court went on to rule, though, that the level of scrutiny applied to

---

[81] Franklin v. Hill, 444 S.E.2d 778 (Ga. 1994).

[82] *See, e.g.*, Friehe v. Schaad, 545 N.W.2d 740 (Neb. 1996) (upholding, under an intermediate level of review, a statute that allowed an unwed mother to withhold consent to adoption while denying an unwed father the same right unless he filed a notice of intent to claim paternity within five days of the child's birth).

[83] Fla. Const. art. I, §2 (1998).

[84] Frandsen v. County of Brevard, 800 So.2d 757, 759–60 (Fla. 5th DCA 2001); *see also*, A Choice for Women, Inc. v. Florida Agency for Health Care Administration, 872 So.2d 970 (Fla. 3rd DCA 2004) (same).

[85] *Frandsen*, at 759, n. 4.

[86] *Id*. The Hawaii case, Baehr v. Lewin, 852 P.2d 44 (Haw. 1993), is discussed *infra* at notes 106–14.

[87] *Frandsen*, at 759–60.

sex classifications could be no less rigorous than that mandated by the United States Supreme Court, namely, intermediate scrutiny.[88]

Pennsylvania is one of the ERA states that takes a particularly strong stand against gender classifications. In 1975, a few years after the ERA was adopted in Pennsylvania, the supreme court of that state invalidated a regulation for high school and junior high school students that disallowed girls to compete or practice with boys in any athletic contest.[89] In finding that the regulation violated the ERA, the Pennsylvania Supreme Court stressed that the aim of the ERA was to remove distinctions based on gender from the law so that men and women had equal legal status.[90] The regulation, therefore, could not be justified on the assertion that girls generally have less athletic ability and are weaker and thus more injury-prone than boys.[91] The presence of certain traits to a greater degree in one sex than the other does not justify classifications based on sex rather than on the particular trait.[92] Concerns about a student's athletic skill, strength, or proneness to injury can be accommodated through a gender-neutral regulation that looks to those factors rather than gender. If an individual student (male or female) is too unskilled, weak, or injury-prone, the student may be excluded from competition for that reason but may not be excluded due to his or her sex without regard for the student's qualifications.[93] In other words, the ERA precludes the use of gender as a proxy for something else. Indeed, to the extent possible, the ERA calls for the elimination of gender-based classifications to differentiate individuals under the law.

In Massachusetts, the supreme court held that the state ERA was offended by an interscholastic athletic regulation that provided that no boy could play on a girls' team.[94] After explaining that that the ERA required the application of strict scrutiny to classifications based on sex,[95] the court went on to conclude that there was no compelling state interest that could justify the challenged regulation.[96] Although there may be

---

[88] Id. at 760.

[89] Commonwealth v. Pennsylvania Interscholastic Athletic Association, 334 A.2d 839 (Pa. 1975).

[90] Id. at 842.

[91] Id. at 842–43.

[92] Id. at 843.

[93] Id.

[94] Attorney General v. Massachusetts Interscholastic Athletic Association, supra note 67.

[95] Id. at 291.

[96] Id. at 293–96.

physical differences between men and women, the court said, they are not so clear or uniform as to justify a regulation that uses gender as a proxy for physical condition.[97] Gender classifications that make no reference to actual skill differentials merely echo "archaic and overbroad generalizations."[98] "Any notion that young women are so inherently weak, delicate or physically inadequate that the state must protect them from the folly of participation in vigorous athletics is a cultural anachronism unrelated to reality."[99]

Thus, Pennsylvania and Massachusetts, as well as other ERA states,[100] have taken a strong stand against the use of gender classifications in school athletic regulations. In states that use intermediate scrutiny to review gender classifications, the courts are not as predisposed against the use of gender classifications in school athletic regulations, nor are they necessarily inclined to approve the use of such classifications. The courts in these states are more willing to accept the assertion that there are physical differences between males and females that justify separate sports teams for males and females, so long as the teams are substantially equivalent.[101] Where there is not substantial equality of the separate teams, however, the courts will not hesitate to strike down a regulation that differentiates between male and female. In Indiana, for instance, the supreme court found that the state constitutional provision proscribing unequal privileges or immunities was violated by a school regulation that barred girls from participating on boys' teams in non-contact sports—in this case, golf.[102] Although there was also a girls' golf team at the plaintiff's school, the court concluded that it was not substantially equal to the boys' team, because its members were not eligible to compete in interscholastic programs.[103] Along similar lines, in West Virginia the state supreme court, applying intermediate scrutiny, ruled that the state equal protection principle was violated by a regulation barring girls from

---

[97] *Id.* at 293.

[98] *Id.* at 293 (quoting Schlesinger v. Ballard, 419 U.S. 498 (1975)).

[99] *Id.* at 294.

[100] *See* Darrin v. Gould, 540 P.2d 882 (Wash. 1975) (state ERA violated by regulation prohibiting girls from playing on high school football team); Blair v. Washington State University, 740 P.2d 1379 (Wash. 1987) (state ERA violated by exclusion of football in assessment of sex equity in collegiate athletic programs).

[101] *See* Israel v. West Virginia Secondary Schools Activities Commission, 388 S.E.2d 480, 484–85 (W. Va. 1989) and cases cited therein.

[102] Haas v. South Bend Community School Corporation, 289 N.E.2d 495 (Ind. 1972).

[103] *Id.* at 499–501.

playing on high school baseball teams.[104] Although there was a girls' softball team, the court found that there were not equal opportunities for boys and girls because softball and baseball are not substantially equivalent.[105]

While its promise was later cut short, one of the most far-reaching interpretations of the ERA occurred in *Baehr v. Lewin*, a 1993 decision where a plurality of the Hawaii Supreme Court took the position that a state statute restricting marriage to opposite-sex couples established a sex-based classification subject to strict scrutiny under the Hawaii ERA.[106] Subsequently on remand, a trial court, applying strict scrutiny as directed by the higher court, found that the statute was not supported by a compelling state interest and hence violated the ERA.[107] However, that decision was countermanded by a state constitutional amendment approved by the voters providing that: "The legislature shall have the power to reserve marriage to opposite-sex couples."[108]

There is some debate as to whether laws, such as the one in *Baehr*, that limit marriage to opposite-sex couples are most appropriately viewed as classifications that discriminate on the basis of sex. As some persons see it, it is more helpful to approach these sorts of marriage laws as classifications that discriminate on the basis of sexual orientation.[109] While the plurality in *Baehr* thought that the Hawaii marriage statute facially discriminated on the basis of sex,[110] other courts assessing similar marriage laws have disagreed. The Supreme Court of Vermont has said that laws restricting marriage to opposite-sex couples are "facially neutral" in regard to gender because they do not single out men or women as a class for disparate treatment, but rather prohibit men and women alike from precisely the same conduct, that is, marrying someone of the same sex.[111] The Washington Court of Appeals has found that the state's refusal to authorize same-sex marriage results from the impossibility of reproduction by same-sex couples, and is not invidious discrimination on account

---

[104] Israel v. West Virginia Secondary Schools Activities Commission, 388 S.E.2d 480, 484–87 (W. Va. 1989).

[105] *Id.* at 485.

[106] Baehr v. Lewin, 852 P.2d 44 (Haw. 1993).

[107] Baehr v. Miike, 910 P.2d 112 (Haw. 1996).

[108] Haw. Const. art. I, §23.

[109] *See* Evan Wolfson, *Crossing the Threshhold: Equal Marriage Rights for Lesbians and Gay Men and the Intra-Community Critique*, 21 N.Y.U. Rev. L. & Soc. Change 567 (1994).

[110] Baehr v. Lewin, 852 P.2d at 59.

[111] Baker v. State, 744 A.2d 864, 880, n. 13 (Vt. 1999).

of sex.[112] While laws restricting marriage to opposite-sex couples certainly can be viewed as drawing classifications on the basis of sex, on the other hand it is debatable whether such laws do so *on account* of sex. Moreover, laws restricting marriage to opposite-sex couples treat male and female equally in the sense of allowing each to marry someone of the opposite gender and disallowing each to marry someone of the same gender. Most state courts that have addressed this question have ruled that laws restricting marriage to opposite-sex couples do not amount to discrimination on the basis of sex.[113] As we shall see, however, several of those courts have gone on to find that it was unconstitutional to deny the benefits and protections of marriage to same-sex couples.[114]

Classifications Based on Sexual Orientation

The United States Supreme Court has decided three cases concerning sexual orientation. In 1986, the nation's high Court decided *Bowers v. Hardwick*, ruling, by a vote of 5–4, that the Due Process Clause was not violated by a Georgia sodomy law making it a crime for persons of the same sex to engage in intimate sexual relations.[115] Seventeen years later, however, in *Lawrence v. Texas*, the Supreme Court saw fit to overrule *Bowers* in striking down a similar Texas law on the ground that it violated the Due Process Clause.[116] Both *Bowers* and *Lawrence* were argued and decided on due process grounds,[117] and the Court did not address the question of whether classifications based on sexual orientation should be considered suspect and therefore subject to heightened scrutiny. Still, it is worth noting, in regard to considerations of equal protection, that in *Lawrence* the Court criticized *Bowers* as unjustly demeaning to gay and lesbian persons.[118]

---

[112] Singer v. Hara, 522 P.2d 1187, 1195 (Wash. Ct. App. 1974).

[113] Baker v. Nelson, 191 N.W.2d 185 (Minn. 1971); Singer v. Hara, *id.*; State v. Walsh, 713 S.W.2d 508 (Mo. 1986); Phillips v. Wisconsin Personnel Commission, 482 N.W.2d 121 (Wis. 1992); Baker v. State, *supra* note 111. These courts also ignore that marriage is considered a fundamental right calling for strict scrutiny. *See* Zablocki v. Redhail, 434 U.S. 374 (1978).

[114] *See infra* at notes 145–81.

[115] Bowers v. Hardwick, 478 U.S. 186 (1986).

[116] Lawrence v. Texas, 539 U.S. 558 (2003).

[117] *Bowers* and *Lawrence* are discussed in Chapters Four and Seven.

[118] *Bowers*, 478 U.S. at 575.

In between *Bowers* and *Lawrence*, the Court decided *Romer v. Evans*, ruling by a vote of 6–3 that the Equal Protection Clause was violated by a Colorado constitutional amendment, adopted in a statewide referendum, that prohibited any legislative, administrative, or judicial action designed to provide protection or entitlement on the basis of a person's sexual orientation.[119] The majority opinion in *Romer* made no mention of the previous decision in *Bowers,* nor did it discuss the issue of whether classifications based on sexual orientation should be considered suspect. The opinion purported to apply some version of minimal scrutiny (no doubt with bite), and proclaimed that "a bare desire to harm a politically unpopular group cannot constitute a legitimate governmental interest."[120] Still, the opinion can be viewed as circumventing or transcending the levels of scrutiny altogether by treating a law that sets a class of persons apart from others on the basis of a personal characteristic as a rare instance of a *per se* violation of the Equal Protection Clause.[121] A state, the Court said, cannot deem a class of persons a stranger to its laws.[122] "A law declaring that in general it shall be more difficult for one group of citizens than for all others to seek aid from the government is in itself a denial of equal protection of the laws in the most literal sense."[123]

Prior to both *Romer* and *Lawrence*, the Supreme Court of Kentucky broke new ground by ruling in a case entitled *Commonwealth v. Wasson* that a statute making it a crime to engage in consensual adult homosexual activity violated the right of privacy[124] implicit in the guarantee of individual liberty in the Kentucky Constitution and also violated the right of equal treatment guaranteed by the Kentucky Constitution.[125] In considering the equal treatment aspect of the case, the Kentucky high court seemed to use an amalgam of the various levels of scrutiny. The court began by noting that classifications based on sexual orientation bear many of the characteristics of a suspect classification.[126] "As subjects of age-old discrimination and disapproval, homosexuals form virtually a discrete and insular minority."[127] Their sexual orientation is in all

---

[119] Romer v. Evans, 517 U.S. 620 (1996).

[120] *Id.* at 620 (quoting United States Dep't of Agriculture v. Moreno, 413 U.S. 528 (1973))

[121] Jeffrey M. Shaman, *Constitutional Interpretation: Illusion and Reality* 84 (2001).

[122] Romer v. Evans, 517 U.S. at 635.

[123] *Id.* at 633.

[124] Same-sex activities and the right of privacy are discussed in Chapter Seven.

[125] Commonwealth v. Wasson, 842 S.W.2d 487 (Ky. 1992).

[126] *Id.* at 499–500 (quoting Laurence Tribe, *American Constitutional Law* 1616 (2d ed. 1988)).

[127] *Id.* at 500.

probability a trait determined by causes beyond their control, and, if not immutable, is extremely difficult to alter.[128] Hence the court held that homosexuals are "a separate and identifiable class for Kentucky constitutional analysis because no class of persons can be discriminated against under the Kentucky Constitution."[129] All persons are entitled to equal treatment, the court continued, unless there is "a substantial governmental interest, a rational basis, for different treatment."[130] In the court's opinion, there was no rational basis to single out homosexual acts for different treatment.[131] The court rejected as "simply outrageous" the arguments of the state that homosexuals are more promiscuous than heterosexuals, are a threat to children, and are more prone to engage in sex acts in public.[132] In fact, in its attempt to justify the statute, the only assertion made by the state that possessed even superficial validity was the assertion that infectious diseases are more readily transmitted by anal intercourse than by other forms of sexual copulation.[133] But that could hardly explain why the statute prohibited homosexual acts aside from anal intercourse or why anal intercourse between a male and female was not prohibited.[134] In the final analysis, the only purpose served by the statute was to single out homosexuals for punishment for engaging in the same activity that heterosexuals were at liberty to perform.[135] In a society "that no longer criminalizes adultery, fornication, or deviate sexual intercourse between heterosexuals" there is no rational basis to single out homosexual conduct for different treatment.[136] Therefore, the court concluded that the statute was an arbitrary denial of equal treatment under the law in violation of the Kentucky Constitution.[137]

Other state courts have considered the question of whether classifications based on sexual orientation should be reviewed with heightened scrutiny on the ground that they bear the characteristics of a suspect classification. The results of these cases have been mixed, although most courts that have addressed the issue have declined to hold that classifications

---

128   *Id.*
129   *Id.*
130   *Id.*
131   *Id.* at 501.
132   *Id.*
133   *Id.*
134   *Id.*
135   *Id.*
136   *Id.*
137   *Id.* at 500.

based on sexual orientation are subject to anything other than rationality review.[138] Indeed, some courts give no more than glancing consideration to the idea that classifications based on sexual orientation should be considered suspect or even quasi-suspect. This occurred in *Singer v. Hara*, where the Court of Appeals of the State of Washington held that it was not unconstitutional to deny a marriage license to same-sex couples.[139] With virtually no explanation, the court summarily rebuffed the appellant's assertion that classifications based on sexual orientation bear many of the characteristics of a suspect classification.[140] The court went on to rule that classifications based on sexual orientation are not suspect and therefore evoke no more than rationality review. "There can be no doubt," the court concluded, that it is rational to restrict marriage[141] to opposite-sex couples because marriage is "the appropriate and desirable forum for procreation and the rearing of children."[142]

Other courts have taken the position that laws that have a discriminatory impact on gay and lesbian persons, such as laws granting benefits only to married persons, do not amount to discrimination based on sexual orientation and therefore are subject only to minimal scrutiny.[143] Thus, in upholding an administrative rule denying family sick leave for an employee to care for her same-sex domestic partner, a Colorado court maintained that the rule "does not discriminate on the basis of sexual orientation ....(or) differentiate between heterosexual and homosexual employees but rather between married and unmarried employees."[144]

---

[138] *See* Singer v. Hara, 522 P.2d 1187, 1196 (Wash. Ct. App. 1974) (upholding law denying marriage licenses to same-sex couples).

[139] *Id.*

[140] "Although appellants present argument to the contrary, we agree with the state's contention that to define marriage to exclude homosexual or any other same-sex relationships is not to create an inherently suspect legislation classification requiring strict judicial scrutiny to determine a compelling state interest." *Id.* at 1196.

[141] Marriage and the right of privacy are discussed in depth in Chapter Six.

[142] *Id.* at 1195–97.

[143] Phillips v. Wisconsin Personnel Commission, 482 N.W.2d 121, 127 (Wis. 1992) (upholding rule limiting health insurance coverage to married couples): "The challenged rule distinguishes between married and unmarried employees, not between homosexual and heterosexual employees." *See also*, Beaty v. Truck Insurance Exchange, 8 Cal. Rptr. 2d 593 (Cal. Ct. App. 1992) (upholding policy denying insurance benefits to same-sex couple): "Whatever this case is about, it is not one involving discrimination on the basis of sexual orientation....To the extent plaintiffs were treated differently than a 'married couple,' it is because they are not married and not because they are homosexuals." *Id.* at 596.

[144] Ross v. Denver Department of Health and Hospitals, 883 P.2d 516, 519–20. (Colo. Ct. App. 1994).

This sort of reasoning, which looks no further than the surface of a law, avoids the use of meaningful scrutiny of laws that have a discriminatory impact on gay and lesbian persons.

In a pioneering decision announced in 1998, *Tanner v. Oregon Health Sciences University*, the Oregon Court of Appeals ruled that sexual orientation was a suspect classification.[145] The court reasoned that:

> Sexual orientation, like gender, race, alienage, and religious affiliation is widely regarded as defining a distinct, socially recognizable group of citizens, and certainly it is beyond dispute that homosexuals in our society have been and continue to be the subject of adverse social and political stereotyping and prejudice.[146]

After concluding that sexual orientation was a suspect class, the court went on to hold that the state equal privileges and immunities clause was violated by a law denying to unmarried gay or lesbian couples the same health and life insurance benefits that were available to married couples. The court found that the law under review could not be justified by any genuine differences between gay or lesbian couples and others to whom the insurance benefits were available.[147] In defending the law, the state argued that the law discriminated on the basis of marital status, not sexual orientation, pointing to the fact that the insurance benefits were available to all married employees-heterosexual and homosexual alike.[148] This was unpersuasive to the court. As the court explained, the Oregon equal privileges and immunities clause prohibits unintentional as well as intentional discrimination.[149] Regardless of the state's intent, the equal privileges and immunities clause may be offended where a law has a disparate impact upon a class of citizens.[150] And because homosexual couples were not permitted to marry, the insurance law in question in *Tanner* had in fact a discriminatory impact upon gay and lesbian couples.[151] As the court put it, the insurance benefits are made available on terms that for gay and lesbian couples "are a legal impossibility."[152]

---

[145] Tanner v. Oregon Health Sciences University, 971 P.2d 435 (Or. Ct. App. 1998).
[146] *Id.* at 447.
[147] *Id.* at 447.
[148] *Id.* at 447–48.
[149] *Id.* at 447.
[150] *Id.*
[151] *Id.* at 448.
[152] *Id.*

Not long after the ruling in *Tanner*, the Supreme Court of Vermont rendered a similar groundbreaking decision concerning discrimination based on sexual orientation. In *Baker v. State*, the high court of that state ruled that by excluding same-sex couples from the benefits and protections of marriage, the state marriage law violated the common benefits clause of the Vermont Constitution, which prohibits special emoluments or advantages that are not shared in common by the entire community.[153] To reach this result, the court abandoned the federal multi-tier model of equal protection, and in its stead adopted a more flexible method of review that relies upon a uniform standard asking whether the law in question bears a reasonable and just relation to a government purpose that serves the common benefits of the community.[154] In applying this standard, the court assesses the significance of the benefits and protections of the challenged law, whether the omission of members of the community from the benefits and protections of the challenged law promotes the government's stated goals, and whether the classification under review is significantly underinclusive or overinclusive.[155]

The state had argued in *Baker* that its marriage law excluding same-sex couples from the benefits and protections incident to marriage was justified by several state interests. First, the state claimed, it had an interest in promoting a permanent commitment between couples who have children to ensure that their offspring are considered legitimate and receive ongoing parental support.[156] The court readily accepted this claim; in fact, the court admitted that it was beyond dispute that the state has an interest in promoting a permanent commitment from couples for the security of their children.[157] However, the court continued, the marriage law was a "significantly underinclusive" means of accomplishing this end, because many couples marry for reasons unrelated to procreation, and have no intent to have children or are not able to have children.[158] The marriage law, then, extends the benefits and protections of marriage to many persons who have no logical connection to the state interest claimed for the marriage law.[159]

---

153 Baker v. State 744 A.2d 864 (Vt. 1999).
154 *Id.* at 873, 878–79.
155 *Id.* at 879.
156 *Id.* at 881.
157 *Id.*
158 *Id.*
159 *Id.*

Furthermore (and perhaps more importantly), there was no explanation as to why the state's interest in promoting a permanent commitment from couples for the security of their children should not include children being raised by same-sex couples.[160] Noting that increasing numbers of children were being raised by same-sex parents, the court saw no reason to exclude these children from the benefits of the marriage law.[161] "(T)o the extent that the state's purpose in licensing marriage was, and is, to legitimize children and provide for their security, the statutes plainly exclude many same-sex couples with respect to these objectives."[162] Thus, persons who were similarly situated in regard to the very purpose of the marriage law nonetheless were treated differently by it.[163] For children being raised by same-sex parents, the law was counterproductive; it exposed them to the precise risks the marriage law was designed to prevent.[164]

The state additionally claimed that because same-sex couples cannot conceive a child on their own, to exclude them from the benefits and protections of the marriage law serves the state interest in promoting a perception of the link between procreation and child rearing.[165] The state claimed that it was justified in sending a public message that procreation and child rearing are intertwined to preclude the notion that mothers and fathers are "mere surplusage."[166] Of dubious factual validity, this assertion was rejected by the court. "Apart from the bare assertion," the court said, "the State offers no persuasive reasoning to support these claims."[167] Indeed, these claims could not explain why married couples who are infertile, nevertheless, are entitled to the full benefit and protection of the marriage laws. As the court pointed out, many married couples who are infertile use assisted-reproductive techniques that involve only one of the married partner's genetic material.[168] "The State does not suggest that the use of these technologies undermines a married couple's sense of parental responsibility, or fosters the perception that they are

---

160 *Id.* at 881–82.
161 *Id.*
162 *Id* at 882.
163 *Id.*
164 *Id.*
165 *Id.*
166 *Id.*
167 *Id.*
168 *Id.*

'mere surplusage.'"[169] Hence, there was no reason to think that the use of the same technologies by a same-sex couple would somehow undermine the bonds of parenthood or society's perception of parenthood.[170]

As the court explained, there was an "extreme logical disjunction between the classification and the stated purposes of the law."[171] That is, excluding same-sex couples from the benefits and protections of the marriage law had little to do with protecting children or maintaining the link between procreation and child rearing. These goals, though laudable, do not provide a reasonable basis for denying the benefits and protections of marriage to same-sex couples who are no differently situated with respect to the goals than their opposite-sex counterparts.[172]

On the other side of the balance, the benefits and protections of marriage denied to same-sex couples were extremely significant. Marriage, the court said, "has long been recognized as a vital personal right."[173] A marriage license provides access to a multitude of legal benefits and protections and marriage is an important social relationship that significantly enhances the quality of life in our society.[174] In light of the great significance of marriage and the many benefits that flow from it, the weak reasons proffered in support of the law were hardly enough to justify it. Therefore, the court concluded that it was unconstitutional to deny the benefits and protections of the Vermont marriage law to same-sex couples.

While ruling that the plaintiffs were entitled the same benefits and protections afforded to opposite-sex couples, the court decided to leave it to the legislature to resolve exactly how those benefits and protections should be extended to same-sex couples.[175] As the court mentioned, this gave the legislature a number of options, one of which was to enact a statute to establish an alternative legal status to marriage for same-sex couples. In response, the Vermont legislature enacted a civil union law providing comprehensive benefits and protections (akin to marriage rights) for same-sex couples.[176]

---

[169] Id.
[170] Id.
[171] Id. at 884.
[172] Id.
[173] Id. at 883.
[174] Id.
[175] Id. at 886.
[176] Vermont Act 91, An Act Relating to Civil Unions, 18 V.S.A. §1204 (2000).

After the decision of the Vermont Supreme Court in *Baker*, several other state supreme courts have ruled that laws denying benefits to same-sex couples violate the constitutional guarantee of equal protection. In Montana, the state supreme court invalidated a policy for the employees of the state university system that disallowed same-sex couples from enrolling for dependent health insurance coverage, while allowing opposite-sex couples, even if they were not married, to enroll for the coverage.[177] Pointing out that the policy classified persons on the basis of sexual orientation rather than marital status, the court concluded that the law was not rationally related to a legitimate state interest and therefore violated the equal protection clause of the Montana Constitution.[178] In Alaska, the supreme court, applying its three-step sliding scale approach, struck down a law denying employee benefits to same-sex couples on the ground that even under minimal scrutiny the law was not substantially related to any of the governmental interests—cost control, administrative efficiency, and promotion of marriage—asserted by the state in defense of the denial of benefits.[179] And in New Jersey, the state supreme court ruled that although same-sex couples do not have a constitutional right to marry, they must be afforded the same rights and benefits enjoyed by married opposite-sex couples.[180] In reaching that result, the court eschewed the "rigid, three-tiered federal equal protection methodology," opting for a more "flexible" test examining each claim "on a continuum that reflects the nature of the burdened right and the importance of the governmental restriction."[181] Using that test, the court concluded that there was no rational basis for denying same-sex couples the benefits and rights available to married opposite-sex couples.

A number of state legislatures, either in response to court decisions or on their own initiative, have enacted civil union or domestic partnership laws for same-sex couples as an alternative to marriage. Following Vermont's lead, California, Connecticut, Hawaii, Maine, and New Jersey all have enacted some sort of civil union or domestic partnership law to extend legal rights to same-sex couples.[182] As we will see in Chapter Seven,

---

[177] Snetsinger v. Montana University System, 104 P.3d 445 (Mont. 2004).

[178] *Id.* at 451–54.

[179] Alaska Civil Liberties Union v. State, 122 P.3d 781 (Alaska 2005).

[180] Lewis v. Harris, 908 A.2d 196 (N.J. 2006).

[181] *Id.* at 212.

[182] *See* "State Policies on Same-Sex Marriage," http://www.stateline.org/live/digitalAssets/5968_Social_Policy.pdf

"The Right of Intimate Association," some states will afford further protection for same-sex couples through constitutional provisions that protect the right of privacy.

Classifications Based on Age

There are various kinds of laws that contain classifications based upon age. Some of these, such as mandatory retirement laws, are aimed at elderly persons. Others, such as curfews, are aimed at the young. Usually, age classifications, whether aimed at the elderly or the young are subject to the most minimal scrutiny, with the result that they are found to be constitutional. Occasionally, though, an age classification will be found to be so irrational that it violates the guarantee of equality.

Mandatory retirement laws are a common form of age classification directed at the elderly. These laws are founded on the notion that old age is accompanied by a decline in skills as well as a variety of disabilities that impair a person's competence. In modern times, though, there has been a good deal of criticism directed to that view of old age and to the choice of "youth over wisdom."[183] While admitting that "age may take its toll,"[184] commentators have pointed out that the traditional view of the elderly is based on stereotypical thinking that demeans older persons and overlooks their individual abilities. In 1967, to counteract unfair treatment of the elderly, the federal government enacted legislation prohibiting employers from discriminating against employees on the basis of age.[185] Since then, there has been a legislative trend away from mandatory retirement. Many states as well as the federal government have raised their mandatory retirement age by five or ten years and a few states have done away with mandatory retirement altogether. This legislative trend has been accompanied by an increasing awareness throughout society of unfair discrimination against the elderly. Despite this awareness and the legislative trend, both federal and state courts have shown an abiding acquiescence toward mandatory retirement laws.

Mandatory retirement laws based on age have been upheld as constitutional by both federal and state courts. On the federal side, the Supreme

---

[183] *See* Hatten v. Rains, 854 F.2d 687, 689 (5th Cir. 1988).
[184] *See* Vance v. Bradley, 440 U.S. 93, 111–12 (1979).
[185] Age Discrimination in Employment Act of 1967, 29 U.S.C. section 621 *et seq.*

Court has concluded in several cases that mandatory retirement laws do not violate the Equal Protection Clause.[186] In each case, the high Court subjected the laws in question to mere rationality review, granting a great deal of deference to the legislature. In declining to use a more heightened form of scrutiny to review age classifications, the Court stated that while the elderly in the nation have suffered some unfair discrimination, they have not experienced "a history of purposeful unequal treatment," nor have they "been subjected to unique disabilities on the basis of stereotyped characteristics not truly indicative of their abilities."[187] In making this assessment, the Court was not entirely realistic about the degree of discrimination inflicted upon elderly persons or its nature. As noted by Justice Marshall in a dissenting opinion, when it comes to employment, the elderly certainly have been subject to repeated arbitrary discrimination based upon overly general stereotypes that stigmatize the elderly as physically and mentally deficient.[188] Still, a majority of the Court ruled that age is not a suspect classification and therefore classifications based on age are to be reviewed with the most minimal scrutiny.

In most instances, the state courts have followed the federal example by using rationality review to assess classifications based on age and uphold them as constitutional. For example, in *O'Neill v. Bane*, the Supreme Court of Missouri ruled that a state mandatory retirement statute requiring magistrates and probate judges to retire at age 70 violated neither the federal nor state equal protection clauses.[189] As the court saw it, there were several rational bases for the statute: it ensured that judges have the health and vitality to competently perform their duties; it avoided the perplexing task of determining which judges are physically and mentally qualified to continue work; it opened up opportunities for younger persons to become judges and bring fresh ideas to the bench; and it assured predictability and ease in administering the pension plan program for judges.[190] The court's opinion, though somewhat more thoughtful than the weakest version of minimal scrutiny, nonetheless, is debatable.

---

[186] Massachusetts Board of Retirement v. Murgia, 426 U.S. 307 (1976); Vance v. Bradley, *supra* note 184; Gregory v. Ashcroft, 501 U.S. 452 (1991).

[187] Massachusetts Board of Retirement v. Murgia, *id.*; *see also* Vance v. Bradley, *id.*; Gregory v. Ashcroft, *id.*

[188] *See Murgia, id.* at 324 (Marshall, J., dissenting).

[189] O'Neill v. Bane, 568 S.W.2d 761 (Mo. 1978). *See also*, Nelson v. Miller, 480 P.2d 467 (Utah 1971); Grinnell v. State, 435 A.2d 523 (N.H. 1981); *In re* Levy, 427 So.2d 844 (La. 1983); Diamond v. Cuomo, 514 N.W.2d 1356 (N.Y. 1987).

[190] *Id.* at 766–67.

Expressly eschewing any need to consider the ability of elderly persons on an individual basis, the opinion followed the old class-based assumption that the skills of the elderly have declined so greatly that the elderly no longer are able to competently perform their duties. The opinion also explicitly adopted a preference for the freshness of youth over the wisdom of experience—a preference that many would question, particularly for a vocation such as the judiciary. Moreover, the opinion offered no explanation whatsoever as to why it was rational to mandate retirement at age 70 for magistrates and probate judges, while allowing other judges—not to mention members of the executive and legislative branches—to continue working past that age.

While *O'Neill v. Bane* represents the general view that classifications based on age are perfectly constitutional, there have been some exceptions to this general trend. A few state courts have been willing to put some bite into rationality review and strike down classifications based on age as violating equality guarantees. In *Arneson v. State*, the Supreme Court of Montana applied an upgraded version of minimal scrutiny in striking down a state law that differentiated on the basis of age in allocating a post-retirement increase (to account for inflation) in certain pension benefits.[191] The law in question provided payments to some beneficiaries but not others depending on their age. Beneficiaries of employees who died while still working were eligible for the increase, but beneficiaries of employees who had retired from work were only eligible for the increase if the beneficiaries were fifty-five years of age or older.[192] In evaluating the law, the court noted that it had previously declined to apply middle tier scrutiny to classifications based on age, and expressly opted to use the "rational basis test."[193] Applying that test, the court concluded that the law was utterly irrational, there being no reason to give the increase to all beneficiaries of deceased workers, but only give the increase to retired workers' beneficiaries who were fifty-five or older.[194] By doing so, the law created an unreasonable classification between persons who were similarly situated.[195] In the court's view, the law was an instance of the legislature picking and choosing who will receive benefits

---

191   Arneson v. State, 864 P.2d 1245 (Mont. 1993).
192   *Id.* at 1248.
193   *Id.*
194   *Id.* at 1248–49.
195   *Id* at 1248.

with absolutely no reason.[196] Even if the legislative purpose was to save money, the court said, it cannot be done on a wholly arbitrary basis.[197] Finding "nothing in the record or by conjecture" to justify the difference in treatment accorded by the law,[198] the court concluded that it violated the Montana equal protection clause.

In *Arneson*, Justice Trieweiler entered a special concurring opinion, "rejoic(ing) in the majority's re-discovery of the rights provided for in the equal protection clause...of Montana's Constitution."[199] In his view, however, classifications based on age should be reviewed under intermediate scrutiny rather than mere, albeit upgraded, minimal scrutiny.[200] No less than intermediate scrutiny was appropriate, said Justice Trieweiler, because age is a "sensitive" if not "suspect" basis for classification.[201] To hold otherwise, he maintained, would be to ignore the import of the Montana Human Rights Act, which provides that the right to be free from discrimination based on age is a civil right.[202] Regardless of that statutory disapprobation of age discrimination, a majority of the Montana Supreme Court was unwilling to elevate its review of age classifications to fully intermediate scrutiny, preferring to take the smaller step of putting some bite into minimal scrutiny when assessing classifications based on age.

Equal protection questions about classifications based on age may also arise where statutes are directed to reducing or offsetting state workers' compensation benefits upon eligibility at age 65 for federal social security retirement benefits. Many states have enacted statutory provisions that reduce state disability or unemployment benefits when an individual becomes 65 and eligible for social security retirement benefits. There is a split of authority in this area; some courts see these offset provisions as consistent with equal protection, while others do not. Although all the states that have considered the issue agree that rationality review is the appropriate level of scrutiny to use for this form of age discrimination, some courts have upheld the laws in question as

---

196 *Id.*
197 *Id.*
198 *Id.*
199 *Id.* at 1249 (Trieweiler, J., concurring).
200 *Id.* at 1252.
201 *Id.* at 1252.
202 *Id.* (citing Montana Human Rights Act, section 49-1-102, Montana Code Annotated).

rational,[203] while other courts have struck them down as irrational.[204] The difference seems to hinge on how a court views the relationship between workers' compensation benefits and social security retirement benefits. Those courts which view workers' compensation benefits and social security as serving the same purpose of substituting for wage loss are inclined to uphold benefit offsets on the ground that they are a rational way of avoiding duplicative benefits. On the other hand, those courts which see workers' compensation benefits and social security retirement benefits as mutually exclusive and not intended to be coordinated are inclined to strike down benefit offsets on the ground that they serve no rational purpose.

Age classifications that discriminate against young persons usually are reviewed with a mild form of minimal scrutiny. The courts ordinarily take the position that youth is not a suspect classification or even a semi-suspect classification, and therefore classifications directed against young people evokes nothing more than rationality review.[205] As a result, the courts have upheld some rather questionable laws that treat minors differently than adults. In a Florida case, for instance, a district court of appeal upheld an anti-graffiti ordinance that prohibited any person under the age of 18 from possessing jumbo markers or spray paint on public property, unless accompanied by a supervising adult.[206] The court was unmoved by the fact that ordinance imposed a criminal penalty upon minors for merely possessing a jumbo marker or spray paint without requiring a showing of intent to create graffiti. Nor was the court moved by the fact that the ordinance imposed this criminal penalty upon minors but not adults. "Youth is not a suspect classification," the court declared, and "review is therefore limited to the rational basis test."[207] In the court's view, the legislature could rationally conclude that the ordinance served to deter incidences of graffiti.[208] When faced with the argument that a more reasonable (not to mention more effective) alternative—indeed,

---

[203] *E.g.*, Injured Workers of Kansas v. Franklin, 942 P.2d 591 (Kan. 1997); Case of Tobin, 675 N.E.2d 781 (Mass. 1997).

[204] *E.g.*, Industrial Claim Appeals Office of the State of Colorado v. Romero, 912 P.2d 62 (Colo. 1996); Pierce v. LaFourche Parish Council, 762 So.2d 608 (La. 2000).

[205] *E.g.*, "Juveniles are neither a suspect class nor a semisuspect class. Thus the rational relationship test applies here...." Washington v. Heiskell, 916 P.2d 366, 371 (Wash. 1996).

[206] D.P. v. State, 705 So.2d 593 (Fla. 1997).

[207] *Id.* at 597.

[208] *Id.*

one that had been adopted in other localities—would be to ban anyone, adult or minor, from possessing jumbo markers or spray paint, the court's response was that if a total ban is permissible, then surely a less extreme measure that applies only to minors also is permissible.[209] This response offers no explanation as to why it is reasonable to single out minors for a criminal penalty while allowing adults to engage in the very same activity with no penalty whatsoever.

A few courts, although adhering to the position that youth is not a suspect classification, have nonetheless managed to strike down laws that discriminate against juvenile offenders. In a 1997 decision, *In re S.L.M.*, the Supreme Court of Montana found that the state equal protection guarantee was violated by a law that, in some instances, subjected juveniles to a longer period of incarceration than adults who committed similar offenses.[210] While following federal rulings to hold that a sentencing policy based on age did not implicate a suspect class, the court relied on state constitutional doctrine to rule that a juvenile's physical liberty was a fundamental right, calling for strict scrutiny.[211] Under strict scrutiny, the court concluded, there certainly was no compelling state interest to treat a juvenile more harshly than his or her adult counterpart. Indeed, it seems that except under the most deferential version of minimal scrutiny there would be no legitimate interest to treat a juvenile more harshly than an adult who committed essentially the same offense. If anything, juveniles should be treated less harshly than adults because juveniles are not considered to possess the same mental capacity as adults, and hence are not held to the same standard of responsibility under the law. The Montana law in question, then, seemed to get things backward and could have been struck down under an enhanced version of minimal scrutiny on the ground that it was completely irrational. Nonetheless, it should be recognized that in the high majority of cases involving classifications against young persons, the courts apply the most minimal scrutiny that leads to finding no constitutional violation.[212]

---

[209] *Id.* at 595–97.

[210] *In re* S.L.M., 951 P.2d 1365 (Mont. 1997). *See also*, State v. Mohi, 901 P.2d 991 (Utah 1995) (striking down a statute that granted discretion to prosecutors to treat some juveniles as adult offenders and proceed against them directly in district or circuit court while leaving other juveniles accused of similar offenses in juvenile court), discussed in Chapter Three.

[211] *In re* S.L.M., *id.* at 1370–72.

[212] *See supra*, at notes 203–7.

Conclusion

We gave seen that in reviewing various classifications state courts in some instances have exercised a more searching form of judicial review than is utilized on the federal side. Race, of course, is the prototypical suspect classification and therefore is subject to the most searching judicial scrutiny whether under the federal or a state constitution. In a few instances state courts have interpreted their state constitutions to go further than federal constitutional law in banning *de facto* racial discrimination, although in one state, California, such action on the part of the state supreme court was counteracted by a statewide initiative amending the state constitution.[213]

In assessing various classifications, state courts are most likely to play a more active role than their federal counterparts when faced with classifications based on gender.[214] A number of state courts have upgraded gender classifications from intermediate to strict scrutiny. In some states this is the result of adopting the ERA, which expressly prohibits gender discrimination, as part of the state constitution. But even in some states that have not adopted the ERA, strict rather than intermediate scrutiny will be used to evaluate classifications based on gender.

Classifications based on sexual orientation have been treated as suspect and therefore subject to heightened scrutiny by a few state courts, although others have adamantly refused to do so.[215] More recently, however, there seems to be an emerging trend on the part of state courts to use some form of meaningful scrutiny to assess the constitutional validity of laws that discriminate against gay and lesbian persons. In reviewing these laws, a growing number of states are opting for a more flexible method of analysis than the rigid federal model.[216] Utilizing this more flexible approach, a number of courts have concluded that laws denying the benefits of marriage to same-sex couples violate the principles of equality established in their state constitutions.[217] These decisions have been bolstered by legislative enactments in some states establishing domestic partnership or civil union laws providing benefits and rights to

---

[213] *See supra* at notes 15–43.
[214] *See supra* at notes 54–114.
[215] *See supra* at notes 124–52.
[216] *See supra* at notes 153–81.
[217] *Id.*

same-sex couples.[218] In line with this trend, as we shall see in Chapter Six, "Civil Unions and Marriage," some states have afforded further protection for gay and lesbian persons through constitutional provisions that protect the right of privacy.[219]

Finally, classifications based on age—whether directed against the young or the elderly—have, with rare exception, been reviewed with very minimal scrutiny by the state courts.[220] Occasionally, though, a state court will eject a bit of bite into minimal scrutiny to strike down an age classification on the ground that it is totally irrational—a result that in all likelihood would not occur on the federal side.

In sum, then, we see that the states have taken significant strides to provide expansive protection against some forms of discrimination that are tolerated more readily on the federal side. A few states have moved beyond federal law to strike down *de facto* racial discrimination. On occasion others have reached beyond federal precedent to invalidate age classifications that discriminate against the elderly or the young. A large number of states have moved forcefully to combat gender discrimination. And an increasing number of states are taking meaningful steps to confront discrimination based on sexual orientation. State constitutional law, then, has become a vibrant source for reviewing legislative classifications to determine if they comport with the guarantee of equality.

---

[218] *See supra* at note 182.
[219] *See* Chapter Seven.
[220] *See supra* at notes 182–212.

CHAPTER THREE

RIGHTS AND PRIVILEGES

State constitutional provisions guaranteeing equality are directed toward the interdiction of unjust discrimination. As such, their primary focus is the prevention of discriminatory classifications. We shall see in subsequent chapters that state constitutional provisions, such as due process clauses or other provisions that guard against the deprivation of liberty, are the primary source of constitutional protection for various rights and privileges. Ordinarily, due process clauses or other provisions safeguarding liberty are utilized to prevent the unjust deprivation of rights or privileges. Of course, the concepts of due process and equal protection overlap each other to a considerable extent, and, as a result, under some circumstances equality provisions may be used to ensure rights or privileges. This is especially so when laws impinge upon rights or privileges in a discriminatory manner. Discriminatory laws that infringe rights or privileges may be subject to constitutional review under equality provisions. Where such laws affect rights that are considered fundamental or entitled to some degree of constitutional status, heightened scrutiny will be evoked. Otherwise, in the absence of a suspect or semi-suspect classification, laws that affect non-fundamental rights or privileges will be reviewed with a very deferential form of minimal scrutiny. On occasion, though, in reviewing laws that discriminate against non-fundamental rights or privileges, minimal scrutiny will be given a bit of bite or upgraded to some degree.

Educational Financing

In the United States, public education is financed primarily through local property taxes. In other words, most of the money used to pay for public education comes from local property taxes in the school districts where the schools are located. The state governments contribute some state funds to local school districts and the federal government contributes a smaller amount of federal funds, but most of the money for public schools comes from local property taxes. So, the majority of funds that are raised to finance public education are obtained from local property taxes.

However, the value of property from one district to another within the same state varies considerably. As a result, the school districts with highly valued property have much more money available for public education than the districts with low valued property. Even when property-poor districts tax themselves at a higher rate than property-rich districts, the variation in assessed valuation of property may be so great, that the property-poor districts still will have less money available for their schools than the property-rich districts. Hence, in many states, more money is spent for the education of students who reside in wealthy districts than is spent for the education of students who reside in poor districts.

The difference in expenditures translates into vast disparities in the substance of educational programs. Charles Benson, Professor of Educational Administration at the University of California at Berkeley, observed that:

> In general, low quality of programs and high tax load were positively correlated. Even by taxing themselves far above the average, poor districts still were able to finance only a meager set of educational offerings. Indeed, the poor places could not, under any reasonable interpretation of public duty, fulfill the minimum state mandated requirements for schools.[1]

Poor districts are forced to hire less qualified teachers and have significantly higher student-teacher ratios. Students in the poor districts attend the shabbiest, most outmoded schools, with the fewest materials for learning. They have fewer course offerings, older books, less equipment, fewer laboratories—whatever the resource or asset, the schools in poor districts have less of it.

---

[1] Charles Benson, *The Economics of School Finance* 156–57 (2d ed. 1968).

In 1973, in *San Antonio Independent School District v. Rodriguez*, the United States Supreme Court ruled that a state educational funding system based primarily on local property taxes that resulted in disparate funding from one district to another did not violate the Equal Protection Clause of the Federal Constitution.[2] The high Court held in *Rodriguez* that education was not a fundamental right and wealth was not a suspect classification, and therefore only minimal scrutiny would be applied in the case. Under minimal scrutiny, the Court concluded that the disparity in financing from district to district was justifiable as a means of enhancing local control of schools. As far as the Supreme Court was concerned, then, disparate financing of public schooling from one district to another did not violate the Federal Equal Protection Clause.

Two years before the Supreme Court's decision in *Rodriguez*, the Supreme Court of California had ruled in *Serrano v. Priest* that the California system of financing public education predominantly through local property taxes was, indeed, a violation of equal protection.[3] Contrary to the United States Supreme Court, the California high court found that education was a fundamental right and that the system of funding public education was so irrational as to violate the principles of equal protection. Nothing could be more irrational, the California court said, than to have the quality of children's education be determined by the value of their parents' and neighbors' property. Two years later, when the United States Supreme Court issued its ruling in *Rodriguez*, the California Supreme Court was asked it to overturn its *Serrano* decision in light of *Rodriguez*. The California Supreme Court declined to do so, noting that its previous decision had been founded on the equal protection clause of the California constitution as well as the Equal Protection Clause of the Federal Constitution.[4] The court explained that while *Rodriguez* of course overruled that part of the California court's decision based on the Federal Equal Protection Clause, *Rodriguez* had no effect upon that part of the court's decision based on the California equal protection clause, which the Court re-affirmed.

The decision of the California Supreme Court in *Serrano II* stands as an early manifestation of the New Judicial Federalism. As the court declares, its main concern is with California law and the full panoply of

---

[2] San Antonio Independent School District v. Rodriguez, 411 U.S. 1 (1973).
[3] Serrano v. Priest (I), 487 P.2d 1241 (Cal. 1971).
[4] Serrano v. Priest (II), 557 P.2d 929 (Cal. 1976).

rights Californians have come to expect as their due.[5] While decisions of the United States Supreme Court are entitled to respect, they will not be followed by the California courts when the protection they afford is less than the protection guaranteed by California law. So, in *Serrano II*, the California Supreme Court concluded on its own that education was a fundamental right, that the school finance system amounted to a suspect classification on the basis of wealth, that strict judicial scrutiny should be used, and that under strict scrutiny the school finance system was unconstitutional.

In *Serrano I*, the California Supreme Court stated unequivocally that it was "convinced that the distinctive and priceless function of education in our society warrants, indeed compels, our treating it as a 'fundamental interest.'"[6] In reaching that conclusion, the court enumerated five reasons why education should be considered fundamental. First, education is essential to preserve an individual's opportunity to compete successfully in a market economy. Second, education is "universally relevant." Third, education continues over a long period of time—12 or 13 years—during which the state government has a sustained and intensive relationship with the student. Fourth, education is unparalleled in the extent to which it molds the personality of our youth. And fifth, education is so important that the state has made it compulsory.[7]

There are additional reasons why education should be considered fundamental. For one, education is the means by which individuals secure other rights. Thus, the Supreme Court of Arkansas has noted that education is "the essential prerequisite that allows our citizens to be able to appreciate, claim and effectively realize their established rights."[8] Also, education enhances the ability of individuals to participate in our democratic system of self-governance. In the words of the United States Supreme Court, education is "the foundation of good citizenship."[9] "It is required in the performance of our most basic public responsibilities, even service in the armed forces."[10]

---

[5] Serrano v. Priest (II), *id*, at 950–52.
[6] Serrano v. Priest (I) *supra* note 3, at 1258.
[7] *Id*. at 1258–59.
[8] DuPree v. Alma School District No. 30, 651 S.W.2d 90, 93 (Ark. 1983).
[9] Brown v. Board of Education, 347 U.S. 483, 493 (1954).
[10] *Id*.

Furthermore, all of the state constitutions include education articles,[11] some of which contain strong language which can be taken to deem education a fundamental right.[12] For example, the Illinois education article states that: "A fundamental goal of the People of the State is the educational development of all persons to the limits of their capacities."[13] Despite this language, the Supreme Court of Illinois used extremely deferential review in upholding the state system of funding education.[14] Some state education articles call for uniformity of schools, which can be taken to call for parity of funding. For instance, the Wisconsin education article states that "The legislature … shall provide … for the establishment of district schools, which shall be as nearly uniform as practical …"[15] Nevertheless, the Wisconsin Supreme Court has rebuffed a challenge to the state education finance system.[16] Other state high courts, however, have not been so quick to brush aside the language of the education articles in their state constitutions. The Supreme Court of Connecticut, for instance, has ruled that in light of the text of the Connecticut education article "it cannot be questioned" that in Connecticut education is a fundamental right.[17]

A state constitutional challenge to a school financing system may be based exclusively on an equality provision, exclusively on an education

---

[11] Ala. Const. art. XIV, 256; Alaska Const. art. VII, 1; Ariz. Const. art. XI, 1; Ark. Const. art. XIV, 1; Cal. Const. art. IX, 1; Colo. Const. art. IX, 2; Conn. Const. art. VIII, 1; Del. Const. art. X, 1; Fla. Const. art. IX, 1; Ga. Const. art. VIII, 1; Haw. Const. art. X, 1; Idaho Const. art. IX, 1; Ill. Const. art. X, 1; Ind. Const. art. VII, 1; Iowa Const. art. IX, 2d, 3; Kan. Const. art. VI, 1; Ky. Const. 183; La. Const. art. VIII, 1; Me. Const. art. VIII, pt.1, 1; Md. Const. art. VIII, 1; Mass. Const. pt. 2, ch. 5, 2; Mich. Const. art. VIII, 2; Minn. Const. art. XIII, 1; Miss. Const. art. VIII, 201; Mo. Const. art. IX, 1(a); Mont. Const. art. X, 1; Neb. Const. art. VII, 1; Nev. Const. art. XI, 2; N.H. Const. pt. 2, art. LXXXIII; N.J. Const. art. VIII, 4, 1; N.M. Const. art. XII, 1; N.Y. Const. art. XI, 1; N.C. Const. art. IX, 2; N.D. Const. art. VIII, 1; Ohio Const. art. VI, 3; Okla. Const. art. XIII, 1; Or. Const. art. VIII, 3; Pa. Const. art. III, 14; R.I. Const. art. XII, 1; S.C. Const. art. XI, 3; S.D. Const. art. VIII, 1; Tenn. Const. art. XI, 12; Tex. Const. art. VII, 1; Utah Const. art. X, 1; Vt. Const. ch. 2, 68; Va. Const. art. VIII, 1; Wash. Const. art. IX, 1; W. Va. Const. art. XII, 1; Wis. Const. art. X, 3; Wyo. Const. art. VII, 1.

[12] North Dakota has a most interesting education article, which says: "A high degree of intelligence, patriotism, integrity, and morality on the part of every voter in a government by the people being necessary in order to insure the continuance of the govt. and the prosperity and happiness of the people, the (legislature) shall make provision for the establishment and maintenance of a system of public schools which shall be open to all children of the state." N.D. Const. art. VIII, §1.

[13] Ill. Const. art. X, sect. 1.

[14] Committee of Educational Rights v. Edgar, 672 N.E.2d 1178 (Ill. 1996).

[15] Wis. Const. art. X, 3.

[16] Kukor v. Grover, 436 N.W.2d 568 (Wis. 1989).

[17] Horton v. Meskill, 376 A.2d 359, 373 (Conn. 1977).

article, or on a combination of the two. One way to combine the two is to use a strongly worded education article to establish that education is a fundamental right under a state constitution, and then use strict scrutiny under an equal protection clause to assess the constitutionality of a school funding system. But some courts, such as the Supreme Court of Illinois, have ruled in education finance suits that education articles are judicially unenforceable, and thus exist as little more than constitutional admonitions for the legislature.[18] A number of state supreme courts, though, have been more willing to enforce their educational articles, either on their own or in combination with an equal protection clause.

There have been suits challenging school financing schemes on state constitutional grounds in forty-three states, and the results are split. In seventeen states the court of last resort has found that property tax-based systems of financing education that result in disparate levels of funding are unconstitutional.[19] On the other hand, twenty-six state supreme courts have upheld such systems, seeing nothing unconstitutional about them.[20] In states where financing systems have been struck down, the courts rely upon either a state equality provision, a state education article, or both. In eight of the states in which an equal protection violation has been found, the state courts have ruled that education is a fundamental right.[21] Three other state supreme courts—those in Wisconsin,[22] Minnesota,[23] and Virginia[24]—have also held that education is a fundamental right, and then went to uphold the school financing systems in their states.

In *Robinson v. Cahill*, the New Jersey system of financing public education, which resulted in inequality from one district to another, was challenged as violating several provisions in the state constitution.[25] One of the challenges was an equal protection challenge, but the New Jersey Supreme Court declined to decide the case on equal protection grounds

---

[18] Committee for Educational Rights v. Edgar, *supra* note 14.

[19] Karen Swenson, *School Finance Reform Litigation: Why Are Some State Supreme Courts Activist and Others Restrained?*, 63 Alb. L. Rev. 1147, 1148–49 (2000).

[20] *Id.* at 1149.

[21] DuPree v. Alma Sch. Dist. No. 30, 651 S.W.2d 90 (Ark. 1983); Serrano v. Priest (I), 487 P.2d 1241 (Cal. 1971); Horton v. Meskill, 376 A.2d 359 (Conn. 1977); Knowles v. State Bd. of Educ. 547 P.2d 699 (Kan. 1976); Rose v. Council for Better Educ., Inc. 790 S.W.2d 186 (Ky. 1989); Robinson v. Cahill, 339 A.2d 193 (N.J. 1975); Seattle School Dist. No. 1 v. State, 585 P.2d 71 (Wash. 1978); Pauley v. Kelly, 255 S.E.2d 859 (W. Va. 1979).

[22] Kukor v. Grover, *supra* note 16.

[23] Skeen v. State, 505 N.W.2d 299 (Minn. 1993).

[24] Scott v. Commonwealth, 443 S.E.2d 138 (Va. 1994).

[25] Robinson v. Cahill, 303 A.2d 273 (N.J. 1973).

because it thought that equal protection analysis was too "unmanageable if it is called upon to supply categorical answers in the vast area of human needs …"[26] The court thought that it would be too difficult to find an objective basis to distinguish education from other basic needs, such as food and lodging, police and fire protection, water and other public health services.[27] If the court ruled that education was a fundamental right and hence entitled to the protection of strict scrutiny under the Equal Protection Clause, it would open the door to similar equal protection challenges against the unequal distribution of those other kinds of services which arguably are no less basic or fundamental than education. So, the court decided not to use the Equal Protection Clause to review the New Jersey method of financing public education.[28]

The court's apprehension about the unmanageability of equal protection review seems unfounded. In fact, there is an objective way to distinguish education from other basic needs, namely, to look to other provisions in the state constitution, particularly the state education article. Unlike the New Jersey Supreme Court, the high courts in a number of other states have been willing to recognize education as a fundamental right by referring to the education articles in their state constitutions. The Supreme Court of Connecticut, for example, used the education article in the state constitution to find that education was a fundamental right that called for strict scrutiny under the state equal protection clause.[29] This analysis combines the state equal protection clause with the state education article. This seems to be a logical means to confine equal protection analysis while remaining true to the dictates of a state's constitution. Indeed, the wording of some state education articles describes education in highly favorable language that virtually designates it as a fundamental right.

Although in *Robinson* the New Jersey Supreme Court was unwilling to recognize education as a fundamental right under the state equal protection clause, it was willing to find heightened constitutional protection for education under another equality provision in the state constitution. The New Jersey Constitution also contains a provision that prohibits "private, local, or special laws" in certain enumerated or listed situations.[30] One of the enumerated situations is in providing for the management

---

[26] *Id.* at 283.
[27] *Id.* at 284.
[28] *Id.* at 287.
[29] Horton v. Meskill, 376 A.2d 359 (Conn. 1977).
[30] N.J. Const. art. IV, sect. 7.

and control of free public schools.[31] So, the New Jersey Constitution contains an equality provision explicitly banning private, local, or special legislation for the management and control of schools.

The New Jersey constitution also contains an education article, which states that, "The legislature shall provide for the maintenance and support of a thorough and efficient system of free public schools for the instruction of all the children in the State between the ages of five and eighteen."[32] According to the education article, the state, and not local school districts, has the responsibility to provide public education.[33] After all, the education article expressly states that the legislature *shall* provide for the maintenance and support of a thorough and efficient system of education for *all the children in the state*. The state may fulfill this obligation directly or by delegating it to local government units, but in either case the state still bears the ultimate responsibility for providing education and for ensuring that the educational system put into effect complies with the requirements of the constitution.[34] And one of those requirements is that there be no local or special laws in the management and control of schools. This requirement, along with the education article, were intended to ensure equal educational opportunity for all children. In fact, the court concluded, equal educational opportunity for children was "precisely in mind" when the provisions were originally adopted.[35] Because the New Jersey system of financing education fell far short of providing statewide equal education opportunity, the court concluded that it was in violation of the state constitution.[36]

Economic Rights

The use of heightened judicial review in cases involving economic matters raises the specter of "Lochnerism." This, of course, refers to the practice, most notably of the United States Supreme Court in the early part of the 20th Century, of incorporating extreme laissez faire economic policy into constitutional provisions, thereby invalidating many remedial statutes

---

[31] N.J. Const. art. IV, sect. 7, para. 9.
[32] N.J. Const. art. VIII, sect. 4, 1.
[33] Robinson v. Cahill, 303 A.2d at 291–92.
[34] *Id.*
[35] *Id.* at 294.
[36] *Id.* at 295–98.

designed to regulate wages, prices, and working conditions. In *Lochner* itself, the Supreme Court ruled that a labor law setting maximum hours of work for bakers unduly interfered with liberty of contract and therefore was a violation of the due process clause of the Fourteenth Amendment.[37] *Lochner* has come to symbolize the excesses of judicial intervention, which saw the Supreme Court equating constitutional provisions with an outmoded, discredited economic policy to the point of inhumanity.[38]

In the federal system, minimal scrutiny was designed to counteract Lochnerism by withdrawing meaningful judicial review from economic matters. Since the 1940s, in both due process and equal protection cases, the Supreme Court has consistently applied the most minimal form of review to economic laws, invariably upholding them as constitutional.[39]

Many states, having also learned the lessons of Lochnerism, follow the federal example in reviewing laws that involve economic matters.[40] In states that conform to the federal pattern, the assertion of economic rights, whether based on due process or equality, usually garners the most minimal constitutional protection.[41] The supreme courts of these states, like the federal Supreme Court, review economic laws with minimal scrutiny that grants extreme deference to the legislature. Tax laws, especially, are reviewed with the most deferential scrutiny and almost always found to be constitutional.[42] Similarly, other kinds of economic laws also are sheltered within the confines of minimal scrutiny and usually are sustained with little more than cursory review.[43]

On the other hand, not all states follow the federal approach of deferential review in evaluating the constitutionality of economic legislation. In some states, review of economic legislation challenged on due process

---

[37] Lochner v. New York, 198 U.S. 45 (1905).

[38] "Justice Peckham's opinion (in *Lochner*) striking down the law has been a continuing source of outrage, both because of the inhumanity of the result and because it contains language that can be reasonably interpreted as violently hostile to all attempts to use the legal system as a conscious mechanism to redress the bargaining position of workers in their dealings with employers." Duncan Kennedy, *Toward an Historical Understanding of Legal Consciousness: The Case of Classical Legal Thought in America, 1850–1940, in Research in Law and Sociology*, Vol. 3 at pp. 9–10 (Steven Spitzer ed., 1980).

[39] *E.g.*, Olsen v. Nebraska, 313 U.S. 236 (1941); Williamson v. Lee Optical of Oklahoma, Inc., 348 U.S. 483 (1955).

[40] *See* Note, *Developments in the Law: The Interpretation of State Constitutional Rights*, 95 Harv. L. Rev. 1463, 1466–67, 1473 (1982).

[41] *Id.*

[42] *See infra* at notes 49–80.

[43] *See infra* at notes 81–162.

or equality grounds is somewhat more forceful than it is in the federal system.[44] A few courts have departed from the norm in economic cases by using an enhanced version of minimal scrutiny to review laws that place caps on the amount of damages recoverable in a tort action.[45] Similarly, a few states have been willing to upgrade minimal scrutiny when considering laws that allocate economic benefits.[46] More frequently, some states have chosen to heighten minimal scrutiny when considering regulatory laws that restrict business competition.[47] And, in the State of Washington, the Supreme Court has seen fit to use a rigorous form of review in assessing laws that bestow special economic entitlements upon a favored few.[48] Thus, there is a developing schism among the states when it comes to reviewing economic legislation under equality provisions; while most states adhere strictly to the federal model of the most minimal scrutiny in examining economic legislation, other states are more rigorous in examining certain kinds of economic legislation.

Tax Laws

In a high majority of cases, tax laws challenged as violating state equality provisions are reviewed with the most minimal variety of scrutiny and are almost always upheld, no matter how irrational they might be.[49] The traditional view, both state and federal, is that tax matters are best left to the legislature-in fact, that tax laws are especially within the province of legislative discretion. As a result, judicial scrutiny under equality provisions is at its most minimal when a taxing statute is challenged.[50] The general view was starkly expressed by the Supreme Court of Connecticut in reiterating that in taxation, even more than other fields, the legislature possesses the greatest freedom to make classifications.[51] When a tax law is

---

[44] *Developments in the Law: The Interpretation of State Constitutional Rights*, 95 Harv. L. Rev. 1463, 1465–74 (1982).

[45] *See infra* at notes 88–101.

[46] *See infra* at notes 113–29.

[47] *See infra* at notes 137–54.

[48] *See infra* at notes 163–71.

[49] *See, e.g.*, Miller v. Heffernan, 378 A.2d 572 (Conn. 1977).

[50] Judicial review of tax laws may even be more minimal than of other economic legislation. *See* Texas Co. v. Cohn, 112 P.2d 522 (Wash. 1941); Hemphill v. Washington State Tax Commission, 400 P.2d 297 (Wash. 1965).

[51] Kellems v. Brown, 313 A.2d 53, 60 (Conn. 1972) (quoting Madden v. Kentucky, 309 U.S. 83, 88 (1940).

challenged, the court recapitulated, the presumption of constitutionality can be overcome only by the most explicit demonstration that a classification amounts to hostile and oppressive discrimination against particular persons or classes.[52] The burden is on the party attacking a tax statute to negative every conceivable basis which might support it.[53]

A Washington case, *Hemphill v. Washington State Tax Commission*, exemplifies the approach usually taken by state courts when tax laws are challenged as violating a state equality provision.[54] In *Hemphill*, the Supreme Court of Washington considered the constitutionality of a state tax on the gross receipts of recreational businesses, such as skating rinks, golf courses, pool and billiard halls, and ski areas. Because the tax exempted bowling alleys, it was challenged as violative of the Federal Equal Protection Clause and the state equal privileges and immunities provision.[55] In the eyes of the Washington Supreme Court, however, there was nothing unconstitutional about the tax. The court was quick to spout the usual rationality review pieties:

> There is a strong presumption that a revenue statute is constitutional, and where there is doubt, it will be resolved in favor of constitutionality. Also, the general rule is that a legislature has the power to make reasonable and natural classifications for purposes of taxation, and that in the exercise of this power the legislature has very broad discretion … (T)he burden is on the challenger to prove that a questioned classification does not rest upon a reasonable basis. … The test is merely whether "any state of facts reasonably can be conceived that would sustain" the classification.[56]

Although conceding that bowling was part of the amusement and recreation industry and that there was little distinction between bowling and other recreational activities that were subject to the tax, the court nonetheless sustained the tax statute by "conceiving" some differences between the two activities. That the differences were either imaginary or irrelevant (or both) did not deter the court from upholding the statute. After all, when it comes to tax laws, the legislature enjoys the widest discretion to make classifications.

---

52 *Id.*
53 *Id.*
54 Hemphill v. Washington State Tax Commission, 400 P.2d 297 (Wash. 1965).
55 *Id.* at 298.
56 *Id.* at 298–99 (omitting citations).

On a few occasions, though certainly not many, state courts have put some bite into equality provisions to strike down tax laws. In a Vermont case, *Oxx v. Vermont Department of Taxes*, the supreme court of that state invalidated a state income tax regulation that "piggybacked" a state tax on a federal one.[57] The tax in question treated all taxpayers who received certain federal recapture benefits as if they had also received corresponding state recapture benefits, when some taxpayers (depending on their state of residence at the time) who received the federal benefits did not in fact receive corresponding state benefits.[58] The tax thus failed to accurately reflect the adjusted gross income of some taxpayers.[59] Purportedly applying rationality review,[60] the court concluded that the tax regulation violated both the Federal Equal Protection Clause and the equality provision in the Vermont Constitution.[61] The decision in *Oxx*, though, is one of the rare exceptions;[62] in the large majority of cases where tax laws are challenged on equal protection grounds, extreme deference remains the norm and the tax laws ordinarily survive the challenge.

In a more recent exception from the norm, *Racing Association of Central Iowa v. Fitzgerald*, the Supreme Court of Iowa struck down a tax law[63] that subsequently withstood rationality review in the eyes of the United States Supreme Court,[64] only to be struck down again by the Iowa high court.[65] The case involved legislation that was designed to provide financial relief for the state riverboat and racetrack industries, both of which were losing significant revenue. Among other things, the legislation eliminated a previous limit on the amount of riverboat gambling and authorized racetracks to operate slot machines (which were already allowed on riverboats). In addition, the legislation set a considerably higher tax

---

[57] Oxx v. Vermont Department of Taxes, 618 A.2d 1321 (Vt. 1992).

[58] *Id.* at 1322–23.

[59] *Id.* at 1325.

[60] *Id.* at 1324.

[61] *Id.*

[62] There is one other case in which the Vermont Supreme Court struck down a tax law. In *Colchester Fire District No. 2 v. Sharrow*, 485 A.2d 134 (Vt. 1984) the court invalidated a tax scheme assessing revenue bond payments for each building that contained a flush toilet. The purpose of the assessment in question was to retire the capital debt, while there was a separate assessment for water consumption. Noting that bond payment assessments bear no relationship to the amount of water used in a building, the court found that the assessment was wholly arbitrary. *Id.* at 135–37. The court concluded that the assessment violated the Federal Equal Protection Clause. *Id.* at 136–37.

[63] Racing Association of Central Iowa v. Fitzgerald, 648 N.W.2d 555 (Iowa 2002).

[64] Fitzgerald v. Racing Association of Central Iowa, 539 U.S. 103 (2003).

[65] Racing Association of Central Iowa v. Fitzgerald, 675 N.W.2d 1 (Iowa 2004).

rate on gambling revenues at racetracks than at riverboats.[66] This disparate tax rate applied to the main gambling activity taking place at both racetracks and riverboats—slot machine gambling. As the Iowa Supreme Court noted, the result of this was that the same activity was being taxed at significantly different rates depending on its location.[67] Although acknowledging that the legislature had broad authority in the realm of taxation, the Iowa court nevertheless noted that even in this area legislation is subject to rational basis review in order to ensure that it is not wholly arbitrary. Seeing no rational explanation whatsoever for the differential tax rate, the court concluded that it violated both the Federal Equal Protection Clause and the state constitutional provision guaranteeing equal privileges and immunities to all citizens.[68]

On appeal, though, the nation's highest court, though saw things differently.[69] First, the Court described the minimalist nature of rationality review, noting that it requires only a plausible explanation for legislation and that it is especially deferential in the context of tax laws. Within the bounds of rationality, the Court explained, the legislature enjoys broad authority to decide whom it wishes to benefit by its tax laws and to what extent. The Court then postulated several possible explanations for the Iowa differential tax rate: The legislature may have wanted to encourage the economic development of river communities by providing incentives for riverboats to remain in the state; the legislature may have wanted to protect the reliance interests of riverboat operators; or the legislature may have wanted to assist the financial position of riverboats.[70] Hence, the high Court concluded that the Iowa law was not so arbitrary or irrational as to violate the Equal Protection Clause. Therefore, the Iowa Supreme Court's judgment to the contrary was reversed and the case was remanded back to that court.

On remand, the Supreme Court of Iowa reinstated its former decision that the tax law violated the state equal privileges and immunities

---

[66] Revenues from slot machines on riverboats were taxed at a maximum rate of 20%; revenues from slot machines at racetracks were taxed at a maximum rate of 36%. *Id.* at 4.

[67] Racing Association of Central Iowa v. Fitzgerald, 648 N.W.2d at 559 (Iowa 2002).

[68] *Id.* at 558–63.

[69] Fitzgerald v. Racing Association of Central Iowa, 539 U.S. 103 (2003). Because the opinion of the Iowa Supreme Court took the position that state and federal equal protection analysis is the same, the United States Supreme Court concluded that the Iowa decision did not rest on independent state law grounds and therefore was within the jurisdiction of the United States Supreme Court. *Id.* at 106.

[70] *Id.* at 108–10.

provision.[71] The court made it clear that the decision of the United States Supreme Court, while entitled to respect, was in no way binding upon the Iowa court in regard to Iowa constitutional law. The meaning of the Iowa equality provision is a matter firmly within the state's sovereign prerogatives to be determined by the Iowa Supreme Court and no other. In exercising the sovereign prerogative of judicial review, the Iowa high court applied constitutional doctrine according to its own lights, ultimately rejecting each rationale proffered by the United States Supreme Court in support of the differential tax rate. The suggestion that the tax law was designed to encourage the economic development of river communities was dismissed by the Iowa court on the ground that it was so inconsistent with the legislative facts as to be implausible.[72] The suggestion that the law was intended to protect the reliance interests of riverboat operators was refuted because the taxation lines were drawn on the basis of where the slot machines were located and not when their owners first invested in them.[73] And the assertion that the law was meant to assist the financial position of riverboats was rejected because it provided no explanation as to why riverboats received more favorable treatment than racetracks when both were in financial straits at the time the tax legislation was enacted.[74] Ultimately, the court returned to the fact that the law in question set disparate tax rates on the same activity—slot machine gambling—depending on where it was located.[75] In the court's opinion there was no reason for that disparity and hence the tax law contravened the Iowa constitutional guarantee of equal privileges and immunities for all citizens.

While the Supreme Court of Iowa may well have been correct that there was no reason to explain the differential tax rate, in reaching that conclusion the court seemed to invest rationality review with more than its typical bite. Indeed, in tax cases rationality review is usually at its most deferential, allowing the legislature extensive latitude to make classifications. Although exceptions occasionally occur, they remain infrequent, as the courts almost always acquiesce to legislative judgments in the field of taxation.

---

[71] Racing Association of Central Iowa v. Fitzgerald, 675 N.W.2d 1 (Iowa 2004).
[72] *Id.* at 9–11.
[73] *Id.* at 11–12.
[74] *Id.* at 12–14.
[75] *Id.* at 15.

A number of state constitutions contain so-called "uniformity clauses" that require taxes to be uniformly levied upon the same class of subjects.[76] Some uniformity clauses apply only to property taxes, while others apply to all taxes.[77] In reviewing the constitutionality of tax laws under uniformity clauses, some state courts invest the clauses with more rigor than is used to review tax laws under equality provisions.[78] For instance, the Indiana Supreme Court has described its uniformity clause as setting a "rigid" standard more demanding than rationality review.[79] Conversely, other states have ruled that their uniformity clauses should be applied with the same sort of deferential rationality review that prevails under the Federal Equal Protection Clause.[80]

Damage Caps

In response to the "tort reform" movement, a number of cases have been filed across the nation challenging the constitutionality of legislation that places caps on the amount of damages recoverable in tort actions. These challenges are based on a variety of state constitutional provisions, including right to remedy or open court guarantees, provisions guaranteeing the right to jury trial, due process clauses, and equality provisions. Most courts are reluctant to overturn damage caps, even in the face of doubts about their efficacy, and in most instances the courts uphold the constitutionality of damage caps, although the number of decisions striking down damage caps as unconstitutional is increasing.[81] In cases where the challenges are successful, the courts most often rely upon right to remedy or open court guarantees as the most appropriate means to strike down damage cap legislation.[82] On occasion, some courts have found that

---

[76] *E.g.*, "All taxes shall be uniform upon the same class of subjects with the territorial limits of the authority levying the tax." Del. Const. art. VIII, sect. 1.

[77] *See* Wade J. Newhouse, *Constitutional Uniformity and Equality in State Taxation* (2d ed. 1984).

[78] *See, e.g.*, Indiana Aeronautics Commission v. Ambassadair, Inc., 368 N.E.2d 1340 (Ind. 1977).

[79] *Id.* at 1343.

[80] *See, e.g.*, Conrad v. State, 16 A.2d 121 (Del. 1940); Leonard v. Thornburgh, 489 A.2d 1349 (Pa. 1985).

[81] *See* Carly N. Kelly & Michelle Mello, *Are Medical Malpractice Caps Constitutional? An Overview of State Litigation*, 33 J.L. Med. & Ethics 515, 515–25 (2005).

[82] *Id.* at 518–20.

damage caps contravene the constitutional right to a jury trial.[83] And a few courts have used equality provisions or due process clauses to strike down damage caps.[84]

In reviewing the constitutionality of damage caps under equality provisions, most courts adopt some variety of rationality review. Using rationality review, courts in several states have upheld damage caps on the ground that they are a rational means of maintaining the availability and quality of health care by reducing its costs, especially the cost of medical malpractice insurance. For example, in upholding a damage cap of $250,000 on noneconomic damages, the Supreme Court of California observed that the state legislature had found that the rising costs of medical malpractice insurance were creating serious problems for the health care system in California, threatening to curtail the availability of medical services in some parts of the state, and that it appeared "obvious" that the damage cap was rationally related to the objective of reducing the costs of malpractice insurance.[85] Along similar lines, the Supreme Court of Virginia upheld a $750,000 cap on all damages, noting that after "careful and deliberate study," the legislature had determined that the cap was the best method to address the significant problem of rising health care costs.[86] In both of these cases the courts applied conventional rationality review to conclude that the legislature had plausible reason to believe that damage caps would reduce the costs of health care.[87]

On the other hand, a few courts have invested rationality review with enough bite to strike down damage caps.[88] These courts have taken the position that there is insufficient evidence to show that damage caps do, in fact, reduce health care costs.[89] This position has been criticized on the ground that under true rationality review the courts should accept the legislative determination that damage caps reduce the costs of health care.[90] Moreover, some studies show that damage caps do decrease health

---

[83] *Id.* at 520–21.

[84] *Id.* at 521–25.

[85] Fein v. Permanente Medical Group, 695 P.2d 665, 680 (Cal. 1985).

[86] Etheridge v. Medical Center Hospitals, 376 S.E.2d 525, 533–34 (Va. 1989).

[87] *See also*, Murphy v. Edmonds, 601 A.2d 102 (Md. Ct. App. 1992) (upholding a $350,000 cap on noneconomic damages after finding that it was a rational method of reducing health care costs and therefore did not violate equal protection).

[88] Farley v. Engelken, 740 P.2d 1058 (Kan. 1987); Best v. Taylor Machine Works, 689 N.E.2d 1057 (Ill. 1997).

[89] Best v. Taylor Machine Works, *id.*

[90] *See* Matthew W. Light, *Who's the Boss?: Statutory Damage Caps, Torts, and State Constitutional Law*, 58 Wash. & Lee L. Rev. 315, 344–53 (2001).

care costs; therefore, in the face of what amounts to inconclusive evidence on this matter, the courts should defer to the legislative judgment.[91]

Now and then courts have used a heightened level of scrutiny in striking down damage caps as violative of the principles of equality. On two occasions, the Supreme Court of New Hampshire has struck down damage cap laws as violating the equal protection guarantee of the state constitution. In *Carson v. Maurer*, the Court ruled that a $250,000 cap on non-economic damages in medical malpractice cases violated the equal protection guarantee,[92] and in *Brannigan v. Usitalo*, the court held that a $875,000 cap on non-economic damages for personal injury claims also violated the equal protection guarantee.[93] In both cases the court found that the right to recover personal injuries was a sufficiently important substantive right to require that restrictions on the right be evaluated by a more rigorous judicial scrutiny than rationality review.[94] The appropriate level of review, the court explained in *Brannigan*, was "middle-tier scrutiny."[95] Under this intermediate standard, the court found that the legislation in question did not bear a fair and substantial relation to its objective because it was "simply unfair and unreasonable to impose the burden of supporting the medical care industry solely upon those persons who are most severely injured and therefore most in need of compensation."[96]

Meanwhile, in the Far West, the Supreme Court of Montana saw fit to combine an equal protection guarantee with a right to remedy guarantee to strike down a statute governing tort actions against the state that barred recovery of non-economic damages and limited recovery of economic damages to $300,000 for each claimant and $1 million for each occurrence.[97] The court took the position that the right to be compensated for physical and mental injury was a fundamental right by virtue of Article II, section 16 of the Montana Constitution guaranteeing a speedy remedy for every injury.[98] Accordingly, strict scrutiny attached, and the court found that the statute violated the guarantee of equal protection of

---

[91] *Id.* at 348–51.
[92] Carson v. Maurer, 424 A.2d 825 (N.H. 1980).
[93] Brannigan v. Usitalo, 587 A.2d 1232 (N.H. 1991).
[94] *Id.* at 1234–35.
[95] *Id.* at 1235.
[96] *Id.* at 1235–36.
[97] White v. State, 661 P.2d 1272 (Mont. 1983).
[98] *Id.* at 1275.

the laws.[99] The state's claim that the statute was necessary to protect the fiscal well-being of the state was rejected by the court as a "bare assertion" unsupported by any evidenced in the record.[100] Therefore, the court concluded that "the strict scrutiny test mandated by the implication of a fundamental right was not satisfied …"[101]

Allocation of Economic Benefits

Traditionally, laws that allocate economic benefits are reviewed by the courts with minimal scrutiny that grants a high degree of deference to the legislature. So, for instance, in *Kelly v. State*, the Supreme Court of Iowa found no violation of equal protection when the state General Assembly granted a 10% pay increase over a three-year period to state employees who were union members, while affording only a 7.5% increase over the same period of time to nonunion state employees.[102] Adhering strictly to the federal model, the Iowa high court declared that "The scrutiny of a challenged statute is the same under both the United States and Iowa Constitutions."[103] Because there is no fundamental right to public employment and because union membership or nonmembership is not a suspect classification, the court applied minimal scrutiny (or rationality review) to the legislative action in question.[104] Under minimal scrutiny, the court concluded that "The State could have rationally determined not to expend equal pay increases to nonunion employees for economic reasons."[105] What those economic reasons might be are not further explicated in the court's opinion. The court's proffered rationale of "economic reasons" is tautological. It furnishes no reason that explains why it might be economically rational for the state to give union employees a larger pay increase than nonunion employees. That the state has a limited amount of funds for pay increases does not explain why the state may allocate more of those funds to one group than another. If there is some reason for the disparate pay rates at issue in *Kelly*, the court's opinion

---

99 *Id.*
100 *Id.*
101 *Id.*
102 Kelly v. State, 525 N.W.2d 409 (Iowa 1994).
103 *Id.* at 411.
104 *Id.*
105 *Id.*

does not say what it is. In other words, the court's opinion pretends that the legislation action is rational, but in no way demonstrates that it is in fact rational. This is the lowest version of minimal scrutiny that accords virtually complete deference to the legislature to regulate economic matters.[106]

Even in those states that have abandoned the federal model of equal protection and taken a more independent view of equality, the assertion of economic rights usually evokes merely a minimal amount of constitutional protection. In Alaska, for example, although the state supreme court has adopted a sliding scale approach that provides enhanced protection for certain individual rights, economic rights still are considered to reside at the low end of the continuum and, hence, are entitled to only a minimal degree of protection.[107] Taking this approach in *Williams v. State*, the Supreme Court of Alaska found no violation of equal protection in an amendment to the state workers' compensation statute that altered the definition of "injury" to exclude stress-related mental injuries from coverage unless the stress was "extraordinary and unusual."[108] Before upholding the amendment, the court noted that Alaska has rejected the federal tiered model in favor of a more flexible sliding scale that may be more protective of individual rights than the federal approach.[109] Nonetheless, the court continued, "Worker's compensation benefits are merely an economic interest, and therefore, are entitled only to minimal protection under (Alaska's) equal protection analysis."[110] In the view of the court, the amendment was constitutional under minimal scrutiny because it was appropriately related to the statutory objective of providing fair disability benefits to workers at a reasonable cost to their employers.[111] The court thought that the amendment rationally served the objective of cutting costs for employers in two ways: by eliminating

---

[106] *See also* McCusker v. Workmen's Compensation Board, 639 A.776 (Pa. 1994) (finding that a statute that cuts off worker compensation benefits if the recipient enters into a "meretricious relationship" is not a denial of equal protection): "It is well settled that in the area of social welfare legislation a court's review of government regulation is deferential." *Id*. at 779.

[107] Williams v. State, 895 P.2d 99, 103–4 Alaska (1995). *See also* Alaska v. Cosio, 858 P.2d 621 (Alaska 1993) (upholding permanent fund dividend regulation requiring recipients of dividends to be physically present in state with intent to remain permanently.).

[108] Williams v. State, 895 P.2d at 101. The amendment also eliminated a presumption of compensability for stress-related mental injury. *Id*.

[109] *Id* at 103.

[110] *Id*. at 104.

[111] *Id*.

claimants who were unusually susceptible to stress-related mental disability; and by minimizing fraud and abuse in claims for stress-related mental injuries.[112]

Under a more searching brand of scrutiny, the court's reasoning would be open to debate. The first justification for the amendment suggested by the court—eliminating claimants who are especially susceptible to stress-related mental disability in order to cut costs—is particularly questionable. If, as the court says, the purpose of the statute is to provide benefits to disabled workers, why should any class of disabled workers be disqualified from receiving benefits? While eliminating claimants who are especially susceptible to stress-related mental disability will cut costs for employers, so will the elimination of any other class of claimants who are particularly susceptible to a mental or physical disability. Why not eliminate claimants who are particularly susceptible to Alzheimer's disease, or heart disease, or cancer? After all, each of those alternatives is an equally or possibly even more effective way of cutting costs to employers. In *Williams*, the court never really explains why, in order to cut costs, it is reasonable to disqualify one class of claimants but not others. Thus, that portion of the court's opinion devolves into the sort of minimal scrutiny that offers little more than a pretense of rationality.

The second justification for the amendment offered by the court—minimizing fraud and abuse in claims of stress-related mental disability in order to cut costs—is also questionable, although probably less so. The question here is a factual one: are claims of stress-related mental disability more prone to fraud and abuse than other claims? If so, it would be rational to exclude them from coverage in order to cut costs. It might be supposed that stress-related claims are in fact more susceptible to fraud and abuse, but it would have been nice to see some explanation or empirical verification of this supposition in the court's opinion, not to mention the legislative record. The court's opinion, though, rather than providing explanation or verification of this justification for the amendment, is content merely to defer to the legislature. *Williams*, then, is yet another example of how deferential rationality review is used to sustain questionable economic legislation.

It is instructive to compare *Williams* with *Breen v. Carlsbad Municipal Schools*, in which the Supreme Court of New Mexico found that the state

---

[112] *Id.*

guarantee of equal protection was violated by a workers' compensation law that provided fewer benefits to workers who suffer mental disabilities than those who suffer physical disabilities.[113] While noting that the law affected economic benefits that do not rise to the level of important rights in the constitutional sense, the court nonetheless chose to apply intermediate scrutiny on the ground that persons who are mentally disabled, though not a suspect class, should be afforded the status of a "sensitive class" because historically they have been subject to discriminatory treatment.[114] Under intermediate scrutiny the court concluded that the law was not substantially related to an important governmental interest. The defendant school district had argued in the case that because mental disability claims are more difficult to diagnose than physical disability claims, the law served the purposes of putting a cap on uncertain claims and preventing fraud. This argument, of course, is similar to the argument accepted under minimal scrutiny by the Alaska Supreme Court in *Williams*. In *Breen*, though, the New Mexico Supreme Court, using intermediate scrutiny, was singularly unconvinced by the argument, noting that there were a number of physical disabilities that were difficult to diagnose and that there were procedural safeguards built into the workers' compensation system to guard against fraud.[115] Accordingly, the court concluded that the disparity in compensation granted to workers who suffer physical injury and those who suffer mental injury amounted to unjust discrimination that contravened the New Mexico guarantee of equal protection of the laws.

The fact patterns in *Kelly*, *Williams*, and *Breen* are instances of a recurring problem in economic cases, that is, the problem of line-drawing in the allocation of limited resources. There are, of course, many different ways to slice a pie of limited size; some are rational, others are not. Perhaps when it comes to economic matters, line-drawing is best left to the legislature and the courts should defer to the legislative judgment by using only

---

[113] Breen v. Carlsbad Municipal Schools, 120 P.3d 413 (N.M. 2005) (Workers who suffered total disability because of a physical injury could receive compensation for the rest of their lives, while workers who suffered total disability because of a primary mental impairment could only receive 100 weeks of compensation; workers who suffered a permanent partial disability because of a physical injury could receive compensation for 700 weeks, while workers who suffered permanent partial disability because of a primary mental impairment could receive only 100 weeks of compensation.).

[114] *Id.* at 419–23.

[115] *Id.* at 426–27.

minimal scrutiny. Still, one wonders if total deference should be practiced by the courts in all cases involving the allocation of economic benefits. There are some instances where the lines drawn by the legislature in allocating benefits appear to be so irrational or so unfairly preferential that they almost cry out for judicial scrutiny with at least a bit of bite.[116]

A few state courts have taken the position that while the legislature should enjoy a great deal of discretion in the allocation of economic benefits, there should be some limit to that discretion.[117] According to this view, the legislature should not be allowed to allocate benefits in a manner that shows no sign of rationality. For instance, in *Arneson v. State*, the Supreme Court of Montana struck down a law that allocated retirement payments to some beneficiaries of workers but not others, depending on the age of a beneficiary.[118] In the view of the court, the law in question was completely arbitrary, there being nothing in the record or even by conjecture to justify the differentiation that it generated.[119] While rejecting the assertion that intermediate scrutiny should be used because the law contained a classification based upon age, the court nonetheless was willing to invest rationality review with a modest but nonetheless meaningful degree of vigor that it does not ordinarily possess.[120] Operating in the mode of minimal scrutiny, the court found that the law under review violated the equal protection clause of the Montana Constitution because the state could not demonstrate that the law was rational. "The legislature cannot arbitrarily pick and choose," the court declared.[121] "Even if the governmental purpose is to save money, it cannot be done on a wholly arbitrary basis."[122]

A few courts have also found that it is unduly arbitrary for farm workers to be excluded from coverage under worker compensation laws.[123]

---

[116] *See, e.g.*, Kotch v. Board of River Pilot Commissioners, 330 U.S. 522 (1947), in which rationality review was used to sustain the administration of Louisiana pilotage laws that granted river pilot licenses to no one other than relatives or friends of incumbent pilots.
[117] *E.g.*, Industrial Claim Appeals Office of the State of Colorado v. Romero, 912 P.2d 62 (Colo. 1996); Pierce v. LaFourche Parish Council, 762 So.2d 608 (La. 2000).
[118] Arneson v. State, 864 P.2d 1245 (Mont. 1993).
[119] *Id.* at 1248.
[120] *Id.*
[121] *Id.*
[122] *Id.*
[123] Gutierrez v. Glaser Crandell Company, 202 N.W.2d 786 (Mich. 1972); Benson v. North Dakota Workmen's Compensation Bureau, 283 N.W.2d 96 (N.D. 1979); *but see*, State *ex rel.* Hammond v. Hager, 503 P.2d 52 (Mont. 1972); Collins v. Day, 644 N.E.2d 72 (Ind. 1994).

Both the supreme courts of Michigan[124] and North Dakota,[125] have concluded that there is no justifiable distinction between agricultural and nonagricultural workers in regard to the risk of injury from their work, and thus there is no reason why farm workers should not be entitled to the same work-related compensation benefits as any other workers.[126] Accordingly, both courts have ruled that to exclude farm workers from worker compensation benefits available to other workers is an unconstitutional denial of equal protection of the laws.[127] Other state supreme courts, however, have taken a different view of worker compensation laws that exclude farm employees from coverage. The supreme courts of Montana[128] and Indiana,[129] adopting the traditional deferential stance, have upheld such laws notwithstanding the lack of any genuine reason why farm workers should be treated differently than other workers. In these states extremely minimal scrutiny carried the day in the review of laws allocating economic benefits.

Regulatory Legislation

The state has a wise scope of authority to regulate business and professional practices in order to protect the public health, safety, and welfare.[130] The right to engage in any trade, occupation, business, or profession

---

[124] "There is no basis for distinguishing the work of a laborer who drives a truck at a factory from a laborer who drives one on the farm…" Gutierrez v. Glaser Crandell Company, 202 N.W.2d 786, 791 (Mich. 1972).

[125] "There are no proper and justifiable distinctions between agricultural employees and nonagricultural employees in relation to the risk of injury from employment." Benson v. North Dakota Workmen's Compensation Bureau, 283 N.W.2d 96, 107 (N.D. 1979).

[126] See also Washington National Insurance Co. v. Board of Review of New Jersey Unemployment Compensation Commission, 64 A.2d 443 (1949) (exclusion of insurance agents from Unemployment Compensation Act violates equal protection provision); DeMonaco v. Renton, 113 A.2d 782 (N.J. 1955) (exclusion of newsboys from Workmen's Compensation Act violates equal protection guarantee).

[127] While the Supreme Court of North Dakota held in Benson that the law in question was unconstitutional, the court did not do so by a sufficient majority to declare a statute unconstitutional according to the North Dakota Constitution. Section 88 of the North Dakota Constitution requires the concurrence of four members of the (five-person) court to declare a statute unconstitutional. In Benson, three members of the court concurred in the majority opinion, one dissented, and one was disqualified. See Benson, 283 N.W.2d 96, at 108, n.*.

[128] State ex rel. Hammond v. Hager, 503 P.2d 52 (Mont. 1972).

[129] Collins v. Day, supra note 123.

[130] See e.g., MRM, Inc. v. City of Davenport, 290 N.W.2d 338 (Iowa 1980); Belle Isle Grill Corp. v. City of Detroit, 666 N.W.2d 271 (Mich. 2003).

necessarily is subject to the regulatory powers of government to safeguard the public interest.[131] While there may be a generalized right to pursue a lawful occupation that is entitled to some degree of constitutional protection, the courts have consistently taken the position that there is not a fundamental right to work in one's chosen profession.[132] In most states, laws regulating or licensing business and professional practices are subject only to rational basis review to ensure that they are not arbitrary or unreasonable. [133]

As noted above, however, not all states are entirely deferential in evaluating the constitutionality of economic legislation. In fact, in applying their equality provisions, some states have opted for more rigorous review of economic legislation than permitted by the federal model.[134] In these states, meaningful review of economic legislation is most likely to occur in cases involving legislation that creates barriers to entering a business or profession, that restricts the modes of business or production methods, or that imposes financial burdens or benefits.[135] It has been suggested that the theme that runs through these cases is that special interest legislation that interferes with fair competition is an abuse of the legislative process and ought to be subject to searching judicial review.[136]

Although occupational licensing statutes ordinarily are subject only to rational basis review, there have been some cases in which such laws are struck down as violating equality provisions. In *D'Amico v. Board of Medical Examiners*, the Supreme Court of California ruled that a law excluding the practice of osteopathic medicine in the state was a denial of equal protection of the laws.[137] While professing to be using no more than minimal scrutiny,[138] the court actively evaluated the underlying factual

---

[131] *See e.g.*, Gillette Dairy, Inc. v. Nebraska Dairy Products Board, 219 N.W.2d 214 (Neb. 1974); Linkus v. Maryland State Board of Heating Ventilation, Air-Conditioning and Refrigeration Contractors, 689 A.2d 1254 (Md. 1997).

[132] Conn v. Gabbert, 526 U.S. 286, 291–92 (1999); Nixon v. Commonwealth, 839 A.2d 277, 288 (Pa. 2003); Amurund v. The Board of Appeals, 143 P.3d 571, 576–77 (Wash. 2006).

[133] *See e.g.*, Wilkerson v. Department of Health and Social Services, 993 P.2d 1018 (Alaska 1999) (upholding regulation denying foster care licenses to persons who had been charged or convicted of certain crimes.); Foley v. Department of Fisheries, 837 P.2d 14 (Wash. 1992) (upholding statute placing restrictions on who may commercially harvest sea urchins.).

[134] *Developments in the Law: The Interpretation of State Constitutional Rights*, 95 Harv. L. Rev. 1463, 1473 (1982).

[135] *Id.* (*see* especially the cases cited at notes 67–69).

[136] *Id.* at 1471–74.

[137] D'Amico v. Board of Medical Examiners, 520 P.2d 10 (Cal. 1974).

[138] *Id.* at 17–19.

basis of the law, finding that osteopathic training was in no way inferior to other medical training in either scope or quality and that practitioners of osteopathy were competent to perform the full range of activities constituting medical science.[139] Therefore, the court concluded that no rational relationship existed between the protection of public health and the exclusion of osteopaths from the practice of medicine.[140]

As compared to the California Supreme Court, the Supreme Court of Alaska was decidedly more frank about upgrading minimal scrutiny when it struck down a law that limited entry into the business of commercial fishing.[141] Noting "mounting discontent" with the "rigid" levels of scrutiny formulated by the United States Supreme Court, the Alaska high court opted for a "more demanding" approach to rationality review.[142] The court then adopted a rational basis test that it described as "fairly rigorous" and "non-deferential."[143] The court explained that it would no longer hypothesize facts to sustain otherwise questionable legislation and that judicial deference to conceivable legislative purposes or imaginable facts would be "strikingly diminished."[144] Accordingly, judicial tolerance of over-inclusive or under-inclusive classifications would be "notably reduced."[145] In applying this enhanced version of rationality review, the court conducted a thorough evaluation of the legislative record in the case before concluding that the law in question did not bear a fair and substantial relationship to a valid state interest, and thus was an unconstitutional denial of equal protection of the laws.[146]

In Illinois, although the state supreme court, wielding a weak variety of rationality review, usually upholds economic legislation,[147] it has drawn the line at licensing statutes that grant monopolistic control over

---

[139] *Id.* at 23–24.

[140] *Id.* at 22–25. *Cf.* Williamson v. Lee Optical of Oklahoma Inc., *supra* note 39 (upholding an Oklahoma law making it unlawful for opticians to fit or replace lenses without a written prescription from a licensed ophthalmologist or optometrist).

[141] Isakson v. Rickey, 550 P.2d 359 (Alaska 1976).

[142] *Id.* at 362.

[143] *Id.*

[144] *Id.*

[145] *Id.*

[146] *Id.* at 363–66.

[147] *See, e.g.,* Illinois Housing Development Authority v. Van Meter, 412 N.E.2d 151, 155 (Ill. 1980) (using rational basis test to uphold a housing statute that was challenged as special legislation): "In the instant case, the category could have been made broader or more precise. Nevertheless, we have found...the amendment is rationally related to a proper legislative purpose."

avenues of entry to certain businesses. In a series of cases,[148] the court struck down three licensing statutes for the plumbing trade because they gave master plumbers "arbitrary and monopolistic control over avenues of entry into the plumbing business."[149] And, in a more recent decision, the court invalidated a licensing statute for private detectives because it gave incumbent members of private detective agencies monopolistic control over individuals who wish to gain entry into the field without upgrading the professional expertise of prospective licensees.[150]

Other kinds of regulatory laws that grant a competitive advantage also have been found wanting under equality provisions. In *Burch v. Foy*, the Supreme Court of New Mexico struck down part of a state minimum wage act that imposed criminal penalties upon employers for failure to pay their employees the minimum wage set by the act.[151] According to the act, variety store employees were to be paid a minimum wage of 75 cents per hour, but drug stores employees doing substantially the same type of work could be paid 50 cents per hour.[152] Because the act gave a competitive advantage to the owners of drug stores, the court concluded that it

---

[148] People v. Brown, 95 N.E.2d 888 (Ill. 1950); Schroeder v. Binks, 113 N.E.2d 169 (Ill. 1953); People v. Johnson, 369 N.E.2d 898 (Ill. 1977). In *Brown* the court struck down a statute that provided that a person could not take the examination to become a master plumber until he had spent five years in the employment of a master plumber as an apprentice and then an additional five years in the employment of a master plumber as a journeyman plumber. The court noted that according to the statute no matter how well-qualified a person might be by instruction or training, that person could never become a licensed apprentice or journeyman or master plumber unless approved by a master plumber. The court concluded that: "The legislature conferred a special privilege upon master plumbers, as a class, when it gave them the arbitrary and exclusive right to determine who shall, or shall not, engage in the vocation of learning the trade of journeyman plumber...." People v. Brown, 95 N.E.2d at 898.

[149] Robert Herman Church v. Illinois, 646 N.E.2d 572, 579 (Ill. 1995).

[150] *Id.* In *Robert Herman Church* the court invalidated a statute requiring all person applying for a license as a private detective to have a minimum of three years experience as a full-time supervisor, manager or administrator for a licenses private alarm contractor agency. The plaintiff, who had 18 years experience as a police officer and operated a private alarm contracting business on a part-time basis, was denied an application for a license. The court found the statute unconstitutional because it granted members of the private alarm contracting trade monopolistic control over entry to the profession and no matter how well-qualified an individual might be, he or she could never become a licensed private detective without approval from a private alarm contractor. *Id.* at 580.

[151] Burch v. Foy, 308 P.2d 199 (N.M. 1957). When viewed from the perspective of employees, the minimum wage act can be considered a law that allocates economic benefits; when viewed from the perspective of employers, such as the plaintiff in the case, who are subject to criminal penalties for failure to pay the minimum wage, the act can be considered a regulatory law that affects competition among businesses.

[152] *Id.* at 200.

---

amounted to "class legislation of the most objectionable kind."[153] For that reason, the court declared that the part of the act relating to drug stores was a denial of equal protection and therefore unconstitutional.[154]

In several states, constitutional challenges have been brought against Sunday closing laws that grant exemptions to certain kinds of businesses. Whether challenged under equality provisions or religion clauses, in most instances the Sunday closing laws have been upheld as constitutional. As far as equality is concerned, most courts have reviewed these laws with minimal scrutiny that gives the legislature broad discretion to draw lines.[155] In a few cases, however, the courts have not been so tolerant of the lines drawn in Sunday closing laws.[156] In *Skag-Way Department Stores, Inc. v. City of Omaha*, the Supreme Court of Nebraska struck down a Sunday closing law because the classifications it drew were unreasonable.[157] As the court pointed out, the law in question discriminated against certain businesses in favor of their competitors.[158] For instance, one section of the law discriminated against the owners of clothing stores by requiring them to close on Sunday while allowing their competitors to remain open on Sunday if the sale of clothing was not their primary business.[159] As the court saw it, the real purpose of the law was not to provide a uniform day of rest, or to promote family unity, or to encourage religious observance; rather, its real purpose was to "enlist the power of the state to protect business interests."[160] Sunday closing laws, the court said, may be proper subjects of legislation, but still the classifications they make must be reasonable.[161] A portion of a class may not be legislated

---

[153] *Id.* at 203.

[154] *Id.*

[155] *See, e.g.*, Goodman v. Kennedy, 329 A.2d 224 (Pa. 1974); Vornado, Inc. v. Hyland, 390 A.2d 606 (N.J. 1978).

[156] *See* Piggly-Wiggly of Jacksonville v. City of Jacksonville, 336 So.2d 1078 (Ala. 1976), in which the Supreme Court of Alabama struck down a Sunday closing law that granted an exemption for food stores that employed no more than four persons. In the court's view, the classification made by the law was completely irrational, there being no reasonable distinction between food stores based upon the number of their employees. *See also*, State v. Ludlow Supermarkets, Inc. 448 A.2d 791 (Vt. 1982), in which the Supreme Court of Vermont struck down a Sunday closing law that discriminated among classes of commercial establishments on the basis of their size.

[157] Skag-Way Department Stores, Inc. v. City of Omaha, 140 N.W.2d 28 (Neb. 1966).

[158] *Id.* at 31–32.

[159] *Id.* at 31.

[160] *Id.* at 32.

[161] *Id.*

against unless there is a reasonable distinction that warrants differential treatment.[162]

Special Entitlements

We have seen that some state supreme courts, although still in the minority, are willing to engage in meaningful review of some economic legislation to ensure that it is not unreasonably discriminatory. Deferential review of economic legislation, though, remains the rule in most states.

It worth considering, however, whether economic legislation that bestows special entitlements upon a favored individual or class ought to be subject to more searching scrutiny in states whose constitutions contain a provision barring special privileges or immunities.[163] After all, the very purpose of such provisions is to preclude the government from giving special treatment to favored individuals or classes; so perhaps the courts ought not to be so deferential when faced with legislation that confers special economic entitlements. In fact, in the State of Washington a less deferential approach to laws granting special favors has been in place for some time. As early as 1905, the Supreme Court of Washington struck down a municipal ordinance on the ground that it violated article 1, section 12 of the state constitution, which prohibits the granting of special privileges or immunities.[164] The ordinance in question banned the peddling of fruits, vegetables, butter, eggs, and other produce within the city limits of Spokane, while exempting from the ban farmers who peddled their own produce. Noting that peddling is no more or less a nuisance when the peddler has produced his own goods, the court concluded that the ordinance amounted to the bestowal of a special privilege, in violation of article 1, section 12 of the state constitution.[165] In later cases, the court similarly struck down laws that granted special privileges to various groups. In one instance, the court invalidated a law that restricted fishing in certain waters while allowing an exception for licensed

---

[162] *Id.*

[163] *See* Jonathan Thompson, *The Washington Constitution's Prohibition on Special Privileges and Immunities: Real Bite for "Equal Protection" Review of Regulatory Legislation?*, 69 Temp. L. Rev. 1247, 1276–78 (1996).

[164] *Ex parte* Camp, 80 P. 547 (Wash. 1905).

[165] *Id.* at 548–49.

operators of gill nets.[166] In another instance, the court struck down an ordinance that required a license for photographers, but only those who were not residents of the city.[167] These laws, like the one in the peddlers' case, were found to confer special privileges in violation of article 1, section 12 of the state constitution.

The Washington Supreme Court has also struck down economic laws that grant special immunities.[168] In *City of Seattle v. Rogers*, the court invalidated an ordinance requiring a costly license to solicit charitable contributions while exempting the Seattle Community Fund from the requirement.[169] And, in *Adams v. Hinkle*, the court struck down a law that required a pre-publication license for dealers of comic books, but expressly exempted the comic section of newspapers.[170] It has been noted that these cases stand in marked contrast to federal deferential review that allows a problem to regulated "one step at a time."[171] Under the federal standard, the laws in both *Rogers* and *Adams* no doubt would be upheld on the ground that the state need not regulate all aspects of a problem at once; rather, it can proceed one step at a time. Whereas, under the more rigorous approach taken by the Supreme Court of Washington, the laws are seen for what they are: the bestowal of special entitlements to a favored few.

Criminal Law

A number of criminal laws have been challenged as violating state equality guarantees. In these cases, the state courts, like their federal counterparts in cases involving the Federal Equal Protection Clause, typically apply rationality review and uphold the challenged laws as constitutional. There are, however, some notable exceptions to this trend.

---

[166] State *ex rel.* Bacich v. Huse, 59 P.2d 1101 (Wash. 1936).

[167] Ralph v. City of Wenatchee, 209 P.2d 270 (Wash. 1949).

[168] Jonathan Thompson notes that the line between "privileges" and "immunities" is blurred, but nonetheless helpful to illuminate patterns in the court's opinions. Jonathan Thompson, *The Washington Constitution's Prohibition on Special Privileges and Immunities: Real Bite for "Equal Protection" Review of Regulatory Legislation?*, 69 Temp. L. Rev. 1247, 1267 (1996).

[169] City of Seattle v. Rogers, 106 P.2d 598 (Wash. 1940).

[170] Adams v. Hinkle, 322 P.2d 844 (Wash. 1958).

[171] Jonathan Thompson, *supra* note 168, at 1273–74.

Disparate Penalties

Various criminal laws that impose disparate penalties for seemingly similar offenses have been challenged under state equality guarantees. The courts, deferring to the legislature, usually rebuff these challenges. The prevalent view is that the judiciary should allow the legislature wide latitude to define criminal conduct and set penalties for it.[172]

Occasionally, though, a court will find that a criminal statute that prescribes different degrees of punishment for the same acts violates the guarantee of equal protection of the laws. In Colorado, the supreme court of that state ruled that equal protection of the laws was denied by a statute that treated reckless manslaughter as a felony while another statute treated criminally negligent homicide as a misdemeanor.[173] The court found that the distinction between recklessness and criminal negligence as defined in the statutes was purely semantic, with the result that the two statutes imposed unequal penalties for what was essentially the same act.[174] Because the law prescribed different degrees of punishment for persons who were similarly situated, the court concluded that it violated the guarantee of equal protection.[175]

A few courts have invalidated laws that set disparate penalties for sex offenses. In California, the state supreme court ruled that the principle of equality was contravened by a sex offender registration statute that treated persons convicted of oral copulation with a minor more severely than persons convicted of sexual intercourse with a minor.[176] The statute required all persons convicted of oral copulation with a minor 16 to 17 years of age to register for life as a sex offender, while leaving registration to the discretion of a trial court for those convicted of sexual intercourse with a minor of the same age. Purporting to apply rationality review, the California court concluded that there was no plausible reason to treat one offense more severely than the other and that, insofar as the statute did

---

[172] As the Supreme Court of Wyoming put it, "We afford substantial deference to the broad authority that legislature necessarily possess in determining the types and limits of punishments for crimes." Garton v. State, 910 P.2d 1348, 1355 (Wyo. 1996).

[173] People v. Calvaresi, 534 P.2d 318 (Colo. 1975).

[174] Id. at 318.

[175] Id. See also, Ciak v. State, 597 S.E.2d 392 (Ga. 2004) (finding equal protection violation by statute that made it unlawful for any state resident, but non-resident, to operate a vehicle with darkly tinted windows).

[176] People v. Hofsheier, 129 P.3d 29 (Cal. 2006).

so, it violated the federal and state equal protection clauses.[177] While the court invalidated the mandatory registration provision of persons convicted of oral copulation with a minor, the impact of it decision was tempered to some degree because, as the court pointed out, those persons still could be required to register if a trial court so ordered. In other words, although the court eliminated the mandatory registration provision, it left in tact the discretionary authority of trial courts to order registration of any sex offender.[178]

In a decision of more telling impact, *State v. Limon*, the Supreme Court of Kansas ruled that equal protection of the laws was infringed by a law that punished criminal voluntary sexual conduct between teenagers of the same sex more harshly than criminal voluntary sexual conduct between teenagers of the opposite sex.[179] The law in question, referred to as the "Romeo and Juliet statute," applied to voluntary sexual acts when the victim was 14 or 15 years old, the offender was less than 19 years of age and less than four years older than the victim, and when the victim and offender were members of the opposite sex.[180] Under the statute, prison terms were shorter and other consequences, such as post-release supervision periods and sex offender registration requirements, were less harsh than they otherwise would be. The defendant in the case, a male who had just turned 18, engaged in a sex act with another male who had just turned 15. After his conviction, the defendant was sentenced to a term of imprisonment of 206 months, which was considered a mitigated term under the Kansas sentencing guidelines. In contrast, if the defendant had been convicted of a sex act with a 15-year-old female, the Romeo and Juliet law would apply and he would have been sentenced to 15 months' imprisonment, at most. As the court noted, because the Romeo and Juliet law did not cover the defendant's crime, he was subject to an "enormous escalation" in the severity of his punishment.[181]

In assessing the constitutionality of the statute, the Kansas court followed federal principles of equal protection, explaining that the Kansas equal protection clause is given much the same effect as its federal counterpart.[182] Accordingly, the court adopted an upgraded version of rationality

---

[177] *Id.* at 36–42.
[178] *Id.* at 42–43.
[179] State v. Limon, 122 P.3d 22 (Kan. 2005).
[180] The statute applied to voluntary sexual intercourse, sodomy, and lewd touching. *Id.* at 24.
[181] *Id.* at 29.
[182] *Id.* at 28.

review similar to that used in several federal cases. Although the state proffered several reasons in an attempt to justify the Romeo and Juliet law, the court rejected them all, ruling that there simply was no rational explanation for the discriminatory aspects of the law.[183] In conclusion, the court declared that the law created a "broad, overreaching, and undifferentiated status-based classification which bears no rational relationship to legitimate State interests," in violation of both the federal and state equal protection clauses.[184]

A number of constitutional challenges have been brought that question disparate statutory penalties for crimes involving drugs. These challenges almost always are rejected. An Alaska decision, *State v. Erickson*, is a typical example.[185] In this case, the defendant attached a criminal statute that classified cocaine as a "narcotic drug."[186] Asserting that cocaine was not a narcotic, the defendant argued that it was more properly classified as an amphetamine. Because the statute in question set forth more severe penalties for the use of narcotics than the use of amphetamines, the defendant argued that the statute denied equal protection of the law. The Alaska Supreme Court, however, found that the statute did not deny equal protection. While admitting that it was clear, as a pharmacologically matter, that cocaine is not a narcotic,[187] the court nonetheless thought that it was permissible for the legislature to classify cocaine as a narcotic because it reasonably could be concluded that cocaine was harmful to health.[188] Professing that it was not its function "to reassess the scientific evidence in the manner of a legislature," the court concluded that there was ample scientific evidence of harm or potential harm from the use of cocaine to sustain the legislative decision to classify cocaine as a narcotic.[189]

In *Erickson*, the court's treatment of the equal protection claim amounts to no more than a minimal form of rationality review, indicative of the latitude usually given the legislature to set penalties for crimes involving drugs. But even when rationality review is given more bite, the

---

[183] *Id.* at 33–38.
[184] *Id.* at 38. *See also*, State v. Denney, 101 P.3d 1257 (Kan. 2004) (finding equal protection violation by statute allowing DNA testing in rape cases by not cases of aggravated criminal sodomy).
[185] State v. Erickson, 574 P.2d 1 (Alaska 1978).
[186] *Id.* at 10–11.
[187] *Id.* at 16.
[188] *Id.* at 17.
[189] *Id.*

courts tend to sustain criminal penalties for drug offenses that are challenged as discriminatory. For instance, in *People v. Kimbrough*, a 1994 decision, the Supreme Court of Illinois upheld a statutory scheme according to which possession of LSD in object or carrier form was punished more severely than possession of considerably smaller amounts of LSD in pure form.[190] The defendant in the case argued that this statutory scheme was irrational, especially in light of the legislative purpose of the statute to punish large-scale drug dealers more severely than petty distributors. In the court's view, however, the statutory scheme was in fact rationally related to its legislative purpose. The court pointed out that it is much easier and more common to sell, transport, store, conceal, and use LSD in the carrier form.[191] Hence, widespread distribution, sale, and abuse of the drug take place in that form.[192] That being so, the court said, the legislature reasonably could determine that LSD in carrier form is more dangerous to society than a much smaller quantity of LSD in pure form.[193] "Therefore, the legislature had a rational basis to punish offenders with smaller quantities of LSD, reduced to object/carrier form, more severely than offenders with greater quantities of the pure, gram form of LSD."[194]

While almost all courts give the legislature a great deal of latitude in drawing lines to punish drug offenses, there is one striking exception to this pattern. In *State v. Russell*, the Supreme Court of Minnesota ruled that the state constitutional principle of equal protection was violated by criminal statutes that penalized possession of crack cocaine much more harshly than possession of the same amount of cocaine powder.[195] Pursuant to the statutes, possession of three grams of crack cocaine carried a penalty of up to twenty years in prison, while possession of the same amount of cocaine powder carried a penalty of up to five years in prison. Early in its opinion, the court noted that the trial court in the case has found that because crack cocaine is used predominantly by blacks and that cocaine powder is used predominantly by whites, the law had a racially discriminatory impact with severe consequences for black persons.[196] The court also was highly critical of the supreme court's approach

---

190   People v. Kimbrough, 644 N.E.2d 1137 (Ill. 1994).
191   *Id*. at 1143.
192   *Id*.
193   *Id*.
194   *Id*.
195   State v. Russell, 477 N.W.2d 886 (Minn. 1991).
196   *Id*. at 887.

to laws that have a racially discriminatory impact, implying that the high court ignored the racially discriminatory impact of many laws and made it virtually impossible to successfully challenge them.[197] To this point, the court's discussion seemed to be leading in the direction of holding that strict scrutiny should be evoked in the case because the statutes in question had a racially disparate impact. Rather than use strict scrutiny, however, the court decided to apply an invigorated version of rationality review. As the court pointed out, in previous cases it had adopted a model of rationality review more stringent than the federal model.[198] Under the Minnesota approach, the court explained, "we have been unwilling to hypothesize a rational basis to justify a classification, as the more deferential federal standard requires."[199] Unlike the federal model, the Minnesota version requires a reasonable connection between the actual, and not merely the hypothetical, effect of the challenged classification and the statutory goals.[200] There was nothing to prevent the court, it proclaimed, from applying this more stringent standard of rationality review as a matter of state law under the state constitution, and it was particularly appropriate to apply the Minnesota stricter version of rational basis review in a case such as the one at hand where the challenged classification "impose(d) a substantially disproportionate burden on the very class of persons whose history inspired the principles of equal protection."[201]

Under this intensified model of rationality review, the state was unable to show an actual justification for the distinction drawn by the statutes between crack cocaine and cocaine powder. The primary justification advanced by the state in support of the distinction was that it served to facilitate prosecution of "street level" drug dealers, there being evidence in the legislative record that possession of three grams of crack cocaine indicates the occurrence of drug dealing.[202] The evidence, however, was purely anecdotal and came from but a single expert witness. This was hardly sufficient to justify the statutory distinction between crack cocaine and cocaine powder. Widely disparate criminal penalties,

---

[197] *Id.* at 888, n. 2.
[198] *Id.* at 888–89.
[199] *Id.* at 889.
[200] *Id.*
[201] *Id.*
[202] *Id.* at 889–90.

the court said, cannot be justified on the anecdotal observations of one expert witness.[203]

The state further argued that the statutory distinction between crack cocaine and cocaine powder was justified because crack cocaine is more addictive, more dangerous, and more likely to lead to violent behavior than cocaine powder. But the state had little evidence to back up this argument, and the evidence that it did have was extremely weak.[204] In the final analysis, the state was unable to show a genuine distinction between crack cocaine and cocaine powder.[205] So, the court concluded that the line drawn by the statutes, imposing disparate penalties, was arbitrary and irrational, in violation of the Minnesota equal protection principle.[206]

State v. Russell is a rare exception to the practice of both state and federal courts to apply the most minimal scrutiny in reviewing the constitutionality of criminal penalties set by the legislature.[207] The vast majority of courts give the legislature wide latitude to set criminal penalties, especially for crimes involving drugs.[208]

Prosecutorial Discretion

The general view is that prosecutors enjoy wide discretion to decide what criminal charges to file against a person and to make other prosecutorial decisions.[209] Courts are disinclined to interfere with prosecutorial discretion, and ordinarily will defer to the decisions made by prosecutors.[210] Though broad, prosecutorial discretion, however, is not unlimited.[211]

---

[203] *Id.* at 890.

[204] *Id.*

[205] *Id.*

[206] *Cf.* State v. Frazier, 631 N.W.2d 432 (Minn. 2001), in which the Court of Appeals of Minnesota, professing to follow the "more stringent rational basis test" of *Russell,* ruled a statute making it a crime to commit certain offenses "for the benefit of a gang" did not violate the equal protection guarantees of the Minnesota Constitution. *Id.* at 434–37.

[207] *E.g.,* State v. Manussier, 921 P.2d 473 (Wash. 1996) (upholding "three strikes" law); United States v. Alton, 60 F.3d 1065 (3d Cir. 1995) (upholding federal sentencing guidelines despite disparate impact on African-Americans); United States v. Fonts, 95 F.3d 373 (5th Cir. 1996) (same).

[208] *E.g.,* State v. Brown, 648 So.2d 872 (La. 1995) (upholding statute enhancing penalty for distributing drugs within one thousand feet of school property); United States v. Alton, *id.*

[209] Andrews v. Willrich, 29 P.3d 880 (Ariz. 2001).

[210] Commonwealth v. Tague, 751 N.E.2d 388 (Mass. 2001).

[211] State v. Salgado, 778 A.2d 24 (Conn. 2001).

On occasion, a particular charging decision made by a prosecutor has been found to run afoul of equal protection principles.

The Supreme Court of Oregon has utilized the state equal privileges and immunities clause to place some limits on the discretion of prosecutors in deciding whether to charge individuals accused of crime through the procedure of information or indictment. Initially, the court ruled that the state constitutional guarantee of equal privileges and immunities was not violated by the coexistence of alternative charging procedures, one of which (indictment) entailed a preliminary hearing while the other (information) did not.[212] Even though the choice of which procedure to use was within the discretion of the prosecutor, the court found that there was nothing inherently unequal about the system of alternative charging devices. In a subsequent decision, *State v. Freeland*, the court refined its previous rulings by explaining that, while a system of alternative charging procedures was not intrinsically unequal, it could amount to a denial of equal treatment if put into effect haphazardly or inconsistently.[213] While not inherently arbitrary, prosecutorial discretion must be exercised in a consistent manner according to permissible criteria so that the right to a particularly procedure such as a preliminary hearing is available on the same terms to all similarly situated persons.[214] Accordingly, the court concluded that the constitutional guarantee of equality was violated where a prosecutor's decision to charge a defendant through the procedure of information rather than indictment was a desultory exercise of discretion that could not be shown to be based on a consistent criterion.[215]

The Oregon high court has also recognized that the state guarantee of equality may restrict prosecutorial discretion in deciding which potential defendants to charge and which to grant immunity as an incentive to testify against others.[216] In *State v. Clark*, the court explained that while the range of prosecutorial discretion in this area is broad, it nonetheless is not without limit.[217] District attorneys are state officers who apply statewide, not local, law and are not immune from judicial scrutiny to ensure that their decisions are consistent with equal protection. The burden, however, is on the defendant to show that a prosecutor's

---

[212] State v. Clark, 630 P.2d 810 (Or. 1981); State v. Edmonson, 630 P.2d 822 (Or. 1981).
[213] State v. Freeland, 667 P.2d 509 (Or. 1983).
[214] *Id.* at 516–17.
[215] *Id.* at 519–20.
[216] State v. Clark, *supra* note 212.
[217] *Id.* at 819.

decision to charge one person and grant another immunity to testify was purely haphazard. Moreover, that a prosecutor has not acted according to previously stated standards is not enough to show impermissible discrimination.[218] As long as the prosecutor can explain why one person was charged and another granted immunity, the prosecutor's decision will not be set aside.[219] For example, in *Clark* where four individuals were implicated in a theft and two of them were granted full immunity from prosecution to testify against another of them, the court found no violation of equal protection because the prosecutor explained that the persons granted immunity had pleaded guilty to other charges while the person charged with theft had instigated additional crimes and was a greater threat to society than his accomplices.[220] This satisfied the court that prosecutor's decision had been made according to permissible criteria that did not violate the guarantee of equality.

Disparate Treatment of Men and Women

Some state courts have struck down criminal laws that treat men and women differently. In Pennsylvania, a state with a strong Equal Rights Amendment, the supreme court has ruled that the sex of a criminal offender may not be considered in either sentencing statutes or the regulations for parole eligibility.[221] The Texas Court of Criminal Appeals has found that the state ERA was violated by a statute that imposed harsher penalties on males than females for driving while intoxicated.[222] Both the Texas Court of Criminal Appeals[223] and the Supreme Court of Illinois[224] have held that the ERA was violated by a statute allowing boys to be tried as adults at the age of seventeen while girls could not be tried as adults until they were eighteen. State courts are split on the issue of whether equality guarantees are violated by statutes that make female but not male prostitution a crime.[225] While some courts have stuck down such

---

[218] *Id.*

[219] *Id.*

[220] *Id.* at 820.

[221] Commonwealth v. Saunders, 331 A.2d 193 (Pa. 1975).

[222] *Ex parte* Tullos, 541 S.W.2d 167 (Tex. Crim. App. 1976).

[223] *Ex parte* Trahan, 591 S.W.2d 837 (Tex. Crim. App. 1979).

[224] People v. Ellis, 311 N.E.2d 98 (Ill. 1974).

[225] Paul Linton, *State Equal Rights Amendments: Making a Difference or Making a Statement?*, 70 Temp. L. Rev. 907, 918 (1997).

statutes, a majority of courts that have considered the issue uphold the statutes, usually on the ground that the greater incidence of female prostitution justifies criminalizing it even though male prostitution is not outlawed.[226]

State courts have consistently rejected equal rights challenges to criminal laws that define rape only as an act committed by a male against a female.[227] The courts articulate a variety of reasons for these gender-based rape laws: differences in physiology between men and women; the relative size and strength of men and women, which makes it difficult for a woman to force a man to have intercourse against his will; the vulnerability of women to pregnancy or injury to their reproductive organs; and statistics showing that male rape of females is a major social problem, while female rape of males is not.[228] Along the same lines, state courts have also upheld statutory rape laws that criminalize male but not female conduct, pointing especially to the profoundly harmful consequences of unwanted pregnancy for young females.[229] Despite the adoption of an ERA in Illinois, the supreme court of that state upheld a criminal statute that made incest between a father and daughter a more serious offense subject to a longer sentence than incest between a mother and son.[230] The court thought the statute was justifiable because the possibility that a female victim may become pregnant adds considerably to the potential harm that may result from incest.[231] Therefore, "the physical and psychological dangers of incest are greater when the offense is committed by a male and the victim is his daughter."[232]

Juvenile Offenders

Usually courts use a mild form of rationality review to evaluate laws dealing with juvenile offenders. In most instances, equality challenges

---

[226] *Id.*

[227] Paul Linton, *State Equal Rights Amendments: Making a Difference or Making a Statement?*, 70 Temp. L. Rev. 907, 916 (1997).

[228] *Id.* at 916–17.

[229] *Id.* at 917.

[230] People v. Boyer, 349 N.E.2d 50 (Ill. 1976). Under the statute, fathers were subject to imprisonment for up to twenty years, while mothers were subject to imprisonment for up to ten years.

[231] *Id.* at 52.

[232] *Id.*

are unavailing against laws regulating juvenile offenders.[233] In a Florida case, for instance, the supreme court of that state upheld a criminal anti-graffiti ordinance that prohibited persons under the age of eighteen from possessing spray paint or jumbo indelible markers on public property.[234] Ruling that youth is not a suspect classification, the court sustained the ordinance under rationality review and explicitly stated that "it is permissible to treat minors differently than adults."

The courts also tend to rebuff equality challenges to laws that create special procedural rules for cases involving juvenile offenders. In a Virginia case, for instance, the supreme court of that commonwealth upheld a procedure whereby juvenile offenders transferred to circuit court to be tried as adults would, after a guilty verdict, have their sentences set by a judge rather than a jury.[235] In the court's opinion, there was no violation of equal protection in granting adults but not juveniles the right to have their sentences fixed by juries. Insisting that the case involved neither a suspect class nor a fundamental right, the court refused to apply heightened scrutiny to the procedure in question.[236] Juveniles, the court maintained, do not constitute a suspect class and although the right to a jury trial on the question of guilt or innocence is fundamental, the right to a jury trial for sentencing is not.[237] Using rationality review, the court concluded that it was permissible for the legislature to opt for judges to sentence juvenile offenders on the rationale that juries could not adequately comprehend the differences in sentencing a juvenile defendant as an adult and the treatment of the same child within the framework of the juvenile court laws.[238]

In *State v. Morales*, the Supreme Court of Connecticut upheld the conviction and sentencing of a child for manslaughter as an adult, even

---

[233] *E.g.*, Washington v. Heiskell, 916 P.2d 366 (Wash. 1996), in which the Supreme Court of Washington upheld a statute that differentiated between sex offenders under the age of fifteen and fifteen or older. The statute allowed sex offenders who were fifteen or older to immediately seek a waiver of registration requirements upon a showing of clear and convincing evidence that future registration was unnecessary. Younger sex offenders had to wait two years to seek a waiver of registration requirements, although they only had to show by a preponderance of the evidence that future registration was unnecessary. The court ruled that "juveniles are neither a suspect class nor a semisuspect class," and used rationality review to uphold the statute. *Id.* at 371.

[234] D.P. v. State, 705 So.2d 593 (Fla. 1997).

[235] Ballard v. Commonwealth of Virginia, 321 S.E.2d 284 (Va. 1984).

[236] *Id.* at 285–86.

[237] *Id.* at 286.

[238] *Id.* at 287.

though he had been acquitted of murder as an adult.[239] The defendant argued that, having been acquitted of murder as an adult, he was similarly situated to juveniles who commit manslaughter, and therefore, there was no rational basis for subjecting him to the more severe penalty for manslaughter committed by an adult. The court, though, rejected this argument, concluding there was "a conceivable rational basis" for differential treatment of those juveniles transferred to the adult criminal docket to stand trial for murder and those who initially are charged with conduct amounting only to manslaughter.[240] In the court's opinion, it was reasonable for the legislature to think that affording a less severe sentence (appropriate for juvenile offenders) to a defendant tried as an adult would damage society's perception of the fair administration of justice.[241] This seems to be a rather weak basis to sustain the treatment of the defendant, acceptable only under the modest form of minimal scrutiny used by the court.

Other courts, however, are more willing to use enhanced scrutiny to review laws that discriminate against juvenile offenders. For instance, in a Montana case, *In re S.L.M.*, the state supreme court applied stringent scrutiny in ruling that the state equal protection guarantee was violated by a law that, in some instances, subjected juveniles to a longer period of incarceration than adults who committed similar offenses.[242] While following the federal position that a sentencing distinction based on age did not implicate a suspect class, the court relied on state constitutional doctrine to rule that a juvenile's physical liberty was a fundamental right, calling for strict scrutiny.[243] Under strict scrutiny, the court concluded, there surely was no compelling state interest to treat a juvenile more harshly than an adult who engaged in the same behavior. As just mentioned, it seems that except under the most deferential form of minimal scrutiny there is no valid interest in penalizing a juvenile more harshly than an adult who committed essentially the same offense. To the contrary, juveniles should be treated less harshly than adults because juveniles are not deemed to possess the same mental capacity as adults, and therefore are not held to the same standard of responsibility under the law. The Montana law under review seemed to get things backward and

---

[239] State v. Morales, 694 A.2d 758 (Conn. 1997).
[240] *Id.* at 764.
[241] *Id.* at 764–65.
[242] *In re S.L.M.*, 951 P.2d 1365 (Mont. 1997).
[243] *Id.* at 1370–72.

could be found completely irrational under an enhanced version of minimal scrutiny.

Juvenile offenders also have been afforded some constitutional protection in Utah. In a 1995 decision, the state supreme court struck down a statute that granted discretion to prosecutors to treat some juveniles as adult offenders and proceed against them directly in district or circuit court while leaving other juveniles accused of similar offenses in juvenile court.[244] In reviewing the statute, the Utah high court applied an upgraded variation of rationality review because the question of whether a juvenile is transferred to the adult criminal system is "critically important."[245] The court then found that the statute violated a provision in the state constitution mandating that "All laws of a general nature shall have uniform operation."[246] Under this provision, for a law to be constitutional it is not enough that it be uniform on its face; what is crucial is that operation of the law be uniform.[247] A law does not operate uniformly, the court explained, if "persons similarly situated" are not "treated similarly."[248] By allowing prosecutors to impose different treatment upon juveniles who committed similar offenses, the statute ran afoul of the uniformity required by the Utah constitution.

Conclusion

We will see in later chapters that in dealing with state constitutional provisions directed to the protection of liberty, state courts have been willing to recognize a number of fundamental rights beyond those countenanced under the Federal Constitution. On the other hand, when dealing with equality provisions, state courts have been more reluctant to exercise their sovereign prerogative to approve any fundamental rights other than the few allowed under federal constitutional law. The major exception to this constraint is in the field of education. Most significantly in contrast to the federal stance, many state courts have taken the position that education is a fundamental right and therefore public school financing

---

[244] State v. Mohi, 901 P.2d 991 (Utah 1995).
[245] *Id.* at 995.
[246] Utah Const. art. I, sect. 24.
[247] State v. Mohi, 901 P.2d at 997.
[248] *Id.*

schemes are to be reviewed with strict judicial scrutiny.[249] Although there is a serious split of authority in the states over this matter and a number of state courts have declined to recognize education as a fundamental right, the fact that so many state courts of last resort have proclaimed education to be a fundamental right and struck down disparate education financing schemes signifies a major trend in this area and one that has had a substantial impact upon the quality of education in many states.

In other areas—those involving economic rights and criminal law—deferential rationality review has been the watchword, although in exceptional situations some states have been willing to intensify rationality review to give it an edge lacking under the federal approach. State courts may sharpen rationality review to assess the constitutionality of economic legislation that restricts the recovery of damages in tort actions, denies benefits for no apparent reason, interferes with fair competition, or grants special entitlements to a favored few.[250] On occasion, a few courts have enhanced rationality review to examine arbitrary tax laws, but this remains a rare exception to the usual practice of applying the most minimal scrutiny in cases reviewing tax laws.[251] In the criminal law arena, state courts may augment rationality review to assay the constitutionality of criminal laws that set forth differential penalties for similar offenses, that treat men and women differently, or that discriminate against juveniles.[252] And in a few decisions, though certainly not many, courts have accentuated rationality review to guard against abuse of prosecutorial discretion.[253] While the vast majority of cases involving economic rights or criminal law still evoke nothing more than the most minimal form of judicial scrutiny, the number of exceptions to this practice increases, albeit slowly, with each passing year.

---

[249] *See supra* at note 19.
[250] *See supra* at notes 81–171.
[251] *See supra* at notes 49–80.
[252] *See supra* at notes 172–208, 221–48.
[253] *See supra* at notes 209–20.

CHAPTER FOUR

THE RIGHT OF PRIVACY

The right of privacy is a broad concept, used in diverse contexts to refer to a variety of claims or entitlements.[1] One of the more significant branches of the right of privacy concerns the right of an individual to make personal decisions about his or her life free from government control; that is, the right of individual autonomy. The right of individual autonomy or privacy potentially may encompass matters such as the right to marry, the right to have a family, the right of reproductive freedom, the right of bodily integrity, the right to ingest substances, the right to refuse medical treatment, the right to physician-assisted suicide, the right to cohabitation, and the right of intimate association.[2]

The concept of privacy (autonomy) often is used interchangeably with the concept of liberty, both referring to a fundamental right of self-determination.[3] The right of privacy is based on the principle that "a person belongs to himself and not others nor to society as a

---

[1] The main branches of the constitutional right of privacy are: (1) the right to be free from unreasonable government surveillance; (2) the right to prevent the collection or dissemination of personal information; and (3) the right of individual autonomy. The focus of this article is on the right of individual autonomy. It also should be noted that in the context of the law of torts, the right of privacy refers to: (1) intrusion into a person's private affairs; (2) public disclosure of non-newsworthy information about an individual; (3) publicity that places an individual in a false light; and (4) appropriation of an individual's name or likeness. *See* William Prosser, *Privacy*, 48 Cal. L. Rev. 383 (1960). For a broad survey of the right to privacy, *see* Richard C. Turkington & Anita L. Allen, *Privacy Law: Cases and Materials* (2d ed. 2002).

[2] "The right of privacy is the right to be left alone. It is a fundamental and compelling interest. It protects our homes, our families, our thoughts, our emotions, our expressions, our personalities, our freedom of communication and our freedom to associate with the people we choose...." City of Santa Barbara v. Adamson, 610 P.2d 436, 439 (Cal. 1980).

[3] *See In re* Guardianship of Browning, 568 So.2d 4, 9–10 (Fla. 1990) (internal quotation marks omitted).

whole."[4] It embodies a sense of "personhood"—an "autonomy of self"[5]— that should remain free from intrusion or coercion by society or the government. It comprehends that there are certain personal decisions concerning one's life that an individual should be able to make for oneself free from interference by the state.[6] Flowing from respect for personal dignity, the right of privacy allows an individual to define his or her own life.

Although the essence of the right of privacy has to do with autonomy of self, in some circumstances there also is a spatial component to the right of privacy directed to protecting the rights of individuals in certain areas or spaces, such as the home or bedroom. According to this notion, there are certain private places that are off limits to the government where an individual should be free to do as he or she chooses.[7] Thus, it might be said that while the gist of the right of privacy concerns the psychological aspect of selfhood, in some instances it is supplemented by the physical aspect of a spatial prerogative.[8]

The right of privacy has developed primarily through decisions of the United States Supreme Court interpreting the Federal Constitution.[9] Over the years the Supreme Court has used the Fourteenth Amendment of the Constitution[10] to formulate an evolving right of privacy that

---

[4] Thornburgh v. American College of Obstetricians & Gynecologists, 476 U.S. 747, 777 n. 5 (Stevens, J. concurring) (quoting Charles Fried, *Correspondence*, 6 Phil. & Pub. Affairs 288–89 (1977)).

[5] The phrase "autonomy of self" is from Lawrence v. Texas, 539 U.S. 558, 562 (2003).

[6] *Browning*, 558 So.2d at 10 (citing Gerald B. Cope, Jr., *To Be Let Alone: Florida's Proposed Right of Privacy*, 6 Fla. St. U. L. Rev. 671, 677 (1978)).

[7] *See generally*, Adam Hickey, Note, *Between Two Spheres: Comparing State and Federal Approaches to the Right to Privacy and Prohibitions Against Sodomy*, 111 Yale L.J. 993 (2002).

[8] "(P)rivacy has been defined as...a "physical and psychological zone within which an individual has the right to be free from intrusion or coercion, whether by government or by society at large." *Browning*, 568 So.2d at 10 (quoting Cope, *supra* note 6, at 677).

[9] "Though the concept of privacy in general has deep roots in state law, the right of "constitutional" privacy in the *Griswold* sense was originally developed by federal courts construing the Federal Constitution and only thereafter adopted by state constitutional amenders and state courts as a matter of state constitutional law. In no state did there exist any independent pre-*Griswold* tradition of constitutional protection for interests of this type. Thus all states which currently protect such rights do so through some process of adoption, explicit or implicit, from federal sources." John M. Devlin, *State Constitutional Autonomy Rights in an Age of Federal Retrenchment: Some Thoughts on the Interpretation of State Rights Derived from Federal Sources*, 3 Emerging Issues in State Constitutional Law 195, 197 (1990).

[10] On one occasion, the Court turned to a "penumbra theory" in lieu of the Fourteenth Amendment in order to protect the right of privacy of a married couple to use contraceptive devices. *See* Griswold v. Connecticut, 381 U.S. 479 (1965).

encompasses certain family rights, reproductive rights, and, most recently, a right of intimate association.[11] Yet the Court has placed definitive limits on family and reproductive rights and also has refused to extend the right of privacy to other areas.[12] There is scant agreement among the justices of the Supreme Court concerning the right of privacy and at times the high Court's commitment to privacy has wavered considerably. As a result of the Court's continuing equivocation in this area, the scope of the right of privacy under the Federal Constitution is considerably uncertain.

Given this uncertainty, it was hardly surprising when a number of states stepped into the breach to revitalize the right of privacy. State constitutions, after all, are an important source of protection for individual rights and liberties, including the right of privacy. Indeed, state constitutions contain various provisions that can be used to protect the right of privacy. Many state constitutions contain due process or law of the land clauses safeguarding liberty that have been interpreted to ensure the right of privacy. Similarly, state constitutional provisions that deny the existence of arbitrary power over individual liberty have been construed to protect the right of privacy.[13] State constitutional provisions guaranteeing equality also are used as a means of protection for the right of privacy. In some states, a right of privacy has been found implicit in constitutional provisions declaring that "All persons are by nature free and independent, and have certain natural and inalienable rights"[14] or stating that "The enumeration in this Constitution of certain rights shall not be construed to deny, impair, or disparage others retained by, the people."[15] In modern times, five states—Alaska, California, Florida, Hawaii, and Montana—have amended their constitutions to expressly protect the right of privacy.[16] These express provisions provide fertile ground for the

---

[11] *See* discussion *infra* at notes 22–93.
[12] *See* discussion *infra* at notes 52–93.
[13] *See, e.g.,* Commonwealth v. Wasson, 842 S.W.2d 487 (Ky. 1992).
[14] N.J. Const., art I, §1.
[15] Ok. Const., art. II, §33.
[16] Jennifer Friesen, *State Constitutional Law: Litigating Individual Rights, Claims, and Defenses,* Vol. 1, pp. 2-4–2-5 (3d ed. 2000). In addition, the constitutions of four states— Hawaii, Illinois, Louisiana, and South Carolina—contain provisions guarding against unreasonable "invasions of privacy," but these provisions are included in sections directed to preventing unreasonable searches or seizures or other unreasonable government surveillance, and were not meant to protect the right of autonomy. *Id.* at 2-5–2-6. The constitutions of Arizona and Washington contain provisions stating that no person shall be disturbed in "his private affairs," but these provisions also are directed to preventing unreasonable searches or seizures or other unreasonable government

recognition of expansive privacy rights, but even where only a more general constitutional provision, such as a due process clause, is available as a source of protection for privacy, some states have been willing to countenance expansive privacy rights.

In recent years, as claims have been made to expand the right of autonomy to new dimensions, the states have differed in their willingness to do so. Some state courts have moved forward to expand the right of a woman to choose to have an abortion, while others have declined to take that course. A number of state courts have recognized the right of intimate association and struck down sodomy laws well before the Supreme Court was willing to do so, while other state courts chose to stand fast with the then prevailing federal approach rebuffing the right of intimate association. Of late, a number of state courts have faced the issue of same-sex marriage or civil union, and have reached various conclusions concerning it. The Supreme Court of Massachusetts became a pioneer by being the first judicial body in the nation to rule that the right of privacy secured by the state Constitution encompassed a right to same-sex marriage.[17] Some twenty-eight years before that, the Supreme Court of Alaska pioneered a different sort of privacy by ruling that the state constitutional guarantee of privacy afforded a right to possess marijuana for personal use in the privacy of one's home,[18] although the court later was unwilling to extend that right to the possession of cocaine.[19] The Alaska ruling was reminiscent of a few earlier cases upholding, on grounds of privacy, a right to smoke cigarettes or to ingest alcoholic beverages. Those decisions, though, fell into desuetude for many years, until they were revived

---

surveillance, and were not meant to protect the right of autonomy. Devlin, *supra* note 9, at 207–10. In one instance, though, the Supreme Court of Arizona ruled that the constitutional provision safeguarding an individual's "private affairs" encompassed the right of individual autonomy to terminate life-sustaining medical care. Rasmussen by Mitchell v. Fleming, 741 P.2d 674 (Ariz. 1987).

[17] Goodridge v. Department of Public Health, 798 N.E.2d 941 (Mass. 2003). Ten years before *Goodridge*, the Supreme Court of Hawaii considered a case challenging the constitutionality of a state marriage law that precluded same-sex marriage. Baehr v. Lewin, 852 P.2d 44 (Haw. 1993). Although the Hawaii Constitution contained a provision expressly guaranteeing the right of privacy, the court held that the provision did not include a right to same-sex marriage. However, the court went on to rule that the statute was presumptively unconstitutional under the state equal protection clause. However, the court's ruling was superseded by an amendment to the Hawaii Constitution providing that the legislature shall have the power to reserve marriage to opposite-sex couples. Haw. Const. art. I, §23.

[18] Ravin v. State 537 P.2d 494 (Alaska 1975).

[19] State v. Erickson, 574 P.2d 1 (Alaska 1978).

as the foundation for regenerating the right of privacy. A few states have gone beyond federal rulings by holding that a man claiming to be the biological father of a child has a constitutional right to establish his paternity. Some states, though not many, have upheld the right of unrelated individuals to live together as a family. States also have been called upon to sanction privacy rights in certain matters concerning adoption, but generally have shied away from doing so. The states have long recognized, first under the common law and later as an aspect of the constitutional right of privacy, a right of bodily integrity which comprehends the right of an individual to refuse medical treatment even if doing so will hasten death. The states have drawn the line, however, at physician-assisted suicide, which has never been considered a common law right or a constitutional one.[20] Thus, considerable variation, not to mention controversy, exists concerning the parameters of the right of privacy in state constitutional law.

The Federal Model of Privacy

The Federal Constitution makes no express provision for a right of privacy. In fact, the word "privacy" (or, for that matter, the word "autonomy") is not mentioned in the Federal Constitution. Nonetheless, the primary development of the right of privacy occurred under the Federal Constitution through decisions of the United States Supreme Court. Although some state conceptions of the right of privacy occurred at an earlier time,[21] they were soon eclipsed by federal doctrine. In more recent times, as we shall see, the pendulum has swung the other way, as a number of states have forged ahead of the Supreme Court in expanding the scope of the right of privacy. But before considering the states' role in the evolution of the right of privacy, attention should be focused on the federal arc of the right of privacy.

The federal right of privacy traces back to 1923 when the Supreme Court decided *Meyer v. Nebraska*.[22] In *Meyer*, the Court struck down, as

---

[20] Oregon is the only state in the nation that has legalized physician-assisted suicide, having done so through a statutory referendum passed in 1997 law authorizing, under some circumstances, physician-assisted suicide for terminally ill persons. Otherwise, though, no state has been willing to recognize a right to physician-assisted suicide. The right to physician-assisted suicide is discussed more fully in Chapter Eight.

[21] *See* discussion *infra* at notes 98–142.

[22] Meyer v. Nebraska, 262 U.S. 390 (1923).

violative of the Due Process Clause of the Fourteenth Amendment, a state law that prohibited the teaching of foreign languages to students below the eighth grade in any school. Although admitting that it had not previously attempted to exactly define the scope of liberty protected by the Due Process Clause,[23] the Court posited that:

> Without doubt, it denotes not merely freedom from bodily restraint but also the right of the individual to contract, to engage in any of the common occupations of life, to acquire useful knowledge, to marry, establish a home and bring up children, to worship God according to the dictates of his own conscience, and generally to enjoy those privileges long recognized at common law as essential to the orderly pursuit of happiness by free men.[24]

The Court then concluded that the Nebraska laws interfered "with the calling of modern language teachers, with the opportunities of pupils to acquire knowledge, and with the power of parents to control the education of their own."[25] A few years later, in *Pierce v. Society of Sisters*, in striking down an Oregon law requiring students to attend public schools, the Court again recognized the fundamental right of parents to control the upbringing of their children.[26] In recognizing, if only in dicta, the right to marry, establish a home, and bring up children, the Court in *Meyer* and *Pierce* initiated a fundamental right that would come to be known, some time later, as the right of privacy or the right of individual autonomy, and that eventually would encompass the right to use contraceptives,[27] the right of a woman to decide for herself to have an abortion,[28] and the right of intimate association.[29]

For a number of years after *Meyer* and *Pierce*, the Supreme Court turned its attention away from the right to marry, establish a home, and bring up children, leaving it in a dormant stage. Then, in 1942, the Court decided a case once again safeguarding, and, in fact, expanding family

---

23 *Id*. at 399.
24 *Id*. The Court also stated that "the individual has certain fundamental rights which must be respected." *Id*.
25 *Id*. at 401.
26 Pierce v. Society of Sisters, 268 U.S. 510 (1925).
27 Griswold v. Connecticut, 381 U.S. 479 (1965).
28 Roe v. Wade, 410 U.S. 113 (1973); Planned Parenthood of Southeastern Pennsylvania v. Casey, 505 U.S. 833 (1992)
29 Lawrence v. Texas, 539 U.S. 558 (2003).

rights, although this time under the Equal Protection Clause, rather than the Due Process Clause.[30] The case was *Skinner v. Oklahoma*, in which the Court struck down a state law providing for compulsory sterilization of individuals convicted for a third time of a felony involving moral turpitude.[31] In *Skinner*, the Court once again recognized a special constitutional status for the right to marry and procreate. "We are dealing here," the Court stated, "with legislation which involves one of the basic civil rights of man. Marriage and procreation are *fundamental* to the very existence and survival of the race."[32] Therefore, the Court continued, any law restricting the right to procreate must be subject to "strict scrutiny."[33]

The importance of marriage was also recognized in a 1965 decision, *Griswold v. Connecticut*, where the Court struck down a law prohibiting the distribution or use of contraceptives.[34] In its opinion, the Court described marriage as "an association for as noble a purpose as any involved in our prior decisions."[35] Moreover, the Court articulated a "right of privacy" surrounding the marriage relationship.[36] Indeed, the Court stated that, "We deal with a right of privacy older than the Bill of Rights."[37] But rather than use the Due Process Clause or even the Equal Protection Clause to protect the right of privacy, the Court chose to fashion a new approach, which has come to be referred to as the "penumbra theory."[38] According to the penumbra theory, various provisions in the Bill of Rights "create zones of privacy."[39] The First Amendment guarantee of freedom of speech, for example, creates a zone of privacy that encompasses freedom of association. The Third Amendment prohibition against quartering soldiers in any house generates another facet of privacy, as do the Fourth Amendment right to be free from unreasonable searches and

---

30 Skinner v. Oklahoma, 316 U.S. 535 (1942).

31 *Id.*

32 *Id.* at 541 (emphasis added).

33 *Id.* at 54.

34 Griswold v. Connecticut, 381 U.S. 479 (1965).

35 *Id.* at 486. The Court further said that: "Marriage is a coming together for better or for worse, hopefully enduring, and intimate to the degree of being sacred. It is an association that promotes a way of life, not causes; a harmony in living, not political faiths, a bilateral loyalty, not commercial or social projects. Yet it is an association for as noble a purpose as any involved in our prior decisions." *Id.*

36 *Id.* at 485–86.

37 *Id.* at 486.

38 *Id.* at 484–85.

39 *Id.* at 484.

seizures and the Fifth Amendment right against self-incrimination.[40] Privacy, then, informs a number of constitutional provisions. Moreover, prior cases interpreting these provisions "suggest that specific guarantees in the Bill of Rights have penumbras formed by emanations from those guarantees that help give them life and substance."[41]

The soundness of the penumbra theory has been the subject of considerable debate, but whatever its cogency may be, the fact remains that in *Griswold*, the Court once again expanded the fundamental right of privacy, this time to include the right of an individual to obtain and use contraceptives.

Seven years after *Griswold*, in *Eisenstadt v. Baird*,[42] the Court specifically upheld the right of an unmarried individual to use contraceptives. In *Eisenstadt*, like *Skinner* before it, the Court relied upon the Equal Protection Clause to protect the right of privacy. Significantly, *Eisenstadt* extended the right of privacy to the individual, whether married or not. As the Court put it, "If the right of privacy means anything, it is the right of the *individual*, married or single, to be free from unwarranted governmental intrusion into matters so fundamentally affecting a person as the decision whether to bear or beget a child."[43]

By now, the right of privacy was an established fundamental right, with a lineage dating back to 1923. At this stage, it encompassed the right of an individual, to marry, have children, control the upbringing of children, and to use contraception. Like other fundamental rights, the right of privacy was to be protected by strict judicial scrutiny that offers little, if any, deference to legislative judgment.[44] Though not absolute, fundamental rights may only be limited upon proof that there is an extremely strong justification for doing so. Any law impinging on a fundamental right will be struck down unless the government can prove that the law in question is precisely tailored to achieve a compelling state interest.[45]

The stage was now set for *Roe v. Wade*.[46] Whether using the Due Process Clause, the Equal Protection Clause, or the penumbra theory, the

---

[40] The Court also pointed out that the Ninth Amendment states that, "The enumeration in the Constitution, of certain rights shall not be construed to deny or disparage others retained by the people." *Id.*

[41] *Id.* at 484.

[42] Eisenstadt v. Baird, 405 U.S. 438 (1972).

[43] *Id.* at 453 (emphasis in original).

[44] Jeffrey M. Shaman, *Constitutional Interpretation: Illusion and Reality* 72 (2001).

[45] *Id.*

[46] Roe v. Wade, 410 U.S. 113 (1973).

Supreme Court had shown an abiding conviction that privacy was a fundamental right. As the Court observed in *Roe*, although the Constitution does not explicitly mention any right of privacy, the Court has recognized that a right of personal privacy, or a guarantee of certain areas or zones of privacy does exist under the Constitution.[47] By 1973, when the Court decided *Roe*, it was ready to return to the Due Process Clause as the source of constitutional protection for the right of privacy. In *Roe*, the Court squarely ruled that the right of privacy is a "fundamental"[48] right "implicit in the concept of ordered liberty"[49] that is grounded in the Due Process Clause of the Fourteenth Amendment.[50] Moreover, the Court stated, the due process fundamental right of privacy was "broad enough to encompass a woman's decision whether or not to terminate her pregnancy."[51] Therefore, the Court concluded, prior to viability of the fetus, a woman had a constitutional right of privacy under the Due Process Clause to choose to have an abortion.

Although *Roe* established the fundamental right of a woman to choose to have an abortion, in subsequent cases the Court ruled that it is not unconstitutional for the government to refuse to subsidize abortion, even if it is subsidizing other medical services, including childbirth.[52] In the view of the Supreme Court, there was no affirmative obligation on the part of the government to fund abortion, even when it had affirmatively chosen to fund childbirth.[53] As a result, the Court concluded that while there was a fundamental right to have an abortion, there was not a fundamental right to have an abortion subsidized by the state.[54]

---

47 *Id*. at 152. To support the existence of this right, the Court cited a number of decisions, including *Meyer, Pierce, Skinner, Griswold*, and *Eisenstadt*. The Court also cited: Stanley v. Georgia, 394 U.S. 557 (1969), which held that an individual has the right to possess obscene material in the privacy of his or her own home; Loving v. Virginia, 388 U.S. 1 (1967), which struck down a state ban on interracial marriage; and Prince v. Massachusetts, 321 U.S. 158 (1944), which recognized that there is a "private realm of family life which the state cannot enter" while upholding a child labor law restricting the right of parents to direct their children to distribute religious literature. *Id*. at 166.

48 *Id*. at 152–54.

49 *Id*.

50 "This right of privacy, whether it be founded in the Fourteenth Amendment's concept of personal liberty and restrictions upon state action, as we feel it is...." *Id*. at 153.

51 *Id*.

52 Williams v. Zbarez, 448 U.S. 358 (1980); Harris v. McRae, 448 U.S. 297 (1980); Poelker v. Doe, 432 U.S. 519 (1977); Maher v. Roe, 432 U.S. 464 (1977).

53 *Maher*, 432 U.S. 473–74.

54 *Id*. at 478–79.

In another group of cases decided after *Roe v. Wade*, the Court considered the constitutionality of state laws requiring parental consent or notification for an unemancipated young woman to have an abortion.[55] In these cases, the Court attempted to reconcile the fundamental right of parents to control the upbringing of their children with the fundamental right of a woman to decide for herself to have an abortion. In a compromise of sorts, the Court ruled that a state may require parental consent or notification for an unemancipated minor to have an abortion, but only if the state creates an alternative procedure—a judicial bypass—so the minor can obtain approval to have an abortion from a judge on the ground that it is in the best interest of the minor or that she is mature enough to make the decision for herself.

Despite attempts to overrule *Roe v. Wade* by various justices on the Court, a majority of the justices have reaffirmed the ruling in *Roe* on numerous occasions, most notably in *Planned Parenthood of Southeastern Pennsylvania v. Casey*, where the Court repeatedly stated that it was reaffirming the "essential holding" of *Roe v. Wade* that prior to viability a woman has a right to choose to have an abortion.[56] The right of privacy, then, including the right of a woman to decide to have an abortion, remains a fundamental right protected by the Due Process Clause of the Fourteenth Amendment. As the Court eloquently explained in *Casey*:

> It is a promise of the Constitution that there is a realm of personal liberty which the government may not enter ....Our law affords constitutional protection to personal relations relating to marriage, procreation, contraception, family relationships, child rearing, and education. These matters, involving the most intimate and personal choices a person may make in a lifetime, choices central to personal dignity and autonomy, are central to the liberty protected by the Fourteenth Amendment. At the heart of liberty is the right to define one's own concept of existence, of meaning, of the universe, and of the mystery of human life.[57]

---

[55] Planned Parenthood of Central Missouri v. Danforth, 428 U.S. 72 (1976); Bellotti v. Baird, 443 U.S. 622 (1979); H.L. v. Matheson, 450 U.S. 398 (1981); Hodgson v. Minnesota, 497 U.S. 417 (1990); Ohio v. Akron Center for Reproductive Health, 497 U.S. 502 (1990).

[56] Planned Parenthood of Southeastern Pennsylvania. v. Casey, 505 U.S. 833, 846, 870 (1992).

[57] *Id.* at 847, 851.

Although reaffirming the essential principle of *Roe v. Wade* that abortion may not be prohibited prior to viability of the fetus, the *Casey* decision modified the ruling in *Roe* to some extent by ruling that some government regulation of abortion was permissible prior to viability so long as the regulation in question does not "unduly burden" a women's right to have an abortion.[58] Under that standard, the Court in *Casey* sustained several provisions regulating abortion, including an informed consent, 24-hour waiting period requirement, while striking down a provision requiring spousal consent on the ground that it unduly burdened a woman's right to choose to have an abortion.[59]

In addition to upholding the reproductive rights of individuals, the Court has decided a number of cases upholding other family rights of individuals, such as the right to marry[60] and the right to live together as an extended family.[61] Clearly, the Court considers procreational and family matters to be fundamental rights protected by the Fourteenth Amendment. The right of privacy, then, includes the right to marry, the right to divorce, the right to have children, the right to use contraceptives, the right to have an abortion, the right to live together as a family, and the right to control the upbringing of one's children. In *Troxel v. Granville*, the Court upheld the right of a parent to control the upbringing of a child by ruling that so long as a parent adequately cares for his or her children, a state court may not intervene in a parental decision to limit visitation of grandparents.[62] There can be no doubt, the plurality opinion stated, that the Due Process Clause of the Fourteenth Amendment protects the fundamental right of parents to make decisions concerning the care, custody, and control of their children.[63] Therefore, so long as a

---

[58] *Id.* at 876. In *Casey*, the Court also rejected the trimester framework that had been established in *Roe*, ruling instead that a state may not prohibit abortion prior to viability of the fetus. *Id.* at 876.

[59] *Id.* at 877. The Court also upheld a provision concerning reporting requirements and another provision requiring parental consent or judicial approval for unemancipated women under the age of eighteen seeking an abortion. *Id.* at 899.

[60] *See* Loving v. Virginia, 388 U.S. 1 (1967); Boddie v. Connecticut, 401 U.S. 371 (1971); Zablocki v. Redhail, 434 U.S. 374 (1978).

[61] *See* Moore v. City of East Cleveland, 431 U.S. 494 (1977).

[62] Troxel v. Granville, 530 U.S. 57 (2000).

[63] *Id.* at 66–67. There was no majority opinion in *Troxel*. Justice O'Connor wrote a plurality opinion joined by Chief Justice Rehnquist and Justices Ginsburg and Breyer. Justices Souter and Thomas concurred in the judgment. Justices Stevens, Scalia, and Kennedy dissented.

parent adequately cares for his or her children, there normally will be no reason for the state to inject itself into the private realm of the family to contravene parental decisions concerning childrearing.[64]

Due to the fundamental importance of family rights, the Supreme Court has allowed that there is a concomitant right of access to the justice system when family rights are at stake. In *Boddie v. Connecticut*, the Court ruled that it was a violation of the Due Process Clause to deny indigent persons access to the courts to obtain a divorce solely because they could not pay the filing fee.[65] The Court noted that the marriage relationship occupies a basic position in our society, and that the state monopolizes the means for legally dissolving marriage. Given those circumstances, the precept of due process of law prohibits a state from denying access to its courts, solely because of inability to pay, to individuals who seek judicial dissolution of their marriages.[66] Following *Boddie*, the Court also ruled that under the Due Process Clause an indigent defendant in a paternity action was entitled to blood tests paid for by the state.[67] More recently, the Court held that in an appeal from an order terminating parental rights, an indigent person was entitled to waiver of fees charged to prepare the record for appeal.[68] In this instance, the Court relied upon the Equal Protection Clause to protect an individual's right of access to the justice system when family rights are at stake.

On occasion, the Court has turned to the past as a source of fundamental rights. Thus, in *Moore v. City of East Cleveland*, a 1977 decision, the plurality opinion concluded that the right to live together in an extended family was fundamental because it was a liberty "deeply rooted in this Nation's history and tradition."[69] Some years later, a reluctant majority of the Court would again look to history in order to "assume" that under the Due Process Clause an individual possessed a right to bodily integrity, which encompassed the right to refuse unwanted medical

---

[64] *Id.* at 68–69.

[65] Boddie v. Connecticut, 401 U.S. 371 (1971).

[66] *Id.* at 374. In subsequent cases, the Court made it clear that the right of access to the courts established in *Boddie* obtained only in situations involving family matters. Accordingly, the Court ruled that due process does not require the waiver of filing fees so that indigent persons might have access to the courts in order to file bankruptcy petitions, United States v. Kras, 409 U.S. 434 (1973), or to seek review of administrative reduction of their welfare payments, Ortwein v. Schwab, 410 U.S. 656 (1973).

[67] Little v. Streater, 452 U.S. 1 (1981).

[68] M.L.B. v. S.L.J., 519 U.S. 102 (1996).

[69] Moore v. City of East Cleveland, *supra* note 61, at 503.

treatment.[70] History, though, can be a double-edged sword, wielded either to accept rights on the basis of their historical pedigree or reject them on the ground that they are not firmly established in our history and tradition. An example of latter occurred in a 1989 decision, *Michael H. v. Gerald D.*, ruling that a biological father did not have a right to visit his child because no such right could be found in the traditions of our society. [71] And in *Washington v. Glucksberg*, the Court ruled an individual did not have a right to physician-assisted suicide, once again because none could be found in the traditions of our society.[72]

In 1969, the Court countenanced a different aspect of privacy by ruling, in *Stanley v. Georgia*, that the private possession of obscene material cannot constitutionally be made a crime, even though distribution of the material may be proscribed.[73] The decision in *Stanley* was based on the First Amendment right of an individual to receive information and ideas which, in the Court's view, takes on an added dimension in the privacy of a person's own home.[74] As the Court put it, "If the First Amendment means anything, it means that a State has no business telling a man, sitting alone in his own house, what books he may read or what films he may watch."[75] Thus, *Stanley* recognizes that the concept of privacy may comprehend a spatial element involving sanctity of the home, an interest related to, though not the same as, the right of individual autonomy.[76]

In a case involving another component of the First Amendment, freedom of association, the Court suggested that because the Bill of Rights was designed to secure individual liberty, it should afford substantial protection for the formation and preservation of "certain kinds of highly personal relationships."[77] As the Court explained, the constitutional shelter granted to these relationships reflects the realization that individuals draw much of their emotional enrichment from close ties with others.[78] "Protecting these relationships from unwarranted state interference

---

[70] Cruzan v. Director, Missouri Department of Health, 497 U.S. 261, 279 (1990).
[71] *See* Michael H. v. Gerald D., 491 U.S. 110 (1989).
[72] Washington v. Glucksberg, 521 U.S. 702, 710–19, 723–26 (1997).
[73] Stanley v. Georgia, 394 U.S. 557 (1969).
[74] *Id*. at 564.
[75] *Id*. at 565.
[76] *See* discussion *infra*, at notes 202–16.
[77] Roberts v. United States Jaycees, 468 U.S. 609, 618–19 (1984).
[78] *Id*., at 619.

therefore safeguards the ability independently to define one's identity that is central to any concept of liberty."[79]

Regard for personal relationships or the sanctity of the home, however, was shunted aside in *Bowers v. Hardwick*, a 1986 decision, in which the Court once again turned to history to cut short the reach of the Due Process Clause, ruling by a vote of 5–4, that the right of privacy does not encompass the right of a consenting adult to engage in homosexual conduct, even in the privacy of his or her home.[80] In upholding the constitutionality of a Georgia criminal law prohibiting sodomy, the majority opinion drew a strict distinction "between family, marriage, or procreation on the one hand and homosexual activity on the other."[81] Taking an historical approach to constitutional interpretation, the Court refused to give constitutional countenance to a right to engage in homosexual conduct because, in the Court's reading of history, such a right was neither "deeply rooted in this Nation's history and tradition" nor "implicit in the concept of ordered liberty."[82]

Seventeen years later, however, *Bowers* was overruled by a 6–3 majority in *Lawrence v. Texas*, in which the Court held that a Texas sodomy statute making it a crime for two persons of the same sex to engage in intimate sexual relations was a violation of the Due Process Clause.[83] Indeed, in *Lawrence* not only did the Court decisively overrule *Bowers*,[84] it also apologized for it, saying that *Bowers* was unjustly demeaning to gay and lesbian persons.[85] And the Court devoted a good part of its opinion in *Lawrence* to explaining why it believed that *Bowers* had been wrongly decided.[86]

In *Lawrence*, the Court dismissed the historical approach that had been taken in *Bowers*, noting that the historical record was more complex than understood in *Bowers* and that the Court's historical analysis in *Bowers* was open to considerable doubt.[87] More importantly, the Court

---

[79] *Id.*

[80] Bowers v. Hardwick, 478 U.S. 186 (1986).

[81] *Id.* at 190–91.

[82] *Id.* at 191–94.

[83] Lawrence v. Texas, 539 U.S. 558 (2003).

[84] The Court stated: "*Bowers* was not correct when it was decided, and it is not correct today. It ought not remain binding precedent. *Bowers v. Hardwick* should be and now is overruled." *Id.* at 578.

[85] *Id.* at 575.

[86] *Id.* at 565–74.

[87] *Id.* at 566–71.

thought that the *Bowers* majority did not take sufficient account of more recent historical developments: "In all events we think that our laws and traditions in the past half century are of most relevance here."[88] Significantly, that more recent tradition showed an emerging awareness that liberty provides substantial protection to adult persons in deciding how to conduct their private lives in matters pertaining to sex. In other words, more recent history showed a trend toward recognizing that the sexual life of consenting adults was a private matter that should be beyond the realm of state authority, at least state criminal authority.[89]

The Court further explained that the liberty component of the Due Process Clause protects persons from unwarranted government intrusions into a dwelling or other private place and also protects other spheres of our lives and existence, beyond the home, where the State should not be a dominant presence.[90] The Court affirmed that:

> Freedom extends beyond spatial bounds. Liberty presumes an autonomy of self that includes freedom of thought, belief, expression, and certain intimate conduct. The instant case involves liberty of the person both in its spatial and more transcendent dimensions.[91]

Quoting *Casey*, the Court once again proclaimed that:

> These matters, involving the most intimate and personal choices a person may make in a lifetime, choices central to personal dignity and autonomy, are central to the liberty protected by the Fourteenth Amendment.[92]

The Supreme Court has yet to develop a consistent theory to determine the scope of the right of privacy under the Fourteenth Amendment. Currently, some of the justices on the high Court believe in adhering strictly to an historical approach which encompasses only those rights that are "deeply rooted in this Nation's history and tradition" or "implicit in the concept of ordered liberty." Other justices, though, are more forward

---

[88] *Id.* at 571–72.
[89] The Court referred to a variety of international, national, and state sources to show the modern trend recognizing that there is liberty to conduct one's private life in matters pertaining to sex. It is particularly noteworthy here that included among those references was the fact that the courts of five different states had declined to follow *Bowers* in interpreting provisions in their state constitutions. *Id.* at 576.
[90] *Id.* at 562.
[91] *Id.*
[92] *Id.* at 574 (quoting Planned Parenthood of Southeastern Pa. v. Casey, 505 U.S. at 851).

looking; they see history as an ongoing phenomena and constitutional interpretation as an evolving process that comprehends the recognition of new rights that are central to personal dignity and autonomy. Although the right of privacy is firmly established as a fundamental right under the Fourteenth Amendment of the Federal Constitution, the Supreme Court remains ambivalent about the right of privacy, embracing it with fervor in one case, rejecting it in another. As a result, the Court's decisions concerning privacy are marked by inconsistency, leaving the scope of the right of privacy under the Federal Constitution far from certain.

The State Conception of Privacy

Under the system of dual sovereignty that exists in this nation, a state court is free to interpret and apply its own state constitution in any way it sees fit so long as it does not contravene federal law.[93] It is a state court's own responsibility to interpret and apply its state constitution independently of federal constitutional doctrine.[94] While decisions of the United States Supreme Court concerning constitutional issues are entitled to respect, they are in no way binding on a state court as it interprets its own state constitutional guarantees.[95] As long as state constitutional protection does not fall below the federal floor, a state court may interpret its own state constitution as it chooses, irrespective of federal constitutional law. Clearly, a state is free as a matter of its own law to grant more expansive rights than is afforded by federal law.[96] State constitutional provisions, such as an express right to privacy guarantee, that have no parallel in the Federal Constitution of course may be interpreted by the states completely independently of federal law. But even state constitutional provisions, such as a due process clause, that do have a federal parallel may be interpreted independently of federal law and more expansively than their federal counterparts. So, for example, in recognizing a right of intimate association under the Kentucky Constitution at a time when

---

93 *See* Chapter One, at notes 43–56.

94 Commonwealth v. Wasson, 842 S.W.2d 487, 492 (Ky. 1992). *See also*, Powell v. State, 510 S.E.2d 18, 22, n. 3 (Ga. 1998).

95 Wasson, *id.*

96 *Id. See also* State v. Fuller, 374 N.W.2d 722, 726 (Minn. 1985) ("It is axiomatic that a state supreme court may interpret its own state constitution to offer greater protection of individual rights than does the federal constitution.").

none existed under the Federal Constitution, the Supreme Court of Kentucky explained that the Bill of Rights in the Federal Constitution represents neither the primary source nor the maximum guarantee of state constitutional liberty, and state constitutional guarantees against intrusive state power do not derive from the Federal Constitution.[97] Thus, state constitutions are a source of rights independent of the Federal Constitution and may be applied by state courts to grant more extensive protection than allowed under the Federal Constitution.

State constitutional conceptions of privacy independent of the federal model began to emerge at a relatively early date. The Supreme Court of Georgia makes the proud boast that when it decided *Pavesich v. New England Life Insurance*[98] in 1905, it became the first court of last resort to recognize the right of privacy.[99] While this may well be so, the *Pavesich* image of privacy was concerned with the right of an individual to keep personal matters away from public scrutiny and had little to do with the right of individual autonomy from government control. True, the Georgia Supreme Court would later link the *Pavesich* vision of privacy to a right of autonomy that included the right of intimate association, but that would not occur until 1998 and even then would require a questionable leap of logic. Meanwhile, just four years after the *Pavesich* decision, the Supreme Court of Kentucky would decide a case, *Commonwealth v. Campbell*, conceiving a remarkably advanced theory of privacy directly regarding individual autonomy.[100] While the *Campbell* conception of privacy would fall into quiescence for decades, it eventually would be revived to play an extremely significant role in extending the right of autonomy to new dimensions. On occasion, state courts also would turn to theories of natural law as support for the existence of a right of privacy. Other visions of the right of privacy would arise in the states at a later date, influenced by the federal model, yet open to a more comprehensive dimension. Through these various conceptions, a number of states would

---

[97] Commonwealth v. Wasson, *supra* note 13, at 492. *See also* Davis v. Davis 842 S.W.2d 588, 600 (Tenn. 1992) ("There is no reason to assume that there is a complete congruency between the federal and Tennessee rights to privacy."); Campbell v. Sundquist, 926 S.W.2d 250, 259 (Tenn. App. 1996), appeal denied (June 10, 1996), appeal denied (Sept. 9, 1996), (same).

[98] Pavesich v. New England Life Insurance, 50 S.E. 68 (1905).

[99] Powell v. State, 510 S.E.2d 18, 21 (Ga. 1998).

[100] Commonwealth v. Campbell, 117 S.W. 383 (Ky. 1909).

mold a vibrant right of privacy flowing from state constitutional law and extending the scope of protection afforded to individual autonomy.

The Right to Be Let Alone

In 1890, Samuel Warren and Louis Brandeis, who at the time were law partners, published an article in the *Harvard Law Review* entitled *The Right of Privacy*.[101] Taking a bold step, the article proposed the creation of a new common law right to be known by that name. As described by the authors, the right of privacy referred to the right of an individual to "protect the privacy of private life," that is, to keep personal matters away from public scrutiny.[102] Warren and Brandeis were particularly concerned about the press intruding into private affairs and publishing personal information that was not of legitimate concern to the public.[103] They viewed members of the press as purveyors of gossip, overstepping the bounds of propriety and decency at every turn by printing photographs and publishing stories that "invade the sacred precincts of private and domestic life."[104]

Warren and Brandeis were ahead of their time by suggesting that privacy was a personal right rather than a property right. They spoke of the need of a person for protection of his or her "thoughts, sentiments, and emotions" and "the more general right of the individual to be let alone."[105] The principle that underlies the right of privacy, they proclaimed, "is in reality not the principle of private property, but that of an inviolate personality."[106] Thirty-eight years later, after becoming an Associate Justice on the United States Supreme Court, Brandeis would author a dissenting opinion in *Olmstead v. United States* (which involved a wiretap of a private telephone conversation), echoing some of the sentiments expressed earlier in *The Right of Privacy*:

> The makers of our Constitution undertook to secure conditions favorable to the pursuit of happiness. They recognized the significance of

---

101 Samuel D. Warren & Louis D. Brandeis, *The Right of Privacy*, 4 Harv. L. Rev. 193 (1890).
102 *Id.* at 215.
103 *Id.*, 195–96, at 214–16.
104 *Id.* at 195–96.
105 *Id.* at 198, 205.
106 *Id.* at 205, 211.

man's spiritual nature, of his feelings and of his intellect. They knew that only a part of the pain, pleasure and satisfactions of life are to be found in material things. They sought to protect Americans in their beliefs, their thoughts, their emotions and their sensations. They conferred, as against the government, the right to be let alone—the most comprehensive of rights and the right most valued by civilized men.[107]

Still, for Warren and Brandeis, the right of privacy had little to do with the autonomy of an individual to make decisions for him- or herself free from government control. What they had in mind was a different sort of privacy, directed to keeping personal information from being exposed to the public, rather than to keeping decisionmaking within the control of an individual.

Warren and Brandeis proposed the creation of a right to recover in tort for the wrongful public exposure of private information. Eventually, their proposal would find fertile soil as a number of states formulated a cause of action under common or statutory law to protect the right of individuals to keep personal matters private.[108] In *Pavesich v. New England Life Insurance*, decided in 1905, the Supreme Court of Georgia became the first court of last resort to recognize a right of privacy similar to the one advocated by Warren and Brandeis.[109] To trace the ultimate source of this right of privacy, the *Pavesich* court turned to natural law, declaring that there is a "right to personal liberty" deriving from natural law that encompasses far more than liberty from physical restraint.[110] It includes the right of individuals to be free in the enjoyment of the faculties with which they have been endowed, "subject only to such restraints as are necessary for the common welfare."[111] In other words, "liberty includes the right to live as one will, so long as that does not interfere with the rights of another or of the public."[112] Therefore, an individual may "live a life of seclusion … or a life of publicity."[113] A person may choose a life that

---

[107] Olmstead v. United States, 277 U.S. 438, 478 (1928) (Brandeis, J., dissenting).

[108] *See* Diane Zimmerman, *Requiem for a Heavyweight: A Farewell to Warren and Brandeis's Privacy Tort*, 68 Cornell L. Rev. 291, 292–93 (1983). On the other hand, Professor Zimmerman also points out that despite an ever-increasing number of claims under the Warren-Brandeis theory, plaintiffs rarely win. *Id.* at 293.

[109] Pavesich v. New England Life Insurance, 50 S.E. 68 (1905).

[110] *Id.* at 70.

[111] *Id.*

[112] *Id.*

[113] *Id.*

keeps him or her constantly in the public gaze or a life shielded from public scrutiny.[114] "Each is entitled to a liberty of choice as to his manner of life, and neither an individual nor the public has a right to arbitrarily take away from him this liberty."[115] Encompassed within an individual's right of personal liberty is the right to exhibit oneself to the public or to "withdraw from the public gaze at such times as a person may see fit."[116] This, then, was the right of privacy, namely, the "right to withdraw from the public gaze as a person may see fit."

After ordaining this right of privacy, the court went on in *Pavesich* to rule that it was a tortious violation of the right of privacy to publish the picture of an individual in an advertisement without his or her consent.[117] Significantly, though, the Georgia high court went a decisive step further than merely recognizing a common law cause of action for violation of the right of privacy. In addition, the court ruled that "liberty of privacy" was *constitutionally* guaranteed by the due process clause of both the Federal and Georgia Constitutions.[118] Indeed, the court declared that:

> The right of privacy within certain limits is a right derived from natural law, recognized by the principles of municipal law, and guaranteed to persons in this state both by the Constitutions of the United States and the state of Georgia, in those provisions which declare that no person shall be deprived of liberty except by due process of law.[119]

The foundation of the court's ruling in *Pavesich* is that the laws of nature afford an individual "the right to live as one will, so long as that does not interfere with the rights of another or of the public." This notion is closely akin to the principle postulated by the English philosopher John Stuart Mill that society has no justification to regulate the behavior of an

---

[114] *Id.*

[115] *Id.*

[116] *Id.*

[117] *Id.* at 73, 79–80. Subsequent decisions delineated the right more precisely. *See* Cabaniss v. Hipsley, 151 S.E.2d 496 (Ga. 1966) (individual has no right of privacy in photograph he or she permitted others to use for publicity purposes); Reece v. Grissom, 267 S.E.2d 839 (Ga. 1980) (individual has no right of privacy against a person who publishes facts that are a matter of public record); Cox v. Brazo, 303 S.E.2d 71 (Ga. 1983) (individual has no right of privacy regarding information publicized by the individual); Tucker v. News Pub. Co., 397 S.E.2d 499 (Ga. 1990) (publication of information about matter of public interest or public investigation does not violate right of privacy).

[118] *Id* at 71 (emphasis added).

[119] *Id.*

individual except to prevent injury to others.[120] As we shall see, that principle has had a profound influence on the Supreme Court of Kentucky, leading it to formulate a constitutional right of privacy directed to protecting the right of an individual to autonomy from governmental dictates in certain aspects of his or her life.[121] On the other hand, the Georgia Supreme Court's decision in *Pavesich* established a constitutional right of privacy directed to affording individuals the right to keep their personal affairs from being publicized. As originally formulated, the *Pavesich* right of privacy was conceptually different than the right of individual autonomy. *Pavesich* concerned the branch of privacy directed to the capacity of an individual to keep personal matters from being aired in public, whereas the right of autonomy is directed to the capacity of an individual to determine aspects of his or her life free from governmental dictates. Nonetheless, in 1998, some ninety-three years after *Pavesich* was decided, the Supreme Court of Georgia made a leap of logic connecting the two kinds of privacy. That leap occurred in *Powell v. State*, in which the Georgia high court held that a state sodomy statute violated the right of privacy guaranteed by the due process clause of the Georgia Constitution.[122] In further ruling that the right of privacy protected by the Georgia due process clause included a right of intimate association, the court reached back to *Pavesich* in order to connect the *Pavesich* image of privacy to the genus of privacy concerned with individual autonomy. Noting that *Pavesich* marked the first time that any court of last resort recognized the right of privacy, the court in *Powell* repeated its previous proud claim that the right of privacy "was birthed by this court" in *Pavesich*.[123] Quoting liberally and approvingly from *Pavesich*, the opinion in *Powell* embraced the principle enunciated in the prior decision that there is a right of personal liberty to live as one will so long as that does not interfere with the rights of others. *Pavesich*, the court said, "ringingly endorsed the 'right to be let alone'" and expressly recognized that "liberty of privacy" is guaranteed by the due process clause of the Georgia Constitution.[124]

---

[120] *See* discussion *infra* at notes 129–42.

[121] *Id.*

[122] Powell v. State, 510 S.E.2d 18 (Ga. 1998).

[123] Powell v. State, 510 S.E.2d at 21. A common law right of privacy in an individual's photographic image was first recognized by an intermediate appellate court in 1901, but that decision was reversed by the state's highest court. Roberson v. Rochester Folding Box Co., 71 N.Y.S. 876 (N.Y. Sup. Crt., App. Div. 1901), rev'd, 64 N.E. 442 (N.Y. 1902).

[124] *Id.* at 21–22.

While admitting that *Pavesich* and its progeny did not delineate the exact bounds of the right of privacy nor its application to sexual behavior, the court nevertheless decided that it was "clear" that consensual sexual behavior of adults conducted in private "is covered by the principles espoused in *Pavesich*."[125] This was clear to the court because such behavior between adults in private is recognized as a private matter by "(a)ny person whose intellect is in a normal condition."[126] Adults who "withdraw from the public gaze," the court continued, to engage in private consensual sex are exercising a right "embraced within the right of personal liberty."[127] Indeed, the court concluded on this point by professing that it could not imagine any other activity that reasonable persons would regard as more private and more deserving of protection from governmental interference than consensual, private, adult sexual activity."[128]

Still, the court's logic is open to question. Granted that the general principle announced in *Pavesich*—there is a right to live as one will so long as it does not interfere with the rights of others—is broad enough to encompass sexual behavior (and a good deal more, for that matter), nonetheless, that principle was adopted in *Pavesich* to forge a right of privacy having to do solely with the capacity of an individual to keep personal matters private, that is, away from public scrutiny. It is quite a leap from that sort of privacy to the kind of privacy directed to personal autonomy. And while it is true that adults may "withdraw from the public gaze" to engage in sex, that seems a bit beside the point. If there should be a right of privacy to engage in sexual activity, its essence has more to do with the right of an individual to determine his or her own sexual behavior free from governmental dictates than with the right of an individual to avoid the prying eyes of others. Certainly, sexual activity may be considered a private matter in part because it normally is conducted behind closed doors, but what essentially endows it with a private nature is that sex is something that should be exclusively within the dominion of an individual to decide for him or herself. Simply put, the government has no business in meddling in an individual's sex life. Yes, sex may be considered a private matter to a certain extent because it usually occurs away

---

[125] *Id.* at 24.
[126] *Id.* (quoting *Pavesich*, 50 S.E. at 69).
[127] *Id.* (quoting *Pavesich*, 50 S.E. at 70).
[128] *Id.*

from the public gaze, but the quintessence of its private nature has more to do with autonomy than seclusion.

So, the leap of logic in *Powell* from one kind of privacy to another was not entirely convincing. That is not to say, however, that the court was wrong in *Powell* to conclude that the right of privacy encompasses a right of intimate association. *Pavesich*, after all, did declare that there is a right to live as one will, so long as it does not interfere with the rights of others—a principle certainly broad enough to include a right of intimate association. The court's failing in *Powell* was simply in not being more forthright in admitting that it was significantly expanding the right of privacy articulated in *Pavesich* to include a new variety of privacy directed to guaranteeing the autonomy of an individual to control his or her own sex life.

The Millian Principle

In 1909, the Court of Appeals of Kentucky decided a case, *Commonwealth v. Campbell*, conceiving a theory of individual autonomy remarkably advanced for its time.[129] In *Campbell*, the court ruled that an ordinance that criminalized possession of intoxicating liquor even for private use was a violation of the Kentucky Bill of Rights. The court's opinion in *Campbell* adopted the principle that the legislature has no authority to restrict the liberty of an individual except where his or her conduct will cause some injury to the public.[130] This precept, the court suggested, flows from the state bill of rights, which declares that seeking safety and happiness is an inalienable right and that the state cannot possess arbitrary power over the lives, liberty, or property of its citizens.[131] Therefore, the question of what a person will drink, or eat, or own, so long as the rights of others are not invaded, "is one which addresses itself alone to the will of the citizen."[132] Thus, the court proclaimed that:

> It is not within the competency of government to invade the *privacy* of a citizen's life and to regulate his conduct in matters in which he

---

[129] Commonwealth v. Campbell, 117 S.W. 383 (Ky. 1909).
[130] *Id.* at 385.
[131] *Id.* at 385, 387.
[132] *Id.*

alone is concerned, or to prohibit him any liberty the exercise of which will not directly injure society.[133]

Quoting liberally from the works of John Stuart Mill, the court incorporated that philosopher's principle that in a just society the only purpose for which power may rightfully be exercised over an individual against his or her will is to prevent harm to others.[134] Hence, the state has no right to compel an individual to do or forbear from doing something merely because others believe it is for the individual's own good, either physical or moral. Indeed, the court continued, the theory of our government is to allow the "largest liberty" commensurate with the public safety.[135] Under our form of government, there is no room for that "inquisitorial and protective spirit" that seeks to regulate the conduct of individuals in matters of no consequence to society or to make individuals conform to standards other than their own, thus crushing individuality.[136]

The court's opinion in *Campbell* was extraordinary, perhaps unique, by treating the possession of alcoholic beverages as a personal right rather than a property right. Virtually all other decisions around that period of time challenging the regulation of alcoholic beverages treated the possession of liquor strictly as a property right.[137] *Campbell*, though, introduced a right not predicated on notions of ownership of things, but rather predicated on the idea that there are certain aspects of personal behavior that are of concern solely to the individual and simply are no business of the government. True, there were some references in *Campbell* to property rights, but the dominant theme in *Campbell* clearly has to do with the personal right of individuals to decide certain matters for themselves, free from governmental dictates. As the court put it, "what a man shall eat and wear, or drink and think" is beyond the authority of the state to regulate.[138]

The principle established in *Campbell* was followed in two subsequent cases decided a few years later. In one of those cases, the Kentucky Court of Appeals ruled that an ordinance regulating cigarette smoking in such broad terms that it could be applied to persons who smoked in the

---

133 *Id* (emphasis added).

134 *Id*. at 386 (quoting John Stuart Mill, *On Liberty*).

135 *Id*. at 387.

136 *Id*.

137 *E.g.*, Eidge v. Bessemer, 51 South. 246 (Ala. 1909); State v. Williams, 61 S.E. 61 (N.C. 1908); State v. Gilman, 10 S.E. 283 (W. Va. 1889); *Ex parte* Brown, 42 S.W. 554 (Tex. 1887).

138 Commonwealth v. Campbell, 117 S.W. at 387.

privacy of their own homes was an "unreasonable interference with the right of the citizen to determine for himself such personal matters."[139] In the other case, the same court declared a statute unconstitutional because it permitted the arrest of an individual for drinking beer in the backroom of an office.[140] In so ruling, the court stated:

> The power of the state to regulate and control the conduct of a private individual is confined to those cases where his conduct injuriously affects others. With his faults or weaknesses, which he keeps to himself, and which do not operate to the detriment of others, the state as such has no concern.[141]

The willingness of the Kentucky Court of Appeals in *Campbell* and its two descendants to adopt the Millian principle that the liberty of an individual may only be restricted to prevent injury to others was an exceptional occurrence, departing from the generally accepted view in other courts. Although courts during that period of time frequently extolled the virtues of individual liberty, the prevailing rule was that individual liberty could be regulated in any way necessary to promote the general welfare, and this was so even though the conduct subject to regulation did not directly harm another person.[142]

Even in Kentucky, *Campbell* and its progeny would fall into decades of desuetude before being revived in 1992 to have a stunning impact in the case of *Commonwealth v. Wasson*, where the Kentucky Supreme Court struck down a criminal sodomy statute on the ground that it violated the right of privacy.[143] In *Wasson*, the court found that the statute, which made it a crime to engage in sexual activity with a person of the same sex, was a violation of the right of privacy that had been recognized as an integral part of the guarantee of liberty in the 1891 Kentucky Constitution since its inception.[144] Moreover, the court relied extensively on *Campbell* to reaffirm the principle that the state has no power to restrict the liberty

---

[139] Hershberg v. City of Barbourville, 133 S.W. 985, 986 (Ky. 1911).

[140] Commonwealth v. Smith, 173 S.W. 340 (Ky. 1915).

[141] *Id.* at 343.

[142] *See, e.g.*, Ah Lim v. Territory, 24 P. 588 (Wash.1890) (statute prohibiting smoking of opium does not violate any constitutional right); Gould v. Gould, 61 A. 604 (Conn. 1905) (statute prohibiting marriage by an epileptic where the woman is under the age of forty-five does not violate constitutional right to liberty).

[143] Commonwealth v. Wasson, 842 S.W.2d 487 (Ky. 1992).

[144] "The right of privacy has been recognized as an integral part of the guarantee of liberty in our 1891 Kentucky Constitution since its inception." *Id.* at 495.

of an individual except where his or her behavior will cause some public harm. There was little doubt, the court concluded in *Wasson*, that the views of John Stuart Mill provided the philosophical underpinnings for reinterpreting the Kentucky Constitution to broaden the protection it affords for individual rights.[145]

The *Wasson* court's reliance on Mill was challenged in a dissenting opinion entered by Justice Wintersheimer, who asserted that the court's understanding of the English philosopher's thought was simplistic[146] and that, in any event, Mill's philosophy was irresponsible and discredited.[147] Justice Wintersheimer also argued that the court's position was based on an overly broad principle—that an individual's liberty may only be restricted when necessary to prevent harm to others—that cannot be applied consistently and neutrally.[148] Consistent application of that principle, he claimed, would lead to constitutional protection for the private use of cocaine, consensual incest, suicide, and prostitution.[149] The first of these examples, however, overlooks that the majority opinion allowed an exception to Mill's principle that would permit the government to intervene in order to prevent self-inflicted harm, such as that which results from failing to wear a seat belt or crash helmet or from ingestion of drugs.[150] The majority thought that this exception was justified not to enforce majoritarian notions of morality, but because the victim of this sort of self-inflicted harm may become a burden to society.[151] Suicide might also fit into this exception, considering that some suicide attempts fail while leaving the victim injured and in need of care by society. Conversely, there are those who believe that there should be a right to commit suicide, at least in some circumstances, such as when an individual is suffering from a terminal illness.[152] As for consensual incest, even under Mill's principle it can justifiably be prohibited because it poses a significant risk of causing serious genetic harm to the children conceived thereby.[153] Finally, while Mill's principle in its pristine form might

---

[145] *Id.* at 497.

[146] Wasson, 842 S.W.2d at 512–13 (Wintersheimer, J., dissenting).

[147] *Id.* at 519.

[148] *Id.* at 514.

[149] *Id.*

[150] Wasson, 842 S.W.2d at 496–97.

[151] *Id.*

[152] The right to physician-assisted suicide is discussed in Chapter Eight.

[153] *See* Y.M. Abdulrazzaq, A. Bener, L.I. Al-Gazali, A.I. Al-Khayat, R. Micallef, & T. Gaber, *A Study of Possible Deleterious Effect Consanguinity*, 51 Clinical Genetics 167 (1997)

provide shelter for prostitution, it is unlikely that the right of privacy would be construed to encompass a commercial activity such as prostitution. Given that the right of privacy is directed to the protection of personal behavior, commercial activity such as prostitution (whether heterosexual or homosexual) may logically be excluded from the scope of its protection. Moreover, there may be justification to regulate prostitution in order to prevent the spread of infectious disease. For these reasons, the courts have been careful not to include prostitution within the right of intimate association.[154]

So, it seems that the examples chosen by Justice Wintersheimer are not all that persuasive in proving his point that Mill's principle is excessively broad and therefore inappropriate as the foundation of a constitutional right. Even if Justice Wintersheimer is correct that the Millian principle is too broad to be applied across the board, there are those who maintain that it may nonetheless be validly applied to protect the right of intimate association. As early as 1955, in advocating the repeal of

---

(study shows statistically significant higher reproductive wastage leading to deleterious effects in offspring in consanguineous couples); Lutfi Jaber, Paul Merlob, Xiangdong Bu, Jerome I. Rotter, & Mordechai Shohat, *Marked Parental Consanguinity as a Cause for Increased Major Malformation in an Israeli Arab Community*, 33 American Journal of Medical Genetics 1 (1992) (study shows that compared to offspring of non-consanguineous parent, children born to first-cousin parents have 2.4–2.7 times higher risk of having major malformations); J. Jancar & S.J. Johnson, *Incest and Mental Handicap*, 34 Journal of Mental Deficiency Research 483 (1990) (study reaffirms that offspring of incestuous unions have higher rates of mental handicap than other children); S.A. Shami, L.H. Schmitt, & A.H. Bittles, *Consanguinity Related Prenatal and Postnatal Mortality of the Populations of Seven Pakistani Punjab Cities*, 26 Journal of Medical Genetics 267 (1989) (study shows highly significant relationship between the degree of inbreeding and mortality); Helen M. Kingston, *ABC of Clinical Genetics*, 298 British Medical Journal (1989) (offspring of incestuous relationships are at high risk of severe abnormality, mental retardation, and childhood death); Muin Khoury, Bernice H. Cohen, Gary A. Chase, & Earl L. Diamond, *An Epidemiologic Approach to the Evaluation of the Effect of Inbreeding on Prereproductive Mortality*, 125 American Journal of Epidemiology 251 (1987) (study shows that compared with offspring of unrelated parents, offspring of first cousin marriages have a higher risk of prereproductive mortality).

[154] *E.g.*, Lawrence v. Texas, *supra* note 5, at 2484 (noting that the sodomy statute found to be unconstitutional did not involve prostitution); Powell v. State, *supra* note 94, at 26 (concluding that a statute that criminalized the performance of "private, unforced, *non-commercial* acts of sexual intimacy" between consenting adults was an unconstitutional violation of the right of privacy) (emphasis added). Gryczan v. State, 942 P.2d 112, 125 (Mont. 1997) (concluding that the right of consenting adults to engage in "private *noncommercial* sexual conduct" lies at the core of Montana's constitutional right of individual privacy) (emphasis added). In *Wasson*, the court explicitly noted that under the sodomy statute found to be unconstitutional it did not matter that "the act is private and involves a caring relationship rather than a commercial one." Wasson, 842 S.W.2d at 488.

criminal penalties for consensual sexual acts conducted in private, the American Law Institute asserted that it is not necessary to endorse the wholesale repeal of all "victimless" crimes in order to recognize that legislating penal sanctions solely to support concepts of morality is a costly enterprise that sacrifices personal liberty, not because an individual's conduct will harm others, but only because it is contrary to majoritarian notions of acceptable behavior.[155]

The Inherent and Unalienable Cornerstone of Liberty

In both the state and federal spheres, constitutional interpretation has had a long, albeit sporadic, flirtation with natural law. In the federal realm, natural law made an early appearance in *Calder v. Bull*, a 1798 Supreme Court decision in which Justice Chase's separate opinion[156] invoked the "*fundamental law*...that flows from the very nature of our free *Republican* governments."[157] In the view of Justice Chase, this fundamental law was independent of and, in fact, higher than the Constitution. Although such an extreme view of law higher than the Constitution has never again been advocated in a Supreme Court opinion, the Court has returned on occasion to natural law theories. From time to time in cases decided in the early 1800s, the high Court would refer to various natural law concepts, such as the "general principles which are common to our free institutions,"[158] "the principles of natural justice," or "fundamental laws of every free government"[159] to inform the meaning of certain constitutional precepts. In the latter part of that century, the Court occasionally used natural law ideology for some decidedly ignoble causes, in one case evoking no less than "the divine ordinance" to justify a law prohibiting

---

[155] ALI, Model Penal Code, Part II, 1980 Ed., pp. 362–63. In 1957, a committee advising the British Parliament also recommended the repeal of law criminalizing homosexual activity. *See* The Wolfenden Report: Report of the Committee on Homosexual Offenses and Prostitution (1963).

[156] At the time, the Supreme Court was still issuing seriatim opinions, a practice that it discontinued not long after *Calder*.

[157] Calder v. Bull, 3 U.S. (3 Dall.) 386, 388 (1798) (emphasis in original).

[158] Fletcher v. Peck, 10 U.S. (6 Cranch) 87, 139 (1810).

[159] Terrett v. Taylor, 13 U.S. (9 Cranch) 43, 52 (1815). See also Corfield v. Coryell, 6 F. Cas. 546, 551 (C.C.E.D. Pa. 1823) (The Article IV privileges and immunities clause protects those interests that are "in their nature, fundamental (and) belong, of right, to the citizens of all free governments.").

women from practicing law,[160] and in another—the infamous *Plessy v. Ferguson*—evoking "the natural order" to justify racial segregation.[161]

Be that as it may, through the 19th Century, the Supreme Court now and then would refer to "the principles of natural justice" or "the fundamental laws of free government" to supply meaning to constitutional provisions. However, the natural law tradition never gained a consistent position in American jurisprudence, and after the Civil War, it exerted little influence upon legal thought in the nation, except in the field of constitutional law,[162] and even in that field its influence would eventually wane.[163]

In 1868, Thomas Cooley, a law professor at the University of Michigan and justice on the Supreme Court of Michigan, published the first edition of his magnum opus, ponderously titled *A Treatise on the Constitution Limitations Which Rest upon the Legislative Powers of the States of the American Union*.[164] It would prove to be extremely influential, perhaps the most important book concerning the law of its time.[165] In a chapter on the formation of state constitutions, Cooley warned that in considering these documents we should not make the mistake of supposing that, because individual rights are safeguarded by state constitutions, those rights owe their origin to them.[166] A constitution, Cooley maintained, is not a fountain of law, nor the origin of rights.[167] Rather, it is merely declaratory of rights that individuals possessed before the constitution was made.[168] A constitution is based on "the pre-existing condition of laws, rights, habits, and modes of thought."[169] It is entirely "derivative" and "presupposes" a social order that precedes it.[170]

---

[160] Bradwell v. State of Illinois, 83 U.S. (16 Wall.) 130, 141 (1873) (Bradley, J., concurring).

[161] Plessy v. Ferguson, 165 U.S. 537, 544 (1896) *overruled by* Brown v. Board of Education 347 U.S. 483 (1954).

[162] *See* Benjamin Fletcher Wright, Jr., *American Interpretations of Natural Law: A Study in the History of Political Thought* 330 (1931).

[163] *See* John Hart Ely, *Democracy and Distrust* 50–52 (1980).

[164] Thomas M. Cooley, *A Treatise on the Constitutional Limitations Which Rest Upon the Legislative Power of the State of the American Union* (1868) (photo reprint 1972).

[165] "Thomas M. Cooley's *Constitutional Limitations*, written in 1868, was the most important book in its time." Lawrence M. Friedman, *A History of American Law* 628 (1985). "Thomas M. Cooley, the most influential constitutional writer of the late nineteenth century...." James W. Ely, Jr., *The Oxymoron Reconsidered: Myth and Reality in the Origins of Substantive Due Process*, 16 Const. Comm. 315, 342 (1999).

[166] Cooley, *supra* note 164, at 95.

[167] *Id.*

[168] *Id.*

[169] *Id.*

[170] *Id.*

Cooley's view of constitutional law was decidedly unrealistic, and supernatural notions such as his about the pre-existence of rights would be swept aside with the rise of the school of Legal Realism in the Twentieth Century. Nevertheless, natural law concepts would not entirely disappear from constitutional interpretation, and occasionally would resurface with significant effect for the emerging right of privacy. From time to time, state courts professed the view that in a free society all persons possess certain fundamental rights that are inherent and unalienable.[171] For example, in 1944, the Supreme Court of Minnesota proclaimed in ringing terms that:

> The entire social and political structure of American rests upon the cornerstone that all men have certain rights which are inherent and inalienable.[172]

A few courts even took the position that these fundamental rights were independent of and, in fact, higher than constitutional proscriptions,[173] although others were quick to point out that as a practical matter it was only those rights that were actually secured by positive law that could be effectively enforced and that a legislative act could not be declared invalid unless found to be in violation of a constitutional mandate.[174] While courts might profess theories of natural law, they seldom put them into practice to recognize new rights, and on the rare occasions when they did so, it was more likely to be in the service of property rights than personal rights.[175]

Personal rights, however, would come to the fore in more modern times, as in *Davis v. Davis*, an extremely significant case decided in 1992 by the Supreme Court of Tennessee.[176] In *Davis*, the high court of Tennessee was confronted with a question of first impression concerning the control of "frozen embryos" that had been created through *in vitro* fertilization by a husband and wife who later were divorced. Sometime after the divorce, the woman requested legal authorization to donate the

---

[171] Dennis v. Moses, 52 P. 333 (Wash. 1898); Ekern v. McGovern, 142 N.W. 595 (Wis. 1913), *overruled* by Boerschinger v. Elkay Enters., Inc. 133 N.W.2d 333 (Wis. 1965).

[172] Thiede v. Town of Scandia Valley et al., 14 N.W.2d 400, 405 (Minn. 1944).

[173] *Dennis*, 52 P. at 339.

[174] Carter v. Craig, 90 A. 598 (N.H. 1914); Lawrence E. Tierney Coal Co. v. Smith's Guardian et al, 203 S.W. 731, 733 (Ky. 1918).

[175] *See e.g.*, *Tierney Coal Co.* 203 S.W. at 734; *Thiede*, 14 N.W.2d at 405–6.

[176] Davis v. Davis, 842 S.W.2d 588 (Tenn. 1992).

frozen embryos to a childless couple, but her former husband was adamantly opposed to this course of action, not wanting to become a reproductive parent beyond the bounds of marriage. In a landmark decision, the court ruled in favor of the man on the ground that under the Tennessee Constitution there was a right of privacy that encompassed a right to procreational autonomy, that is, a right to decide for oneself to become a parent or to not become a parent.

In reaching this result, the Supreme Court of Tennessee established the right of privacy as a fundamental right inherent in the concept of liberty guaranteed by the state constitution. The court began its analysis by admitting that the right of privacy is not specifically mentioned in either the Federal or Tennessee Constitution.[177] Nevertheless, the court said, there is "little doubt" that the right of privacy is grounded in the concept of liberty reflected in both documents.[178] Turning first to the federal side, the Tennessee court pointed out that in *Meyer v. Nebraska*, the United States Supreme Court explained that the liberty component of the Fourteenth Amendment due process clause comprehends fundamental rights essential to the orderly pursuit of happiness by free men.[179] Subsequently, in *Griswold v. Connecticut*, the nation's high Court noted that the concept of liberty protects those personal rights that are fundamental and is not limited to rights specifically enumerated in the document.[180] Moreover, the right of privacy that is "inherent" in the constitutional concept of liberty was identified in the dissenting opinion of Justice Brandeis in *Olmstead v. United States* as "the right to be let alone—the most comprehensive of rights and the right most valued by civilized men."[181]

After discussing the expansive scope of liberty under the Federal Constitution, the Tennessee court observed that the protection of fundamental rights is not confined to federal constitutional law. "The entire social and political structure of the nation," the court said, "rests upon the cornerstone that all men have certain rights that are inherent and inalienable."[182] Among those rights is the right of "personal liberty."[183] Hence, it

---

[177] *Id.* at 598.
[178] *Id.*
[179] *Id.* at 599. *Meyer v. Nebraska* is discussed *supra*, at notes 22–25.
[180] *Id. Griswold v. Connecticut* is discussed *supra*, at notes 34–42.
[181] *Id.* The Brandeis opinion in *Olmstead v. United States* is discussed *supra*, at notes 106–7.
[182] *Id.* (quoting Thiede v. Town of Scandia Valley, 14 N.W.2d 400, 405 (Minn. 1944)).
[183] *Id.*

is not surprising that the concept of liberty plays a central role in the Tennessee Constitution. Liberty is twice expressly secured by Article I, Section 8 of the Constitution, which states that "no man shall be . . . disseized of his freehold, *liberties* or privileges...or deprived of his life, *liberty* or property, but by...the law of the land."[184] In fact, the notion of liberty is so deeply embedded in the Tennessee Constitution that it, alone among American constitutions, gives the people the right to resist, to the extent of overthrowing, the government, should it transgress individual liberty.[185]

Although the Tennessee Constitution makes no explicit mention of a right to privacy or autonomy, the court, taking a line of analysis similar to the penumbra approach of *Griswold v. Connecticut*,[186] thought that a right of privacy was reflected in several provisions of the constitution's declaration of rights, namely, those sections that guarantee freedom of worship and freedom of speech and press and those that prohibit unreasonable searches and seizures and the quartering of soldiers in any house without consent of the owner.[187] Privacy, then, is a value that underlies several constitutional sections and thereby informs the liberty clauses of the declaration of rights. Obviously, the drafters of the 1796 Tennessee Constitution were unable to foresee a need to construe the liberty clauses of the document to apply to choices surrounding *in vitro* fertilization. Still, the court thought that there was "little doubt" that the drafters did foresee the need to protect individuals from unwarranted governmental interference into matters such as the one before the court that involve intimate questions of personal and family concern.[188] Based on the language and development of the state constitution, the court had "no hesitation" in concluding that the liberty clauses of the Tennessee

---

[184] Tenn. Const. art. 1, §8 (emphasis added).

[185] Davis v. Davis, 842 S.W.2d at 599–600, (referring to Tenn. Const. art. 1): "*Section 1. All power inherent in the people–Government under their control.* That all power is inherent in the people, and all free governments are founded on their authority, and instituted for their peace, safety, and happiness; for the advancement of those ends they have at all times, an inalienable and indefeasible right to alter, reform, or abolish the government in such manner as they may think proper. *Section 2. Doctrine of nonresistance condemned.* That government being instituted for the common benefit, the doctrine of non-resistance against arbitrary power and oppression is absurd, slavish, and destructive of the good and happiness of mankind."

[186] The penumbra theory of *Griswold v. Connecticut* is discussed *supra*, at notes 34–42.

[187] *Davis*, 842 S.W.2d at 600.

[188] *Id.*

Declaration of Rights guarantee and protect a right of individual privacy.[189]

More specifically, the court held that under the Tennessee Constitution, the right of procreational autonomy was a vital part of the right of privacy. In the court's view, a right to procreational autonomy was "inherent in our most basic concepts of liberty" and therefore was an essential aspect of the right of privacy secured by the Tennessee Constitution.[190] In subsequent cases, the Supreme Court of Tennessee extended the right of privacy established in *Davis* to include various parental rights in the care and custody of their children.[191] The court further developed the right of privacy to augment certain abortion rights beyond those allowed under the Federal Constitution.[192] In addition, relying on the authority of *Davis*, the Court of Appeals of Tennessee, broadened the right of privacy to encompass the right of intimate association.[193]

Penumbrae Redux

Although notions of pre-existent natural law hold little sway in contemporary jurisprudence, the idea that there are—or, at least, should be—certain inherent rights still maintains a certain appeal, although one that is more theoretically acceptable if the rights can be shown to have some connection, even a loose one, to positive law. So, it should have come as no surprise when courts turned to the penumbra theory as a foundation for recognizing the right of privacy. The penumbra theory can be considered a coalescence of natural and positive law in that it

---

[189] *Id.*

[190] *Id.* at 600–601. The further specified that the right of procreational autonomy is composed of two rights of equal significance, the right to procreate and the right to avoid procreation. *Id.* at 601.

[191] Simmons v. Simmons, 900 S.W.2d 682 (Tenn. 1995) (parents have fundamental right to care and custody of child; therefore state may not override parents' decision to deny visitation rights to grandparents); Hawk v. Hawk, 855 S.W.2d 573 (Tenn.1993) (same); Nale v. Robertson, 871 S.W.2d 674 (Tenn. 1994); (biological father has fundamental interest in care and custody of child; therefore petition of father to legitimate child must be decided prior to petition of other person to adopt child).

[192] Planned Parenthood of Middle Tennessee v. Sundquist, 38 S.W.3d 1 (Tenn. 2000).

[193] Campbell v. Sundquist, 926 S.W.2d 250 (Tenn. App. 1996), (statute criminalizing consensual criminal activity by adult persons of the same sex violates constitutional right to privacy).

allows the recognition (or creation) of rights that underlie (or inhere in) constitutional provisions.

We have just seen that in *Davis v. Davis* the Supreme Court of Tennessee relied in part on the penumbra theory to establish a constitutional basis for the right of privacy. In several other states, the courts have been willing to rely more exclusively on the penumbra theory to formulate a constitutional foundation for the right of privacy. In Texas, a constitutional right of privacy was first recognized in a case entitled *Texas Employees Union v. Texas Department of Mental Health & Mental Retardation*, a 1987 decision in which the Supreme Court of Texas ruled that a mandatory policy requiring employees of a state agency to take polygraph tests violated privacy rights protected by the state constitution.[194] In elaborating a constitutional right of privacy, the Texas high court observed that while the state constitution contains no express guarantee of privacy, it does contain several provisions similar to those in the Federal Constitution that have been identified as implicitly creating "zones of privacy."[195] Section 19 of the Texas Bill of Rights precludes the arbitrary deprivation of life and liberty. Section 8 guarantees freedom to speak, write, or publish. Section 10 prohibits compulsory self-incrimination and section 9 secures the sanctity of an individual's home and person against unreasonable intrusion. The Texas Constitution also safeguards liberty of religious conscience. In the court's view, each of these provisions gave rise to "a concomitant zone of privacy."[196] Therefore, the court did not doubt that a right of individual privacy was implicit among those "general, great, and essential principle of liberty and free government" created by the Texas Bill of Rights.[197]

In Arkansas, the state supreme court used the penumbra theory in recognizing a right of privacy while striking down a sodomy statute that prohibited intimate behavior by persons of the same sex.[198] After acknowledging that the Arkansas Constitution did not specifically enumerate a right of privacy, the court began its analysis by evoking a provision in the Arkansas Constitution, which states that "the enumeration of rights shall

---

[194] Texas State Employees Union v. Texas Department of Mental Health & Mental Retardation, 746 S.W.2d 203 (Tex. 1987).
[195] *Id.* at 205.
[196] *Id.*
[197] *Id.*
[198] Jegley v. Picado, 80 S.W.3d 332 (Ark. 2002). The penumbra theory of *Griswold v. Connecticut* is discussed *supra* at notes 34–42.

not be construed to deny or disparage others retained by the people."[199] This suggests that certain rights may be recognized under the constitution in addition to those specifically enumerated in it. With this apparent authorization for a flexible interpretation of the state constitution, the court then turned to the language of other constitutional provisions to determine whether a right of privacy was "inherent" in the constitutional guarantees of the Arkansas constitution.[200] Liberty is mentioned several times in the state constitution, most appositely in Article 2, which states that no Arkansan will be deprived of life, liberty, or property without due process of law. Other parts of the document protect various aspects of privacy, such as the right of persons to be secure in their homes and to be free from unreasonable searches and seizures. The constitution guarantees equality of all persons before the law and prohibits the granting of any privilege or immunity not equally by all citizens. In addition to the rights granted by the constitution, the court examined the development of the right of privacy in state statutes and regulations, noting that privacy is mentioned in over eighty statutes enacted by the legislature and plays an important role in many areas of both the criminal and civil law of the state.[201] So, in considering the constitution along with statutes, rules, and case law, the court concluded that a right of privacy was "implicit in the Arkansas Constitution."[202]

Spatial Privacy: The Home as Sanctuary

As originally conceived, the right of privacy was based on the principle of individual autonomy or self-determination. In other words, the right of privacy was addressed to the right of an individual to control his or her own life. Occasionally, though, one or another early case might acknowledge, almost in passing, a spatial element to the right of privacy. For example, in *Hershberg v. City of Barbourville*, decided in 1911, a Kentucky appellate court struck down an ordinance banning the smoking of cigarettes within city limits, on the ground that the ordinance unreasonable interfered with "the right of the citizen to determine for himself such personal matters."[203]

---

[199] *Jegley*, 80 S.W.3d at 346–47 (quoting to Ark. Const. art. 2, §29).
[200] *Id.* at 347.
[201] *Id.* at 347–49.
[202] *Id.* at 349–50.
[203] Hershberg v. City of Barbourville, 133 S.W. 985, 986 (Ky. 1911).

While the court certainly was concerned with the principle of self-determination, it also noted that the ordinance was "so broad as to prohibit one from smoking a cigarette in his own home."[204] Spatial considerations further were apparent in the court's observation that if the ordinance had prohibited smoking cigarettes on the streets of the city, a different question would be presented.[205] Thus, in concluding that ordinance was an unreasonable invasion of personal liberty, the court was influenced by considerations of space as well as considerations of personhood.

In later years, state courts from time to time in appropriate cases have relied upon a notion of place in regard to the right of privacy. In 1975, the Supreme Court of Alaska ruled that the right of privacy expressly guaranteed by the state constitution included the right of an individual to possess marijuana for personal consumption at home. Emphasizing the spatial aspect of privacy, the court reasoned that the right of privacy obtains with special force within the home, thus providing constitutional shelter for certain activities that occur there even though those activities might not be protected when they occur elsewhere. As the court explained, many activities may be conducted lawfully within the privacy and confines of the home, although they may be prohibited when conducted in public.[206] Referring to federal decisions formulating the right of privacy, the court noted that privacy takes on an added dimension within the home. For example, in *Griswold v. Connecticut*, while upholding the right to receive birth control information, the Supreme Court described the marital bedroom as a "sacred precinct." And in *Stanley v. Georgia*, in ruling that there was a right to possess obscene materials in one's own household, the nation's high Court emphasized the home as the "situs" of protected activities.[207] "(A) State has no business," the Court proclaimed, "telling a man, sitting alone in his own house, what books he may read or what films he may watch."[208] As a later case affirmed, *Stanley* was not based on the notion that there was constitutional protection for obscene material, but rather upon the principle that "a man's home is his castle."[209]

---

[204] *Id.*

[205] *Id.*

[206] *Id.* at 985–86, n. 40.

[207] Stanley v. Georgia, *supra* note 47.

[208] *Id.* at 565.

[209] *Ravin*, 537 P.2d at 503. Although this principle is expressed in sexist and elitist terms, its point is well taken: a person's home should be his or her safehold.

In the view of the Alaska Supreme Court, the home was a special place with enhanced constitutional status:

> If there is any area of human activity to which a right to privacy pertains more than any other, it is the home. The importance of the home has been amply demonstrated in constitutional law....In Alaska we have also recognized the distinctive nature of the home as a place where the individual's privacy receives special protection....The home, then, carries with it associations and meanings which make it particularly important as the situs of privacy. Privacy in the home is a fundamental right, under both the federal and Alaska constitutions....[210]

The spatial aspect of privacy also has been recognized by the Court of Appeals of Tennessee in ruling that the state's Homosexual Practices Act criminalizing same-sex activity violated the state constitution by impinging upon the right of privacy.[211] In holding that the right of privacy embraced a right of intimate association, the court turned to the spatial aspect of privacy, noting that the sanctity of the home has long been recognized under both federal and Tennessee law and that both bodies of law have drawn distinctions between actions committed in the privacy of the home and those committed in public.[212] Accordingly, the court concluded that an adult's right to engage in consensual, noncommercial sexual activity in the privacy of the home was a matter of intimate personal concern lying at the heart of Tennessee's protection of the right of privacy.[213]

It has been asserted that an approach to privacy focused on its spatial aspect is preferable to an approach focused on individual autonomy, because the spatial approach is less value-laden.[214] This may or may not be so, but the more important point is that the spatial approach does not capture the essence of the right of privacy nearly as well as an approach that emphasizes the psychological aspects of selfhood. As the Supreme

---

[210] *Id.* at 504. The court added that: "We do not mean by this that a person may do anything at anytime as long as the activity takes place within a person's home....(T)his right must yield when it interferes in a serious manner with the health, safety, rights and privileges of others or with the public welfare. No one has an absolute right to do things in the privacy of his own home which will affect himself or others adversely." *Id.*

[211] Campbell v. Sundquist, *supra* note 97.

[212] *Id.* at 261–62.

[213] *Id.* at 262.

[214] Note, *Between Two Spheres, supra* note 7, at 1024–30.

Court explained in *Lawrence v. Texas*, the right of privacy encompasses an autonomy of self that transcends spatial bounds.[215] The essence of privacy revolves around personality and selfhood—the idea of what it means to be a person with control over the intimate aspects of one's own life. While the spatial component of privacy should not be overlooked, neither should it be inflated to supplant the principle of self-determination. Although it is true that in certain places, most notably the home, there should be an enhanced right of privacy, nevertheless the core aspect of privacy goes to personality rather than space. Privacy is about self, more than place.

Constitutional Situs and Methodology

Whatever theory is used to formulate it, the right of privacy must be connected to a constitutional provision in order to have status as a constitutional right. In the federal system, the right of privacy, at one time located within the penumbra emanating from several constitutional provisions,[216] has been established as an aspect of "liberty" within the protection of the Due Process Clause of the Fourteenth Amendment.[217] In the state systems, a variety of provisions have been evoked as the constitutional source of the right of privacy. A number of states have ruled that a right of privacy is encompassed with the protection of "liberty" afforded by a due process clause, a law of the land clause, or other constitutional provisions that forbid the exercise of arbitrary power over individual liberty.[218] In fact, the term "privacy" frequently is used interchangeably with the term "liberty," and courts regularly have turned to constitutional guarantees of liberty to embrace the right of privacy.[219] State constitutional guarantees of equality also may be relied on as a source of protection for

---

[215] Lawrence v. Texas, *supra* note 5, at 562.

[216] *See* discussion *supra* at notes 34–42.

[217] *See* discussion *supra* at notes 42–52.

[218] *See, e.g.*, Commonwealth v. Wasson, 842 S.W.2d 487 (Ky. 1992).

[219] "Privacy" has been used interchangeably with the common understanding of the notion of "liberty," and both imply a fundamental right of self-determination subject only to the state's compelling and overriding interest. *In re* Guardianship of Browning, *supra* note 3, at 9–10.

the right of privacy.[220] In some states, a right of privacy has been found implicit in constitutional provisions declaring that, "All persons are by nature free and independent, and have certain natural and inalienable rights,"[221] or stating that, "The enumeration of rights in this constitution shall not be construed to deny or impair others retained by, and inherent in, the people."[222] In more recent times, five states have amended their constitutions to expressly guarantee the right of privacy.[223] Finally, as described before, some states have declined to tie the right of privacy to a single specific constitutional provision, preferring instead to use the penumbra theory to designate privacy as an animating value that underlies different parts of the state constitution.

The enactment of constitutional provisions expressly guaranteeing a right of privacy has the effect of ordaining privacy as a fundamental right. Privacy may also be endowed as a fundamental right by recognizing it as such under a more general constitution provision, such as a provision guaranteeing that liberty may not be denied arbitrarily or without due process of law. While fundamental rights are not absolute, they may not be restricted unless the government can demonstrate that it has extremely strong justification for doing so. Any law that impinges upon a fundamental right will be subject to strict judicial scrutiny and will be struck down unless the government can show that the law is necessary to accomplish a compelling state interest.

As described in Chapter One, "Equality," strict scrutiny is one of three methods that the courts use to review the constitutionality of legislation.[224] A somewhat less rigorous form of judicial review, intermediate scrutiny, requires that legislation be narrowly tailored to serve an important or substantial state interest. Though less demanding than strict scrutiny, the intermediate tier of review nonetheless provides a meaningful methodology for assessing the constitutionality of legislation. Not so minimal scrutiny, the least rigorous form of review, which is also referred

---

[220] *See, e.g.,* Doe v. Maher, 515 A.2d 134 (Conn. 1986) (using state equal protection clause in part to strike down regulation denying Medicaid funding for abortions); Commonwealth v. Wasson, *supra,* note 218 (using state equal protection clause in part to strike down law making it a crime to engage in consensual adult homosexual activity).

[221] N.J. Const., art I, §1.

[222] Miss. Const., art. III, §32.

[223] *See supra* note 16 and accompanying text.

[224] The levels of scrutiny are described in detail in Chapter One, at notes 45–87.

to as "rationality review" because it requires only that legislation possess a modicum of rationality to be constitutional. Under minimal scrutiny, legislation is presumed to be constitutional and will not be struck down unless shown to bear no rational relationship to any legitimate state interest. In practice, there are two varieties of minimal scrutiny, the most common of which is completely deferential to the legislature and reduces minimal scrutiny to virtually no scrutiny at all that provides nothing more than a pretense of rationality to legislation. The other form of minimal scrutiny, which makes an occasional appearance, also is deferential, but not completely so. It renders the review of legislation a bit more genuine.

Minimal scrutiny operates by granting deference to the legislature, but under strict or intermediate scrutiny such deference is inappropriate either because the legislation under review is tainted by a suspicious property (such as racial or gender bias) or because it impinges upon the exercise of a basic right (such as the right to vote) of constitutional magnitude—in other words, a fundamental right. Hence, the designation of privacy as a fundamental right, either expressly or implicitly, is extremely consequential because it brings into play strict judicial scrutiny of legislative action. Once privacy is recognized as a fundamental right within the protection of strict scrutiny, it then becomes extremely important to define the right of privacy to determine exactly what activities it encompasses, which accordingly will be entitled to the highest degree of constitutional protection.

Conclusion

Although theories of privacy as a state constitutional prerogative began to evolve at a relatively early date, they were later eclipsed by a developing federal constitutional right of privacy that predominated throughout the nation for several decades. At some point, however, the commitment of the United States Supreme Court to the concept of self-determination began to waver, and the Court became reluctant to allow further development of the right of privacy. To this day, the nation's highest court remains equivocal concerning the right of autonomy and therefore its ambit under the Federal Constitution is uncertain. While uncertainty regarding privacy persists in the federal realm, a number of states have stepped into the breach to engender a state constitutional right of privacy, more vital and expansive than the federal model of privacy. The state conception of autonomy builds on the federal model, but remolds and extends it into new areas.

The principle of liberty runs deep in the waters of state constitutional law. Many state constitutions provide protection for liberty in their due process or law of the land clauses. Other constitutions simply, but forcefully, mandate that liberty may not be arbitrarily denied by the state. Under these constitutional provisions, the right of privacy is a fundamental aspect of liberty that may not be restricted except for the most compelling of reasons. In modern times, other states have chosen to enshrine autonomy as a fundamental right by amending their constitutions to expressly guarantee the right of privacy. But whatever route is taken, many states have seen fit to elevate privacy as a fundamental right, entitled to the highest degree of constitutional protection.

Accordingly, states have taken the lead in recognizing the right of intimate association[225] as well as a right to same-sex marriage or civil union.[226] When the United States Supreme Court circumscribed a woman's right to choose to have an abortion, a number of state courts went in the opposite direction to allow a wider scope for reproductive freedom.[227] State courts have also taken a more expansive view of parental rights and the right of individuals to live together.[228] A small number of states, taking a broad view of individual autonomy, have endorsed a right to ingest substances.[229] Also, the states have always been in the forefront in recognizing, as an important component of self-determination, a right of bodily integrity that includes the right to refuse medical treatment, even if doing so will result in death.[230] Thus, state constitutional law has proven to be a vital source of protection for the right of privacy.

While the federal conception of privacy has remained dormant, if not constricted, the state right of privacy has become dynamic, and, hence, more responsive to the evolving needs of a changing society. It now is the state courts that lead the movement to recognize new rights by expanding the conception of self-determination. As we learned in Chapter One in

---

[225] *See* Chapter Seven.
[226] *See* Chapter Six.
[227] *See* Chapter Five.
[228] *See* Chapter Five.
[229] *See* Chapter Eight.
[230] *See* Chapter Eight.

regard to equality, the right of privacy is no longer a predominantly federal construct. To appreciate the full scope of the right of autonomy in the United States, state constitutional law, no less than federal constitutional law, must be taken into account. Like equality, the right of privacy is now a joint federal and state enterprise.

CHAPTER FIVE

FAMILY RIGHTS

Reproductive Freedom

In 1973, the United States Supreme Court decided *Roe v. Wade*, establishing a right of privacy under the Fourteenth Amendment of the Federal Constitution that encompasses the right of a woman to choose to have an abortion.[1] Although the high Court continues to adhere to the central premise of *Roe* that prior to viability a woman has the right to choose to have an abortion, other decisions of the Court have allowed some limits to be placed on a woman's right to choose to have an abortion. These decisions limiting a woman's right to reproductive freedom have found favor in some states, but not in others. Several states have been willing to interpret their state constitutions to embrace rights of reproductive autonomy going beyond those recognized by the Supreme Court of the United States.

Public Funding of Abortions

On the federal side, the Supreme Court has repeatedly held that under the Fourteenth Amendment of the Federal Constitution it is not impermissible for the government to refuse to subsidize abortion, even if it is subsidizing other medical services, including childbirth.[2] From the perspective of the Supreme Court, there is no affirmative obligation on the

---

[1] Roe v. Wade, 410 U.S. 113 (1973).
[2] Williams v. Zbarez, 448 U.S. 358 (1980); Harris v. McRae, 448 U.S. 297 (1980); Poelker v. Doe, 432 U.S. 519 (1977); Maher v. Roe, 432 U.S. 464 (1977).

part of a state to fund abortion, even when it has affirmatively chosen to fund childbirth.[3] The Court applies minimal scrutiny in these cases on the rationale that while there is a fundamental right to choose to have an abortion, there is not a fundamental right to have an abortion subsidized by the state.[4] Using minimal scrutiny, the Court has upheld government refusals to fund abortion on the ground that they are rationally related to the legitimate state interest of protecting potential life and encouraging childbirth.[5] The Court's rationale that there is a fundamental right to have an abortion but not one subsidized by the government has been criticized as a sophism that makes it impossible for indigent women to exercise their constitutional right to have an abortion. That is, when the state finances the costs of childbirth, but not the costs of abortion, it realistically forecloses an indigent woman from choosing to have an abortion even though she has a constitutional right to do so.[6] In actuality, this seriously erodes the principle of *Roe v. Wade* that pregnant women have a fundamental right to decide whether to have an abortion.[7]

State courts are split on the issue of abortion funding, some of them adhering to the federal position upholding restrictions on abortion funding,[8] while others have taken a more expansive view in striking down such restrictions.[9] In several states whose constitutions contain express guarantees of privacy, the courts have departed from federal precedent to invalidate restrictions on abortion funding.[10] These courts have been quick to recognize that by expressly guaranteeing the right of privacy, their state constitutions provide more extensive protection for reproductive autonomy than does the Federal Constitution. In other states whose constitutions do not expressly safeguard privacy, courts have turned to constitutional provisions protecting liberty or guaranteeing equality to assess the constitutionality of laws that exclude abortion

---

3 *Maher*, 432 U.S. at 473–74.

4 *Id.* at 478–79.

5 Maher v. Roe, 432 U.S. at 478 (1977).

6 Committee to Defend Reproductive Rights v. Myers, 625 P.2d 779, 799 (Cal. 1981).

7 Maher v. Roe, 432 U.S. at 484 (Brennan, J., dissenting).

8 *See, e.g.*, Doe v. Director of Michigan Department of Social Services, 487 N.W.2d 166 (Mich. 1992); Bell v. Low Income Women of Texas, 95 S.W.3d 253 (Tex. 2002).

9 *See, e.g.*, American Academy of Pediatrics v. Lundgren, 940 P.2d 797 (Cal. 1997); Doe v. Maher, 515 A.2d 134 (Conn. 1986).

10 American Academy of Pediatrics v. Lundgren, 940 P.2d 797 (Cal. 1997); Valley Hospital Association v. Mat Su Coalition for Choice, 948 P.2d 963 (Alaska 1997); Simat Corp. v. Arizona Health Care Cost Containment System, 56 P.3d 28 (Ariz. 2002).

from subsidized health care benefits.[11] Under this approach, several state courts, finding federal precedent in this area to be unpersuasive, have rejected it and proceeded to take a more expansive view of reproductive autonomy.[12]

In striking down a regulation that denied Medicaid funding for abortions except those medically necessary to save the life of a mother, the Supreme Court of Connecticut found that the regulation violated the state due process clause, the state equal protection clause, and the state Equal Rights Amendment.[13] Early in its opinion, the court noted that since it was proceeding solely under the state constitution, federal decisions concerning abortion funding were not controlling.[14] Finding it difficult to accept the rationale of the Supreme Court in abortion funding cases, the Connecticut court chose to apply strict scrutiny under the state equal protection clause because the challenged regulation impinged on the fundamental right to choose whether to have an abortion.[15] Through the lens of strict scrutiny, the court concluded that the state could not show a compelling interest to justify the regulation.[16] While protecting potential human life may be an important state interest, it is not compelling enough under strict scrutiny to outweigh the fundamental right of a woman to choose to have an abortion.[17]

The Connecticut court was well aware that the denial of funds for abortion had a severe impact upon poor women in desperate need of medical care.[18] Referring to "the poor woman's dilemma," the court noted that "if the pregnant poor woman finds herself requiring an abortion to

---

[11] Committee to Defend Reproductive Rights v. Myers, 625 P.2d 779 (Cal. 1981); Doe v. Maher, 515 A.2d 134 (Conn. 1986).

[12] *Id.*

[13] Doe v. Maher, 515 A.2d 134 (Conn. 1986). *See also,* Moe v. Secretary of Administration, 417 N.E.2d 387 (Mass. 1981) (struck down restrictions on Medicaid-eligible pregnant women for funding of medically necessary abortions); New Mexico Right to Choose/ NARAL v. Johnson, 975 P.2d 841 (N.M. 1998) (state equal rights amendment required Medicaid funding for medically necessary abortions); Right to Choose v. Byrne, 450 A.2d 925 (N.J. 1982) (equal protection violation to withhold Medicaid funds for women who needed abortions to protect their health, not just their life); Committee to Defend Reproductive Rights v. Myers, 625 P.2d 779 (Cal. 1981) (struck down abortion funding restrictions because of interference with constitutional right to choose).

[14] Doe v. Maher, 515 A.2d at 152.

[15] *Id.* at 159.

[16] *Id.*

[17] *Id.* at 157.

[18] *Id.* at 153–55.

preserve her health, she has no place to turn."[19] The cruelty of this situation was demonstrated by a number of cases the court described involving indigent women who were in dire need of medical services.[20] While not suggesting that poverty is a suspect classification, the court did call attention to the fact that the exclusion of abortion from health care funding has serious consequences for the poor.[21]

The court further thought that the denial of funding for abortion amounted to discrimination on the basis of sex that violated the state Equal Rights Amendment. As the court explained, since only women become pregnant, discrimination against pregnancy by not funding abortion when it is medically necessary and when all other medical expenses are paid by the state for both men and women amounts to sex-based discrimination.[22] Because pregnancy is a condition unique to women, "any classification which relies on pregnancy as the determinative criterion is a distinction based on sex."[23] That being so, the court then ruled that the appropriate standard of review under the state ERA must be strict scrutiny.[24] Having previously decided that there was no compelling state interest to justify the regulation, the court concluded that it violated the Connecticut equal protection clauses and, "more specifically," the Connecticut ERA.[25]

Other states, though, have taken a different position, content to conform to the federal approach by applying minimal scrutiny to uphold laws that exclude abortion from health care funding. The Supreme Court of Pennsylvania, for example, held that a statute denying public funding for abortion while subsidizing other health care services did not violate

---

[19] *Id.* at 153.

[20] *Id.* at 154–55.

[21] *See also*, Committee to Defend Reproductive Rights v. Myers, 625 P.2d 779, 799 (Cal. 1981): "Indeed, the statutory scheme before us is all the more invidious because its practical effect is to deny to poor women the right of choice guaranteed to the rich. An affluent woman who desires to terminate her pregnancy enjoys the full right to obtain a medical abortion, regardless of the opposition of any legislative majority. By contrast, when the state finances the costs of childbirth, but will not finance the termination of pregnancy, it realistically forces an indigent pregnant woman to choose childbirth even though she has the constitutional right to refuse to do so."

[22] *Id.* at 159.

[23] *Id.*

[24] *Id.* at 161.

[25] *Id.* at 162.

the ban on special legislation in the state constitution.[26] Although the court professed that it was not shy about interpreting the Pennsylvania Constitution more generously than the Federal Constitution, it declined to do so in this instance.[27] Taking its cue from the federal abortion funding cases, the Pennsylvania court ruled that the appropriate standard of review was one of rationality,[28] because the statute affected neither a fundamental right nor a suspect class.[29] In conformity with federal rulings, the court professed that it had never held that financial need alone designates a suspect class for purposes of equal protection analysis.[30] Adopting the federal slant, the court professed that the statute only affected "the purported right to have the state subsidize the individual exercise of a constitutionally protected right."[31] Such a right, the court said, is found nowhere in the state constitution and therefore cannot be considered fundamental.[32] Using minimal scrutiny, the court had "no hesitation" in concluding the statute in question served the legitimate state interest of preserving potential life.[33]

The Pennsylvania court also ruled that the statute denying funding for abortion did not violate the state Equal Rights Amendment. Although the court had previously ruled that the thrust of the ERA was to eliminate sex as a basis for distinction under the law, in this instance the court saw no distinction based on sex.[34] "The mere fact that only women are affected by this statute does not necessarily mean that women are being discriminated against on the basis of sex."[35] The basis for the distinction made by the statute, according to the court, was not sex, but abortion.[36] Moreover,

---

[26] Fischer v. Department of Public Welfare, 502 A.2d 114 (Pa. 1985). *See also*, Doe v. Director of Michigan Department of Social Services, 487 N.W.2d 166 (Mich. 1992) (upholding statute that restricted abortion funding); Hope v. Perales, 634 N.E.2d 183 (N.Y. 1994) (statute that provided benefits to indigent women for childbirth but not for abortion did not interfere with right to reproductive choice).

[27] *Id*. at 121–23.

[28] "(A)s the United States Supreme Court concluded in *Harris*, we think the proper standard of review is one of rationality." *Id*. at 123.

[29] *Id*. at 121–22.

[30] *Id*.

[31] *Id*. at 121.

[32] *Id*.

[33] *Id*. at 123. Alternatively, the court also concluded that the state interest in preserving potential human life was an important interest that would satisfy intermediate scrutiny if that was the appropriate level of review. *Id*. at 122–23.

[34] *Id*. at 124–25.

[35] *Id*. at 125.

[36] *Id*.

the ERA "does not prohibit differential treatment among the sexes when, as here, that treatment is reasonably and genuinely based on physical characteristics unique to one sex."[37]

It is apparent from the foregoing cases that the states are seriously divided in regard to the constitutionality of laws that exclude abortion from subsidized health care services. In some states, the courts have accepted these laws, on the premise that they do not implicate a woman's fundamental right to choose to have an abortion. In a number of other states, however, the courts have struck down these restrictions on abortion funding, viewing them as unconstitutional burdens upon the fundamental right of reproductive autonomy.

Abortion Rights of Minors

In *In re T.W.*, the Supreme Court of Florida struck down a state statute that required a minor who wanted an abortion to obtain either parental consent or, alternatively, to obtain approval from a court by showing that she was mature enough to make the decision for herself or that the abortion was in her best interest.[38] In striking down the statute, the court ruled that the state constitutional privacy provision, which had been added to the Florida Constitution to expressly protect the right of privacy, encompassed a woman's right to terminate a pregnancy and extended that right to minors.[39] The court's decision, extending reproductive freedom to minors, goes beyond decisions of the United States Supreme Court, which have upheld statutes similar to the one invalidated in *T.W.* However, the Florida court declined to follow federal decisions because, unlike the Federal Constitution, the Florida Constitution contains a provision explicitly protecting the right of privacy. The Florida privacy guarantee was adopted as a constitutional amendment by the voters of the state in 1980 and, as the court noted, is worded very broadly, not being limited by words like "unreasonable" or "unwarranted" before the phrase "governmental intrusion," in order to render the right of privacy as strong as possible.[40] Indeed, as the court described it, the citizens of Florida opted for more protection from government intrusion than is

---

37 *Id.* (quoting People v. Salinas, 551 P.2d 703, 706 (Colo. 1976)).
38 *In re* T.W., A Minor, 551 So.2d 1186 (Fla. 1989).
39 *Id.* at 1191–93.
40 *Id.* at 1191–92.

provided by the Federal Constitution and did so by adopting a provision that is "intentionally phrased in strong terms."[41] Because the citizens of the state exercised their prerogative to amend the state constitution to explicitly provide for a strong right of privacy not found in the United States Constitution, the court could only conclude that the right was "much broader" in scope than that of the Federal Constitution.[42]

In the court's view, there was little doubt that the privacy amendment encompassed the right of a woman to decide to have an abortion. The court pointed out that choosing whether to have an abortion was exceptionally personal, having to do with a woman's control of her own body.[43] Along with the decision of a terminally ill individual to discontinue medical treatment,[44] it is one of the most profound and intimate decisions concerning one's body that a person can make. Choosing whether to have an abortion has "specific physical, psychological, and economic implications of a uniquely personal nature for each woman ....' [F]ew decisions are more personal and intimate, more properly private, or more basic to individual dignity and autonomy.'"[45]

Next, the court held that the right to freedom of choice concerning abortion applied to minors because the constitutional amendment guaranteeing privacy said so.[46] The amendment stated that the right of privacy belonged to "every natural person." The court saw this language as unambiguous. Minors are natural persons in the eyes of the law and therefore must be considered with the ambit of the privacy guarantee.[47]

Having determined that minors have a fundamental right of privacy under the Florida Constitution, the court turned to the question of whether the statute requiring parental consent or judicial approval could be supported by a compelling state interest. In accord with federal decisions, the court noted that there was a state interest in protecting potential

---

[41] *Id.* at 1191.

[42] *Id.* at 1191–92 (quoting Winfield v. Division of Pari-Mutual Wagering, 477 So.2d 544, 548, (Fla. 1985).

[43] *Id.* at 1192–93.

[44] *Id.* at 1192. The right of an individual to discontinue medical treatment is discussed in Chapter 8.

[45] *T.W.* 551 So.2d at 1193 (quoting Thornburgh v. American College of Obstetricians and Gynecologists, 476 U.S 747, 772 (1986), *overruled in part by* Planned Parenthood of Southeastern Pennsylvania v. Casey, 505 U.S. 833 (1992)).

[46] *Id.* at 1193.

[47] *Id.*

life in the fetus, which becomes compelling at the point of viability when the fetus is capable of meaningful life outside the womb.[48] There also was a compelling state interest in protecting the health of the mother, but given that abortion is a relatively safe procedure through the first stages of pregnancy, it also did not become compelling until a later time.[49] Because the statute in question operated from the point of conception on, it could not be justified on the basis of state interests that did not become compelling until a later stage of pregnancy.

The court also considered the question of whether the statute could be justified on the basis of a state interest in protecting the well-being of immature minors who, because of their youth, lack the experience, perspective, and judgment to make difficult decisions without parental guidance. In sustaining similar statutes, the United States Supreme Court pointed to the state interest in safeguarding immature minors who lack the ability to make critical decisions on their own. The Florida court, however, thought that in those cases the nation's highest court had applied a "relaxed" standard, calling for something short of the compelling state interest required under the Florida Constitution in all cases where the right to privacy is implicated.[50] While the Florida court agreed that safeguarding immature minors was a worthy objective, it was not recognized as sufficiently compelling to justify a parental consent requirement in other contexts.[51] For instance, a state statute expressly allowed an unwed pregnant minor to consent to medical or surgical care for herself or for her child, and her consent is valid and binding as if she had achieved her majority. The court pointed out that under this statute, with the exception of abortion, a minor may consent, without parental approval, to any medical procedure involving her pregnancy or her child—no matter how dire the possible consequences. Under Florida case law, minor parents also have the right to remove a life support system from an infant in a permanent coma.[52] Considering the wide authority that the state grants in other contexts to minors to make life-or-death decisions concerning their selves or their children without parental consent, the court could

---

[48] *Id.*
[49] *Id.*
[50] *Id.* at 1194–95.
[51] *Id.* at 1195.
[52] *Id.*

not discern a compelling interest on the part of the state to protect minors only where abortion was concerned.[53] As the court put it:

> We fail to see the qualitative difference in terms of impact on the well-being of a minor between allowing the life of an existing child to come to an end and terminating a pregnancy, or between undergoing a highly dangerous medical procedure on oneself and undergoing a far less dangerous procedure to end one's pregnancy .... Although the state does have an interest in protecting minors, the "selective approach employed by the legislature evidences the limited nature of the ... interest being furthered by these provisions."[54]

Informed Consent and Waiting Periods

In *Planned Parenthood of Southeastern Pennsylvania v. Casey*, the United States Court modified to some degree its previous ruling in *Roe v. Wade* by holding that some government regulation of abortion was permissible even prior to viability so long as the regulation in question does not "unduly burden" a women's right to have an abortion.[55] Under that standard, the Court in *Casey* sustained several provisions regulating abortion, including an informed consent, 24-hour waiting period requirement.[56]

The high Court's decision in *Casey* was found wanting by the Supreme Court of Tennessee, which, in *Planned Parenthood of Middle Tennessee v. Sundquist*, rejected the undue burden approach and went on to strike down an informed consent and waiting period requirement.[57] The Tennessee court's ruling in *Sundquist* traces back to its previous decision in *Davis v. Davis*, when the court first held that procreational autonomy was an aspect of the right of privacy encompassed in the concept of

---

[53] The court also noted that the state's adoption act contained no requirement that a minor obtain parental consent for minors before giving up a child up for adoption, "even though this decision clearly is fraught with intense emotional and societal consequences." *Id.*

[54] *Id.* (quoting Ivey v. Bacardi Imports, Co., 541 So.2d 1129, 1139 (Fla. 1989)).

[55] Planned Parenthood of Southeastern Pa. v. Casey, 505 U.S. 833 (1992). While modifying the ruling in *Roe*, the Court also emphatically reaffirmed the essential principle of *Roe* that abortion may not be prohibited prior to viability of the fetus. *Id.* at 846, 870.

[56] The court struck down one provision requiring spousal consent on the ground that it unduly burdened a woman's right to choose to have an abortion. *Id.* at 877.

[57] Planned Parenthood of Middle Tennessee v. Sundquist, 38 S.W.3d 1 (Tenn. 2000).

liberty guaranteed by the Tennessee Declaration of Rights.[58] In *Davis*, it will be remembered,[59] the court was faced with an issue concerning the control of "frozen embryos" that had been created through *in vitro* fertilization by a husband and wife who later were divorced. Subsequent to the divorce, the woman sought legal authorization to donate the frozen embryos to a childless couple, but her former husband was adamantly opposed to this course of action, not wanting to become a reproductive parent outside of marriage. In a landmark decision, the court ruled in favor of the man on the ground that under the Tennessee Constitution there was a right to procreational autonomy, that is, a right to decide for oneself whether to become a parent. In reaching this result, the Supreme Court of Tennessee established the right of procreational autonomy as a fundamental right guaranteed by the state Constitution.

Adhering to that principle, in *Sundquist* the Tennessee court rejected the undue burden approach of *Casey* on the ground that it was too subjective—"essentially no standard at all"—and therefore did not provide adequate protection for the fundamental right of procreational autonomy.[60] In the court's view, the undue burden approach "offers our judges no real guidance and engenders no expectation among the citizenry that governmental regulation of abortion will be objective, evenhanded, or well-reasoned."[61] Indeed, the undue burden approach "would relegate a fundamental right of the citizens of Tennessee to the personal caprice of an individual judge."[62] Disdainful of such a weak approach, the court opted to adhere to the settled standard of strict scrutiny because it provides a more appropriate measure of protection for the fundamental right of procreational autonomy.[63] In fact, the court adopted a good deal of language and reasoning from a pre-*Casey* Supreme Court decision, *Akron v. Akron Center for Reproductive Health*, that had applied strict scrutiny in striking down an informed consent and waiting period requirement, only to be overruled in part nine years later in *Casey*.[64]

In *Sundquist*, the Tennessee Supreme Court, applying strict scrutiny, found that neither the informed consent nor the waiting period requirement

---

[58] Davis v. Davis, 842 S.W.2d 588 (Tenn. 1992).
[59] *Davis* is fully discussed in Chapter Four.
[60] Sundquist, *supra* note 57, at 16.
[61] *Id.* at 16–17.
[62] *Id.*
[63] *Id.*
[64] Akron v. Akron Center for Reproductive Health, 462 U.S. 416 (1983).

were constitutionally justifiable. The informed consent requirement was constitutionally flawed because it required that before a woman consents to an abortion, she must be orally informed of certain information about the procedure by her attending physician. While agreeing that it was important for a woman who is contemplating abortion to be adequately informed about it, the court pointed out that there was no need for the information to be provided by the attending physician.[65] Evidence showed that it was standard practice throughout the medical community for health care professionals other than the attending physician to provide the necessary counseling and that the attending physician's function was to ensure that the patient had received the appropriate information.[66] "The State's interest is in ensuring that the woman's consent is informed and unpressured; the critical factor is whether she obtains the necessary information and counseling from a qualified person, not the identity of the person from whom she obtains it."[67] Since it was not necessary for the physician personally to convey the information to the woman, the court concluded that the requirement was not narrowly tailored to further a compelling state interest. Furthermore, in a departure from *Casey*, the Tennessee court found that the requirement should not be upheld under the less exacting undue burden approach; given that a woman could be fully informed by another health care professional, the only apparent purpose for requiring a physician to impart the information was to place a "substantial obstacle" in the path of a woman seeking an abortion.[68]

The waiting period requirement, which mandated a two-day wait before a woman could sign a consent form to have an abortion, was also constitutionally deficient. While acknowledging that a woman should have sufficient time to reflect upon her decision to have an abortion, the court thought that the two-day waiting period was so "arbitrary and inflexible" that it could not be sustained as constitutional.[69] The court explained that what was a sufficient time for reflection varies with each individual woman and that most women have seriously contemplated their decision to have an abortion before making their initial appointment with a doctor. "To mandate that she wait even longer insults the

---

[65] Sundquist, *supra* note 57, at 21–22.
[66] *Id.* at 22.
[67] *Id.* (quoting Akron v. Akron Center for Reproductive Health, 462 U.S. at 448 (1983)).
[68] *Id.*
[69] *Id.* at 22–23 (quoting *Akron*, 462 U.S. at 450).

intelligence and decisionmaking capabilities of a woman ....."[70] On the other side of the balance, the court found that the two-day waiting period exacerbated the financial and psychological burdens of having an abortion since many women must travel long distances and take time off from work to have the procedure.[71] The waiting period was especially difficult for indigent women and women who suffer from abusive relationships. So, the court concluded that the waiting period requirement was not narrowly tailored to achieve a compelling state interest. Moreover, again departing from *Casey*, the court found that the waiting period requirement should not be sustained under the less rigorous undue burden approach because the requirement was intended as and had the effect of placing a "substantial obstacle" in the path of a woman seeking an abortion.[72]

Family Relations

Parental Rights

In the year 2000, the United States Supreme Court broadened the federal privacy rights of parents by ruling that so long as a parent adequately cares for his or her children, a state may not intervene in a parental decision to limit grandparent visitations.[73] Even before that ruling, however, several states had recognized under their state constitutions that the right of privacy of parents might be violated by court orders mandating grandparent visitation contrary to parental wishes.[74] For example, in *Hawk v. Hawk*, decided in 1993, the Supreme Court of Tennessee ruled that a state statute permitting estranged grandparents "reasonable" visitation rights if found to be in the best interests of a child violated the state constitutional right to privacy in parenting decisions.[75] Referring to Tennessee's historically strong protection of parental rights as well as federal precedent, the court was convinced that parents have a fundamental right to care for their children, which is secured by the liberty clauses of the

---

[70] *Id.* at 23.
[71] *Id.* at 23–24.
[72] *Id.* at 24.
[73] Troxel v. Granville, 530 U.S. 57 (2000).
[74] Hawk v. Hawk, 855 S.W.2d 573 (Tenn. 1993); Von Eiff v. Azicri, 750 So.2d 510 (Fla. 1998).
[75] Hawk v. Hawk, *id.*

Tennessee declaration of rights.[76] Noting that the right of privacy is not expressly mentioned in either the federal or state constitution, the court nonetheless thought that there was "little doubt" that it was grounded in the concept of liberty reflected in both documents.[77] The notion of individual liberty is "deeply embedded" in the Tennessee Constitution and encompasses the right to "personal autonomy," which fully protects the right of parents to care for their children without unwarranted state intervention.[78]

In another matter concerning parental rights, a few states have gone beyond federal rulings by holding that a man claiming to be the biological father of a child born to a woman married to another man has a constitutional right to establish his paternity.[79] Thus, contrary to the United States Supreme Court's decision in *Michael H. v. Gerald D.*,[80] the Supreme Court of Texas granted standing to a professed biological father to challenge the so-called marital presumption that a child born to a married woman was presumed to be her husband's legitimate child. Pointing out that in previous decisions it had recognized that the "natural right" existing between parent and child is one of "constitutional dimensions,"[81] the court ruled that a biological father's interest in his child was a fundamental aspect of individual liberty entitled to a high degree of constitutional protection.

The court went on to find that, in the circumstances of the case, the marital presumption was a violation of the due course of law guarantee in the Texas Constitution. The marital presumption, which traces back to the English common law, was originally designed to protect children from the harsh consequences of a finding of illegitimacy, which could nullify a child's right to support or inheritance. As the Texas court remarked, perhaps the marital presumption had merit at an earlier time when the true biological father of a child could not be established with

---

76 *Id.* at 478–79.

77 *Id.* at 479 (quoting Davis v. Davis, 842 S.W.2d 588, 598 (Tenn. 1992)).

78 *Id.* (quoting Davis v. Davis, 842 S.W.2d 588, 598 (Tenn. 1992)).

79 *In the Interest of* J.W.T., 872 S.W.2d 189 (Tex. 1994); *see also*, State *ex rel.* Roy Allen S. v. Stone, 474 S.E.2d 554 (W. Va. 1996) (recognizing a right, if certain qualifications are met, of a putative biological father to establish paternity of a child born to a woman married to another man); *but see* Evans v. Steelman, 970 S.W.2d 431 (Tenn. 1998) (upholding a statute allowing standing to putative fathers to legitimate children born out of wedlock, while not allowing similar standing to putative fathers of children born to married women).

80 Michael H. v. Gerald D., 491 U.S. 110 (1989).

81 *In the Interest of* J.W.T., 872 S.W.2d at 194–95.

near certainty and when illegitimacy carried a significant legal and social stigma, but this is no longer the case.[82] The marital presumption is "out of place in a world in which blood tests can prove virtually beyond a shadow of a doubt who sired a particular child and in which the fact of illegitimacy no longer plays the burdensome and stigmatizing role it once did."[83]

Still, the court did not say that the state constitution guaranteed every purported biological father the right to establish paternity.[84] The court did rule, though, that a person claiming to be a natural father may not be arbitrarily prevented from attempting to establish his paternity, especially after offering early and unqualified acceptance of parental duties, as the avowed father had done in this case.[85] In conclusion, the court specified that standing to establish paternity is "constitutionally mandated" if near the time of the child's birth a biological father both acknowledges responsibility for child support or other care and maintenance and makes a serious and continuous effort to establish a relationship with the child.[86]

Adoption

Privacy claims regarding adoption usually involve either the question of who may adopt or the question of whether adopted children may obtain access to their adoption records. Adoption is primarily a statutory matter and most questions concerning adoption are determined through statutory interpretation. In most states, the adoption statutes do not expressly address the question of whether gay or lesbian persons may adopt a child.[87] In some states, the courts have interpreted these statutes to permit gay or lesbian adoptions, while courts in other states have interpreted their statutes to preclude gay or lesbian adoptions.[88] In a few states, the adoption statutes specifically permit gay or lesbian adoptions, but in three states statutes specifically bar such adoptions.[89]

---

[82] *Id.* at 197.

[83] *Id.* at 197, n. 24 (quoting Brennan, J., dissenting in *Michael H.*, 491 U.S. at 140).

[84] *Id.* at 198.

[85] *Id.*

[86] *Id.* at 195.

[87] Martin R. Gardner, *Adoption by Homosexuals in the Wake of Lawrence v. Texas*, 6 J. L. & Fam. Stud. 19 (2004).

[88] *Id.* at 23.

[89] *Id.*

Constitutional challenges to laws barring gay or lesbian adoption have not been successful in either federal or state court.[90] State courts inclined to uphold a right to gay or lesbian adoption do so on grounds of statutory interpretation without finding it necessary to reach the constitutional issue. State courts disinclined to countenance a right to gay or lesbian adoption occasionally have reached the constitutional issue and have rejected the assertion that there is constitutional protection for gay or lesbian adoption.[91]

In *Florida Department of Health and Rehabilitative Services v. Cox*, the Court of Appeals of Florida sustained the constitutionality of a statutory provision barring gay or lesbian adoption, rejecting the assertion that it violated the express guarantee of privacy in the state constitution.[92] The court took the position that because adoption was a statutory privilege, it could not be a fundamental right.[93] To the court's way of thinking, adoption was not the same as choosing to have a natural family, because a person who asks the state for the privilege of adopting a child does not have a fundamental right arising from an existing family relationship.[94] Be that as it may, the court's reasoning is extremely dubious. Marriage and divorce are also "privileges" granted by the state, but that does not make them any less fundamental. Given the personal nature of adoption, its importance to the individual, and its integral place in family life, it seems especially deserving of constitutional recognition as a fundamental right. Indeed, it seems fair to say that a prospective parent has a fundamental interest in adopting a child and the child has a fundamental interest in being adopted, neither of which should be infringed except for compelling reasons. Nevertheless, on appeal, the Supreme Court of

---

[90] In the federal system, despite the Supreme Court's decision in Lawrence v. Texas, 539 U.S. 558 (2003), upholding a fundamental right to intimate association, the Court of Appeals for the Eleventh Circuit ruled that a law precluding adoption by gay or lesbian persons violated neither the Due Process Clause nor the Equal Protection Clause of the Fourteenth Amendment. Lofton v. Secretary of the Department of Children and Family Services, 358 F.3d 804 (11th Cir. 2004); *see also*, Lindley for Lindley v. Sullivan, 889 F.2d 124, 131 (7th Cir.1989) ("there is no fundamental right to adopt").

[91] Two state courts have upheld laws barring gay or lesbian adoption, seeing no violation of the federal constitution, without considering whether the state constitution might offer more expansive protection for adoption rights. *In re* Angel Lace, 516 N.W.2d 678 (Wis.1994); *In the Matter of* T.K.J. and K.A.K., 931 P.2d 488 (Colo. App. 1996).

[92] Florida Department of Health and Rehabilitative Services v. Cox, 627 So.2d 1210 (Fla. Ct. App. 1993).

[93] *Id.* at 1216.

[94] *Id.*

Florida approved the ruling of the Court of Appeals that adoption was not a fundamental right within the constitutional guarantee of privacy, although the higher court did remand the case for further proceedings to determine if the statute barring gay or lesbian adoption could be sustained under equal protection rationality review.[95]

Both adopted persons and birth parents have brought suits claiming a right of privacy concerning information contained in adoption records.[96] Obviously, adoptees claim a right of privacy to obtain access to the records, while birth parents claim a right of privacy to keep the records sealed. Both claims are usually based on the informational component of the right of privacy, but occasionally they also address the autonomy component of privacy.[97] In any case, no court has ever found a constitutional right of privacy to adoption records for either adoptees or birth parents.[98] On one hand, statutes denying access to adoption records have been upheld as constitutional;[99] on the other hand, statutes allowing disclosure of adoption records also have been upheld as constitutional.[100] So, while adopted persons do not have a fundamental right to learn the identity of their biological parents, neither do the parents have a fundamental right to keep their identity confidential.

In recent times, a number of states have enacted statutes unsealing birth and adoption records to allow adopted children access to those records when they reach a certain age. Some of these statutes have been unsuccessfully challenged by birth parents claiming a violation of their right of privacy. In *Doe v. Sundquist*, the Supreme Court of Tennessee upheld a state law allowing an adopted person to obtain access to his or her adoption records against a claim by a group of birth parents who

---

95 Cox v. Florida Department of Health and Rehabilitative Services, 656 So.2d 902 (Fla. 1995). While approving other portions of the Court of Appeals' opinion, The Supreme Court of Florida held that the record was insufficient to determine if the statute could be sustained under equal protection rationality review. Therefore, the higher court remanded the case for further proceedings to complete the factual record solely on that issue. *Id.* To date, there are no further reported decisions in the case.

96 Kathleen Caswell, *Opening the Door to the Past: Recognizing the Privacy Rights of Adult Adoptees and Birthparents in California's Sealed Adoption Records While Facilitating the Quest for Personal Origin and Belonging*, 32 Golden Gate L. Rev. 271, 288 (2002).

97 Informational privacy concerns the right of an individual to obtain information or to keep information confidential; whereas autonomy concerns the right of an individual to make personal decisions free from governmental control.

98 *Id.*

99 *In re* Adoption of S.J.D., 641 N.W.2d 794 (Iowa 2002).

100 Doe v. Sundquist, 2 S.W.3d 919 (Tenn. 1999); Does v. State, 993 P.2d 822 (Or. Ct. App. 1999).

contended that the law violated their right of privacy.[101] The parents posited that the law implicated two branches of the right of privacy: family autonomy and informational privacy.[102] They claimed that the law violated their right to familial privacy by impeding a birth parent's freedom to determine whether to raise a family. In addition, they claimed that the law violated their right to informational privacy by authorizing the release of personal and confidential information against their will.

Neither claim was convincing to the court. Although the court once again recognized that the concept of liberty is "deeply embedded" in the Tennessee Constitution and encompasses the right to "individual privacy,"[103] the court did not believe that the state law in question improperly impinged upon an incident of familial autonomy. While the decision of whether to carry a pregnancy to term clearly implicates the right of autonomy, the court suggested that the decision of whether to surrender a child for adoption was a different matter.[104] The right of adoption is statutory and was created to protect the interests of children whose parents are unable or unwilling to care for them.[105] It was not created to advance the right of parents to procreate.[106] Moreover, the court was not certain that the decision to bear a child would be affected by the prospect that adoption records may be disclosed years later. While that prospect may have some bearing on the decision to bear a child, the court thought that it was too speculative to conclude that it interfered with the right to procreational privacy.[107] This was especially so given that the prospect of disclosure was not entirely new in Tennessee, having been allowed in more limited circumstances for some time.

Finally, the court rejected the contention that law violated a right to informational privacy by authorizing the release of personal information. In Tennessee, confidentiality of records is a statutory matter and not a constitutional one.[108] In other words, informational privacy is not recognized as a fundamental right in Tennessee.

---

[101] Doe v. Sundquist, 2 S.W.3d 919 (Tenn. 1999).
[102] *Id.* at 925–26.
[103] *See id.; see also* Hawk v. Hawk, 855 S.W.2d 573, 579 (Tenn. 1993).
[104] Doe v. Sundquist, at 926.
[105] *Id.*
[106] *Id.*
[107] *Id.*
[108] *Id.*

In Iowa, the state supreme court ruled that an adopted person did not have a constitutional right to see his or her adoption records.[109] The adoptee in this case asserted a free speech right to obtain information, including private information such as adoption records, but the court rebuffed the assertion, noting that state and federal courts have uniformly rejected the argument that adoptees have a fundamental right to learn the identities of their biological parents.[110] The court further maintained that the right to privacy and information claimed by adoptees directly conflicted with the privacy interests of birth parents to be left alone.[111] Given these conflicting interests, the court concluded that it was rational to preclude access to adoption records in order to protect the integrity of the adoption process.[112]

In the decisions refusing to recognize a fundamental right of privacy concerning adoption records, the reasoning of the courts is less than satisfactory. Given the impact of adoption information on both adoptees and birth parents, one could certainly argue that both parties have a fundamental interest concerning adoption records. As far as an adopted child is concerned, information about one's origins goes to the core of an individual's sense of "personhood."[113] Discovering information about one's biological parents is a function of identity formation and may be essential to developing a fully integrated self-image.[114] In some cases, it also is important for an adoptee to learn the identity of his or her biological parents for medical reasons.[115] Although medical information might be available without revealing the identity of the birth parents, an adoptee is more likely to obtain a complete medical history if allowed to contact the birth parents directly. In any event, knowing whom one's biological parents are is an intensely personal matter that lies at the heart of self-identity. Thus, there would seem to be sound reason to recognize a fundamental privacy interest on the part of an adopted child to know the identity of his or her birth parents. It is exactly these sort of considerations that have led quite a few states to enact statutes allowing adopted

---

[109] *In the Matter of* S.J.D., 641 N.W.2d 794 (Iowa 2002).

[110] *Id.* at 802–3.

[111] *Id.*

[112] *Id.*

[113] Kathleen Caswell, *supra* note 96, at 284–85, 293–94.

[114] Mills v. Atlantic City Department of Vital Statistics, 372 A.2d 646, 651 (N.J. Super. 1977).

[115] Kathleen Caswell, *supra* note 96, at 285–86.

children access to their adoption records, thereby obviating the necessity of raising these concerns as constitutional interests.

On the other side of the equation, birth parents also have strong privacy interests in keeping their identity confidential. The decision to place a child for adoption is an intensely personal one involving an individual's deepest sentiments about parenthood and family. Revealing a birth parent's identity may well have a profound and lasting impact upon the parent's life. Placing a child for adoption would seem to be the sort of intimate family decision that should be a matter of individual autonomy free from governmental interference. Birth parents, as well as adopted children, have much at stake here.

Perhaps, then, the courts would have been more convincing had they acknowledged a fundamental right of privacy concerning adoption records on the part of both adoptees and birth parents and then attempted to balance these rights. Had the courts done so, in all probability the results in the cases would turn out the same: neither laws denying access to adoption records nor laws allowing access to the records would be found to be unconstitutional. But at least the courts' reasoning would be more honest in recognizing the significance of the personal interests involved in matters of adoption information.

Cohabitation as a Family

Although the United States Supreme Court has held that the right of privacy includes the right of extended family members to live together,[116] the high Court has refused to extend the same right to persons who are not related by blood, marriage, or adoption. In *Village of Belle Terre v. Borass*, the Court found that no privacy rights were implicated by a zoning ordinance that prohibited more than two unrelated persons from living together in a single-family residence.[117] Applying minimal scrutiny, the Court sustained the ordinance as constitutional. Several state courts, however, going beyond *Belle Terre*, have struck down similar ordinances on the ground that they violate privacy or due process provisions in their

---

[116] Moore v. City of East Cleveland, 431 U.S. 494 (1977).
[117] Belle Terre v. Borass, 416 U.S. 1 (1974).

state constitutions.[118] In widening the scope of privacy beyond *Belle Terre*, the California Supreme Court observed that the federal right of privacy in general appears to be narrower than what the voters of the state approved when they specifically added a right of privacy to the state constitution.[119] The California Constitution ensures a fundamental right of privacy not only in one's family but also in one's home, comprehending the right to live with whomever one wishes or, at least, to live in an alternate family with persons not related by blood, marriage, or adoption.[120]

Several courts have found that zoning ordinances that bar unrelated persons from living together violate due process because they are not rationally related to a legitimate state interest.[121] Municipalities often attempt to justify these zoning ordinances by arguing that the ordinances serve the goal of controlling population density and the problems associated with it, such as noise, pollution, and parking and traffic difficulties. As the courts have pointed out, however, restricting the occupancy of a house to related persons bears no reasonable relationship to the goal of controlling population density or the problems associated with it.[122] Reducing population density does not depend on whether the occupants of a house are related; rather, it depends on the size of a house and its lot and the number of people who live in it.[123] In terms of controlling population density, zoning ordinances that restrict unrelated persons from living together are both over- and under-inclusive. They are over-inclusive by prohibiting single housekeeping units which are not, in fact, overcrowded and they are under-inclusive by failing to prohibit single housekeeping units which are, in fact, overcrowded.[124] As a result, the ordinances "indiscriminately regulate where no regulation is needed and fail to regulate where regulation is most needed."[125] Population density is more effectively dealt with by zoning ordinances that limit the number of occupants in a home by requiring a minimum amount of space or floor

---

[118] State v. Baker, 405 A.2d 368 (N.J. 1979); City of Santa Barbara v. Adamson, 610 P.2d 436 (Cal. 1980).

[119] City of Santa Barbara v. Adamson, *id.* at 440, n. 3.

[120] *Id.* at 439–40.

[121] Delta v. Dinolfo, 351 N.W.2d 831 (Mich. 1984); McMinn v. Town of Oyster Bay, 488 N.E.2d 1240 (N.Y. 1985).

[122] *McMinn, id.* at 1243.

[123] *Id.*

[124] "Under the instant ordinance, twenty male cousins could live together, motorcycles, noise, and all, while three unrelated clerics could not. A greater example of over- and under-inclusiveness we cannot imagine." Delta v. Dinolfo, *supra* note 121, at 841–42.

[125] *Id.* at 842.

area per occupant. But zoning ordinances that restrict unrelated persons from living together simply are not a rational means of controlling population density or its associated problems.

Municipalities also attempt to justify zoning ordinances restricting unrelated persons from living together as a means of preserving the character of traditional single-family neighborhoods. Courts have recognized this as a legitimate government objective, but not one that can be accomplished by arbitrarily limiting the definition of a family to exclude a household that is a family in every sense except biologically.[126] If a household is the functional equivalent of a "natural family," it may not be excluded from a single-family neighborhood. As the New York Court of Appeals explained, a zoning ordinance that limits occupancy of single-family homes to related persons has the effect of excluding many households that pose no threat to the goal of preserving the character of the traditional single-family neighborhood.[127] The traditional character of a neighborhood can be more appropriately preserved by restricting certain uses of buildings to disallow, for instance, hotels, boarding houses, or clubs.[128] As a general proposition, zoning ordinances are much less suspect when they focus on the use of structures rather than who are the users. But a zoning ordinance that restricts unrelated persons from living together is not rationally related to the goal of preserving the character of traditional single-family neighborhoods.

---

[126] McMinn v. Town of Oyster Bay, *supra* note 121, at 1243.
[127] *Id.*
[128] City of Santa Barbara v. Adamson, *supra* note 118, at 441.

CHAPTER SIX

CIVIL UNIONS AND MARRIAGE

Although there is a split of authority on the issue, some state courts have ruled that it is unconstitutional to deny gay or lesbian couples the civil benefits and rights that are available to heterosexual couples who are married. For the most part, these rulings are based on state constitutional provisions guaranteeing equality,[1] although they also raise considerations regarding marriage that pertain to the right of privacy.

In *Tanner v. Oregon Health Sciences University*, a 1998 decision, the Oregon Court of Appeals ruled that the state equal privileges and immunities clause was violated by a law denying to unmarried gay or lesbian couples the same health and life insurance benefits the were available to married opposite-sex couples.[2] The court's decision was based on the premise that sexual orientation was a suspect classification calling for strict judicial scrutiny.[3] The court reasoned that sexual orientation, like gender, race, alienage, and religious affiliation is widely regarded as defining a distinct, socially recognizable group of citizens, and that homosexuals in our society have been and continue to be the subject of adverse social and political stereotyping and prejudice.[4] Using strict scrutiny, the court found that the law under review could not be justified by any

---

[1] *See* the discussion of laws that classify on the basis of sexual orientation in Chapter Two.

[2] Tanner v. Oregon Health Sciences University, 971 P.2d 435 (Or. Ct. App. 1998).

[3] *Id.* at 447.

[4] *Id.* at 447. *But see*, Singer v. Hara, 522 P.2d 1187 (Wash. Ct. App. 1974), (ruling that classifications based on sexual orientation were not suspect and therefore evoke no more than minimal scrutiny. With virtually no explanation, the court summarily dismissed the appellants' assertion that classifications based on sexual orientation bear many of the characteristics of a suspect classification and went on to hold that it was not unconstitutional to deny a marriage license to couples of the same sex).

genuine differences between gay or lesbian couples and others to whom the insurance benefits were available.[5] In defending the law, the state argued that the law discriminated on the basis of marital status, not sexual orientation, pointing to the fact that the insurance benefits were available to all married employees—heterosexual and homosexual alike.[6] This was unpersuasive to the court. As the court explained, the Oregon equal privileges and immunities clause prohibits unintentional as well as intentional discrimination.[7] Regardless of the state's intent, the equal privileges and immunities clause may be offended where a law has a disparate impact upon a class of citizens.[8] And because homosexual couples were not permitted to marry, the insurance law in question in fact had a discriminatory impact upon gay and lesbian couples.[9] As the court put it, the insurance benefits are made available on terms that for gay and lesbian couples "are a legal impossibility."[10]

In *Baker v. State*, the Supreme Court of Vermont ruled that by excluding same-sex couples from the benefits and protections of marriage, the state marriage law violated the common benefits clause of the Vermont Constitution, which prohibits special emoluments or advantages that are not shared in common by the entire community.[11] In reaching this result, the court concluded that the law in question did not bear a reasonable and just relation to a government purpose that served the common benefits of the community.[12] The state had argued in *Baker* that its marriage law excluding same-sex couples from the benefits and protections incident to marriage was justified by several state interests. First, the state claimed, it had an interest in promoting a permanent commitment between couples who have children to ensure that their offspring are considered legitimate and receive ongoing parental support.[13] The court readily accepted this claim; in fact, the court admitted that it was beyond dispute that the state has an interest in promoting a permanent commitment from couples for the security of their children.[14] However, the court

---

[5] *Tanner*, 971 P.2d at 447.
[6] *Id.* at 447–48.
[7] *Id.* at 447.
[8] *Id.*
[9] *Id.* at 448.
[10] *Id.*
[11] Baker v. State 744 A.2d 864 (Vt. 1999).
[12] *Id.* at 873, 878–79.
[13] *Id.* at 881.
[14] *Id.*

continued, the marriage law was a "significantly underinclusive" means of accomplishing this end, because many couples marry for reasons unrelated to procreation, and have no intent to have children or are not able to have children.[15] The marriage law, then, extends the benefits and protections of marriage to many persons who have no logical connection to the state interest claimed for the marriage law.[16]

Furthermore (and perhaps more importantly), there was no explanation as to why the state's interest in promoting a permanent commitment from couples for the security of their children should not include children being raised by same-sex couples.[17] Noting that increasing numbers of children were being raised by same-sex parents, the court saw no reason to exclude these children from the benefits of the marriage law.[18] "(T)o the extent that the state's purpose in licensing marriage was, and is, to legitimize children and provide for their security, the statutes plainly exclude many same-sex couples with respect to these objectives."[19] Thus, persons who were similarly situated in regard to the very purpose of the marriage law nonetheless were treated differently by it.[20] For children being raised by same-sex parents, the law was counterproductive; it exposed them to the precise risks the marriage law was designed to prevent.[21]

The state additionally claimed that because same-sex couples cannot conceive a child on their own, to exclude them from the benefits and protections of the marriage law serves the state interest in promoting a perception of the link between procreation and child rearing.[22] The state claimed that it was justified in sending a public message that procreation and child rearing are intertwined to preclude the notion that mothers and fathers are "mere surplusage."[23] Of dubious factual validity, this assertion was rejected by the court. "Apart from the bare assertion," the court said, "the State offers no persuasive reasoning to support these claims."[24] Indeed, these claims could not explain why married couples who are infertile nevertheless are entitled to the full benefit and protection

---

[15] *Id.*
[16] *Id.*
[17] *Id.* at 881–82.
[18] *Id.*
[19] *Id* at 882.
[20] *Id.*
[21] *Id.*
[22] *Id.*
[23] *Id.*
[24] *Id.*

of the marriage laws. As the court pointed out, many married couples who are infertile use assisted-reproductive techniques that involve only one of the married partner's genetic material.[25] "The State does not suggest that the use of these technologies undermines a married couple's sense of parental responsibility, or fosters the perception that they are 'mere surplusage.'"[26] Hence, there was no reason to think that the use of the same technologies by a same-sex couple would somehow undermine the bonds of parenthood or society's perception of parenthood.[27]

As the court explained, there was an "extreme logical disjunction between the classification and the stated purposes of the law."[28] That is, excluding same-sex couples from the benefits and protections of the marriage law had little to do with protecting children or maintaining the link between procreation and child rearing. These goals, though laudable, do not provide a reasonable basis for denying the benefits and protections of marriage to same-sex couples who are no differently situated with respect to the goals than their opposite-sex counterparts.[29]

On the other side of the balance, the benefits and protections of marriage denied to same-sex couples were extremely significant. Marriage, the court said, "has long been recognized as a vital personal right."[30] A marriage license provides access to a multitude of legal benefits and protections and marriage is an important social relationship that significantly enhances the quality of life in our society.[31] In light of the great significance of marriage and the many benefits that flow from it, the weak reasons proffered in support of the law were hardly enough to justify it. Therefore, the court concluded that it was unconstitutional to deny the benefits and protections of the Vermont marriage law to same-sex couples. While ruling that the plaintiffs were entitled the same benefits and protections afforded to opposite-sex couples, the court decided to leave it to the legislature to resolve exactly how those benefits and protections should be extended to same-sex couples.[32] As the court mentioned, this gave the legislature a number of options, one of which was to enact a

---

25 *Id.*
26 *Id.*
27 *Id.*
28 *Id.* at 884.
29 *Id.*
30 *Id.* at 883.
31 *Id.*
32 *Id.* at 886.

"domestic partnership" statute to establish an alternative legal status to marriage for same-sex couples.[33]

The decisions in *Baker* and *Tanner* extend the legal benefits of marriage, but not necessarily the right to marry itself, to same-sex couples. In other words, the decisions mandate the extension of something short of marriage—civil union or domestic partnership—to gay or lesbian couples. In *Baehr v. Lewin*, however the Supreme Court of Hawaii went a decisive step further, although its ruling would later be countermanded by a constitutional amendment.[34] Before enactment of the amendment, however, the high court of Hawaii ruled in *Baehr* that a state statute restricting marriage to opposite-sex couples was subject to strict scrutiny and would be struck down unless shown to be justified by a compelling state interest.[35] Subsequently on remand, a trial court, applying strict scrutiny as directed by the Hawaii high court, found that the statute was not supported by a compelling state interest and hence was unconstitutional.[36]

Although the Hawaii constitution of 1978 contains a provision expressly guaranteeing the right of privacy,[37] the Hawaii Supreme Court chose to base its decision on the state equal protection clause.[38] To interpret the privacy provision in the state constitution, the court looked to the intent of its framers and found a portion in the committee report of the Constitutional Convention stating that the privacy provision was meant to protect a right "similar to the privacy right discussed in cases such as *Griswold v. Connecticut, Eisenstadt v. Baird, Roe v. Wade,* etc."[39] Because the committee report referred to federal decisions regarding privacy, the court concluded that at a minimum the Hawaii provision was meant to encompass all of the fundamental rights expressly recognized as within the right of privacy by the United States Supreme Court.[40] That surely included the right to marry, the court acknowledged, but only the right to marry someone of a different sex.[41] In fact, the United States

---

[33] *Id.*

[34] Baehr v. Lewin, 852 P.2d 44 (Haw. 1993), *superseded by constitutional amendment,* Haw. Const. art I, §23.

[35] *Id.* at 67.

[36] Baehr v. Miike, 910 P.2d 112 (Haw. 1996), *superseded by constitutional amendment,* Haw. Const. art. I, §23.

[37] "The right of the people to privacy is recognized and shall not be infringed without the showing of a compelling state interest." Haw. Const. art I, §6 (1978).

[38] Baehr v. Lewin, 852 P.2d at 67.

[39] *Id.* at 55–57.

[40] *Id.*

[41] *Id.*

Supreme Court has never recognized a fundamental right of privacy to enter a same-sex marriage. Moreover, the Hawaii Supreme Court was unwilling to expand the right of privacy to include same-sex marriages, because, turning to federal conceptions of fundamental rights, it did not believe that a right to same-sex marriage was "rooted in the traditions or collective conscience of our people" or "implicit in the concept of ordered liberty."[42]

On the other hand, the court ruled that under the Hawaii equal protection clause the right to a same-sex marriage was protectable by strict scrutiny and could only be limited upon proof of a compelling state interest.[43] The court began its analysis of the equal protection issue by noting that the equal protection clauses of the United States and Hawaii Constitutions "are not mirror images of one another."[44] Indeed, the Hawaii Constitution contains two phrases not included in the federal equal protection clause that were particularly relevant here. The Hawaii equal protection clause states "no person shall be denied the equal protection of the laws, nor be denied the enjoyment of the person's *civil rights* or be discriminated against in the exercise thereof because of race, religion, *sex*, or ancestry."[45] As the court pointed out, it has long been recognized that marriage is a basic or fundamental *civil right*.[46] Moreover, the express wording of the Hawaii equal protection clause makes sex a suspect classification.[47] So, according to the language of the Hawaii equal protection clause, there are two reasons for applying strict scrutiny: the presence of a fundamental right—marriage—and the presence of a suspect classification—sex. Therefore, the court concluded that strict judicial scrutiny should be applied to the Hawaii marriage law, and it should be struck down unless shown to be narrowly tailored to achieve a compelling state interest.[48] All to no avail, however, because five years later the voters of Hawaii approved a legislative amendment to the state constitution providing that "The legislature shall have the power to reserve marriage to opposite-sex couples."[49]

---

42 *Id.* at 56–57.
43 *Id.* at 58–67.
44 *Id.* at 59.
45 Haw. Const. art. I, §5 (1978) (emphasis added).
46 *Id.* at 60.
47 *Id.*
48 *Id.* at 67.
49 Haw. Const. art. I, §23.

It is interesting that the Hawaii high court chose to base its decision on the state equal protection clause rather than the express privacy provision in the Hawaii Constitution. Arguably, the express guarantee of the right of privacy would be the more appropriate language to embrace a right to same-sex marriage. But, as the court explained, the history of the privacy provision indicated that its framers did not intend it for that purpose. Still, it seems inconsistent to follow federal conceptions of privacy ("the traditions and collective conscience of our people," "the concept of ordered liberty") to interpret a state constitutional privacy provision that has no analogue whatsoever in the Federal Constitution while declining to follow federal law when interpreting a state equal protection clause that does have a federal analogue, but not one that is a "mirror image." Presumably, the court's explanation for this inconsistency would be that the intent of the framers of the privacy provision pointed to federal criteria, whereas no similar intent underlay the state equal protection clause, the language of which was certainly amenable enough to encompass same-sex marriage.

In *Goodridge v. Department of Public Health*, a momentous decision announced in 2003, the Supreme Court of Massachusetts ruled that under the Massachusetts constitution, the commonwealth could not deny the right to marry to persons of the same sex.[50] In the introduction to its opinion, the court noted that, on one hand, many people hold deep-seated religious, moral, and ethical convictions against same-sex marriage, while, on the other hand, many people hold equally strong religious, moral, and ethical convictions that same-sex couples should be allowed to marry.[51] The court's concern, however, was with the Massachusetts Constitution. Quoting the United States Supreme Court's decision in *Lawrence v. Texas*, the Massachusetts high court stated that "Our obligation is to define the liberty of all, not to mandate our own moral code."[52] "Barred access to the protection, benefits, and obligations of civil marriage," the court continued, "a person who enters into an intimate exclusive union with another of the same sex is arbitrarily deprived of membership in one of our community's most rewarding and cherished institutions. That exclusion is incompatible with the constitutional principles of respect for individual autonomy and equality under law."[53]

---

[50] Goodridge v. Department of Public Health, 798 N.E.2d 941 (Mass. 2003).
[51] *Id.* at 948.
[52] *Id.*
[53] *Id.* at 949.

In reaching its decision, the court referred to several provisions of the Massachusetts Constitution, which are worth noting here to show the extent of protection afforded to liberty and equality expressed in the state constitution.[54] Article 1 of the Massachusetts Constitution declares that "All people are born free and equal and have certain natural, essential and unalienable rights; among which may be reckoned the right of enjoying and defending their lives and liberties; that of acquiring, possessing and protecting property; in fine, that of seeking and obtaining their safety and happiness. Equality under the law shall not be denied or abridged because of sex, race, color, creed, or national origin." Article 6 provides that "No man, nor corporation, or association of men, have any other title to obtain advantages, or particular and exclusive privileges, distinct from those of the community, than what arises from the consideration of services rendered to the public." Article 7 says: "Government is instituted for the common good; for the protection, safety, prosperity, and happiness of the people; and not for the profit, honor, or private interest of any one man, family or class of men." Article 10 states: "Each individual of the society has a right to be protected by it in the enjoyment of his life, liberty and property, according to standing laws." And, Article 12 provides that "No subject shall be deprived of his property, immunities, or privileges, put out of the protection of the law ... or deprived of his life, liberty, or estate, but by the judgment of his peers, or the law of the land." So, the wording of the Massachusetts Constitution provides extensive and ringing protection for liberty and equality.[55]

In regard to the Massachusetts Constitution, the court observed that it protects matters of personal liberty just as zealously, and often more so, than the Federal Constitution, even where both constitutions use essentially the same language.[56] This is an aspect of our federal system and it is "(f)undamental to the vigor of our federal system of government" that state courts are "absolutely free" to interpret state constitutional provisions

---

[54] *Id.* at 950, n. 7.

[55] The court also referred to article 16, which provides that, "The right of free speech shall not be abridged," and article 4, which states that "full power and authority are hereby given and granted to the said general court, from time to time, to make, ordain, and establish all manner of wholesome and reasonable orders, laws, statutes, and ordinances, directions and instructions, either with penalties or without; so as the same shall be not repugnant or contrary to this constitution, as they shall judge to be for the good and welfare of this Commonwealth." *Id.* at 951, n. 8.

[56] *Id.* at 959.

to accord greater protection to individual rights than do similar provisions of the federal constitution.[57]

Early in its opinion, the court noted that civil marriage is a secular institution, governed by civil law and not by religious law.[58] Religions, of course, are free to choose what marriages they will or will not sanctify, but as far the legal aspects of a marriage are concerned, that is strictly governed by the law of the state, and in Massachusetts no religious ceremony has ever been required to validate a marriage.[59]

Marriage, the court observed, is extremely important to individuals; in fact, it is one of the most important intimate or personal aspects of an individual's life.[60] As the court explained,

> (Marriage) bestows enormous private and social advantages on those who choose to marry … It is an association that promotes a way of life…because it fulfils yearnings for security, safe haven, and connection that express our common humanity…The decision of whether and whom to marry is among life's momentous acts of self-definition.[61]

The court noted that tangible as well as intangible benefits flow from marriage.[62] The legal status of marriage brings with it valuable property rights and other benefits, a number of which the court enumerated in its opinion.[63] As the court described, the benefits accessible only by way of marriage are enormous, "touching nearly every aspect of life and death."[64] Given the many concrete benefits of marriage as well as its "intimately personal significance" the United States Supreme Court and several state supreme courts have recognized that it is a basic civil right fundamental to our very existence and survival.[65] Without the right to choose to marry, a person "is excluded from the full range of human experience and denied full protection of the laws."[66] Because civil marriage is integral to the lives of individuals as well as to the welfare of the community, the law assiduously

---

[57] *Id.*
[58] *Id.* at 948, 954.
[59] *Id.* at 954.
[60] *Id.* at 954–55.
[61] *Id.* (quoting Griswold v. Connecticut, 381 U.S. 479, 486 (1965)).
[62] *Id.* at 955.
[63] *Id.* at 955–57.
[64] *Id.* at 955.
[65] *Id.* at 957.
[66] *Id.*

safeguards the right of an individual to marry against undue government incursion.[67]

The court also pointed out that for centuries in the United States white and black Americans were prohibited by law from marrying, but that long history did not avail when the Supreme Court of California struck down a prohibition of interracial marriage in 1948 in *Perez v. Sharp* or when the United States Supreme Court struck down an anti-miscegenation law in 1967 in *Loving. v. Virginia*.[68] Comparing the Massachusetts law barring same-sex marriage to the anti-miscegenation laws struck down in *Perez* and *Loving*, the court noted stated that:

> In this case, as in *Perez* and *Loving*, a statute deprives individuals of access to an institution of fundamental legal, personal, and social significance—the institution of marriage—because of a single trait: skin color in Perez and Loving, sexual orientation here. As it did in Perez and Loving, history must yield to a more fully developed understanding of the invidious quality of the discrimination.[69]

In *Goodridge*, the plaintiffs challenged the Massachusetts marriage law under both the equality guarantee and the liberty-due process guarantee of the Massachusetts Constitution, which, the court noted, frequently overlap one another in regard to matters relating to marriage, family, or the upbringing of children.[70] Of course, there was a question of what level of scrutiny to apply—strict or minimal (rational basis). The commonwealth had argued that rationality review should be used because there was no fundamental right or suspect classification implicated, while the plaintiffs had argued that strict scrutiny should be used because the marriage law amounted to a sex-based suspect classification that impinged on a fundamental right—marriage. The court, though, surprisingly, avoided that issue by ruling that the marriage ban could not survive rational basis review under either the due process or equal protection clause.[71] It was quite remarkable that the court did not take the step of holding that marriage was a fundamental right within the protection of strict judicial scrutiny. After all, the court had gone through an extensive analysis showing how important marriage was to an individual and had

---

[67] *Id.*
[68] *Id.* at 958.
[69] *Id.*
[70] *Id.* at 953.
[71] *Id.* at 961.

described marriage as "among the most basic" of rights and of "funda-mental importance."[72] The court also observed that even the United States Supreme Court, as well as several state courts, had recognized that mar-riage is a basic civil right fundamental to our very existence.[73] Moreover, by ruling that marriage was a fundamental right, strict scrutiny would be evoked, affording a more penetrating medium by which to examine the state interests offered in support of the prohibition of same-sex marriage. Be that as it may, the court stopped short of actually ruling that there was a fundamental right to marriage, and instead struck the statute down on the ground that it could not survive rational basis review.[74]

Under rationality review, the Massachusetts Department of Public Health asserted a number of possible rationales for prohibiting same-sex marriage, none of which satisfied the court as sufficient to uphold the Massachusetts restriction on same-sex marriage.[75] The first rationale offered by the Department for prohibiting same-sex marriage was to pro-vide a favorable setting for procreation. The court rejected this rationale on the ground that it was a pretense that mischaracterized the purposes of the state marriage laws.[76] As the court explained, the Massachusetts laws of marriage do not sanction procreative heterosexual intercourse between married persons above other forms of adult intimacy or other ways of creating a family. There is no requirement that applicants for a marriage license attest to their ability or intention to conceive children through intercourse. Fertility is not a condition of marriage, nor lack of it grounds for divorce. People who never consummate their marriage and never plan to do so nonetheless are still married. Indeed, "People who cannot stir from their deathbed may marry." While many, perhaps most, married couples have children together, "it is the exclusive and permanent commitment of the marriage partners to one another, not the begetting of children, that is the *sine qua non* of civil marriage."[77]

Furthermore, the Commonwealth actively supports bringing children into a family regardless of whether the intended parent is married or not, whether the child is adopted or born into the family, whether technology was used as an aid to conceive the child, and whether the parent or partner

---

[72] *Id.* at 957.
[73] *Id.*
[74] *Id.* at 961.
[75] *Id.* at 962–64.
[76] *Id.* at 962.
[77] *Id.* at 961.

is heterosexual, homosexual, or bisexual.[78] Thus, the attempt to designate procreation as the foundation of marriage[79] overlooks the more comprehensive way in which courts have considered the complex and interrelated aspects of personal autonomy, marriage, family, and child rearing. The jurisprudence of the Commonwealth recognizes that, "in these nuanced and fundamentally private areas of life, such a narrow focus is inappropriate."[80]

To presume that procreation is the basis of marriage "singles out the one unbridgeable difference between same-sex and opposite-sex couples, and transforms that difference into the essence of legal marriage."[81] This has the same flaw as the Colorado law struck down by the United States Supreme Court in *Romer v. Evans* of identifying persons by a single trait and denying them protection across the board on the basis of that single trait. Moreover, this has the effect of impermissibly conferring "an official stamp of approval on the destructive stereotype that same-sex relationships are inherently unstable and inferior to opposite-sex relations and are not worthy of respect."[82]

As the court observed, the first rationale offered by the Department of Public Health in support of prohibiting same-sex marriage (to provide a favorable setting for procreation) shaded imperceptibly into its second rationale, which was to ensure that children are raised in an optimal setting, one that the Department asserted could only be provided by opposite-sex parents.[83] Along the same lines, one of the dissenting justices insisted that the state had an imported interest in ensuring an optimal social structure within which to bear and raise children.[84] In answer to this argument, the court readily admitted that protecting the welfare of children was a paramount state policy, but nonetheless concluded that restricting marriage to opposite-sex couples could not plausibly further the policy of protecting children.[85] Noting that the demographic changes

---

[78] *Id.* at 962.

[79] In a dissenting opinion, Justice Cordy described procreation as "the source of a fundamental right to marry." *Id.* at 987 (Cordy, J., dissenting). He insisted that procreation was "essential to the Supreme Court's denomination of the right to marry as fundamental." *Id.*

[80] *Id.* at 962 (majority opinion).

[81] *Id.*

[82] *Id.*

[83] *Id.*

[84] *Id.* at 998–1000 (Cordy, J., dissenting).

[85] *Id.* at 962 (majority opinion).

of the past century have all but obliterated the notion of an average American family, the court pointed out that composition of families varies considerably from household to household. In response to the changing characteristics of the American family, the Commonwealth of Massachusetts has "moved vigorously to strengthen the modern family in its many variations."[86] Furthermore, the court has previously repudiated the power of the state to treat children differently based on the circumstances of their birth and has recognized that the standard of the best interests of a child should not be determined by a parent's sexual orientation or marital status.[87]

The Department of Public Health offered no evidence to show that barring same-sex marriage will lead to an increase in the number of couples who decide to enter into opposite-sex marriages in order to have children.[88] So, there was no rational relationship between the marriage statute and the Department's professed purpose of ensuring the "optimal" setting for child-rearing. In addition, the Department readily conceded that individuals in same-sex couples may be excellent parents.[89] Same-sex couples (including several of the plaintiff couples in the case) have children for the same reasons as other persons—to love them, to care for them, to nurture them. However, the exercise of child rearing by same-sex couples is made infinitely more difficult by "their status as outliers to the marriage laws."[90] Although it is extremely important to establish a child's parentage as soon as possible, same-sex couples are forced to undergo what can be a long and intrusive process of adoption by a second parent in order to establish their joint parentage. The children of same-sex couples are deprived of significant marital benefits that bring financial security to all members of a family.[91] Hence, the Massachusetts marriage laws actually work at cross purposes to the state's goal of enhancing the welfare of children; the exclusion of same-sex couples from marriage does nothing to benefit the children of opposite-sex marriages, while denying children of same-sex couples immeasurable benefits that ensue from a stable family edifice. As the court put it,

---

[86] *Id.* at 963.
[87] *Id.*
[88] *Id.*
[89] *Id.*
[90] *Id.*
[91] *Id.*

No one disputes that the plaintiff couples are families, that many are parents, and that the children they are raising, like all children, need and should have the fullest opportunity to grow up in a secure, protected family unit. Similarly, no one disputes that, under the rubric of marriage, the State provides a cornucopia of substantial benefits to married parents and their children. The preferential treatment of civil marriage reflects the Legislature's conclusion that marriage 'is the foremost setting for the education and socialization of children' precisely because it 'encourages parents to remain committed to each other and to their children as they grow.[92]

Therefore, the court concluded that it was not reasonable to penalize children by denying them the benefits of state law for no other reason that the state disapproves of their parents' sexual orientation.

The third rationale advanced by the Department of Public Health was to preserve scarce state and private financial resources.[93] The Department argued that it was rational to assume that partners of same-sex couples tended to be more financially independent of one another than married spouses were of each other and therefore less needy of public marital benefits, such as tax advantages, or private marital benefits, such as insurance coverage.[94] That assumption, however, is an over-generalization that bears little factual support. There are many same-sex partners who are not financially independent of one another and many married spouses who are. As the court pointed out, numerous same-sex couples have children and other dependents, such as aged parents, in their care, who are no less needy than the dependents of married couples.[95] Moreover, state law does not condition eligibility for public or private benefits for married individuals on a showing of financial dependence on each other. To the contrary, benefits are available to married couples without regard to whether they mingle their funds or actually depend on each other for support.[96] And there is no reason why those benefits should not be available to same-sex couples on the same basis.

The Department of Public Health further asserted that it was justifiable to prohibit same-sex marriage because to allow same-sex marriage would

---

[92] *Id.* at 964.
[93] *Id.*
[94] *Id.*
[95] *Id.*
[96] *Id.*

trivialize or diminish the institution of marriage as it has historically been understood.[97] Like the Department's other arguments, this one was rejected by the court. While admitting that a decision allowing same-sex marriage certainly would mark a significant change in the definition of marriage, the court maintained that it would not harm the fundamental value of marriage in our society.[98] To the contrary, such a decision would enhance the value of marriage by manifesting how it important it was to all people. The court opined that recognizing the right of an individual to marry a person of the same sex would not diminish the validity or dignity of opposite-sex marriage any more than recognizing the right of an individual to marry a person of a different race devalues the marriage of a person who marries someone of her own race.[99] If anything, granting the right to marry to same-sex couples will reinforce the importance of marriage as a social institution. "That same-sex couples are willing to embrace marriage's solemn obligations of exclusivity, mutual support, and commitment to one another is a testament to the enduring place of marriage in our laws and in the human spirit."[100]

Having failed to convince the court that disallowing same-sex marriage served any reasonable state interests, the Department then claimed that the expansion of marriage to include same-sex couples would lead to interstate conflict.[101] In response to that argument, the court said that it would not presume to direct another state how to respond to the court's decision, but considerations of comity should not deter the court from according the residents of Massachusetts the full measure of protection available under the state constitution. "The genius of our Federal system is that each State's Constitution has vitality specific to its own traditions and that, subject to the minimum requirements of the Fourteenth Amendment, each State is free to address difficult issues of individual liberty in the manner its own Constitution demands."[102]

Several amici curiae briefs were submitted in the case, some of which asserted that prohibiting same-sex marriage reflects a consensus among the community that homosexual conduct is immoral.[103] The court, though, disagreed, noting that Massachusetts, as evidenced by a number

---

97 *Id.* at 965.
98 *Id.*
99 *Id.*
100 *Id.*
101 *Id.* at 967.
102 *Id.*
103 *Id.*

of statutes and court decisions, has a strong affirmative policy of preventing discrimination on the basis of sexual orientation.[104]

In concluding that the Department of Public Health could not properly justify the ban of same-sex marriage, the court stated that many of the propositions advanced by the Department were "starkly at odds with the comprehensive network of vigorous, gender-neutral laws promoting stable families and the best interests of children."[105] "The marriage ban," the court continued, "works a deep and scarring hardship on a very real segment of the community for no rational reason."[106] Indeed, given the absence of a reasonable relationship between the marriage ban and any state interest in protecting the public health, safety, or general welfare, the court could only conclude that the ban was rooted in irrational prejudice against gay and lesbian persons.[107] Therefore, the court ruled that the Massachusetts law prohibiting same-sex marriage was a violation of "the basic premises of individual liberty and equality under law protected by the Massachusetts Constitution."[108]

As mentioned above, the majority in *Goodridge* found it unnecessary to evoke strict judicial scrutiny in the case, stopping short of declaring that marriage was a fundamental right.[109] Nor did the majority indicate that the state marriage laws contained the sort of classification, based on gender or sexual orientation, calling for heightened scrutiny.[110] Several other justices, though, addressed those issues in concurring and dissenting opinions. In a separate opinion concurring in the court's decision, Justice Greaney maintained that the case should be decided under what he referred to as "traditional equal protection analysis," which clearly called for the application of strict scrutiny on the ground that marriage is a fundamental right.[111] Relying on precedent, Justice Greaney maintained that it was indisputable that marriage was a fundamental right entitled to the protection of strict scrutiny.[112] Indeed, marriage was "one of the vital personal rights essential to the orderly pursuit of happiness by free men."[113]

---

[104] *Id.*
[105] *Id.* at 968.
[106] *Id.*
[107] *Id.*
[108] *Id.*
[109] *Id.* at 961.
[110] *See id.*
[111] *Id.* at 970 (Greaney, J., concurring).
[112] *Id.*
[113] *Id.* (quoting Loving v. Virginia, 388 U.S. 1, 12 (1967)).

None of the dissenting justices questioned the premise that marriage is a fundamental right, but they argued that the fundamental right to marry does not encompass the right to marry someone of the same sex. In separate dissenting opinions, both Justices Cordy and Spina asserted that marriage was the civil union between a single man and a single woman.[114] According to this view, the marriage laws of Massachusetts did not restrict the right of any individual to marry; all persons were free to enter into the institution of marriage—marriage being a union between a man and a woman.

Clearly, the dissenting justices were taking the position that marriage, as a matter of definition, is the union of a man and a woman, and both justices were presuming that it is constitutional to define marriage in that way. Highly tautological, this position begs the question of whether marriage can properly be defined by the state as precluding same-sex unions. As Justice Greaney explained in his concurring opinion, to define marriage as a union between a man and woman is "conclusory and bypasses the core question" presented by the case.[115] This case, he said, "calls for a higher level of legal analysis," one that confronts and reexamines "ingrained assumptions" concerning the "roles of men and women within the institution of marriage."[116]

In response, the dissenters made an attempt to rationalize their position, but the reasons they offered were open to considerable question. Justice Cordy contended that marriage (between a man and woman) should be considered a fundamental right only because it is associated with procreation.[117] As described above, the majority opinion dismissed this contention on the ground that it reduces the essence of marriage to a single element, thereby ignoring the importance of marriage as an intimate union between two individuals.[118] To focus on procreation as the foundation of marriage ignores the comprehensive nature of marriage and the numerous deeply personal benefits it provides for individuals.[119]

The dissenters also argued that the right to same-sex marriage should not be considered fundamental because it is not "deeply rooted this

---

[114] *Id.* at 975 (Spina, J., dissenting); *Id.* at 984–85 (Cordy, J., dissenting).
[115] *Id.* at 972–73 (Greaney, J., concurring).
[116] *Id.* at 973.
[117] *Id.* at 984–85 (Cordy, J., dissenting).
[118] *Id.* at 954–57 (majority opinion).
[119] *Id.*

Nation's history."[120] As Justice Cordy put it, "although the institution of marriage is deeply rooted in the history and traditions of our country,… the right to marry someone of the same sex is not."[121] This approach, however, has its drawbacks. By looking to the past, it makes constitutional interpretation a static process, strictly precluding the recognition of new rights. Such a severe approach would have foreclosed the possibility of recognizing interracial marriage as a fundamental right because, like same-sex marriage, it was not deeply rooted in the nation's history or tradition. Courts, however, do not always use history in such a restrictive manner. Indeed, there is considerable debate concerning the role that history should play in determining the meaning of a constitution, and many decisions, both state and federal, take a more progressive approach to constitutional interpretation recognizing that the meaning of constitutional provisions develops over time. While history has much to teach us, it is important to remember that history is an ongoing process. It is a myth to think that the meaning of a constitution is fixed at some point in the past.[122] History itself is evolutionary and in turning to history to interpret a constitution, the meaning of constitutional provisions also will evolve.

In addition to the presence of a fundamental right, heightened judicial scrutiny might also be evoked in a case due to the presence of a suspect or semi-suspect classification. In his concurring opinion, Justice Greaney further suggested that strict scrutiny should be applied in *Goodridge* because the Massachusetts marriage law amounted to a classification based on sex.[123] The marriage law, he said, constrained a person's choice of a spouse because of his or her own sex and hence constituted discrimination on the basis of gender.[124] Not so, retorted Justice Spina, who took the position that the marriage law created no distinction between the sexes, but treated men and women precisely the same.[125] The law, he asserted, "does not create any disadvantage identified with gender, as both men and women are similarly limited to marrying a person of the

---

[120] *Id.* at 976–77 (Spina, J., dissenting) (quoting Moore v. City of East Cleveland, 431 U.S. 494, 503 (1977) (plurality opinion).

[121] *Id.* at 984 (Cordy, J., dissenting).

[122] *See* Jeffrey M. Shaman, *Constitutional Interpretation: Illusion and Reality* 11–20 (2001).

[123] *Goodridge*, 798 N.E.2d at 971 (Greaney, J., concurring).

[124] *Id.*

[125] *Id.* at 974 (Spina, J., dissenting).

opposite sex."[126] Justice Spina's position sounds strikingly similar to the argument once proffered to support anti-miscegenation laws and rejected by the United States Supreme Court in *Loving v. Virginia*.[127] There it was claimed that the state law banning interracial marriage was not racially discriminatory because it treated the white and black races precisely the same, both were similarly limited to marrying a person of the same race. The Supreme Court, however, was unpersuaded by that claim, noting that the miscegenation law "rest(ed) solely upon distinction drawn according to race" and therefore were subject to the "most rigid scrutiny."[128]

Be that as it may, the onus of the Massachusetts marriage law seems to be more in the nature of discrimination based on sexual orientation than gender-based discrimination. After all, the impact of the law falls entirely upon gay and lesbian persons who want to enter into a same-sex marriage.[129] Gay and lesbian persons are denied the right to marry the partner of their choice while heterosexual individuals are not. In its practical effect, the law seems to discriminate on the basis of sexual orientation, more so than on the basis of gender.

Nevertheless, in his dissenting opinion, Justice Spina further claimed that the state marriage law did not discriminate on the basis of sexual orientation.[130] Under the law, he claimed, no one is disqualified from marrying on the basis of sexual orientation; all persons are free to marry "within the institution of marriage."[131]

This, of course, overlooks that the marriage laws have a discriminatory impact on the basis of sexual orientation; gay and lesbian individuals are denied the right to marry the partner of their choice while heterosexual persons are not. Furthermore, in claiming that there is no discrimination here, Justice Spina is merely repeating the same tautological argument he previously made, an argument that begs the question by assuming that marriage can be nothing more than a union between a man and a woman.

In stark contrast to Justice Spina, Justice Greaney thought that the Massachusetts marriage law created "a straightforward case of

---

[126] *Id.*

[127] Loving v. Virginia, 388 U.S. 1 (1967).

[128] *Id.* at 11.

[129] *See supra* at notes 2–10 (discussion of Tanner v. Oregon Health Sciences University, ruling that state law denying gay and lesbian couples health and insurance benefits available to opposite-sex married couples had discriminatory impact on basis of sexual orientation.)

[130] *Goodridge*, 798 N.E.2d at 975 (Spina, J., dissenting).

[131] *Id.*

discrimination that disqualifies an entire group of citizens and their families from participation in an institution of paramount legal and social importance."[132] Justice Greaney pointed out that the rights of couples to have children, adopt, and be foster parents, regardless of sexual orientation or marital status, was firmly established in Massachusetts, yet the state's refusal to recognize same-sex marriage created a system in which the children of same-sex couples were unable to partake in the many legal protections and social benefits readily available to other children.[133] "The continued maintenance of this caste-like system," said Justice Greaney, "is irreconcilable with, indeed, totally repugnant to, the State's strong interest in the welfare of all children...."[134]

Justice Greaney stated that he did not doubt the sincerity of deeply held moral or religious beliefs in the traditional view that marriage can only be a union between a man and a woman.[135] Nonetheless, he said, neither tradition nor individual conviction can justify the continuation of a hierarchy in which same-sex couples and their families are deemed less worthy of social and legal recognition than others.[136] Taking a humanistic approach, he observed that:

> The plaintiffs are members of our community, our neighbors, our coworkers, our friends....(T)heir professions include investment advisor, computer engineer, teacher, therapist, and lawyer. (They) volunteer in our schools, worship beside us in our religious houses, and have children who play with our children, to mention just a few ordinary daily contacts. We share a common humanity and participate together in the social contract that is the foundation of our Commonwealth. Simple principles of decency dictate that we extend to the plaintiffs, and to their new status, full acceptance, tolerance, and respect. We should do so because it is the right thing to do.[137]

After concluding that there was no justification for denying same-sex couples the right to marry, the court granted the plaintiffs' request to declare that barring same-sex marriage was in violation of the

---

[132] *Id.* at 970 (Greaney, J., concurring).
[133] *Id.* at 972.
[134] *Id.*
[135] *Id.* at 971, 973.
[136] *Id.* at 973.
[137] *Id.*

Massachusetts Constitution.[138] In addition, following the lead of a previous decision by the Court of Appeals of Ontario, the court decided to "refine" the common-law meaning of marriage so as to construe civil marriage as referring to the voluntary union of two persons as spouses, thus allowing same-sex marriage.[139]

As might be expected, the court's ruling that it violated the constitution for the commonwealth not to allow same-sex marriage was denounced as usurping the role of the legislature, which, it was claimed, should have the sole authority to control the definition of marriage.[140] Building on that theme, it was stressed that such a dramatic change in social institutions should only occur at the behest of the people through the democratic process.[141] The court, though, thought that these arguments misunderstood the role of the judiciary in exercising judicial review.[142] As the court explained, the Massachusetts Constitution places limits on what the legislature can do, and it is the function of the judiciary to insure that those limits are enforced.[143] To claim that the court was usurping the role of the legislature was to misunderstand the nature and purpose of judicial review. While the court admitted that considerable deference was owed to the legislature to decide social and policy issues, nonetheless it is the traditional and settled function of courts to enforce constitutional norms.[144] If complete deference was granted to the legislature, the judiciary would be divested of its constitutional authority to resolve challenges to laws concerning marriage, child rearing, and family relations; the courts would be powerless to invalidate unconstitutional laws, including those, for example, that mandate forced sterilization, prohibit miscegenation, or otherwise restrict an individual's right of privacy.[145] This, of course, would be contrary to our constitutional tradition.

Sometime after the decision in *Goodridge*, the Massachusetts legislature requested an advisory opinion[146] from the Massachusetts Supreme

---

[138] *Id.* at 953 (majority opinion).
[139] *Id.*
[140] *Id.* at 1003–5 (Cordy, J., dissenting).
[141] *Id.* at 977 (Spina, J., dissenting).
[142] *Id.* at 965–67 (majority opinion).
[143] *Id.* at 966.
[144] *Id.*
[145] *Id.* at 966–67.
[146] Each branch of the Massachusetts legislature as well as the governor and the executive council has authority to require advisory opinions from the supreme court on important questions of law. Mass. Const., art. II, ch. III.

Court concerning a bill pending before the legislature that would allow civil unions for same-sex couples but prohibit same-sex marriage. In response to the legislative request, the court issued an opinion declaring that civil union was not an adequate substitute for civil marriage and that to continue to disallow same-sex marriage would be a violation of the state constitution.[147] In other words, nothing short of marriage itself for same-sex couples would suffice to comply with the court's previous ruling. In the court's eyes, there was a wide gulf between civil union and civil marriage, a "dissimilitude" that was far from innocuous and that had the effect of assigning same-sex couples to "second class status."[148] The bill in question purported to make civil union parallel to civil marriage, yet separate from it, leading the court to observe that "separate is seldom, if ever, equal."[149] The court acknowledged that federal law currently barred recognition by the federal government of same-sex marriages and also permitted other states to refuse to recognize same-sex marriages.[150] But that does not mean, the court continued, that state constitutional protections should not be made available to their fullest extent in Massachusetts.[151] By excluding same-sex couples from civil marriage, the bill under consideration would have the effect of maintaining and fostering "a stigma of exclusion that the Constitution prohibits."[152]

The decision of the Massachusetts Supreme Court in *Goodridge* had a stunning impact across the nation, arousing strong feelings both for and against it. There were demonstrations, counter demonstrations, debates, editorials, articles, and discussions across the nation.[153] Even the President weighed in, calling for a federal constitutional amendment that would ban same-sex marriage.[154] After *Goodridge* was decided, city officials in California, New Mexico, Oregon, and New York authorized the issuance of marriage licenses to same-sex couples, but courts in all four states subsequently voided those actions.[155] In New York, lower court

---

[147] Opinion of the Justices to the Senate, 802 N.E.2d 565, 570 (2004).

[148] *Id.*

[149] *Id.* at 569.

[150] *Id.* at 570.

[151] *Id.* at 571.

[152] *Id.* at 570.

[153] *See* Kavan Peterson, *Wash., New York Say No to Gay Marriage*, March 29, 2005, http://www.stateline.org/live/details/story?contentId=20695

[154] Elisabeth Bumiller, *Bush Backs Ban in Constitution on Gay Marriage*, <u>New York Times</u>, Feb. 25 2004, at A1.

[155] *See* Peterson, *supra* note 153.

judges created confusion across the state by issuing conflicting decisions concerning the constitutionality of laws barring same-sex marriage, resulting in appeals to the state's highest court, which eventually ruled that the state marriage laws that allowed only opposite-sex couples to marry did not violate the New York Constitution.[156]

In May of 2004, same-sex couples began to marry in Massachusetts and each year since then thousands of same-sex marriages have been performed in the Commonwealth.[157] Not too long after the *Goodridge* decision, the Massachusetts legislature voted to amend the state constitution to ban same-sex marriage, but allow civil unions; however, under the state constitution, the legislature must re-approve the measure a second time and then submit it to a statewide vote before it may go into effect. Since that initial vote, the Commonwealth's legislature has had a change of heart, rejecting efforts to amend the constitution to prohibit same-sex marriage. In 2007, the legislature voted 151 to 45 against the proposed constitutional amendment, which needed 50 favorable votes to be presented to the voters in a referendum.[158] As a consequence, further attempts to enact the amendment will have to be started anew, and any amendment cannot possibly be on the ballot until 2012.[159] So, same-sex marriage remains valid in Massachusetts and continues to be performed there.

In several other states, the legislatures have enacted civil union or domestic partnership laws that provide legal benefits to same-sex couples. The Vermont legislature, in response to the state supreme court's decision in *Baker v. State*, enacted a civil union law providing comprehensive benefits and protections (akin to marriage rights) for same-sex couples. In addition to Vermont, three other states—Connecticut, New Hampshire, and New Jersey—have enacted laws authorizing civil unions.[160] Of those states, New Hampshire earned the distinction of becoming the first state to allow same-sex unions without being under a court order or the threat of one to do so.[161]

---

[156] Hernandez v. Robles, 855 N.E.2d 1 (N.Y. 2006).
[157] *Gay marriage ripe for decision in 3 courts*, www. stateline.org (updated June 15, 2007).
[158] Pam Belluck, *Massachusetts Gay Marriage to Remain Legal*, New York Times, June 15, 2007.
[159] *Id.*
[160] *Same-sex marriage and alternatives*, www.stateline.org (updated May 31, 2007).
[161] *New Hampshire Senate Approves Civil Unions*, New York Times, April 26, 2007.

California, Hawaii, Maine, Oregon, and Washington all have adopted domestic partnership laws that provide certain legal rights to same-sex couples.[162]

The decision in *Goodridge* gave renewed impetus to the Defense of Marriage Act (DOMA),[163] originally enacted by Congress in 1996, in reaction to the Hawaii Supreme Court's decision in *Baehr v. Lewin*, which had paved the way for same-sex marriage in that state until the citizens of Hawaii voted to amend the state constitution to allow the legislature to reserve marriage to opposite-sex couples. For purposes of federal law, DOMA defines marriage as the legal union of a man and a woman as husband and wife.[164] In addition, DOMA authorizes a state to refuse to give effect to same-sex marriages performed in another state. Since the enactment of this federal law, 42 states have adopted their own version of DOMA, similarly defining marriage as the union of a man and woman and barring recognition of same-sex marriages performed in another state.[165] Twenty-seven of those states have enacted DOMA as amendments to their state constitutions, thereby precluding the courts in those states from finding a prohibition of same-sex marriage to be unconstitutional.[166] In some of those states, the constitutional amendments also ban same-sex civil unions or similar partnership laws.[167]

Since *Goodridge* was decided, courts in several states have declined to follow it.[168] In *Morrison v. Sadler*, the Supreme Court of Indiana, in ruling that a prohibition of same-sex marriage did not violate the state constitution, expressly declined to follow *Goodridge*. The Indiana court was critical of the majority analysis in *Goodridge*, suggesting that it was faulty by purporting to apply rationality review while actually using a more strict form of scrutiny.[169] This was inconsistent with the approach taken in

---

[162] *Same-sex marriage and alternatives*, www.stateline.org (updated May 31, 2007).

[163] Defense of Marriage Act, Pub. L. No. 104–199, 110 Stat. 2419 (1996) (codified at 1 U.S.C. §7 (2000) and 28 U.S.C. §1738C (2000)).

[164] *Id.*

[165] *Same-sex marriage and alternatives*, www.stateline.org (updated May 31, 2007).

[166] *Id.*

[167] *Id.*

[168] Morrison v. Sadler, 821 N.E.2d 15 (Ind. 2005); Seymour v. Holcomb, 790 N.Y.S.2d 858 (N.Y. Sup. Crt. 2005). *See also*, Lewis v. Harris, 875 A.2d 259, 273–74 (N.J. 2005) (declining to follow *Goodridge*, but noting that New Jersey had enacted a Domestic Partnership Act that entitled same-sex couples to many of the same legal benefits enjoyed by married opposite-sex couples); Hernandez v. Robles, 855 N.E.2d 1 (N.Y. 2006).

[169] *Morrison, id.* at 28–9.

Indiana, which affords "substantial deference" to legislative classifications.[170] Under the extremely deferential approach followed in Indiana, the burden is "entirely" on the plaintiffs to overcome the presumption of constitutionality granted to legislation.[171] That being so, the court found in *Morrison* that the plaintiffs had failed to show that the prohibition of same-sex marriage was manifestly unreasonable or arbitrary.[172] There was, the court said, an inherent difference between opposite-sex and same-sex couples that rationally distinguished them—the ability to procreate "naturally."[173] In the court's view, the state had a legitimate interest in restricting marriage to opposite-sex couples in order to encourage "responsible procreation" within "the relatively stable institution of marriage."[174] Accepting that it was not unreasonable for the state to favor "marital procreation,"[175] the Indiana high court concluded that the state marriage laws were not unconstitutional.[176]

Other courts, applying minimal scrutiny, also have found that it is reasonable for a state to prohibit same-sex marriage in order to encourage procreation and child-rearing within the marital relationship.[177] "There can be no doubt," one court proclaimed, that it is rational to restrict marriage to opposite-sex couples because marriage is "the appropriate and desirable forum for procreation and the rearing of children."[178]

Of course, that rationale is only acceptable under an extremely deferential form of minimal scrutiny. Under more meaningful scrutiny, considerable doubt exists concerning the reasonableness of a state prohibiting same-sex marriage in order to encourage procreation and child-rearing within a marital relationship. To start, that rationale assumes that state policy favors procreation and child-rearing within an opposite-sex marriage despite a number of indications to the contrary. First, as pointed out in *Goodridge*, neither an intent nor ability to procreate is a requirement of marriage, which suggests that encouraging procreation within a marital

---

[170] *Id.* at 29. The court also described this as a "high degree of deference." *Id.* at 31.
[171] *Id.* at 21.
[172] *Id.* at 22.
[173] *Id.* at 31.
[174] *Id.* at 28–31.
[175] The court used this phrase several times in its opinion. *See, e.g., id.* at 23.
[176] *Id.* at 29–31.
[177] *See, e.g.,* Standhardt v. Superior Court, 77 P.3d 451, 463–64 (Ct. App. Ariz. 2003); Singer v. Hara, 522 P.2d 1187, 1195–97 (Wash. Ct. App. 1974).
[178] Singer v. Hara, 522 P.2d at 1195.

relationship may not be so important to the state.[179] Moreover, in most states the law manifestly encourages all types of families. As was true in Massachusetts, many states actively support bringing children into a family regardless of whether the intended parent is married or not, whether the child is adopted or born into the family, whether technology was used as an aid to conceive the child, and whether the parent or partner is heterosexual, homosexual, or bisexual.[180] In today's world, there are many different kinds of families and most states countenance all types of families, especially because it is in the best interest of children to do so. These aspects of state law belie the assumption that state policy favors procreation and child-rearing within a traditional family over other ways of creating a family.

In addition, prohibiting same-sex marriage hardly advances the goal of encouraging procreation and child-rearing within the marital relationship. As the court found in *Goodridge*, it is implausible to suggest that allowing same-sex marriage will lead to a decrease in the number of persons who decide to enter into opposite-sex marriages in order to have children.[181] Nor will same-sex marriage otherwise harm traditional families. Allowing same-sex marriage in no way interferes with procreation or child-rearing within opposite-sex marriage, but it does harm same-sex couples and their children by denying them legal benefits, financial security, and making child-rearing more difficult. Excluding same-sex couples from marrying does nothing to benefit the children of opposite-sex marriages or their parents, but it does deprive children of same-sex couples the considerable benefits that flow from a stable family structure. In truth, limiting marriage to opposite-sex couples does virtually nothing to advance procreation and child-rearing within marriage, but it does cause considerable harm to the members of same-sex families.

---

[179] Goodridge v. Department of Public Health, 798 N.E.2d 941, 961 (Mass. 2003).
[180] *Id.* at 962–64.
[181] *Id.* at 962–63.

CHAPTER SEVEN

THE RIGHT OF INTIMATE ASSOCIATION

Sexual Relations Between Consenting Adults (Married or Not)

At common law, sodomy, which usually referred to oral or anal sexual intercourse or sex with an animal, was a crime. At one time or another, all of the states adopted various criminal laws forbidding sodomy and many states also criminally prohibited fornication and adultery. Until 1961, all states outlawed sodomy.[1] Some sodomy statutes proscribed all oral or anal intercourse, including that between a married man and woman. Other sodomy statutes applied only to contact between unmarried persons and yet other statutes applied only to contact between persons of the same sex.[2] However, it was not until 1971 that any state singled out same-sex activity as a crime, and only nine states did so.[3] In 1955, the American Law Institute promulgated the Model Penal Code, which took the position that consensual sexual relations conducted in private should not be made a crime.[4] By 2003, all but 13 of the states had repealed their laws prohibiting sodomy.[5] In nine of those states the sodomy laws applied to opposite-sex as well as same-sex activity.[6]

In 1977, in *State v. Saunders*, the supreme court of New Jersey ruled that a state fornication statute that prohibited sexual intercourse between

---

[1] *See* Bowers v. Hardwick, 478 U.S. 186, 193 (1986), *overruled by* Lawrence v. Texas, 539 U.S. 558 (2003).

[2] Jennifer Friesen, *State Constitutional Law: Litigating Individual Rights, Claims, and Defenses* 2–72 (3d ed. 2000).

[3] Lawrence v. Texas, *supra* note 1.

[4] *Id.* at 572 (citing American Law Institute, Model Penal Code, §213.2, comment 2, (1980)).

[5] *Id.* at 573.

[6] *Id.*

a man (married or single) and an unmarried woman violated the right of privacy protected by both the state and Federal Constitutions.[7] Turning first to federal decisions, the court traced the development of the right of privacy under the Federal Constitution, noting that its scope encompassed the right of individual autonomy concerning intimate human activities and relationships.[8] By the time of the court's decision, it was settled that the right of privacy guaranteed by the Federal Constitution had an analogue in the New Jersey Constitution that protected the fundamental right of consenting adults to engage in private sexual relations.[9] Sexual relations between consenting adults, married or not, were considered a matter of fundamental personal choice, an integral aspect of an individual's right to decide private matters free from unwarranted governmental intrusion.[10]

In upholding this fundamental right to privacy, the court rejected the state's argument that its statute served the compelling interests of preventing venereal disease and the propagation of illegitimate children. The statute was not an effective means of preventing venereal disease and, in fact, may have been counter productive of that goal by deterring affected persons from coming forward for treatment, for fear that they would be criminally prosecuted.[11] Along the same lines, the court concluded that the statute could not be justified as a means of preventing the propagation of illegitimate children because it did very little to accomplish that goal.[12]

The court also was unimpressed by the state's argument that by preventing illicit sex the statute encouraged marriage and protected public morals. Whether or not abstention from sexual relations was likely to induce persons to marry, the statute was not a permissible method of fostering marriage.[13] To allow the state to coerce people into marriage would undermine the very autonomy that lies at the core of the right of privacy.[14] The decision to marry is of a highly personal nature that should be free from official coercion or sanction and beyond the regulatory

---

7 State v. Saunders, 381 A.2d 333 (N.J. 1977).
8 *Id.* at 337–39.
9 *Id.* at 341.
10 *Id.* at 339–41.
11 *Id.* at 341–42.
12 *Id.* at 342.
13 *Id.*
14 *Id.*

power of the state.[15] Nor was the statute a permissible means of upholding public morals. As the court put it:

> Fornication may be abhorrent to the morals and deeply held belief of many persons. But any appropriate "remedy" for such conduct cannot come from legislative fiat. Private personal acts between two consenting adults are not to be lightly meddled with by the State. The right of personal autonomy is fundamental to a free society. Persons who view fornication as opprobrious conduct may seek strenuously to dissuade people from engaging in it. However, they may not inhibit such conduct through the coercive power of the criminal law ....[T]he liberty which is the birthright of every individual suffers dearly when the State can so grossly intrude on personal autonomy.[16]

A few years after the *Saunders* decision in New Jersey, two courts in other states struck down sodomy statutes that criminalized "deviate sexual intercourse" (oral or anal sex) between persons who were not husband and wife.[17] In *Commonwealth v. Bonadio*, the Supreme Court of Pennsylvania ruled that the statute in question exceeded the proper bounds of the state police power and violated state and federal equal protection clauses.[18] Referring to the philosophy of John Stuart Mill, the court took the position that the state had no authority to regulate individual behavior that caused no harm to others.[19] The court maintained that the police power of the state does not include the authority to enforce moral dictates regulating the private conduct of consenting adults.[20] Many issues that are thought to be matters of morals are subject to debate, and there is no sufficient state interest that justifies legislation of moral standards simply because a particular belief has majority approval.[21] Notions of morality are relative; they change with the times and their

---

[15] *Id.*

[16] *Id.* at 342–43.

[17] Commonwealth v. Bonadio, 415 A.2d 47 (Pa. 1980); People v. Onofre, 415 N.E.2d 936 (N.Y. 1980). *See also*, State v. Pilcher, 242 N.W.2d 348 (Iowa 1976) (ruling that an Iowa sodomy statute was an unconstitutional violation of the federal right of privacy to the extent that it attempted to criminalize consensual sexual acts performed in private by adult persons of the opposite sex).

[18] Commonwealth v. Bonadio, *id.*

[19] *Id.* at 50.

[20] *Id.*

[21] *Id.*

social context.[22] Thus, the court concluded that although "deviate sexual intercourse" may be considered by some to be an abhorrent crime against nature and a sin against God, it is not properly within the realm of the state's police power.[23]

The Pennsylvania high court further ruled that by making "deviate" acts criminal only when performed by unmarried persons, the statute in question infringed the right to equal protection of the laws guaranteed by the state and Federal Constitutions, there being absolutely no reason to prohibit unmarried persons from engaging in certain sexual behavior while allowing married persons to engage in the very same behavior.[24] As the court said, to suggest that deviate acts are heinous if performed by unmarried persons but acceptable when done by married persons lacks even a rational basis.[25]

In *People v. Onofre*, the Court of Appeals of New York held that a state penal law proscribing "deviate sexual intercourse" between persons not married to one another violated the right of privacy and the right to equal protection of the laws guaranteed by the Federal Constitution.[26] Noting that previous decisions of the United States Supreme Court established a constitutional right of privacy or autonomy to make certain personal decisions free from governmental interference, the New York court interpreted those decisions to extend to the right of an unmarried individual to engage in consensual acts of sexual intimacy, so long as they were non-commercial and occurred in private.[27] And because these acts were non-commercial and occurred in private, the state would not be heard to assert that the law forbidding the acts served to advance public morality. In the court's view, the regulation of intimate sexual behavior out of view of the public and with no commercial component did nothing to advance the cause of public morality.[28] Finally, the court found that there was no rational explanation for the law's discrimination between married and unmarried persons.[29] Accordingly, the court ruled that the New York law

---

[22] *Id.*
[23] *Id.*
[24] *Id.* at 51.
[25] *Id.*
[26] People v. Onofre, *supra* note 17.
[27] *Id.* at 939–41.
[28] *Id.* at 941.
[29] *Id.* at 942–43.

violated the right of unmarried persons to equal protection of the laws as well as violating their right of privacy.

These decisions were part of a growing recognition that an individual's sex life was a private matter that simply was no business of the government. As such, they established a firm basis for expanding the right of privacy to include sexual activities. The right of privacy, then, comprehended a right of intimate association.

Gay and Lesbian Sexual Relations

In 1986, the United States Supreme Court decided *Bowers v. Hardwick*, upholding the constitutionality of a Georgia criminal law prohibiting sodomy and ruling that the right of privacy does not encompass the right of a consenting adult to engage in homosexual conduct, even in the privacy of his or her home.[30] Decided by the slimmest of margins, *Bowers* was viewed by many as an egregious decision that took an excessively cramped view of the Due Process Clause of the Fourteenth Amendment that was intolerant to the point of cruelty.[31] Eventually the high Court would end up apologizing for its decision in *Bowers* and would unceremoniously overrule it in *Lawrence v. Texas*.[32] But it would take seventeen years for the Court to do so, and in the meantime a number of state courts would step into the breach by turning to their state constitutions to protect the right of intimate association and strike down laws making sodomy a crime. In fact, those state decisions would play a role in convincing the Supreme Court that its decision in *Bowers* had been in error and should be overruled.[33]

---

[30] Bowers v. Hardwick, 478 U.S. 186 (1986), *overruled* by Lawrence v. Texas, 539 U.S. 558 (2003).

[31] *See, e.g.,* Daniel O. Conkle, *The Second Death of Substantive Due Process,* 62 Ind. L.J. 215 (1987); Thomas B. Stoddard, *Bowers v. Hardwick: Precedent by Personal Predilection,* 54 U. Chi. L. Rev. 648 (1987); William N. Eskridge, Jr., *Hardwick and Historiography,* 1999 U. Ill. L. Rev. 631 (1999).

[32] *Lawrence,* 539 U.S. at 578.

[33] In explaining its willingness to overrule *Bowers,* the Supreme Court stated: "The foundations of *Bowers* have sustained serious erosion from our recent decisions in *Casey* and *Romer.* When our precedent has been thus weakened, criticism from other sources is of greater significance. In the United States criticism of *Bowers* has been substantial and continuing, disapproving of its reasoning in all respects, not just as to its historical assumptions. (Citations omitted.) The courts of five different States have declined to follow it in interpreting provisions in their own state constitutions parallel to the Due Process Clause of the Fourteenth Amendment. (Citations omitted.)" *Lawrence,* 539 U.S. at 576.

In the seventeen year interim between *Bowers* and *Lawrence*, courts in five states (one of which was Georgia) rejected both the reasoning and result of *Bowers* to strike down criminal laws that punished adult consensual homosexual activity as violating either state constitutional provisions that expressly protect the right of privacy or more general constitutional provisions that have been interpreted to protect the right of privacy.[34] The first decision of a state supreme court to do so was *Commonwealth v. Wasson*, in which the Supreme Court of Kentucky ruled that a statute making it a crime to engage in sexual activity with a person of the same sex violated the right of individual liberty guaranteed by the Kentucky Constitution and the right of equal treatment also guaranteed by the Kentucky Constitution.[35]

In *Wasson*, the Kentucky Supreme Court emphatically refused to march in lock step with the United States Supreme Court in determining whether there was a constitutional right to engage in intimate sexual relations with a person of the same sex.[36] The Kentucky high court proclaimed that under the system of dual sovereignty that exists in the nation, it is the court's own responsibility to interpret and apply the state constitution independently of federal constitutional doctrine[37] The Bill of Rights in the Federal Constitution represents neither the primary source nor the maximum guarantee of state constitutional liberty, and state constitutional guarantees against intrusive state power do not derive from the Federal Constitution.[38] While decisions of the United States Supreme Court concerning individual rights are entitled to respect, they are in no

---

[34] Jegley v. Picado, 80 S.W.3d 332 (Ark. 2002); Powell v. State, 510 S.E.2d 18 (Ga. 1998); Gryczan v. State, 942 P.2d 112 (Mont. 1997); Campbell v. Sundquist, 926 S.W.2d 250 (Tenn. App. 1996), appeal denied (June 10, 1996), appeal denied (Sept. 9, 1996); Commonwealth v. Wasson, 842 S.W.2d 487 (Ky. 1992). In addition, a Texas intermediate appellate court rejected *Bowers* in declaring a same-sex sodomy statute unconstitutional. State v. Morales, 826 S.W.2d 201 (Tex. App. 1992). However, that decision was later vacated for lack of jurisdiction by the Texas Supreme Court, 869 S.W.2d 941 (Tex. 1994).

[35] Commonwealth v. Wasson, 842 S.W.2d 487, 500–501 (Ky. 1992). *Wasson* actually was the second state decision to reject *Bowers*. The first was State v. Morales, *id.*, which was decided seven months before *Wasson*. *Morales*, though, was an intermediate appellate court decision and, as previously noted, was later overruled for lack of jurisdiction. *Id.* Mention should also be made of *State v. Ciuffini*, 395 A.2d 904 (N.J. Super. Ct. 1978), a decision of the Appellate Division of the New Jersey Superior Court prior to *Bowers*, ruling that a statute criminalizing same-sex activity was a violation of the right of privacy.

[36] *Id.* at 492.

[37] *Id.*

[38] *Id.*

way binding on the Kentucky Supreme Court.[39] So long as state constitutional protection does not fall below the federal floor, a state is free as a matter of its own law to grant more expansive rights than is dictated by federal law.[40]

Moreover, the court thought that there were several special considerations in this particular case calling for independence from federal law. First, there were structural and textual differences between the Federal Bill of Rights and the Kentucky one, which suggested a different path for Kentucky than the one taken in *Bowers*.[41] More significantly, Kentucky had a rich and compelling tradition of protecting individual liberties from government intrusion that could be traced back at least as far as the Debates of the Kentucky Constitutional Convention of 1890 and to cases from the era when that Constitution was adopted.[42] The Kentucky Supreme Court first recognized the constitutional concept of personal liberty in 1909, when it decided *Commonwealth v. Campbell*, which ruled that an ordinance that made it a crime to possess intoxicating liquor, even for private use, was a violation of the Kentucky Bill of Rights.[43] The court's opinion in *Campbell* established the principle that the state has no authority to restrict the liberty of an individual except where his or her conduct will cause some harm to the public.[44] This prescription, the court indicated in *Campbell*, is based on the state Bill of Rights, which declares that seeking safety and happiness is an inalienable right and that the state cannot possess arbitrary power over the lives, liberty, or property of its citizens.[45] Taking a page (or two) from the philosophy of John Stuart Mill, the court adopted his belief that in a just society the only purpose for which power may rightfully be exercised over an individual against his or her will is to prevent harm to others.[46] The government, therefore, possesses no authority to invade the "privacy" of a person's life to regulate conduct in matters that concern the individual alone and do not directly injure society.[47]

---

[39] *Id.*

[40] *Id.*

[41] *Id.*

[42] *Id.*

[43] Commonwealth v. Campbell, 117 S.W. 383 (Ky. 1909).

[44] *Id.* at 385.

[45] *Id.*

[46] *Id.* at 386 (quoting John Stuart Mill, *On Liberty*).

[47] *Id.*

When *Wasson* was decided, it was apparent that *Campbell* and its progeny made a deep impression on the Kentucky Supreme Court, leading it to believe that the authority of the state over an individual is limited to those situations where his or her conduct injuriously affects other persons. The "clear implication" of previous decisions, the high court said in *Wasson*, "is that immorality in private which does 'not operate to the detriment of others,' is placed beyond the reach of state action by the guarantees of liberty in the Kentucky Constitution."[48] Therefore, the court concluded that, "The right of privacy has been recognized as an integral part of the guarantee of liberty in our 1891 Kentucky Constitution since its inception."[49]

In *Wasson*, after concluding that the right of privacy was an integral aspect of the guarantee of liberty in the state constitution, the court turned its attention to the guarantee of equality in the state constitution, noting that the Kentucky law criminalizing intimate sexual relations with a person of the same sex discriminated against homosexuals.[50] That is, the law proscribed "deviate" sexual activity between persons of the same sex, but did not proscribe the very same activity when engaged in by persons of the opposite sex. In the court's view, then, the essential issue presented by the case was not whether sexual activity traditionally viewed as immoral could be punished, but whether it could be punished solely on the basis of sexual orientation.[51]

In determining that issue, the court rebuffed the argument made by the Commonwealth that homosexuals were not a protected class under the state constitution.[52] To the contrary, the court explained that classifications based on sexual orientation bear many of the characteristics of a suspect classification deserving of special constitutional protection.[53] "As subjects of age-old discrimination and disapproval, homosexuals form virtually a discrete and insular minority."[54] Their sexual orientation is in all probability a trait determined by causes beyond their control, and, if not immutable, is extremely difficult to alter.[55] Hence, the court held that

---

[48] Commonwealth v. Wasson, 842 S.W.2d at 496.
[49] *Id.* at 495.
[50] Commonwealth v. Wasson, 842 S.W.2d at 499.
[51] *Id.*
[52] *Id.* at 499–500.
[53] *Id.* at 499–500 (quoting Laurence Tribe, *American Constitutional Law* 1616 (2d ed. 1988)).
[54] *Id.* at 500.
[55] *Id.*

homosexuals are "a separate and identifiable class for Kentucky constitutional analysis because no class of persons can be discriminated against under the Kentucky Constitution."[56] All persons are entitled to equal treatment, the court continued, unless there is "a substantial governmental interest, a rational basis, for different treatment."[57]

In the court's opinion, there was no rational basis to single out homosexual acts for different treatment.[58] The court rejected as "simply outrageous" the arguments of the state that homosexuals are more promiscuous than heterosexuals, are a threat to children, and are more prone to engage in sex acts in public.[59] In fact, in its attempt to justify the statute, the only assertion made by the state that possessed even superficial validity was the assertion that infectious diseases are more readily transmitted by anal intercourse than by other forms of sexual copulation.[60] But that could hardly explain why the statute prohibited homosexual acts aside from anal intercourse or why anal intercourse between a male and female was not prohibited.[61]

In the final analysis, the only purpose served by the statute was to single out homosexuals for punishment for engaging in the same activity that heterosexuals were at liberty to perform.[62] In a society "that no longer criminalizes adultery, fornication, or deviate sexual intercourse between heterosexuals," there was no rational basis to single out homosexual conduct for different treatment.[63] Therefore, the court concluded that the statute was an arbitrary denial of equality and liberty in violation of the Kentucky Constitution.[64]

As the first decision of a state supreme court to reject *Bowers*, the Kentucky Supreme Court's ruling in *Wasson* set an example for other states to emulate, and a number of them were quick to do so. Several state supreme courts, like their counterpart in Kentucky, were inclined to establish an historical basis for the right of privacy. Proudly claiming to be a "pioneer in the realm of the right of privacy," the Supreme Court of Georgia recounted the "long and distinguished history" of the right of

---

[56] *Id.*

[57] *Id.*

[58] *Id.* at 501.

[59] *Id.*

[60] *Id.*

[61] *Id.*

[62] *Id.*

[63] *Id.*

[64] *Id.* at 500.

privacy in Georgia that dated back to 1905.[65] The Supreme Court of Arkansas, looking to state constitutional language and case law, as well as state statutes and rules, concluded that Arkansas enjoyed a "rich and compelling tradition of protecting individual privacy."[66] And in Tennessee, the Court of Appeals, referring to the drafters of the 1796 state constitution, the language of the document, and its later development, found "a strong historic commitment by the citizens of this State to individual liberty and freedom from governmental interference in their personal lives."[67] Others states, where the historical pedigree for the right of privacy was not so venerable, still were not deterred from recognizing a constitutional foundation for the right of privacy. In Montana, the task was in part straightforward, given that the state constitution contained a provision expressly guaranteeing the right of privacy.[68] What was more difficult was to construe the constitutional guarantee of privacy to encompass a right of intimate association, which the Supreme Court of Montana was able to accomplish by resorting to (of all things!) federal precedent generally defining the right of privacy and then stretching the contours of that definition beyond the then prevailing federal bounds.[69]

In the five state cases rejecting *Bowers* and recognizing a right of intimate association prior to the Supreme Court's decision in *Lawrence v. Texas*, the courts turned to a variety of constitutional provisions to find a home for the right of privacy. In Montana, the choice was obvious because, as just noted, that state's constitution contains a provision that expressly secures the right of privacy. In several other states, the courts determined that the right of privacy was within the scope of "liberty" afforded protection by their respective state constitutions. The Supreme Court of Kentucky determined that the right of privacy was part of the liberty guaranteed by several sections in the state bill of rights, most notably section 1, which states that all persons have the "right of enjoying and defending their lives and liberties," and section 2, which states that "absolute and arbitrary power over the lives, liberty and property of freemen exists nowhere in a republic."[70] In both Georgia and Tennessee, courts ruled that the right of privacy was an aspect of liberty guaranteed

---

[65] Powell v. State, *supra* note 34, at 21–22.
[66] Jegley v. Picado, *supra* note 34, at 346–50.
[67] Campbell v. Sundquist, *supra* note 34.
[68] Gryczan v. State, *supra* note 34.
[69] *Id.* at 122–23.
[70] Commonwealth v. Wasson, *supra* note 35, at 494.

by the constitutional mandate that no person shall be deprived of liberty except by due process of law.[71] Whereas in Arkansas, the state supreme court adopted an approach reminiscent of the "penumbra theory" used by the United States Supreme Court in *Griswold v. Connecticut.*[72] The court believed that a flexible approach similar to the one utilized in *Griswold* was warranted by a provision in the Arkansas Constitution stating that "the enumeration of rights shall not be construed to deny or disparage others retained by the people."[73] Noting that privacy was a value underlying a number of provisions in the state constitution, as well as many state statutes, the court concluded that the right of privacy was "implicit in the Arkansas Constitution."[74]

In interpreting the right of privacy to encompass a right of intimate association, courts have referred to various theories of privacy. As noted above, in *Wasson*, the Supreme Court of Kentucky based its ruling recognizing a right of intimate association on the Millian principle that individual liberty may only be restricted in order to prevent harm to others. That principle also influenced the Supreme Court of Georgia in its decision upholding the right of intimate association. Liberty, the Georgia court proclaimed, includes "the right to live as one will, so long as that will does not interfere with the right of another or of the public."[75] In the view of the Georgia high court, that aspect of privacy was tied to another aspect of privacy, namely, the right to be let alone, which of course has a long history in Georgia.[76] The right of personal liberty, the court explained, embraces the right to withdraw from the public gaze at such times as a person may see fit.[77] There is a "right to be let alone" so long as (a person) was not interfering with the rights of other individuals or of the public.[78]

Courts also have turned to notions of spatial privacy as a theoretical basis for establishing a right of intimate association. In striking down a law prohibiting same-sex contact, the Court of Appeals of Tennessee pointed to the "sanctity of the home," and declared that an adult's right to

---

71 Powell v. State, *supra* note 34, at 21; Campbell v. Sundquist, *supra* note 34, at 259.
72 Jegley v. Picado, *supra* note 34. The penumbra theory of *Griswold v. Connecticut* is discussed in Chapter Four.
73 *Jegley*, *supra* note 34, at 346–47 (referring to Ark. Const. art. 2, section 29).
74 *Id.* at 349–50.
75 Powell v. State, *supra* note 34, at 22.
76 *See* Chapter Four.
77 Powell v. State, *supra* note 34, at 22.
78 *Id.*

engage in consensual, noncommercial sexual activities in the privacy of the home lies at "the heart of Tennessee's protection of the right of privacy."[79] The Supreme Court of Montana, in striking down a statute criminalizing same-sex activity, combined the idea of spatial privacy with the right to be let alone.[80] As the court explained, there is an expectation of privacy in the bedroom, according to which individuals "fully and properly expect that their consensual sexual activities will not be subject to the prying eyes of others or to governmental snooping or regulation."[81] An individual's sexual activities, therefore, should remain "personal and private."[82]

Once the right of intimate association is afforded constitutional status, whether by a provision expressly guaranteeing privacy such as the one in Montana, by a more general protection of liberty, or by the penumbra theory, it will be treated as a fundamental right entitled to the most exacting degree of constitutional protection. As previously noted, fundamental rights are not absolute, but they may only be restricted upon the showing that the restriction in question is necessarily related to a compelling state interest. In the five cases upholding the right of intimate association, a number of claims were presented asserting that there were compelling reasons that justified restricting the right of intimate association through criminal laws prohibiting sodomy. In all of the cases, these claims were rejected.

Public Health

In some instances, the state has argued that laws prohibiting sexual relations between persons of the same sex serve a compelling state interest by preventing the spread of infectious diseases, particularly AIDS. While readily admitting that the prevention of disease is a compelling state interest, courts have found that criminal laws directed at same-sex activities do very little to serve that interest. To begin with, the assertion that AIDS can be contained by laws prohibiting same-sex contact rests "on faulty logic and invalid assumptions about the disease."[83] It assumes that

---

[79] Campbell v. Sundquist, *supra* note 34, at 261–62.
[80] Gryczan v. State, *supra* note 34.
[81] *Id.* at 122.
[82] *Id.*
[83] *Id.* at 123.

all same-sex activity risks spread of the disease, while conversely assuming that heterosexual sexual activity does not. This overlooks that sexual contact between women has an extremely low incidence of HIV transmission and heterosexual contact accounts for a significant proportion of HIV transmission.[84] In fact, heterosexual contact is the now the chief means of transmitting HIV in the United States.[85]

Criminal laws that target same-sex conduct tend to be grossly over- and under-inclusive. They prohibit all same-sex activity even though the people involved are disease free, practicing safe sex, or engaging in the kind of sexual contact that does not spread disease.[86] The Supreme Court of Montana noted that its statute proscribing deviate sexual conduct went so far as to define "deviate sexual relations" as including "sexual contact" between two persons of the same sex, which could encompass such innocuous activity as touching, caressing, and kissing.[87] While prohibiting same-sex activities that pose little, if any, risk of spreading disease, sodomy statutes often are not directed toward heterosexual activity that does pose a risk of spreading disease. It makes little sense to criminalize certain homosexual contact, such as anal intercourse, on the ground that it poses a health risk, while allowing the very same contact between a man and a woman. By criminalizing certain same-sex behavior not associated with the spread of AIDS or HIV but at the same time excluding high-risk heterosexual contact, statutes aimed only at same-sex contact bear a tenuous relationship to the goal of preventing disease.[88]

Moreover, in practical effect, criminal statutes that prohibit same-sex activity may well be counterproductive to public health goals.[89] According to public health officials, some gay persons infected with sexually transmitted diseases do not seek medical treatment or report their conditions due to fear of prosecution under criminal laws.[90] Public health experts generally agree that criminal sanctions are ineffective as a deterrent and can be extremely harmful to public education and other efforts to prevent disease.[91] As a means of changing behavior in this area, education and

---

[84] *Id.* at 124.

[85] *Id.*

[86] Campbell v. Sundquist, *supra* note 34, at 263.

[87] Gryczan v. State, *supra* note 34, at 124.

[88] *Id.*

[89] Campbell v. Sundquist, *supra* note 34, at 263–64.

[90] *Id.* at 264.

[91] Gryczan v. State, *supra* note 34, at 124.

counseling are decidedly more effective than criminal statutes, which frequently undermine public health efforts by causing people to conceal and distort information and by interfering with public education programs.[92] When all is said and done, criminal laws proscribing sexual behavior do precious little, if anything at all, toward promoting the public health.

Social Morality

It also has been argued that laws prohibiting same-sex activity are justified by the state interest in advancing social morality. According to this argument, the state has a compelling interest in protecting public morals and the legislature may enact laws that reflect the moral judgments and values of a majority of the citizenry. This argument, though, has not prevailed in the cases upholding the right of intimate association. In one case, a Texas court observed that it is disingenuous for the state to suggest that its statute forbidding same-sex contact serves to advance public morality when the state readily concedes that it rarely, if ever, enforces the statute.[93] In other cases, the courts, while admitting the right of the legislature to enact laws reflecting prevailing notions of morality, nonetheless have not found the advancement of morality compelling enough to override the fundamental right of intimate association.[94] The courts have observed that the authority of the legislature to make policy is defined by the state constitution and the ability of the legislature to regulate morals is not without constitutional limits.[95] Noting that what is considered to be "moral" changes with time and is dependent upon societal background, the courts have been reluctant to allow the legislature to enforce the morality of the majority upon individuals whose conduct does no harm to others.[96] Fundamental rights, after all, may not be restricted simply because the majority disapproves, no matter how strongly, of particular behavior. A bare desire to harm a politically unpopular group does not amount to a legitimate state

---

92 *Id.*

93 State v. Morales, 826 S.W.2d 201, 205 (Tex. App. 1993).

94 *See* Campbell v. Sundquist, *supra* note 34, at 264–66; Gryczan v. State, *supra* note 34, at 124–26; Powell v. State, *supra* note 34, at 25–26; Jegley v. Picado, *supra* note 34, at 351–53.

95 Gryczan v. State, *supra* note 34, at 125.

96 *Id.* The court continued: "Spiritual leadership, not the government, has the responsibility for striving to improve the morality of individuals." *Id.*

interest, let alone a compelling one.[97] By itself, moral repugnance does not rise to a compelling state interest strong enough to override the fundamental right of privacy.[98] Absent an interest more compelling than a distaste of what is perceived to be offensive and immoral, sexual activity within the right of privacy may not be restricted.[99] "There are certain rights so fundamental that they will not be denied to a minority no matter how despised by society."[100] Thus, those courts that have recognized a fundamental right of intimate association have uniformly concluded that the enforcement of majoritarian notions of morality does not constitute a compelling state interest strong enough to override the right of individuals to engage in consensual homosexual or lesbian sexual activity.

Other State Interests

In *Campbell v. Sundquist*, in attempting to justify its statute prohibiting homosexual practices, the state advanced other several state interests that were soundly rejected by the court. The court dismissed two of these purported state interests on the ground that they were neither compelling nor even constitutionally valid. The state's claim that same-sex practices could be restricted because they did not lead to procreation was rejected on this basis with the court noting that the right of privacy includes the right to engage in intimate sexual activities regardless of whether they lead to procreation.[101] The court could have added that this purported state interest could not explain why the state did not prohibit heterosexual activities that did not lead to procreation.

The state also tried to claim an interest in outlawing same-sex conduct in order to discourage a lifestyle that is socially stigmatized and hence leads to higher rates of suicide, depression, and substance abuse.[102] The court dismissed this condescending argument, ruling that the asserted state interest, like the previous one, was neither compelling nor

---

97 Jegley v. Picado, *supra* note 34, at 352 (quoting United States Department of Agriculture v. Moreno, 413 U.S. 528, 534 (1973)).
98 Powell v. State, *supra* note 34, at 26.
99 Gryczan v. State, *supra* note 34, at 125–26.
100 *Id.* at 126.
101 Campbell v. Sundquist, *supra* note 34, at 262–63.
102 *Id.* at 263.

even constitutionally valid.[103] Denying an individual a constitutional right merely because exercise of that right may subject the individual to private prejudice and bias operates to impermissibly give legal effect to that private prejudice and bias.[104] In addition, the state's argument on this point suffered from other flaws. It was based on the erroneous (and insulting) assumption that there was a uniform homosexual lifestyle practiced by most homosexuals, and it was not supported by sufficient evidence in the record to demonstrate that the statute in fact advanced the interest claimed for it.[105]

Finally, the state made another condescending and insulting argument in claiming that its statute was justified in order to prevent homosexuals from entering into short lived, shallow, and promiscuous relationships that weaken the "fabric" of society.[106] The court summarily rejected this argument with the terse observation that there was insufficient evidence in the record to show that homosexual relationships are short lived and shallow or that they weaken the "fabric" of the community.[107]

Conclusion

In surveying the various claims proffered in the name of justifying state criminal laws prohibiting same-sex activity, one is struck by several recurring patterns. For one thing, a number of the claims have little factual support to substantiate them. They frequently are based on nothing more than prejudicial stereotypes about gay and lesbian persons that have scant basis in reality. Moreover, the claims often are overly broad; they proscribe some same-sex activity that clearly is not within the rationale put forth for the proscription. In addition, claims commonly are made to justify criminalizing same-sex activity while opposite-sex couples are left free to engage in the very same activity. These recurring defects of the claims made to justify prohibiting same-sex conduct cause one to suspect that the claims are little more than pretext designed to rationalize prejudice against gay and lesbian persons. In any event, the questionable nature of the claims have lead several courts to conclude that laws prohibiting

---

[103] *Id.*
[104] *Id.* (citing O'Connor v. Donaldson, 422 U.S. 563, 575 (1975)).
[105] *Id.*
[106] *Id.*
[107] *Id*

same-sex contact serve no purpose other than the illegitimate one of singling out gay and lesbian persons for disfavored treatment.[108] Thus, these
courts are in agreement that there is no compelling state interest that can
justify laws that make it a crime to engage in same-sex activity.[109]

In delineating a right of intimate association, the courts have been
careful to exclude commercial sexual activities, such as prostitution and
solicitation, from the scope of the right.[110] When presented with constitutional challenges to laws regulating commercial sexual activities, several
courts have ruled that such activities are not part of the right of intimate
association.[111] Courts have sought to distinguish commercial sexual activities from noncommercial sexual behavior in several ways. Prostitution
and solicitation, though usually transacted in private, often are negoti-
ated in public and frequently are connected with other criminal activity.[112] Although intimate, they are impersonal.[113] But perhaps the most
persuasive cause to allow the regulation of prostitution and solicitation is
to prevent the spread of infectious disease.[114] For these reasons, the courts
are agreed that laws prohibiting prostitution or solicitation do not uncon-
stitutionally infringe the right to intimate association.

In the seventeen-year span between *Bowers* and *Lawrence*, not all state
courts that encountered the constitutional issue of sodomy laws regulating
same-sex act activities departed from the federal mold to strike down such
laws. In *State v. Smith*, for example, the Supreme Court of Louisiana, faced

---

[108] Commonwealth v. Wasson, *supra* note 35, at 500–501; Jegley v. Picado, *supra* note 34, at 352–54; Campbell v. Sundquist, *supra* note 34, at 262–65.

[109] *Wasson, id.; Jegley, id.; Campbell, id.*

[110] E.g., Lawrence v. Texas, *supra* note 30, at 2484 (noting that the sodomy statute found to be unconstitutional did not involve prostitution); Powell v. State, *supra* note 34, at 26 (concluding that a statute that criminalized the performance of "private, unforced, *non-commercial* acts of sexual intimacy" between consenting adults was an unconstitutional violation of the right of privacy) (emphasis added). Gryczan v. State, *supra* note 34, at 125 (concluding that the right of consenting adults to engage in "private *noncommercial* sexual conduct" lies at the core of Montana's constitutional right of individual privacy) (emphasis added). In *Wasson*, the court explicitly noted that under the sodomy statute found to be unconstitutional it did not matter that "the act is private and involves a caring relationship rather than a commercial one." Wasson, 842 S.W.2d at 488.

[111] State v. Mueller, 671 P.2d 1351 (Haw. 1983); State v. Grey, 413 N.W.2d 107 (Minn. 1987); Howard v. State, 527 S.E.2d 194 (Ga. 2000).

[112] State v. Gray, 413 N.W.2d 107, 114 (Minn. 1987) (quoting State v. Price, 237 N.W.2d 813, 818 (Iowa 1976)).

[113] *Id.*

[114] *Id.* It has been pointed out, however, that a less restrictive means of preventing the spread of disease would be to register prostitutes and require them to undergo period medical exams. *See* Jennifer Friesen, *supra* note 2, at 2-77.

with a constitutional challenge to a statute criminalizing "crime against nature," chose to uphold the statute.[115] Noting that oral and anal sex have been criminally prohibited by Louisiana law in one form or another, for nearly two hundred years, the court maintained that no reasonable person could consider the result of voting to ratify a general constitutional guarantee of "liberty" or "privacy" would be to divest the legislature of the authority to continue the specific statutory proscription against sodomy.[116] In the court's view, the question was not one of what was good or wise for the people of Louisiana, but rather what the voters intended when they adopted the constitution by referendum, and there was no evidence to show that the voters meant to deprive the legislature of authority to deal with this matter.[117] The state constitution, said the court, should not be subject to "judicial amendment" on the basis of what a majority of the court happens to believe at any given time is enlightened social policy.[118] Stating that it was not inclined to discover new constitutional rights, the court squarely ruled that the Louisiana Constitution did not provide a right of privacy for consenting adults to engage in sexual activities.[119]

Despite the decision of the Louisiana Supreme Court in *State v. Smith*, the right of intimate association continued to gain favor throughout the nation, eventually culminating in the Supreme Court's ruling in *Lawrence*, establishing a federal constitutional right to intimate association under the Due Process Clause of the Fourteenth Amendment.[120] The high Court's decision in *Lawrence* was influenced by the state decisions that preceded it in recognizing the right to intimate association.[121] In no small sense, the ruling in *Lawrence* vindicated those state courts that were first able to comprehend the fundamental nature of the right to intimate association. The state rulings recognizing the right of intimate association prior to *Lawrence* stand as important precedent in their respective jurisdictions, firmly establishing the right of intimate association as a matter of state constitutional law. They also stand as powerful examples of state court independence in the constitutional realm, reaffirming the moment of state constitutions as a source of protection for individual liberty.

---

[115] State v. Smith, 766 So.2d 501 (La. 2000).
[116] *Id.* at 506, 508.
[117] *Id.* at 508–9.
[118] *Id.* at 510.
[119] *Id.* at 510–12.
[120] Lawrence v. Texas, *supra* note 30.
[121] *Id.* at 571–72, 576.

CHAPTER EIGHT

THE RIGHT OF BODILY INTEGRITY

The Right to Refuse Medical Treatment and the Right to Die

The right of an individual to control his or her own body is deeply rooted in our nation's history and tradition. At common law, every person of adult years and sound mind had "the right to determine what shall be done with his own body"[1] and any touching of one person by another without consent or legal justification was a battery.[2] Indeed, well over a century ago, the Supreme Court proclaimed that, "No right is held more sacred, or is more carefully guarded, by the common law, than the right of every individual to the possession and control of his own person, free from all restraint and interference of others, unless by clear and unquestionable authority of law."[3] Thus, at common law there was a right to control one's own person, that is, a right of bodily integrity.

The common law right to control one's own body encompassed the right to refuse medical treatment. Any attempt to alter or invade an individual's body without consent was considered tortious,[4] and a surgeon who performed an operation without the patient's informed consent committed an assault, for which the surgeon was liable in damages.[5]

The right of an individual to refuse medical treatment comprehends the right to refuse life-sustaining treatment.[6] Numerous courts have

---

[1] Schloendorff v. Society of New York Hospital, 105 N.E.2d 92, 93 (N.Y. 1914), *overruled by* Bing v. Thunig, 143 N.E.2d 3 (N.Y. 1957).

[2] Cruzan v. Director, Missouri Department of Health, 497 U.S. 261, 269 (1990).

[3] Union Pacific Railway Co. v. Botsford, 141 U.S. 250, 251 (1891).

[4] Jarvis v. Levine, 418 N.W.2d 139, 149 (Minn. 1988).

[5] *Schloedorff, supra* note 1. *See also, Cruzan, supra* note 2: "The informed consent doctrine has become firmly entrenched in American tort law."

[6] *See In re* Farrell, 529 A.2d 404, 410 (1987).

recognized that there is a right to refuse or terminate medical treatment even if doing so will hasten death.[7] An individual's decision to refuse or terminate life-support treatment is not considered an attempt to commit suicide, but rather the exercise of a personal right.[8] Simply put, there is a right to choose death by refusing or terminating life-sustaining medical treatment. While the right is not absolute, there is general agreement that it is an essential element of personal autonomy and that, absent extraordinary circumstances, it outweighs countervailing state interests, including the state interest in preserving life.[9]

While some states still rely exclusively on the common law to protect the right to refuse medical treatment, other states have chosen to incorporate that right as an aspect of the state constitutional protection for the right of privacy.[10] In some states where the constitution contains a provision expressly guaranteeing the right of privacy, the courts have naturally turned to those provisions and interpreted them to embrace the right of an individual to refuse medical treatment.[11] In other states, where an express privacy guarantee is not contained in the state constitution, the courts have invoked more general constitutional provisions that safeguard "rights" or "liberty" to provide constitutional status for the right of an individual to refuse medical treatment.[12] The right to refuse medical treatment also has been recognized in some states as an aspect of

---

[7] *Id.*

[8] *Id.* at 411.

[9] *See, e.g.,* Zant v. Prevatte, 286 S.E.2d 715 (Ga. 1982), (holding that the state's interest in preserving human life did not amount to a compelling state interest sufficient to override a prisoner's right to refuse to eat or submit to medical treatment for starvation).

[10] Jennifer Friesen, *State Constitutional Law: Litigating Individual Rights, Claims, and Defenses,* at 2-55 to 2-56.

[11] Rasmussen by Mitchell v. Fleming, 741 P.2d 674 (Ariz. 1987); *In re* Guardianship of Grant, 747 P.2d 445 (Wash. 1987); Hondroulis v. Schuhmacher, 553 So.2d 398 (La. 1988); Conservatorship of Drabick, 200 Cal. App. 3d 185 (Cal. 1988); *In re* Guardianship of Browning, 568 So.2d 4 (Fla. 1990).

[12] *In re* Caulk, 480 A.2d 93, 94 (N.H. 1984) (N.H. Const. pt. I, art. 2: All men have certain natural, essential and inherent rights—among which are, the enjoying and defending life and liberty...); *In re* Brown, 478 So.2d 1033, 1040 (Miss. 1985) (Miss. Const. Art. 3, §32: The enumeration of rights in this constitution shall not be construed to deny and impair others retained by, and inherent in, the people); State v. McAfee, 385 S.E.2d 579, 580 (Ga. 1989) (Ga. Const. Art. I, Sec. I, Par. I: No person shall be deprived of life, liberty, or property except by due process of law). *See also, In the Matter of* Lawrance, 579 N.E.2d 32, 39 (Ind. 1992) (Noting that the common law right to refuse medical treatment "has evolved in a legal culture governed by the Indiana Constitution, which begins by declaring that the liberty of our citizens is inalienable").

religious liberty, protected by state constitutional guarantees of religious freedom.[13]

Although there clearly is a right to terminate medical treatment even if it results in death, there is a question as to how that right may be exercised for an individual who is unconscious or incompetent to exercise the right on his or her own. Almost all of the states have enacted "living will" statutes that allow individuals to execute a declaration calling for the withdrawal of life-sustaining medical treatment if the individual is in a terminal condition and unable to make his or her own medical decisions.[14] In the absence of a living will, some states allow a family member or appointed guardian to evoke the right to terminate medical treatment for an unconscious or incompetent person, but only on a showing by clear and convincing evidence that this is what the person would have wanted.[15] Other states apply a less exacting standard which allows termination of medical treatment if it is shown to be consistent with the person's wishes, even though the evidence to that effect is not clear and convincing.[16] Where there is scant evidence of the individual's wishes, some states allow a family member or guardian to make the decision to terminate treatment if he or she believes it would be in the best interests of the individual.[17] Despite these various approaches to how the right to refuse treatment may be exercised in the case of an unconscious or incompetent person, under each approach the paramount goal is to effectuate the wishes of the individual. Whatever approach is chosen, the fact remains that all individuals, whether competent or not to express their wishes, have a right to choose death by refusing or terminating life-sustaining medical treatment.[18]

The courts, however, have drawn the line at physician-assisted suicide, refusing to accept it as an aspect of personal autonomy. On the federal side, the Supreme Court ruled in *Washington v. Glucksberg* that there is

---

[13] *In re* Milton, 505 N.E.2d 255 (Ohio 1987).

[14] David L. Sloss, Note, *The Right to Choose How to Die: A Constitutional Analysis of State Laws Prohibiting Physician-Assisted Suicide*, 48 Stan. L. Rev. 937, 945 (1996).

[15] Jennifer Friesen, *supra* note 10, at 2-57. In *Cruzan v. Director, Missouri Dept. of Health, supra* note 2, the Supreme Court ruled that it did not violate the Federal Constitution for a state to adopt this standard of proof.

[16] Jennifer Friesen, *id.*

[17] *Id.*

[18] "The recognition of (the right to refuse medical treatment) must extend to the case of an incompetent, as well as a competent, patient because the value of human dignity extends to both." Superintendent of Belchertown State School v. Saikewicz, 370 N.E.2d 417, 427 (Mass. 1977).

not a fundamental right to physician-assisted suicide under the Due Process Clause of the Fourteenth Amendment and therefore a state may—as some forty-nine states do—prohibit the act of aiding a person to commit suicide.[19] In *Glucksberg*, the Court took the position that physician-assisted suicide should not be recognized as a fundamental liberty under the Due Process Clause because it was not a right that is "deeply rooted in our nation's history and tradition."[20] To the contrary, the Court observed, the common law tradition has punished or otherwise disapproved of both suicide and assisting suicide for over 700 years.[21] Moreover, while bans on assisted-suicide have been re-examined in more recent times, they have been generally reaffirmed.[22] In a companion case to *Glucksberg*, *Vacco v. Quill*, the Court further ruled that it was not a violation of the Equal Protection Clause for a state to prohibit physician-assisted suicide while allowing patients to refuse life-sustaining medical treatment.[23] Thus, the high Court has drawn a strict line between the refusal of life-sustaining medical care and physician-assisted suicide, by definitively ruling that the latter is not a fundamental right under the Federal Constitution.

In 1997, the voters of Oregon enacted the Death With Dignity Act, which authorizes, under some circumstances, physician-assisted suicide for terminally-ill persons.[24] Oregon, though, is the only state in the nation that has legalized physician-assisted suicide, and, in fact, most states have expressed disapproval of it one way or another, even while continuing to recognize the right to refuse life-sustaining medical treatment.[25] The few state courts that have faced the constitutional question of physician-assisted suicide have declined to recognize it as an aspect of the right of privacy.[26]

In a 1989 decision involving the right to an abortion, the Supreme Court of Florida made the following statement:

> Of all decisions a person makes about his or her body, the most
> profound and intimate relate to two sets of ultimate questions: first,

---

[19] Washington v. Glucksberg, 521 U.S. 702 (1997).
[20] *Id.* at 721.
[21] *Id.* at 711.
[22] *Id.* at 716.
[23] Vacco v. Quill, 521 U.S. 793 (1997).
[24] Death with Dignity Act, Or. Rev. Stat. §§127.800 to .897 (2006).
[25] *See, e.g.,* Krischer v. McIver, 697 So.2d 97, 100 (Fla. 1997).
[26] *See* Donaldson v. Lungren, 4 Cal. Rptr. 2d 59 (Cal. 1992); *Krischer, id.*

whether, when, and how one's body is to become the vehicle for another human being's creation; second, when and how—this time there is no question of "whether"—one's body is to terminate its organic life.[27]

Despite that statement and despite the fact that the Florida Constitution contains a provision expressly protecting the right of privacy, eight years later the same court ruled in *Krischer v. McIver* that the state constitution did not countenance a right to physician- assisted suicide.[28] Measured by the same criteria used in cases involving the right to refuse medical treatment, the court concluded that there were three state interests that were "so compelling" that they "clearly outweigh(ed)" an individual's right to physician-assisted suicide.[29] These interests were the preservation of life, the prevention of suicide, and the maintenance of the integrity of the medical profession.[30]

The court also asserted that there was a distinction between the right to refuse medical treatment and the right to commit physician-assisted suicide. As the court saw it, the latter was not treatment in the traditional sense, but rather was "an affirmative act designed to cause death."[31] This attempt to distinguish physician-assisted suicide from an individual's right to refuse medical treatment has a certain logic, but only in a formal sense and, moreover, only in regard to an individual's right to initially refuse medical treatment. On the other hand, the termination of life-sustaining treatment already in place, like physician-assisted suicide, is an affirmative act designed to cause death. Thus, the court's rationale cannot explain, even on a formal basis, why physician-assisted suicide should be treated differently than the individual right to terminate life-sustaining medical treatment.

Moreover, the attempt by the court to portray physician-assisted suicide as an "affirmative act" somehow different from other actions is not entirely coherent. As a practical matter, it frequently is arbitrary to designate an occurrence as either an affirmative act or an act of omission.[32]

---

[27] *In re* T.W., A Minor, 551 So.2d 1186, 1192 (Fla. 1989) (*citing* Laurence Tribe, *American Constitutional Law* 1337–38 (2d ed. 1988)).

[28] Krischer v. McIver, 697 So.2d 97 (Fla. 1997).

[29] *Id.* at 103.

[30] *Id.* at 103–4.

[31] *Id.* at 102.

[32] Richard Sherlock *For Everything There Is a Season: The Right to Die in the United States*, 1982 B.Y.U. L. Rev. 545, 550–53 (1982).

Consider the example of disconnecting a respirator—is it an affirmative act (turning off a machine) or an act of omission (failing to provide air)?[33] Is a patient who refuses food actively starving or merely omitting to eat?[34] These examples illustrate that in many instances an occurrence can be considered either an affirmative act or an act of omission, depending upon the perspective by which it is viewed.

Most importantly, the court's attempt to differentiate physician-assisted suicide from either the initial refusal to accept medical care or the later decision to terminate life-sustaining care is formalistic and fails to address the question of *why* an individual should have the right to choose death by the presumably passive means of refusing medical care, but not by the apparently more active means of physician-assisted suicide. That an occurrence is active or passive does not determine if it is morally justifiable.[35]

The court further attempted to differentiate physician-assisted suicide from the termination of life-sustaining medical treatment by citing a report from the American Medical Association, which stated that when life-sustaining treatment is declined, "the patient dies primarily because of an underlying disease (that) is simply allowed to take its natural course. With assisted suicide, however, death is hastened by the taking of a lethal drug or other agent."[36]

This attempt to distinguish physician-assisted suicide from the refusal or withdrawal of life-sustaining treatment also is specious. For one thing, it overlooks that the refusal or withdrawal of life-sustaining treatment, no less than assisted suicide, hastens death. Moreover, like the previous argument, it is formalistic and fails to offer any explanation as to why an individual should have the right to choose death by refusing medical care, but not by physician-assisted suicide. Given this failure, the AMA's statement seems little more than a bald assertion that in the case of withdrawal of life-sustaining support, a physician should not be held liable for the patient's death.[37]

---

[33] Note, *Physician Assisted Suicide and the Right to Die with Assistance*, 105 Harv. L. Rev. 2021, 2028 (1992).

[34] *Id.*

[35] *See* James Rachels, *The End of Life* 111–14 (1986).

[36] *Krischer*, 697 So.2d at 102 (quoting *Council on Ethical and Judicial Affairs, American Medical Association, Report I-93-8*, at 2 (1992), *reprinted in* 267 JAMA 2229–33 (1992)).

[37] *See* Note, *Physician Assisted Suicide and the Right to Die with Assistance*, 105 Harv. L. Rev. 2021, 2028–29 (1992).

In a dissenting opinion in the *Krischer* case, Justice Kogan took issue with the seemingly neat distinction the majority drew between "dying by natural causes" and death by suicide.[38] He observed that in the past it was possible to distinguish death by natural causes and death by suicide, but advances in modern technology and medicine have to a great extent diminished that distinction. With the development of modern science and technology, "dying no longer falls into the neat categories our ancestors knew."[39] The distinction drawn by the majority between "active" and "passive" death makes little sense in the context of modern science and, in fact, drawing a dividing line between physician-assisted suicide and refusing life-sustaining treatment has become next to impossible.[40] As Justice Kogan explained, "Terminal illness is not a portrait in blacks and whites, but unending shades of gray, involving the most profound of personal, moral, and religious questions."[41]

Justice Kogan's point is well-taken, especially in light of the Florida Supreme Court's previous pronouncement that deciding to end one's life is one of the most profound and personal decisions that an individual can make. That being so, it is extremely difficult, if not impossible, to draw a line between the right to refuse life-sustaining medical care and an equivalent right to physician-assisted suicide.

The Right to Ingest Food, Beverages, or Other Substances

Some of the earliest cases recognizing a right of individual autonomy concerned the right of a person to ingest food, beverages, or other substances. As described in Chapter Four, "The Right of Privacy," in *Commonwealth v. Campbell*, decided in 1909, the Court of Appeals of Kentucky ruled that an ordinance making it a crime to possess intoxicating liquor even for private use was a violation of the Kentucky Bill of Rights.[42] The court's ruling in *Campbell* was based on the principle that the state has no authority to restrict the liberty of an individual except where his or her conduct will cause some injury to the public.[43] The court

---

[38] *Krischer*, 697 So.2d at 109–11 (Kogan, J., dissenting).
[39] *Id.* at 109 (Kogan, J., dissenting).
[40] *Id.* at 110–11 (Kogan, J., dissenting).
[41] *Id.* at 111. (Kogan, J., dissenting).
[42] Commonwealth v. Campbell, 117 S.W. 383 (Ky. 1909).
[43] *Id.* at 385, 387.

reasoned that this precept flows from the state Bill of Rights, which declares that seeking safety and happiness is an inalienable right and that the state cannot possess arbitrary power over the lives, liberty, or property of its citizens.[44] Accordingly, the state has no right to compel an individual to do or forbear from doing something merely because others believe it is for the individual's own good.[45] The state has no authority to invade private aspects of a person's life or to regulate conduct which causes no harm to others. Therefore, the question of what a person may eat or drink, so long as the rights of others are not affected, "is one which addresses itself alone to the will of the citizen."[46]

The principle of autonomy established in *Campbell* was followed a few years later when the Kentucky Court of Appeals invalidated an ordinance regulating cigarette smoking.[47] The court explained that the ordinance was so broad that it could be applied to persons who smoked in the privacy of their own homes and therefore was an "unreasonable interference with the right of the citizen to determine for himself such personal matters."[48] In the opinion of the court, the government had no right to regulate personal conduct occurring within the privacy of the home that does not injuriously affect others.[49]

For the most part, however, these early cases recognizing the right of an individual to ingest various substances were an exception to the rule. Although courts during that period of time often sang the praises of individual liberty, the prevailing rule was that individual liberty could be regulated in any way necessary to promote the general welfare, and this was so even though the conduct subject to regulation did not directly harm another person.[50] Thus, few other decisions during this period recognized a right of the individual to ingest substances.

---

44 *Id.*

45 *Id.* at 386.

46 *Id.* at 385.

47 Hershberg v. City of Barbourville, 133 S.W. 985, 986 (1911). *See also* Commonwealth v. Smith, 173 S.W. 340 (1915), (declaring a statute to be an unconstitutional violation of the right of privacy because it permitted the arrest of an individual for drinking beer in the backroom of an office).

48 *Hershberg*, 133 S.W. at 986.

49 *Id.* at 343; *see also Smith*, 173 S.W. at 343.

50 *See, e.g.,* Ah Lim v. Territory, 24 P. 588 (Wash.1890) (statute prohibiting smoking of opium does not violate any constitutional right); Gould v. Gould, 61 A. 604 (Conn. 1905) (statute prohibiting marriage by an epileptic where the woman is under the age of forty-five does not violate constitutional right to liberty).

Nor have the courts shown much inclination in more recent times to countenance a right to ingest substances as part of the right of privacy. Several courts across the nation have rejected claims that there is a fundamental right of privacy to possess or smoke marijuana.[51]

In a departure from the general trend, however, in 1975 the Supreme Court of Alaska ruled in *Ravin v. State* that the state constitutional guarantee of privacy was violated by a criminal statute prohibiting possession of marijuana by an adult for personal consumption at home.[52] In reaching that result, the court took the unusual position that while there was not a general right to ingest marijuana, there was a limited right to possess it for consumption at home.[53] Noting that the Alaska Constitution had been amended in 1972 to expressly guarantee the right of privacy, the court nonetheless thought that the amendment could not be read to make possession or ingestion of marijuana a fundamental right.[54] The right to ingest food, beverages, or other substances, the court said, must yield to the legitimate needs of the state to protect the health and welfare of its citizens.[55] Distinguishing a case in which the court had previously struck down a school hair-length regulation,[56] the court suggested that unlike personal appearance, the use of marijuana is not "a highly personal matter" or "something of critical importance" to an individual.[57] So, the court concluded, there was not a "general fundamental constitutional right" to possess or ingest marijuana.[58]

On the other hand, the court thought that the constitutional guarantee of privacy applies with special force within the home, thus providing constitutional sanctuary for certain activities that occur there, even though those activities would not be protected when they occur outside the home.[59] Emphasizing the spatial aspect of privacy, the court pointed out that many activities may be conducted lawfully within the privacy and confines of the home, although they be prohibited when are conducted elsewhere.[60]

---

51 *E.g.*, Commonwealth v. Leis, 243 N.E.2d 898 (Mass. 1969); State v. Kantner, 493 P.2d 406 (Haw. 1972).
52 Ravin v. State, 537 P.2d 494 (Alaska 1975).
53 *Id*. at 504.
54 *Id*. at 502.
55 *Id*. at 501–2, 509.
56 Breese v. Smith, 501 P.2d 159 (Alaska 1972).
57 *Ravin* 537 P.2d. at 500–502.
58 *Id*. at 502.
59 *Id*. at 503.
60 *Id*.

The home is a special place that makes it "particularly important as the situs of privacy."[61] The "distinctive nature" of the home marks it as an area where an individual's privacy receives "special protection."[62]

In fact, the privacy amendment to the state constitution was intended to provide particular recognition to the home.[63] Affording enhanced constitutional protection to the home was consonant with the character of life in Alaska, which traditionally has been a haven for persons who prize their individuality and have chosen to live in Alaska to achieve a measure of control over their own lifestyles that is not possible in other states.[64] Hence, the court recognized that under the constitutional guarantee of privacy there was a fundamental right to possess marijuana for personal use at home that could only be restricted if the state could demonstrate a sufficient justification to do so.[65]

As it turned out, this was a burden that the state could not meet. The state had argued that the use of marijuana causes aggressive criminal behavior, can be physically or psychologically addictive, leads to the use of more dangerous drugs, and is harmful in other respects to the health of the person using it.[66] None of these assertions, however, could be supported by empirical evidence.[67] As the court said, "It appears that there is no firm evidence that marijuana, as presently used in this country, is generally a danger to the user or to others."[68] The one significant risk of using marijuana that was shown by empirical evidence was that it could impair the driving ability of persons under its influence.[69] Therefore, the court ruled that there was a sufficient justification to prohibit a person from possessing or ingesting marijuana while driving.[70] Otherwise, however, there was no showing that use of marijuana was a health hazard or caused harmful behavior.[71]

Given the lack of evidence showing any harmful effects of marijuana use, the court speculated that implicit in the state's argument was the

---

[61] *Id.* at 504.
[62] *Id.* at 503.
[63] *Id.*
[64] *Id.*
[65] *Id.* at 504.
[66] *Id.* at 504–9.
[67] *Id.*
[68] *Id.* at 508.
[69] *Id.*
[70] *Id.* at 510–11.
[71] *Id.*

assumption that the state had authority to protect an individual "from his own folly" by controlling conduct even though it does no harm to others.[72] Such an assumption, the court suggested, would be wrong.[73] It is basic to a free society, the court explained, that the state cannot impose its own notions of morality, propriety, or fashion on individuals when the public has no legitimate interest in the affairs of those individuals.[74] While the right of an individual to do as he or she pleases is not absolute, it can only be made to yield in the face of a genuine harm to the public welfare.[75] "A state cannot simply decide what is in a person's best interest and compel it."[76] In the absence of evidence showing that marijuana posed a real health hazard (except while driving) either to those who use it or to other persons, the court concluded that the constitutional guarantee of privacy protected the right of an individual to possess marijuana for personal consumption at home.[77]

Courts in other states have declined to follow *Ravin*. In Hawaii, for example, the supreme court refused to recognize a right to use marijuana at home,[78] despite the fact that the Hawaii Constitution, like Alaska's, contains a provision expressly guaranteeing privacy, which the court had previously interpreted to encompass the right to possess obscene materials in the privacy of one's home, as well as the correlative right to purchase such materials for use in the home.[79] In the court's eyes, though, that previous ruling was distinguishable from the case at hand because it was grounded on privacy in the home in conjunction with another interest of constitutional magnitude, freedom of speech. The court was disinclined to extend the right of privacy to include possession of marijuana in the home, and dismissed *Ravin* with the observation that it was based, at least in part, on social and cultural factors unique to Alaska,

---

[72] *Id.* at 508.

[73] *Id.* at 509.

[74] *Id.*

[75] *Id.*

[76] *Id.* (citing State v. Lee, 465 P.2d 573, 578 (Haw. 1970) (Abe, J., dissenting)).

[77] *Id.* at 511.

[78] State v. Mallan, 950 P.2d 178 (Haw. 1998).

[79] State v. Kam, 748 P.2d 372 (Haw. 1988). It is worth noting that *Kam* went beyond United States Supreme Court rulings in this area, by recognizing a right to purchase obscene materials for use in the home. Although the United States Supreme Court recognized in *Stanley v. Georgia*, 394 U.S. 557 (1969), a right to possess obscene materials at home, it later ruled in *United States v. Reidel*, 402 U.S. 351 (1971), that there was not a right to purchase the materials.

which stands alone in upholding the right to possess marijuana for use at home.

In the state of Washington, the Court of Appeals declined to follow *Ravin*, primarily because, unlike Alaska, Washington does not have an express privacy provision in its state constitution, nor does case law in the state support such a strong right to privacy.[80] The court maintained that, except for *Ravin*, cases discussing the right of privacy in the home limit that right to activities involving important or fundamental rights, such as freedom of speech, which do not include possession of marijuana.[81] Finding *Ravin* unpersuasive, the court concluded that in Washington the right of privacy did not comprehend a right to use marijuana in one's home.[82]

Some years later, in *Seeley v. State* the Supreme Court of Washington refused to countenance a right of privacy for a terminally ill cancer patient to smoke marijuana for medicinal purposes.[83] The patient, who wished to be able to smoke marijuana because it provided the most relief from the nausea and vomiting resulting from chemotherapy, filed suit seeking a declaratory judgment that the state statute prohibiting the use of marijuana violated the privileges and immunities clause of the Washington Constitution.[84] However, the court ruled that in the context of the case, the state privileges and immunities clause provided no more protection than its federal counterpart, the Equal Protection Clause of the Fourteenth Amendment, and that neither of them afforded protection for the right to smoke marijuana, even for medicinal purposes.[85] Although the plaintiff claimed only a limited right to smoke marijuana for medical treatment (rather than a general right to smoke it), the court rejected his claim on the ground that there is not a fundamental right to obtain drugs of unproven efficacy.[86] Seeing no fundamental right in the case, the court opted for minimal scrutiny and went on to conclude that it was not

---

[80] State v. Anderson, 558 P.2d 307, 309 (Wash. Ct. App. 1976).

[81] *Id.* at 310.

[82] *Id.*

[83] Seeley v. State, 940 P.2d 604 (Wash. 1997).

[84] "No law shall be passed granting to any citizen, class of citizens, or corporation other than municipal, privileges or immunities which upon the same terms shall not equally belong to all citizens, or corporations." Wash. Const., Art. I, sect. 12.

[85] Seeley, 940 P.2d at 608–11.

[86] *Id.* at 612–13.

irrational for the legislature to prohibit smoking marijuana because there was some evidence to suggest that it was harmful to health.[87]

The decision in *Seeley* represents the majority view concerning the right to ingest food, beverages, or other substances. Very few states have been willing to recognize this right as an aspect of the right of privacy. A few relatively early decisions recognized a right to consume alcoholic beverages and to smoke cigarettes. And, of course, the Alaska Supreme Court later ruled that there was a fundamental right to possess marijuana for personal use in the privacy of one's home. Otherwise, however, the states have been disinclined to accept a right to ingest substances as part of the constitutional right of privacy.

---

[87] *Id.* at 613–17.

CHAPTER NINE

BACKLASH AND ADVANCEMENT

Since the 1970s, constitutional law has moved in two opposite directions in the United States. On the federal side, it has become increasingly conservative and antipathetic to the recognition of new individual rights; on the state side, it has become increasingly progressive and receptive to the recognition of new individual rights. This, of course, has been made possible by the system of government in the United States composed of dual sovereignty shared by the state and federal governments. As a result of dual sovereignty, those state courts that chose to do so were free to interpret their state constitutions expansively while the federal courts had embarked on a path of restrictive interpretation of the federal constitution. With the rise of the New Judicial Federalism, state courts have reaffirmed their independence from federal constitutional law and created a vibrant body of state constitutional law.

Admittedly, not all of the states have joined in the New Judicial Federalism. Some have chosen to hew closely to federal constitutional law, refusing to open their state constitutions to any new possibilities beyond those required by the federal document. Others have taken one or two steps on their own, while adhering to federal law in the vast majority of cases. But a significant number of states have celebrated their independence to create a substantial body of state constitutional law that goes well beyond the federal constitutional doctrine to establish rights of the individual that flow from state constitutions.

Many states have exercised their sovereign independence to create a conception of equality that transcends the federal model of equal protection of the laws.[1] State constitutional equality evolves from the federal

---

[1] *See* Chapter One.

construct of equal protection, but reshapes and extends it into new areas beyond the dimensions of federal equal protection.[2] In cases involving equality, a number of state courts have seen fit to recognize more expansive individual rights than those able to gain favor in the federal system.[3] For example, the supreme courts of both California and Connecticut took a strong stand against *de facto* racial segregation in public schools, despite the adamant refusal of the United States Supreme Court to do so.[4] A number of state courts—some of them buoyed by the adoption of a state Equal Rights Amendment—have taken a more forceful position against gender discrimination than prevails in the federal courts.[5] Some state courts have gone beyond their federal counterparts to strike down laws that discriminate against gay or lesbian persons.[6] A few state courts have put bite into rationality review to strike down classifications based on age,[7] and one state court even used a sharpened version of rationality review to invalidate a statute that discriminated against adopted persons.[8]

Notwithstanding the position of the United States Supreme Court to the contrary, numerous state courts have taken the position that education is a fundamental right and therefore public school financing schemes are to be reviewed with strict scrutiny.[9] As a consequence, a growing number of state courts of last resort have concluded that state systems of financing education that result in disparate levels of funding are unconstitutional.[10] State courts also are more willing than federal ones to sharpen their review of (and in some cases strike down) discriminatory economic legislation.[11] On occasion, state courts may enhance rationality review to examine the constitutionality of criminal laws that provide differential penalties or treatment for similar offenses.[12] State courts have struck down laws that eliminated welfare benefits,[13] restricted the recovery

---

[2] *See id.*

[3] *See id.*

[4] *See* Chapter Two at notes 15–43. The force of the California rulings was subsequently nullified to some degree by an initiative amending the state constitution. See *infra* at notes 27–28.

[5] *See id.* at notes 354–403.

[6] *See id.* at notes 124–37, 145–52.

[7] *See id.* at notes 191–212.

[8] *See id.* at note 100.

[9] *See* Chapter Three at notes 3–10, 21–24.

[10] *See id.* at notes 18–24.

[11] *See id.* at notes 57–76, 88–96, 113–29, 134–71.

[12] *See id.* at notes 172–84, 195–208.

[13] *See* Chapter One at notes 129–40.

of damages in tort actions,[14] or gave undue discretion to prosecutors to treat juvenile offenders as adults.[15]

So, while the federal conception of equality remains relatively static, if not regressive, its state counterpart is dynamic and therefore responsive to the evolving needs of a changing society. Since the rise of the New Judicial Federalism, it has been the state courts that have been the standard-bearer for equal rights. In state courts across the nation, equality is a vibrant and progressive concept, open to diverse possibilities.

At the same time, the states have exercised their sovereign prerogative to create a conception of liberty that surpasses the federal notion of liberty.[16] The principle of liberty has deep roots in state constitutional law, manifest in a strong commitment to the right of privacy or individual autonomy—the right of an individual to make personal decisions about his or her life free from government control.[17] In interpreting various constitutional provisions safeguarding liberty, state supreme courts have recognized that the right of privacy is a fundamental aspect of liberty that may not be restricted except for the most compelling of reasons.[18] In modern times, some states have chosen to enshrine autonomy as a fundamental right by amending their constitutions to expressly guarantee the right of privacy.[19] Whatever method is used, though, many states have seen fit to elevate privacy as a fundamental right, entitled to the highest degree of constitutional protection.[20]

Consequently, states have taken the lead in giving constitutional protection to the right of intimate association[21] as well as the right to same-sex marriage or civil union.[22] When the United States Supreme Court narrowed a woman's right to choose to have an abortion, a number of state courts went in the opposite direction to provide a wider compass for reproductive freedom.[23] State courts have also taken a more expansive view of parental rights and the right of individuals to live together.[24]

---

[14] *See* Chapter Three at notes 88–101.
[15] *See* Chapter One at note 146.
[16] *See* Chapter Four.
[17] *See id.*
[18] *See id.* at notes 216–30.
[19] *See id.* at note 223.
[20] *See id.* at notes 216–30.
[21] *See* Chapter Seven.
[22] *See* Chapter Six.
[23] *See* Chapter Five.
[24] *See* Chapter Five.

The states have always been in the forefront in recognizing, as an important component of self-determination, a right of bodily integrity that includes the right to refuse medical treatment, even if doing so will result in death.[25] A few states, taking a broad view of individual autonomy, have sanctioned a right to ingest substances.[26] Thus, state constitutional law has proven to be a wellspring of protection for the right of privacy.

The right of privacy has traversed a course in our federal system similar to the one traversed by equality. That is, while the federal notion of privacy has become dormant, if not constricted, the state right of privacy has become dynamic and hence more amenable to the evolving needs of contemporary society. It is now state courts that are in the vanguard of the movement to cultivate a comprehensive constitutional right of privacy. Both privacy and equality thrive most abundantly in the domain of state constitutional law.

Not everything is positive in that domain, however. The advances of equality and privacy achieved through the New Judicial Federalism have, in some instances, been greeted with disapproval. Some states have encountered a legislative or popular backlash against the recognition of certain new rights by state courts. In California, for instance, after the state supreme court ruled that the state equal protection clause requires schools to remedy *de facto* as well as *de jure* racial segregation in schools, the electorate voted to add a provision to the state equal protection clause declaring that, with respect to school assignment or transportation, nothing in the California Constitution imposed any obligation or responsibility on the state which exceeds those imposed by the Equal Protection Clause of the Federal Constitution.[27] Apparently, the people of the Golden State, in this instance, were opposed to the extension of state constitutional rights beyond those required under the Federal Constitution. Still, the constitutional amendment tying the state equal protection clause to the federal one seemed a strange way to counteract the state court rulings, especially given that five years before the electorate had added a provision to the state constitution declaring that, "Rights guaranteed by this Constitution are not dependent on those guaranteed by the United States Constitution."[28]

---

[25] *See* Chapter Eight.

[26] *See* Chapter Eight.

[27] *See* Chapter Two at notes 319–21.

[28] Cal. Const. art. I, §24 (1974). The Rhode Island Constitution contains an identical provision. R.I. Const. art I, §24 (1986).

There has been backlash, too, in response to state court rulings requiring the equalization of school financing. Here the backlash has come primarily in the form of legislative recalcitrance to enact laws genuinely reforming school finance systems so as to comply with court rulings.[29] In some states, the legislature has dragged its heels to avoid true reform or has enacted one law after another that amount to nothing more than a shallow pretense of reform.[30] This legislative recalcitrance is reminiscent of—though perhaps not as severe as—the resistance shown by Southern states to the Supreme Court's decision in *Brown v. Board of Education* striking down racial segregation in public schools.[31] There, too, state legislatures procrastinated or enacted phony desegregation plans to avoid compliance with a constitutional mandate of equality.[32] In more recent times, a similar legislative defiance—in this instance to court-ordered reform of school finance systems—can be seen in some states. New Jersey, for example, presents an extreme instance of legislative resistance to court-ordered educational reform. In 1973, the New Jersey Supreme Court first ruled that the state system of public school financing, which caused gross disparities in the funding of schools from one district to another, violated the state constitution.[33] The court's decision was met with persistent antipathy by the state legislature. As described by one commentator, "After twenty-five years, ten additional New Jersey Supreme Court opinions, and three major legislative overhauls, the New Jersey Supreme Court was faced with an education system that displayed little, if any improvement."[34] When the litigation continued, the New Jersey high court issued yet another opinion, including a mandate for an ambitious and expansive plan of reform[35] that finally prompted the state legislature and executive branch to fund and implement programs bringing

---

29 *See* Paula J. Lundberg, *State Courts and School Funding: A Fifty-State Analysis*, 63 Albany L. Rev. 1101 (2000); John Dayton & Anne Dupre, *School Funding Litigation: Who's Winning the War?*, 57 Vand. L. Rev. 2351 (2004).
30 *Id.*
31 *See* Robert McKay, "*With All Deliberate Speed*," 31 N.Y.U. L. Rev. 991 (1956); Lucas A. Powe, Jr., *The Road to Swann: Mobile County Crawls to the Bus*, 51 Tex. L. Rev. 505 (1973).
32 *See, e.g.,* Griffin v. County School Board of Prince Edward County, 377 U.S. 218 (1964); Green v. County School Board, 391 U.S. 430 (1968).
33 Robinson v. Cahill, 303 A.2d 273 (1973).
34 Alexandra Greif, *Politics, Practicalities, and Priorities: New Jersey's Experience Implementing the Abbott V Mandate*, 22 Yale Law & Policy Rev. 615, 615 (2004).
35 Abbott v. Burke (V), 710 A.2d 450 (N.J. 1998).

some measure of reform to the state school system.[36] The New Jersey experience can be considered a partial success, albeit one that took decades and interminable litigation to achieve.

In other states, educational reform of school financing has not taken such an arduous course; not all state legislatures are so resistant to real reform.[37] Some state legislatures have been more willing than others to comply with the court decisions calling for equalization of school financing.[38] In response to court decisions in a number of states, the legislature has reallocated school funds to reduce the degree of disparity from one school district to another.[39] At the opposite end of the spectrum from New Jersey, the experience in Kentucky shows that educational reform need not be attended by conflict between the legislature and judiciary. In 1989, the Supreme Court of Kentucky decided *Rose v. Council for Better Education*, in which the plaintiffs challenged the Kentucky system of school financing, claiming that it caused "inadequacies, inequities, and inequalities" throughout the state in violation of the state constitution.[40] Upon assessing the state school system, the Kentucky high court found not only that the state system of funding schools was unconstitutional, but in addition ruled that the entire system of common schools in the state was invalid.[41] In response, the Kentucky legislature promptly implemented a new financing system that directed a higher proportion of state money to poor districts.[42] This resulted in dramatic improvement of the school system in Kentucky—so dramatic that it has been described as transforming "one of the worst state education systems to the forefront of the national education reform movement."[43]

As might be expected, the extent to which funding disparities have been reduced varies from state to state, but in some states substantial

---

[36] *See* New Jersey Department of Education, Report to the Legislature on the Progress of Abbott School Districts (Oct. 1997) http://www.state.nj.us/njed/abbotts/archives/abbreport.shtml. *See also*, Greif, *supra* note 34, at 626–57.

[37] See Gail F. Levine, *Meeting the Third Wave: Legislative Approaches to Recent Judicial School Finance Rulings*, 28 Harvard Journal on Legislation 507 (1991); Kimberly D. Bartman, *Public Education in the 21st Century: How Do We Ensure That No Child Is Left Behind?*, 12 Temp. Pol. & Civ. Rts. L. Rev., 95, 113–19 (2002).

[38] *See id.*

[39] *See id.*

[40] Rose v. Council for Better Education Inc., 790 S.W.2d 186 (Ky. 1989).

[41] *Id.* at 215.

[42] *See* Molly A. Hunter, *All Eyes Forward: Public Engagement and Educational Reform in Kentucky*, 28 Journal of Law and Education 485 (1999).

[43] Bartman, *supra* note 37, at 115.

progress has been achieved toward equalization of school funding.[44] The efforts of state courts to engender equality in school financing, though certainly not entirely successful, have nonetheless been the impetus for significant reform in a fair number of states.[45] If nothing else, state court rulings in this area have heightened awareness of the injustice and inefficiency of inequality in public school financing, and in some states have led to meaningful reform of educational financing.

Backlash has occurred, too, in response to state court decisions granting constitutional protection to same-sex marriage. The first decision to do so, *Baehr v. Lewin*,[46] announced by the Supreme Court of Hawaii in 1993, was countermanded by a state constitutional amendment adopted by the voters of Hawaii.[47] Because of the ruling in *Baehr*, a proposed amendment to the Florida Constitution that would have expressly barred discrimination on the basis of "sex" was replaced for fear that it would lead Florida courts to accord constitutional protection for same-sex marriage, as had occurred in Hawaii.[48] The *Baehr* decision also was the impetus for the enactment of the Defense of Marriage Act, a federal statute defining marriage, for purposes of federal law, as the legal union of a man and a woman as husband and wife.[49]

Considerably more backlash was engendered in response to the decision of the Supreme Court of Massachusetts in *Goodridge v. Department of Public Health*, ruling that the under Massachusetts Constitution same-sex couples could not be denied the right to marry.[50] As described in Chapter Six, "Civil Unions and Marriage," *Goodridge* provoked an intense emotional reaction throughout the nation, arousing strong feelings both for and against it.[51] There were demonstrations, counter demonstrations, debates, editorials, articles, and discussions across the country. Even the President weighed in, calling for a federal constitutional amendment that

---

44 *Id.* at 113–19.

45 *See* Levine, *supra* note 37.

46 Baehr v. Lewin, 852 P.2d 44 (Haw. 1993).

47 *See* Chapter Two at notes 106–8.

48 *See id.* at notes 83–88. In its place, an amendment was adopted stating: "All natural persons, female and male alike, are equal before the law...." Fla. Const. art. I, §2 (1998).

49 Defense of Marriage Act, Pub. L. No. 104–199, 110 Stat. 2419 (1996) (codified at 1 U.S.C. §7 (2000) and 28 U.S.C. §1738C (2000)).

50 Goodridge v. Department of Public Health, 798 N.E.2d 941 (Mass. 2003). *Goodridge* is discussed in depth in Chapter Six at notes 50–179.

51 *See* Chapter Six at notes 153–66.

would ban same-sex marriage.[52] A number of states enacted laws defining marriage as the union of a man and woman and barring recognition of same-sex marriages performed in another state.[53] By now, some forty-two states have adopted such laws, twenty-seven of them as amendments to their state constitutions, thereby precluding the courts in those states from finding a prohibition of same-sex marriage to be unconstitutional.[54] In some of those states, the constitutional amendments also ban same-sex civil unions or similar partnership laws.[55]

The backlash engendered by *Goodridge* was hardly surprising. *Goodridge*, after all, takes the New Judicial Federalism to its furthest reach and concerns an extremely sensitive topic. It was bound to provoke an intense reaction. But what is perhaps more surprising was the counter-reaction to the *Goodridge* backlash and the staying power of the decision itself. Immediately after the decision, there were calls to amend the Massachusetts Constitution to counteract the ruling in *Goodridge* and at first it appeared that the Massachusetts legislature was determined to do exactly that. Initially the legislature voted to amend the state constitution to ban same-sex marriage (although allow civil unions); however, to amend the state constitution, the legislature must re-approve a measure a second time and then submit it to a statewide vote before it may go into effect. After the initial vote approving the amendment, the Commonwealth's legislature had a change of heart, rejecting efforts to amend the constitution to prohibit same-sex marriage. In 2007, the legislature voted 151 to 45 against the proposed constitutional amendment, which needed 50 favorable votes to be presented to the voters in a referendum.[56] Any further attempts to enact the amendment will have to be started anew, and the amendment could not possibly be on the ballot until 2012.[57] So, same-sex marriage remains valid in Massachusetts and continues to be performed there. In fact, since May of 2004, when same-sex couples began to marry in Massachusetts, thousands of same-sex marriages have been performed in the Commonwealth every year.[58]

---

[52] Elisabeth Bumiller, *Bush Backs Ban in Constitution on Gay Marriage*, New York Times, Feb. 25 2004, at A1.

[53] *Same-sex marriage and alternatives*, www.stateline.org (updated May 31, 2007).

[54] *Id.*

[55] *Id.*

[56] Pam Belluck, *Massachusetts Gay Marriage to Remain Legal*, New York Times, June 15, 2007.

[57] *Id.*

[58] *Gay marriage ripe for decision in 3 courts*, www. stateline.org (updated June 15, 2007).

While Massachusetts remains the only state to countenance same-sex marriage, several other states have adopted civil union or domestic partnership laws that provide legal benefits to same-sex couples. The Vermont legislature, in response to the state supreme court's decision in *Baker v. State* ruling that same-sex couples could not constitutionally be denied the legal benefits and protection of marriage, enacted a civil union law providing comprehensive benefits and protections (akin to marriage rights) for same-sex couples.[59] In addition to Vermont, three other states—Connecticut, New Hampshire, and New Jersey—have enacted laws authorizing civil unions.[60] Of those states, New Hampshire earned the distinction of becoming the first state to allow same-sex unions without being under a court order or the threat of one to do so.[61] California, Hawaii, Maine, Oregon, and Washington all have adopted domestic partnership laws that provide certain legal rights to same-sex couples.[62]

At the same time, same-sex civil unions, if not same-sex marriage, has gained increasing approval with the public. A poll conducted in mid-2004 showed that 28% of Americans thought that gay and lesbians should be allowed to marry, while an addition 29% believed that gays and lesbians should be permitted to form civil unions.[63] Overall then, 57% of Americans supported some type of legal status for same-sex couples.[64] Nor should it be overlooked that same-sex couples can now marry in Belgium, the Netherlands, and many Canadian provinces, while many other nations grant some sort of legal status to same-sex couples.[65] Given all of these developments, it is undeniable that *Goodridge* and other cases such as *Baker v. State* have had a tremendous impact upon society that will continue to be felt in years to come. Despite the backlash it evoked, the decision of the Massachusetts Supreme Court in *Goodridge* prevailed,

---

[59] Baker v. State 744 A.2d 864 (Vt. 1999). *Baker* is discussed in depth in Chapter Six at notes 11–33.

[60] *Same-sex marriage and alternatives*, www.stateline.org (updated May 31, 2007).

[61] *New Hampshire Senate Approves Civil Unions*, <u>New York Times</u>, April 26, 2007.

[62] *Same-sex marriage and alternatives* (updated May 31, 2007).

[63] CBS News, *Poll: Most Oppose Same-Sex Unions*, May 30, 2004, www.cbsnews.com/stories/2004/05/08/opinions/polls/printable620258.shtml. (Author's note: Ironically, the title of this article is misleading; it suggests that a majority of the people oppose any sort of same-sex unions, which is not the case. The article should have been entitled: *Most Oppose Same-Sex* Marriage. Or: *Most* Favor *Same-Sex Unions*.).

[64] *Id.*

[65] Linda J. Lacey, D. Marianne Blair, *Symposium Foreword: Coping With the Aftermath of Victory*, 40 Tulsa L. Rev 371, 372 (2005).

bringing significant change to the Commonwealth and extending its influence to other regions.

State court rulings concerning same-sex marriage, the equalization of school financing, and *de facto* racial segregation have been subject to varying degrees of backlash. Rulings in other areas emblematic of the New Judicial Federalism, have been accepted more readily. For example, many state supreme courts have taken a strong stand against gender discrimination with little or no resistance from the public or from the other branches of government.[66] In those states that have adopted the Equal Rights Amendment,[67] the courts enjoy the mandate of an explicit constitutional amendment in support of their rulings against gender discrimination; but in other states as well where the courts have taken a forceful position against gender discrimination, their decisions have been met for the most part with approval.[68] State court decisions expanding the rights of women to choose to have an abortion also have been met with relative approval or, at least, little opposition. There has been general acceptance by the public of court decisions that strike down laws restricting abortion funding[69] or laws calling for informed consent and a waiting period.[70] Even rulings that grant minors the right to choose abortion have not evoked much negative reaction.[71] State court rulings upholding the right of intimate association also have gained public acceptance. Although court decisions striking down sodomy laws met with some amount of disapproval, a majority of the public seemed to recognize that laws criminalizing homosexual conduct were excessively harsh and that a right of intimate association was essential in a free society. State court decisions upholding the right of intimate association gained favor with the public and influenced the United States Supreme Court to finally follow suit. In some states, then, certain rights have been accepted by the public as an integral part of the evolving nature of equality and liberty. Overall, the New Judicial Federalism seems to be steadily progressing. Undeniably, in some areas there has been serious backlash, but even there gains

---

[66] *See* Chapter Two at notes 65–172, 88–100.
[67] Twenty states have amended their constitutions to include an Equal Rights Amendment specifically barring gender discrimination. *See Id.* at note 63.
[68] *See id.* at notes 78–81.
[69] *See* Chapter Five at notes 9–25.
[70] *See id.* at notes 57–72.
[71] *See id.* at notes 38–54.

eventually have been made. In other areas, public approval has come more readily, and the progression has been more constant.

With the rise of the New Judicial Federalism, equality and liberty have found fertile fields in state courts throughout the nation. Not all states have joined the movement, and among those that have joined, there has been varying degrees of commitment. Nonetheless, the movement has been dramatic, finding its strongest expression in the protection of the most basic of individual rights, equality and liberty. State courts have invested equality and liberty with new meaning that has made for a more just society by enhancing the lives of countless individuals. In re-invigorating state constitutional law, state courts have surpassed the federal courts as the guardians of equality and liberty. The achievement of the state courts in expanding individual rights represents the highest fulfillment of the federal system, as each state is able to exercise its sovereign prerogative to safeguard equality and liberty according to its own vision. With its course already well set, the advancement of equality and liberty will endure as the great attainment of the Golden Age of State Constitutional Law.

TABLE OF CASES

A Choice for Women, Inc. v. Florida Agency for Heath Care Administration, 872 So.2d 970 (Fla. 3d DCA 2004), 57

Abbott v. Burke (V), 710 A.2d 450 (N.J. 1998), 247

Abington School District v. Schempp, 374 U.S. 201 (1963), xiii

Adams v. Hinkle, 322 P.2d 844 (Wash. 1958), 107

Adams v. North Carolina Department of Natural and Economic Resources, 249 S.E.2d 402 (N.C. 1978), 36

Ah Lim v. Territory, 24 P. 588 (Wash.1890), 145, 236

Akron v. Akron Center for Reproductive Health, 462 U.S. 416 (1983), xv, 172–73

Alabama State Federation of Labor v. McAdory, 18 So.2d 810 (Ala. 1944), 35

Alaska Civil Liberties Union v. State, 122 P.3d 781 (Alaska 2005), 69

Alaska Pacific Assurance Company v. Brown, 687 P.2d 264 (Alaska 1984), 19

Alaska v. Cosio, 858 P.2d 621 (Alaska 1993), 97

Alden v. Maine, 527 U.S. 706 (1999), xix

Alvarez v. Chavez, 886 P.2d 461 (N.M. Ct. App. 1994), 18

Ambach v. Norwick, 441 U.S. 68 (1979), xviii, 6

American Academy of Pediatrics v. Lundgren, 940 P.2d 797 (Cal. 1997), 164

Amurund v. The Board of Appeals, 143 P.3d 571 (Wash. 2006), 102

Anderson v. Martin, 375 U.S. 399 (1964), 5, 46

Anderton v. City of Milwaukee, 52 N.W. 95 (Wis. 1892), 31, 32

Andrews v. Willrich, 29 P.3d 880 (Ariz. 2001), 113

Archer v. Mayes, 194 S.E.2d 707 (Va. 1973), 56

Arlington Heights v. Metropolitan Housing Corp., 429 U.S. 252 (1977), 47

Arneson v. State, 864 P.2d 1245 (Mont. 1993), 72–73, 100

Attorney General v. Massachusetts Interscholastic Athletic Association, 393 N.E.2d 284 (Mass. 1979), 55, 58

Baehr v. Lewin, 852 P.2d 44 (Haw. 1993), 57, 60, 124, 189, 208, 249

Baehr v. Miike, 910 P.2d 112 (Haw. 1996), 60, 189

Baker v. Nelson, 191 N.W.2d 185 (Minn. 1971), 61

Baker v. State, 744 A.2d 864 (Vt. 1999), 16, 20, 31, 44, 60–61, 66, 186, 207, 251

Ballard v. Commonwealth of Virginia, 321 S.E.2d 284 (Va. 1984), 117

Beaty v. Truck Insurance Exchange, 8 Cal. Rptr. 2d 593 (Cal. Ct. App. 1992), 64

Bell v. Low Income Women of Texas, 95 S.W.3d 253 (Tex. 2002), 164

Belle Isle Grill Corp. v. City of Detroit, 666 N.W.2d 271 (Mich. 2003), 101

Belle Terre v. Borass, 416 U.S. 1 (1974), 181–82

Bellotti v. Baird, 443 U.S. 622 (1979), 130

Benson v. North Dakota Workmen's Compensation Bureau, 283 N.W.2d 96 (N.D. 1979), 100–101

Best v. Taylor Machine Works, 689 N.E.2d 1057 (Ill. 1997), 94

Bierkamp v. Rogers, 293 N.W.2d 577 (Iowa 1980), 37

Bing v. Thunig, 143 N.E.2d 3 (N.Y. 1957), 229

Blair v. Washington State University, 740 P.2d 1379 (Wash. 1987), 59

Boddie v. Connecticut, 401 U.S. 371 (1971), 131, 132

Boerschinger v. Elkay Enters., Inc. 133 N.W.2d 333 (Wis. 1965), 150

Bolling v. Sharpe, 347 U.S. 497 (1954), 4, 11

Bowers v. Hardwick, 478 U.S. 186 (1986), 12, 40, 61–62, 134–35, 211, 215–17, 219–20, 227

Bradwell v. State of Illinois, 83 U.S. (16 Wall.) 130 (1873), 53, 149

Brannigan v. Usitalo, 587 A.2d 1232 (N.H. 1991), 95

Breen v. Carlsbad Municipal Schools, 120 P.3d 413 (N.M. 2005), 98–99

Breese v. Smith, 501 P.2d 159 (Alaska 1972), 237

Brown v. Board of Education, 347 U.S. 483 (1954), xiii, 5, 10, 39, 46, 82, 149, 247

Buck v. Bell, 274 U.S. 200 (1927), 39

Burch v. Foy, 308 P.2d 199 (N.M. 1957), 104

Butte Community Union v. Lewis, 712 P.2d 1309 (Mont. 1986), 21–22

Cabaniss v. Hipsley, 151 S.E.2d 496 (Ga. 1966), 140

Calder v. Bull, 3 U.S. (3 Dall.) 386 (1798), 148

Campbell v. Sundquist, 926 S.W.2d 250 (Tenn. App. 1996), 137, 153, 157, 216, 220–222, 223, 224, 225, 227, 236

Carson v. Maurer, 424 A.2d 825 (N.H. 1980), 95

Carter v. Craig, 90 A. 598 (N.H. 1914), 150

Case of Tobin, 675 N.E.2d 781 (Mass. 1997), 74

Ciak v. State, 597 S.E.2d 392 (Ga. 2004), 108

City of Cleburne v. Cleburne Living Center, Inc., 473 U.S. 432 (1985), 12, 40

City of Dover v. Imperial Casualty & Indemnity Co., 575 A.2d 1280 (N.H. 1990), 23

City of Santa Barbara v. Adamson, 610 P.2d 436 (Cal. 1980), 121, 182, 183

City of Seattle v. Rogers, 106 P.2d 598 (Wash. 1940), 107

Civil Rights Commission v. Travelers Ins. Co., 759 P.2d 1358 (Colo. 1988), 56

Colchester Fire District No. 2 v. Sharrow, 485 A.2d 134 (Vt. 1984), 90

Collins v. Day, 644 N.E.2d 72 (Ind. 1994), 17, 34, 36, 100, 101

Columbus Board of Education v. Penick, 443 U.S. 449 (1979), 47

Committee of Educational Rights v. Edgar, 672 N.E.2d 1178 (Ill. 1996), 83, 84

Committee to Defend Reproductive Rights v. Myers, 625 P.2d 779 (Cal. 1981), 164–165, 166

Commonwealth v. Bonadio, 415 A.2d 47 (Pa. 1980), 213

Commonwealth v. Campbell, 117 S.W. 383 (Ky. 1909), 137, 143–144, 217, 235

Commonwealth v. Leis, 243 N.E.2d 898 (Mass. 1969), 237

Commonwealth v. Pennsylvania Interscholastic Athletic Association, 334 A.2d 839 (Pa. 1975), 58

Commonwealth v. Saunders, 331 A.2d 193 (Pa. 1975), 115

Commonwealth v. Smith, 173 S.W. 340 (Ky. 1915), 145, 236

Commonwealth v. Tague, 751 N.E.2d 388 (Mass. 2001), 113

Commonwealth v. Wasson, 842 S.W.2d 487 (Ky. 1992), xxii, 62, 123, 136–137, 145–47, 158, 159, 216, 218–220, 227

Commonwealth v. Werner, 280 S.W.2d 214 (Ky. 1955), 31

Conn v. Gabbert, 526 U.S. 286 (1999), 102

Conrad v. State, 16 A.2d 121 (Del. 1940), 93

Conservatorship of Drabick, 200 Cal. App. 3d 185 (Cal. 1988), 230

Corfield v. Coryell, 6 F. Cas. 546 (C.C.E.D. Pa. 1823), 148

Corn v. New Mexico Educators Federal Credit Union, 889 P.2d 234 (N.M. Ct. App. 1994), 18

Cox v. Brazo, 303 S.E.2d 71 (Ga. 1983), 140

Cox v. Florida Department of Health and Rehabilitative Services, 656 So.2d 902 (Fla. 1995), 178

Craig v. Boren, 429 U.S. 190 (1976), xiv, 6, 40, 53, 54

Crawford v. Board of Education, 551 P.2d 28 (Cal. 1976), 47, 48

Crego v. Coleman, 615 N.W.2d 218 (Mich. 2000), 16

Cruzan v. Director, Missouri Department of Health, 497 U.S. 261 (1990), 133, 229, 231

Cutinello v. Whitley, 641 N.E.2d 360 (Ill. 1994), 38

D'Amico v. Board of Medical Examiners, 520 P.2d 10 (Cal. 1974), 102

Dandridge v. Williams, 397 U.S. 471 (1970), xv, 6, 13

Darrin v. Gould, 540 P.2d 882 (Wash. 1975), 59

Davis v. Davis, 842 S.W.2d 588 (Tenn. 1992), 137, 150, 152, 154, 171–72, 175

Delta v. Dinolfo, 351 N.W.2d 831 (Mich. 1984), 182

DeMonaco v. Renton, 113 A.2d 782 (N.J. 1955), 101

Dennis v. Moses, 52 P. 333 (Wash. 1898), 150

Diamond v. Cuomo, 514 N.W.2d 1356 (N.Y. 1987), 71

Doe v. Commonwealth's Attorney, 425 U.S. 901 (1976), 12

Doe v. Department of Social Services, 487 N.W.2d 166 (Mich. 1992), 16

Doe v. Director of Michigan Department of Social Services, 487 N.W.2d 166 (Mich. 1992), 164, 167

Doe v. Maher, 515 A.2d 134 (Conn. 1986), 159, 164, 165

Doe v. Sundquist, 2 S.W.3d 919 (Tenn. 1999), 178, 179

Does v. State, 993 P.2d 822 (Or. Ct. App. 1999), 178

Donaldson v. Lungren, 4 Cal. Rptr. 2d 59 (Cal. 1992), 232

D.P. v. State, 705 So.2d 593 (Fla. 1997), 74, 117

Duncan v. Louisiana, 391 U.S. 145 (1968), xiii

Dundee Mortgage, Trust Investment Co. v. School District No. 1, Multnomah County, 19 F. 359 (C.C.D. Or. 1884), 35

DuPree v. Alma School District No. 30, 651 S.W.2d 90 (Ark. 1983), 82, 84

Eidge v. Bessemer, 51 South. 246 (Ala. 1909), 144

Eisenstadt v. Baird, 405 U.S. 438 (1972), 128, 129, 189

Ekern v. McGovern, 142 N.W. 595 (Wis. 1913), 150

Elfbrandt v. Russell, 384 U.S. 11 (1966), xiv

Engel v. Vitale, 370 U.S. 421 (1962), xiii

Estate of Cargill v. Rochester, 406 A.2d 704 (N.H. 1979), 23

Etheridge v. Medical Center Hospitals, 376 S.E.2d 525 (Va. 1989), 94

Evans v. Steelman, 970 S.W.2d 431 (Tenn. 1998), 175

Ex parte Brown, 42 S.W. 554 (Tex. 1887), 144

Ex parte Trahan, 591 S.W.2d 837 (Tex. Crim. App. 1979), 115
Ex parte Tullos, 541 S.W.2d 167 (Tex. Crim. App. 1976), 115

Farley v. Engelken, 740 P.2d 1058 (Kan. 1987), 94
Federal Maritime Commission v. South Carolina State Ports Authority,
    535 U.S. 743 (2002), xix
Fein v. Permanente Medical Group, 695 P.2d 665 (Cal. 1985), 94
Fischer v. Department of Public Welfare, 502 A.2d 114 (Pa. 1985), 167
Fitzgerald v. Racing Association of Central Iowa, 539 U.S. 103 (2003), 90, 91
Fletcher v. Peck, 10 U.S. (6 Cranch) 87 (1810), 148
Florida Department of Health and Rehabilitative Services v. Cox, 627 So.2d 1210
    (Fla. Ct. App. 1993), 177, 178
Foley v. Connelie, 435 U.S. 291 (1978), xviii
Foley v. Department of Fisheries, 837 P.2d 14 (Wash. 1992), 102
Foster v. Sunnyside Valley Irrigation District, 687 P.2d 841 (Wash. 1984), 25
Frandsen v. County of Brevard, 800 So.2d 757 (Fla. 5th DCA 2001), 57
Franklin v. Hill, 444 S.E.2d 778 (Ga. 1994), 56, 57
Friehe v. Schaad, 545 N.W.2d 740 (Neb. 1996), 56, 57
Frontiero v. Richardson, 411 U.S. 677 (1973), xiv, 39, 53, 54
F.S. Royster Guano Co. v. Virginia, 252 U.S. 412 (1920), 45
Fullilove v. Klutznick, 448 U.S. 448 (1980), 11

Garton v. State, 910 P.2d 1348 (Wyo. 1996), 108
Gillette Dairy, Inc. v. Nebraska Dairy Products Board, 219 N.W.2d 214 (Neb. 1974), 102
Goodman v. Kennedy, 329 A.2d 224 (Pa. 1974), 105
Goodridge v. Department of Public Health, 798 N.E.2d 941 (Mass. 2003), 124, 191–94,
    200–202, 203, 205–8, 209–10, 249–51
Gora v. City of Ferndale, 576 N.W.2d 141 (Mich. 1998), 15
Gould v. Gould, 61 A. 604 (Conn. 1905), 145, 236
Graham v. Richardson, 403 U.S. 365 (1971), 11, 40
Green v. County School Board, 391 U.S. 430 (1968), 247
Gregory v. Ashcroft, 501 U.S. 452 (1991), 71
Griffin v. County School Board of Prince Edward County, 377 U.S. 218 (1964), 247
Griffin v. Illinois, 351 U.S. 12 (1956), xv, 6, 12
Grinnell v. State, 435 A.2d 523 (N.H. 1981), 71
Griswold v. Connecticut, 381 U.S. 479 (1965), 122, 126, 127–129, 151, 152, 154, 156, 189,
    193, 221
Gryczan v. State, 942 P.2d 112 (Mont. 1997), 147, 216, 220, 222–225, 227
Gutierrez v. Glaser Crandell Company, 202 N.W.2d 786 (Mich. 1972), 100, 101

Haas v. South Bend Community School Corporation, 289 N.E.2d 495 (Ind. 1972), 59
Hale v. Portland, 783 P.2d 506 (Or. 1989), 34
Harper v. Virginia State Board of Elections, 383 U.S. 663 (1966), xv, 6, 11, 12
Harris v. McRae, 448 U.S. 297 (1980), xv, 129, 163
Hatten v. Rains, 854 F.2d 687 (5th Cir. 1988), 70
Hawk v. Hawk, 855 S.W.2d 573 (Tenn.1993), 153, 174, 179
Hemphill v. Washington State Tax Commission, 400 P.2d 297 (Wash. 1965), 88, 89
Henderson v. Henderson, 327 A.2d 60 (Pa. 1974), 55
Hernandez v. Robles, 855 N.E.2d 1 (N.Y. 2006), 207, 208

Hershberg v. City of Barbourville, 133 S.W. 985, 986 (Ky. 1911), 145, 155, 236
Hirabayashi v. United States, 320 U.S. 81 (1943), 11
H.L. v. Matheson, 450 U.S. 398 (1981), 130
Hodgson v. Minnesota, 497 U.S. 417 (1990), 130
Holden v. James, 11 Mass. 396 (1814), 29
Hondroulis v. Schuhmacher, 553 So.2d 398 (La. 1988), 230
Hope v. Perales, 634 N.E.2d 183 (N.Y. 1994), 167
Horton v. Meskill, 376 A.2d 359 (Conn. 1977), 50, 83, 85
Howard v. State, 527 S.E.2d 194 (Ga. 2000), 227
Hughes v. State, 653 A.2d 241 (Del. 1994), 5

Illinois Housing Development Authority v. Van Meter, 412 N.E.2d 151 (Ill. 1980), 35, 103
In re Adoption of S.J.D., 641 N.W.2d 794 (Iowa 2002), 178
In re Angel Lace, 516 N.W.2d 678 (Wis.1994), 177
In re Belmont Fire Protection District, 489 N.W.2d 1385 (Ill. 1986), 38
In re Brown, 478 So.2d 1033 (Miss. 1985), 230
In re Caulk, 480 A.2d 93 (N.H. 1984), 230
In re Farrell, 529 A.2d 404, 410 (1987), 229
In re Guardianship of Browning, 568 So.2d 4 (Fla. 1990), 121, 158, 230
In re Guardianship of Grant, 747 P.2d 445 (Wash. 1987), 230
In re Leach, 34 N.E. 641 (Ind. 1893), 53
In re Levy, 427 So.2d 844 (La. 1983), 71
In re Milton, 505 N.E.2d 255 (Ohio 1987), 231
In re S.L.M., 951 P.2d 1365 (Mont. 1997), 75, 118
In re T.W., A Minor, 551 So.2d 1186 (Fla. 1989), 168, 169, 233
In the Interest of J.W.T., 872 S.W.2d 189 (Tex. 1994), 175
In the Matter of Girard, 200 P.2d 593 (Cal. 1921), 45
In the Matter of Lawrance, 579 N.E.2d 32 (Ind. 1992), 230
In the Matter of S.J.D., 641 N.W.2d 794 (Iowa 2002), 180
In the Matter of T.K.J. and K.A.K., 931 P.2d 488 (Colo. App. 1996), 177
Indiana Aeronautics Commission v. Ambassadair, Inc., 368 N.E.2d 1340 (Ind. 1977), 93
Industrial Claim Appeals Office of the State of Colorado v. Romero, 912 P.2d 62
    (Colo. 1996), 74, 100
Injured Workers of Kansas v. Franklin, 942 P.2d 591 (Kan. 1997), 74
Isakson v. Rickey, 550 P.2d 359 (Alaska 1976), 19, 103
Israel v. West Virginia Secondary Schools Activities Commission, 338 S.E.2d 480
    (W. Va. 1989), 4, 45, 56, 59, 60
Ivey v. Bacardi Imports, Co., 541 So.2d 1129 (Fla. 1989), 171

Jackson v. Pasadena City School District, 382 P.2d 878 (Cal. 1963), 47, 48
James v. Valtierra, 402 U.S. 137 (1971), xv, 12
Jarvis v. Levine, 418 N.W.2d 139 (Minn. 1988), 229
Jefferson v. Hackney, 406 U.S. 535 (1972), xv, 6, 13
Jegley v. Picado, 80 S.W.3d 332 (Ark. 2002), 154, 155, 216, 220, 221, 224, 225, 227

Kellems v. Brown, 313 A.2d 53 (Conn. 1972), 88
Kelly v. State, 525 N.W.2d 409 (Iowa 1994), 15, 45, 96, 99
Keyes v. School District No. 1, 413 U.S. 189 (1973), 47
Kimel v. Florida Board of Regents, 528 U.S. 62 (2000), xix

Knowles v. State Board of Education 547 P.2d 699 (Kan. 1976), 84

Korematsu v. United States, 323 U.S. 214 (1944), 11, 39, 40

Kotch v. Board of River Pilot Commissioners, 330 U.S. 522 (1947), 100

Krischer v. McIver, 697 So.2d 97 (Fla. 1997), 232–34, 235

Kukor v. Grover, 436 N.W.2d 568 (Wis. 1989), 83, 84

Lalli v. Lalli, 439 U.S. 259 (1978), 11

Lawrence E. Tierney Coal Co. v. Smith's Guardian et al, 203 S.W. 731 (Ky. 1918), 150

Lawrence v. Texas, 539 U.S. 558 (2003), 61, 62, 122, 126, 134, 147, 158, 177, 191, 211, 215, 216, 220, 227, 228

Leonard v. Thornburgh, 489 A.2d 1349 (Pa. 1985), 93

Lewis v. Harris, 875 A.2d 259 (N.J. 2005), 208

Lewis v. Harris, 908 A.2d 196 (N.J. 2006), 69

Lienhard v. State, 417 N.W.2d 119 (Minn. 1987), 23

Lindley for Lindley v. Sullivan, 889 F.2d 124 (7th Cir.1989), 177

Lindsey v. Normet, 405 U.S. 56 (1972), xv, 6, 13

Linkus v. Maryland State Board of Heating Ventilation, Air-Conditioning and Refrigeration Contractors, 689 A.2d 1254 (Md. 1997), 102

Little v. Streater, 452 U.S. 1 (1981), 132

Lochner v. New York, 198 U.S. 45 (1905), 87

Lofton v. Secretary of the Department of Children and Family Services, 358 F.3d 804 (11th Cir. 2004), 177

Longanacre v. Crabtree, 350 S.E.2d 760 (W.Va. 1986), 4

Loving v. Virginia, 388 U.S. 1 (1967), xiii, 5, 46, 129, 131, 200, 203

Low Income Women of Texas v. Bost, 38 S.W.3d 689 (Tex. Ct. App. 2000), 55

Lujan v. Colorado State Board of Education, 649 P.2d 1005 (Colo. 1982), 56

Lynden Transport, Inc. v. State, 532 P.2d 700 (Alaska 1975), 19

MacCallum v. Seymour, 686 A.2d 935 (Vt. 1996), 17, 43

Madden v. Kentucky, 309 U.S. 83 (1940), 88

Maher v. Roe, 432 U.S. 464 (1977), 129, 163, 164

Malabed v. North Slope Borough, 70 P.3d 416 (Alaska 2003), 51, 52

Mandell v. Haddon, 121 S.E.2d 516 (Va. 1961), 36

Massachusetts Board of Retirement v. Murgia, 427 U.S. 307 (1976), xv, 6, 12, 13, 71

Mathews v. Lucas, 427 U.S. 495 (1976), 11

McCusker v. Workmen's Compensation Board, 639 A.776 (Pa. 1994), 97

McLaughlin v. Florida, 379 U.S. 184 (1964), 38

McMinn v. Town of Oyster Bay, 488 N.E.2d 1240 (N.Y. 1985), 182, 183

Meech v. Hillhaven West, Inc., 776 P.2d 448 (Mont. 1989), 31

Meyer v. Nebraska, 262 U.S. 390 (1923), 125–26, 129, 151

Michael H. v. Gerald D., 491 U.S. 110 (1989), 133, 175, 176

Miller v. Heffernan, 378 A.2d 572 (Conn. 1977), 88

Miller v. Rosenberg, 749 N.E.2d 946 (Ill. 2001), 38

Mills v. Atlantic City Department of Vital Statistics, 372 A.2d 646 (N.J. Super. 1977), 180

Mills v. Habluetzel, 456 U.S. 91 (1982) xv, 11

Mississippi University for Women v. Hogan, 458 U.S. 718 (1982), 40

M.L.B. v. S.L.J., 519 U.S. 102 (1996), 132

Moe v. Secretary of Administration, 417 N.E.2d 387 (Mass. 1981), 165

Moore v. City of East Cleveland, 431 U.S. 494 (1977), xiv, 131, 132, 181, 202

Morrison v. Sadler, 821 N.E.2d 15 (Ind. 2005), 208–9

MRM, Inc. v. City of Davenport, 290 N.W.2d 338 (Iowa 1980), 101

Murphy v. Edmonds, 601 A.2d 102 (Md. Ct. App. 1992), 94

Nale v. Robertson, 871 S.W.2d 674 (Tenn. 1994), 153

Nelson v. Miller, 480 P.2d 467 (Utah 1971), 71

New Mexico Right to Choose/NARAL v. Johnson, 975 P.2d 841 (N.M. 1998), 165

New York Times Co. v. Sullivan, 376 U.S. 254 (1964), xiv

Nixon v. Commonwealth, 839 A.2d 277 (Pa. 2003), 102

North Ottawa Community Hospital v. Kieft, 578 N.W.2d 267 (Mich. 1998), 16

Nyquist v. Mauclet, 432 U.S. 1 (1977), 11

O'Connor v. Donaldson, 422 U.S. 563 (1975), 226

Ohio v. Akron Center for Reproductive Health, 497 U.S. 502 (1990), 130

Olmstead v. United States, 277 U.S. 438 (1928), 138, 139, 151

Olsen v. Nebraska, 313 U.S. 236 (1941), 87

Olsen v. State ex rel. Johnson, 554 P.2d 139 (Or. 1976), 25, 26

O'Neill v. Bane, 568 S.W.2d 761 (Mo. 1978), 71–72

Orr v. Orr, 440 U.S. 268 (1979), 6

Ortwein v. Schwab, 410 U.S. 656 (1973), 6, 132

Oxx v. Vermont Department of Taxes, 618 A.2d 1321 (Vt. 1992), 90

Oyoma v. California, 332 U.S. 633 (1948), 11

Pace v. State, 648 So.2d 1302 (La. 1995), 56

Page v. Welfare Commissioner, 365 A.2d 1118 (Conn. 1976), 55

Palmore v. Sidoti, 466 U.S. 429 (1984), xiii, 10

Pan-Alaska Construction, Inc. v. State, 892 P.2d 159 (Alaska 1995), 19

Pauley v. Kelly, 255 S.E.2d 859 (W. Va. 1979), 84

Pavesich v. New England Life Insurance, 50 S.E. 68 (1905), 137, 139–143

People v. Boyer, 349 N.E.2d 50 (Ill. 1976), 116

People v. Brown, 95 N.E.2d 888 (Ill. 1950), 104

People v. Calvaresi, 534 P.2d 318 (Colo. 1975), 108

People v. Ellis, 311 N.E.2d 98 (Ill. 1974), 56, 115

People v. Hofsheier, 129 P.3d 29 (Cal. 2006), 108

People v. Johnson, 369 N.E.2d 898 (Ill. 1977), 104

People v. Kimbrough, 644 N.E.2d 1137 (Ill. 1994), 111

People v. Onofre, 415 N.E.2d 936 (N.Y. 1980), 213, 214

People v. Salinas, 551 P.2d 703 (Colo. 1976), 55, 168

Perez v. Sharp, 198 P.2d 17 (Cal. 1948), 194

Personnel Administrator of Massachusetts v. Feeney, 442 U.S. 256 (1979), 6

Phillips v. Wisconsin Personnel Commission, 482 N.W.2d 121 (Wis. 1992), 61, 64

Pierce v. LaFourche Parish Council, 762 So.2d 608 (La. 2000), 74, 100

Pierce v. Society of Sisters, 268 U.S. 510 (1925), 126, 129

Piggly-Wiggly of Jacksonville v. City of Jacksonville, 336 So.2d 1078 (Ala. 1976), 105

Planned Parenthood of Central Missouri v. Danforth, 428 U.S. 72 (1976), 130

Planned Parenthood of Middle Tennessee v. Sundquist, 38 S.W.3d 1 (Tenn. 2000), 153, 171–73

Planned Parenthood of Southeastern Pennsylvania v. Casey, 505 U.S. 833 (1992), 126, 130–31, 135, 169, 171–74

Plessy v. Ferguson, 165 U.S. 537 (1896), 149
Plummer v. Donald M. Drake Co., 320 P.2d 245 (Or. 1958), 25
Plyer v. Doe, 457 U.S. 202 (1982), 18
Poelker v. Doe, 432 U.S. 519 (1977), 129, 163
Police Department of the City of Chicago v. Mosley, 408 U.S. 92 (1972), 19
Powell v. Pennsylvania, 127 U.S. 678 (1888), 46
Powell v. State, 510 S.E.2d 18 (Ga. 1998), 136, 137, 141, 143, 147, 216, 220, 221, 224, 225, 227
Prince v. Massachusetts, 321 U.S. 158 (1944), 129
Puget Sound Gillnetters Association v. Moos, 603 P.2d 819 (Wash. 1979), 35

Racing Association of Central Iowa v. Fitzgerald, 648 N.W.2d 555 (Iowa 2002), 90, 91
Racing Association of Central Iowa v. Fitzgerald, 675 N.W.2d 1 (Iowa 2004), 90, 92
Railroad Co. v. Morris, 65 Ala. 193 (1880), 32
Ralph v. City of Wenatchee, 209 P.2d 270 (Wash. 1949), 107
Rasmussen by Mitchell v. Fleming, 741 P.2d 674 (Ariz. 1987), 124, 230
Ravin v. State, 537 P.2d 494 (Alaska 1975), 124, 156, 237–40
Reece v. Grissom, 267 S.E.2d 839 (Ga. 1980), 140
Reed v. Reed, 404 U.S. 71 (1971), 11
Regents of the University of California v. Bakke, 438 U.S. 265 (1978), 39
Right to Choose v. Byrne, 450 A.2d 925 (N.J. 1982), 165
Rivera v. Gerner, 448 A.2d 508 (N.J. 1982), 23
Roberson v. Rochester Folding Box Co., 71 N.Y.S. 876 (N.Y. Sup. Crt., App. Div. 1901), 141
Robert Herman Church v. Illinois, 646 N.E.2d 572, 579 (Ill. 1995), 104
Roberts v. United States Jaycees, 468 U.S. 609, (1984), 133
Robinson v. Cahill, 303 A.2d 273 (N.J. 1973), 25, 84, 85–86, 247
Robinson v. Cahill, 339 A.2d 193 (N.J. 1975), 84
Roe v. Wade, 410 U.S. 113 (1973), xiv–xvi, 126, 128, 129–31, 163, 164, 171, 189
Romer v. Evans, 517 U.S. 620 (1996), 12, 40, 62, 196, 215
Rose v. Council for Better Education, Inc., 790 S.W.2d 186 (Ky. 1989), 84, 248
Ross v. Denver Department of Health and Hospitals, 883 P.2d 516 (Colo. Ct. App. 1994), 64
Ross v. Moffit, 417 U.S. 600 (1974), 6
Rutgers Council of AAUP Chapters v. Rutgers, 689 A.2d 828 (N.J. 1997), 20

San Antonio Independent School District v. Rodriguez, 411 U.S. 1 (1973), xv, xix, xx, 6, 10, 12, 13, 81
San Francisco Unified School District v. Johnson, 479 P.2d 669 (Cal. 1971), 47
Schilling v. Bedford City Memorial Hospital, Inc., 303 S.E.2d 905 (Va. 1983), 56
Schlesinger v. Ballard, 419 U.S. 498 (1975), 59
Schloendorff v. Society of New York Hospital, 105 N.E.2d 92 (N.Y. 1914), 229
Schroeder v. Binks, 113 N.E.2d 169 (Ill. 1953), 104
Schweiker v. Wilson, 450 U.S. 221 (1981), 12
Scott v. Commonwealth, 443 S.E.2d 138 (Va. 1994), 84
Seattle School District No. 1 v. State, 585 P.2d 71 (Wash. 1978), 84
Seeley v. State, 940 P.2d 604 (Wash. 1997), 240–41
Serrano v. Priest (I), 487 P.2d 1241 (Cal. 1971), xix, 81, 82, 84
Serrano v. Priest (II), 557 P.2d 929 (Cal. 1976), xix, xx–xxi, 21, 81, 82
Seymour v. Holcomb, 790 N.Y.S.2d 858 (N.Y. Sup. Crt. 2005), 208
Shapiro v. Thompson, 394 U.S. 618 (1969), xv, 6, 12
Sharpless v. Mayor of Philadelphia, 21 Pa. 147 (1853), 33

Shaw v. Reno, 509 U.S. 630 (1993), xv

Sheff v. O'Neill, 678 A.2d 1267 (Conn. 1996), 48–50

Sherbert v. Verner, 374 U.S. 398 (1963), xiv

Simat Corp. V. Arizona Health Care Cost Containment System, 56 P.3d 28 (Ariz. 2002), 164

Simmons v. Simmons, 900 S.W.2d 682 (Tenn. 1995), 153

Singer v. Hara, 522 P.2d 1187 (Wash. Ct. App. 1974), 61, 64, 185, 209

Sioux City Bridge Co. v. Dakota County, 260 U.S. 441 (1923), 40

Skag-Way Department Stores, Inc. v. City of Omaha, 140 N.W.2d 28 (Neb. 1966), 105

Skeen v. State, 505 N.W.2d 299 (Minn. 1993), 84

Skinner v. Oklahoma, 316 U.S. 535 (1942), 127, 128, 129

Snetsinger v. Montana University System, 104 P.3d 445 (Mont. 2004), 69

Sosna v. Iowa, 419 U.S. 393, (1975), xviii

Southwest Washington Chapter, National Electrical Contractors Association v. Pierce County, 667 P.2d 1092 (Wash. 1983), 55

Standhardt v. Superior Court, 77 P.3d 451 (Ct. App. Ariz. 2003), 209

Stanley v. Georgia, 394 U.S. 557 (1969), 129, 133, 156, 239

Stanton v. Stanton, 421 U.S. 7 (1975), 6

State v. Adams, 522 P.2d 1125 (Alaska 1974), 19

State v. Anderson, 558 P.2d 307 (Wash. Ct. App. 1976), 240

State v. Baker, 405 A.2d 368 (N.J. 1979), 182

State v. Brown, 648 So.2d 872 (La. 1995), 113

State v. Chevalier, 744 A.2d 597 (N.J. Super. A.D. 2001), 56

State v. Ciuffini, 395 A.2d 904 (N.J. Super. Ct. 1978), 216

State v. Clark, 630 P.2d 810 (Or. 1981), 26, 27, 114

State v. Denney, 101 P.3d 1257 (Kan. 2004), 110

State v. Edmonson, 630 P.2d 822 (Or. 1981), 27, 114

State v. Erickson, 574 P.2d 1 (Alaska 1978), 18, 19, 110, 124

State v. Frazier, 631 N.W.2d 432 (Minn. 2001), 113

State v. Freeland, 667 P.2d 509 (Or. 1983), 45, 114

State v. Fuller, 374 N.W.2d 722, 726 (Minn. 1985), 136

State v. Gilman, 10 S.E. 283 (W. Va. 1889), 144

State v. Gilmore, 511 A.2d 1150 (N.J. 1986), 56

State v. Grey, 413 N.W.2d 107 (Minn. 1987), 227

State v. Kam, 748 P.2d. 372 (Haw. 1988), 239

State v. Kantner, 493 P.2d 406 (Haw. 1972), 237

State v. Lee, 465 P.2d 573, 578 (Haw. 1970), 239

State v. Limon, 122 P.3d 22 (Kan. 2005), 109

State v. Ludlow Supermarkets, Inc., 448 A.2d 791 (Vt. 1982), 105

State v. Mallan, 950 P.2d 178 (Haw. 1998), 239

State v. Manussier, 921 P.2d 473 (Wash. 1996), 113

State v. McAfee, 385 S.E.2d 579 (Ga. 1989), 230

State v. Mohi, 901 P.2d 991 (Utah 1995), 23, 44, 75, 119

State v. Morales, 826 S.W.2d 201 (Tex. App. 1992), 216, 224

State v. Morales, 694 A.2d 758 (Conn. 1997), 117–18

State v. Mueller, 671 P.2d 1351 (Haw. 1983), 227

State v. Pilcher, 242 N.W.2d 348 (Iowa 1976), 213

State v. Price, 237 N.W.2d 813 (Iowa 1976), 227

State v. Russell, 477 N.W.2d 886 (Minn. 1991), 5, 111–13

State v. Salgado, 778 A.2d 24 (Conn. 2001), 113

State v. Saunders, 381 A.2d 333 (N.J. 1977), 211–12

State v. Smith, 766 So.2d 501 (La. 2000), 227–28

State v. Walsh, 713 S.W.2d 508 (Mo. 1986), 61

State v. Williams, 61 S.E. 61 (N.C. 1908), 144

State v. Wylie, 516 P.2d 142 (Alaska 1973), 19

State Administrative Board of Election Laws v. Supervisors of Elections of Baltimore City, 679 A.2d 96 (Md. 1996), 4

State *ex rel.* Bacich v. Huse, 59 P.2d 1101 (Wash. 1936), 35, 107

State *ex rel.* Hammond v. Hager, 503 P.2d 52 (Mont. 1972), 100, 101

State *ex rel.* Roy Allen S. v. Stone, 474 S.E.2d 554 (W. Va. 1996), 175

State *ex rel.* Warren v. Nusbaum, 208 N.W.2d 780 (Wis. 1973), 33

Sugarman v. Dougall, 413 U.S. 634 (1973), xviii, 11

Superintendent of Belchertown State School v. Saikewicz, 370 N.E.2d 417, 427 (Mass. 1977), 231

Tanner v. Oregon Health Sciences University, 971 P.2d 435 (Or. Ct. App. 1998), 17, 65–66, 185, 186, 189, 203

Terrett v. Taylor, 13 U.S. (9 Cranch), 43 (1815), 148

Texas Co. v. Cohn, 112 P.2d 522 (Wash. 1941), 88

Texas State Employees Union v. Texas Department of Mental Health & Mental Retardation, 746 S.W.2d 203 (Tex. 1987), 154

Thiede v. Town of Scandia Valley et al., 14 N.W.2d 400, (Minn. 1944), 150, 151

Thornburgh v. American College of Obstetricians & Gynecologists, 476 U.S. 747 (1986), xv, 122, 169

Trimble v. Gordon, 430 U.S. 762 (1977), 11, 40

Troxel v. Granville, 530 U.S. 57 (2000), 131, 174

Truillo v. City of Albuquerque, 965 P.2d 305 (N.M. 1998), 18

Tucker v. News Pub. Co., 397 S.E.2d 499 (Ga. 1990), 140

Union Pacific Railway Co. v. Botsford, 141 U.S. 250 (1891), 229

United States v. Alton, 60 F.3d 1065 (3d Cir.1995), 113

United States v. Carolene Products Co., 304 U.S. 144 (1938), 10, 40

United States v. Fonts, 95 F.3d 373 (5th Cir. 1996), 113

United States v. Kras, 409 U.S. 434 (1973), 6, 132

United States v. Reidel, 402 U.S. 351 (1971), 239

United States v. Virginia, 518 U.S. 515 (1996), 40

United States Department of Agriculture v. Moreno, 413 U.S. 528 (1973), 40, 62, 225

Vacco v. Quill, 521 U.S. 793 (1997), 13, 232

Valley Hospital Association v. Mat Su Coalition for Choice, 948 P.2d 963 (Alaska 1997), 164

Vance v. Bradley, 440 U.S. 93 (1979), xv, 6, 12, 70, 71

Vanzant v. Waddel, 10 Tenn. 260 (1829), 31, 32

Von Eiff v. Azicri, 750 So.2d 510 (Fla. 1998), 174

Vornado, Inc. v. Hyland, 390 A.2d 606 (N.J. 1978), 105

Washington v. Davis, 426 U.S. 229 (1976), 47

Washington v. Glucksberg, 521 U.S. 702 (1997), 13, 133, 231–32

Washington v. Heiskell, 916 P.2d 366 (Wash. 1996), 74, 117

Washington National Insurance Co. v. Board of Review of New Jersey Unemployment
    Compensation Commission, 64 A.2d 443 (1949), 101
Washington Statewide Organization of Stepparents v. Smith, 536 P.2d 1202 (Wash. 1975), 35
White v. State, 661 P.2d 1272 (Mont. 1983), 23, 95
Wilkerson v. Department of Health and Social Services, 993 P.2d 1018 (Alaska 1999), 102
Williams v. State, 895 P.2d 99 (Alaska 1995), 19, 97
Williams v. Zbarez, 448 U.S. 358 (1980), xv, 129, 163
Williamson v. Lee Optical of Oklahoma, Inc., 348 U.S. 483 (1955), 26, 87, 103
Winfield v. Division of Pari-Mutual Wagering, 477 So.2d 544 (Fla. 1985), 169

Younger v. Harris, 401 U.S. 37 (1971), xviii

Zablocki v. Redhail, 434 U.S. 374 (1978), xiv, 61, 131
Zant v. Prevatte, 286 S.E.2d 715 (Ga. 1982), 230

INDEX

Abortion. *See* Family rights
Age discrimination, 70–74
Alito, Samuel, xvi
American Law Institute, 148, 211
Autonomy. *See* Privacy, right of

Backlash, 243–53
Bodily integrity, right of
  right to ingest food, beverages, or other
    substances, 235–41
  right to refuse medical treatment and
    right to die, 229–35
Brandeis, Louis, 138–39, 151
Brennan, William, xvii, 164, 176

Civil union, 68–76, 124, 161, 189, 201,
  206–7, 245, 251
Classifications
  age, 12, 14, 70–75, 100
  gender, xiv, 6, 10–11, 14, 17, 26, 39–40,
    53–61, 200–203, 252 (*see also* Sexual
    discrimination)
  mental illness, 12, 14
  mental retardation, 12–14
  race, 2, 3, 10–11, 16, 24, 32, 39, 46–53,
    65, 76, 127, 185, 190–92, 203,
    246–47, 252 (*see also* Racial
    discrimination)
  sexual orientation, 12, 14, 17, 43, 60,
    61–70
  wealth, 12, 14, 81, 82
Cooley, Thomas, 45, 149
Criminal law
  disparate penalties, 108–13

disparate treatment of men and women,
  115–16
juvenile offenders, 116–19
prosecutorial discretion, 113–15

Death with Dignity Act, 232
Defense of Marriage Act (DOMA),
  208, 249
Domestic partnership. *See* Civil union
Dual sovereignty, xix, 136, 216, 243

Economic rights
  allocation of economic benefits, 96–101
  damage caps, 93–96
  Lochnerism, 86–87
  regulatory legislation, 101–6
  special entitlements, 106–7
  tax laws, 88–93
Educational financing, xix–xxi, 79–86,
  247–249
Equal Rights Amendment (ERA), xxii, 2,
  54–55,115, 165–67, 244, 252
Equality. *See also* Classifications
  equal protection of the laws, xiii–xv 1, 3,
    4, 15–16, 32, 34, 38–42, 109, 190,
    214–15, 243
  federal model, 8–15, 53, 76, 88, 96, 97,
    102, 112
  special privileges or immunities, 28–38
  state conception, 15–28
  state constitutions, 1–6
  state development, 44–46
Exacting scrutiny, 11, 39, 55, 222. *See also*
  Heightened scrutiny; Strict scrutiny

Family rights
  abortion rights of minors, 168–71, 252
  adoption, 18, 57, 125, 176–81
  cohabitation as a family, 181–83
  family relations, 174–76, 205
  informed consent and waiting periods,
    171–73, 229, 252
  parental rights, 132, 153, 161, 174–76, 254
  public funding of abortions, 163–68, 252
  reproductive freedom, 121, 161,
    163–68, 252
Fourteenth Amendment, xiii–xvi, 1, 4–5,
    20, 25, 34–35, 38, 41, 46, 48, 87, 122,
    126, 129, 130–31, 135–36, 151, 158,
    163, 177, 199, 215, 228, 232, 240
Fundamental rights, xv, xx, 6, 12–15, 41,
    79, 119, 126, 128, 131–32, 150–51, 159,
    189, 190, 222, 224, 240

Gender discrimination. See Sexual
    discrimination

Heightened scrutiny, 13, 15, 17, 39, 43, 61,
    63, 76, 79, 117, 200. See also Exacting
    scrutiny; Intermediate scrutiny; Strict
    scrutiny

Intermediate scrutiny, 10–13, 18, 22, 24,
    39–40, 43, 56–59, 73, 76, 99–100,
    159–60, 167. See also Heightened
    scrutiny
Intimate association, right of
  gay and lesbian sexual relations,
    215–21, 251
  sexual relations between consenting
    adults, 211–15, 251
Levels of scrutiny
  federal model, 8–15, 53, 76, 88, 96, 97,
    102, 112
  right of privacy, and, 121–25
  state approach, 19–30

Marriage, 44, 60–70, 124–46, 189–210, 236,
    249–52. See also Defense of Marriage
    Act (DOMA)
Mill, John Stuart, 140, 144, 146, 213, 217
Minimal scrutiny, xiii, xv–xvi, 7–12, 16, 20,
    24–25, 37–39, 66, 72, 80, 82, 88–93, 95,
    97, 126–34, 143, 148–49, 151, 197, 214,

    216–17, 230, 248, 263, 306. See also
    Rationality review
Model Penal Code, 148, 211
New Judicial Federalism, xiii–xxii, 7–8, 16,
    42, 81, 243–53

O'Connor, Sandra Day, xvi

Penumbra theory. See Privacy, right of
Privacy, right of
  constitutional amendments, xxii, 30, 51,
    54, 208, 250
  constitutional situs and methodology,
    158–60
  cornerstone of liberty, 148–53
  federal model, xiv–xviii, 125–36
  Millian principle, 143–48
  penumbra theory, 122, 127–28, 152–54,
    159, 221–22
  right to be let alone, 138–43
  spatial privacy, 155–58, 222
  state conception, 113–43
  state development, 123–24

Quasi- (or semi-) suspect classification,
    10–12, 14, 54, 64, 79, 117–118, 202

Racial discrimination, 5, 38–39, 40, 46–53,
    76–77, 246–47, 252. See also
    Classifications, race
Rationality review, xviii, 9, 14, 17–19,
    22–23, 43, 56, 64, 71–74, 89–96, 98,
    100, 103, 107–8, 110, 112, 116–17, 120,
    160, 178, 194–95, 208, 244. See also
    Minimal scrutiny
Rehnquist, William, xv–xvi, 131
Roberts, John, xvi

Same-sex marriage. See Marriage
Sexual discrimination, 6, 54–56, 251–252.
    See also Classifications, gender
Sexual orientation, discrimination based
    on, 60–70, 185–86, 194–97, 249–251
Scalia, Antonin, xvi
School financing. See Educational financing
Semi-suspect classification. See Quasi-
    (or semi-) suspect classification
Sexual relations between consenting adults,
    211–13

Sexual relations of same-sex couples,
60–64, 215–21
Sodomy, 61, 109, 124, 134, 141, 145, 147,
154, 211–23, 227–28
Strict scrutiny, 9–13, 17, 19, 21, 23, 34, 40,
43, 47, 52, 54–58, 60–61, 75–76, 82,
84–85, 95–96, 112, 118, 127, 159–60,
165–66, 172, 185, 189–90, 194–95, 200,
202, 244. See also Exacting scrutiny;
Heightened scrutiny
Suicide, physician-assisted, 234–35
Suspect classification, 10–15, 17, 26–27,
39–40, 46, 53–56, 61–65, 71, 73–76, 79,

81–82, 96, 99, 117–118, 166–167, 185,
190, 194, 202, 218

United States Supreme Court, xv–xxii, 4–5,
8, 15, 26, 37, 48, 53, 58, 61, 80–82,
90–92, 103, 122, 125, 136, 138, 151,
160–68, 174, 181, 189, 193–96, 203,
214–16

Warren, Earl, viii, 5, 46
Warren, Samuel, 138